Parallax

Also Available from Bloomsbury

New Realism and Contemporary Philosophy, ed. Gregor Kroupa and Jure Simoniti

Beckett and Dialectics: Be It Something or Nothing, ed. Eva Ruda

The Dialectics of Music: Adorno, Benjamin, and Deleuze, Joseph Weiss

Is There an Object Oriented Architecture? Engaging Graham Harman, ed. Joseph Bedford

Parallax

The Dialectics of Mind and World

Edited by
Dominik Finkelde, Slavoj Žižek, and Christoph Menke

BLOOMSBURY ACADEMIC
LONDON • NEW YORK • OXFORD • NEW DELHI • SYDNEY

BLOOMSBURY ACADEMIC
Bloomsbury Publishing Plc
50 Bedford Square, London, WC1B 3DP, UK
1385 Broadway, New York, NY 10018, USA
29 Earlsfort Terrace, Dublin 2, Ireland

BLOOMSBURY, BLOOMSBURY ACADEMIC and the Diana logo are
trademarks of Bloomsbury Publishing Plc

First published in Great Britain 2021
This paperback edition published 2023

Cover image: Distorted reflection of Seattle Space Needle
reflected in office building window, October 2006
(© Stephen Finn / Alamy Stock Photo)

A catalogue record for this book is available from the British Library.

Library of Congress Cataloging-in-Publication Data

Names: Finkelde, Dominik, editor. | Žižek, Slavoj, editor. |
Menke, Christoph, 1958- editor.
Title: Parallax: the dialectics of mind and world / edited by Dominik
Finkelde, Christoph Menke, and Slavoj Žižek.
Description: London, UK; New York, NY, USA: Bloomsbury Academic, 2021. |
Includes bibliographical references and indexes. |
Identifiers: LCCN 2021004127 (print) | LCCN 2021004128 (ebook) |
ISBN 9781350159624 (hb) | ISBN 9781350172043 (epdf) |
ISBN 9781350172050 (ebook)
Subjects: LCSH: Dialectic.
Classification: LCC B105.D48 P37 2021 (print) |
LCC B105.D48 (ebook) | DDC 146/.32–dc23
LC record available at https://lccn.loc.gov/2021004127
LC ebook record available at https://lccn.loc.gov/2021004128

ISBN: HB: 978-1-3501-5962-4
PB: 978-1-3502-5337-7
ePDF: 978-1-3501-7204-3
eBook: 978-1-3501-7205-0

Typeset by Integra Software Services Pvt. Ltd.

To find out more about our authors and books visit www.bloomsbury.com
and sign up for our newsletters.

Contents

Preface

Hegel and the Ethical Parallax

Slavoj Žižek

Parallax is not just the unsurpassable ontological feature of an inconsistent universe, it is also operative in the very heart of our ethical experience—let's try to demonstrate this through a recent representative reading of the ethical implications of Hegel's thought.

In his last masterpiece *The Spirit of Trust*,[1] Robert Brandom focuses on the notion of "forgiving recollection" deployed by Hegel toward the end of the chapter on Spirit in his *Phenomenology*: the gap that separates the acting subject and its severe judge is overcome through their reconciliation when not only the agent confesses his sin but the judge also confesses the unilaterality of his own position, his participation in what he condemns: Evil is also the gaze which sees evil everywhere around it. Brandom's notion of forgiving recollection is very useful today: it enables us to see what is false in precisely those who advocate tolerance and reject "hate speech." Is today an exemplary case of a rigid moral judgment not a politically correct subject who sternly condemns those who are accused of practicing "hate speech"?

But there are clear limits to this notion of forgiving recollection. "Hegel incorporates, adapts, and transforms the traditions he inherits—what we will come to recognize as the way he recollectively forgives them" (514). To be brutal in a simplified way: can we also "recollectively forgive" Hitler? And if the answer is no, is this because Hitler cannot be in this sense forgiven or because we ourselves are not yet at the high enough level of ethical reflection to do it? The only way to avoid regression to the position of a "beautiful soul" (which passes judges from an external position exempted from its object) is to endorse the second option—that our castigation of Hitler as evil must be a reflexive determination of the Evil that persists in ourselves, that is, of the non-reflected particularity that persists in our own position from which we pass judgments. Let us note that many rightist revisionists today try to enact precisely such a recollective forgiving of Hitler: yes, he made terrible mistakes, he committed horrible crimes, but in doing this, he was just fighting for the ultimately good cause (against the capitalist corruption for him embodied in Jews) in a wrong way. (It is easy to construct a more rational and not rightist-revisionist version of how we who condemn Nazism should also ask forgiveness: not only was anti-Semitism by far not limited to Germany but was very strong in the nations that were at war with Germany; not only did the obvious injustice of the treaty of Versailles as an act of revenge against the defeated Germany also contribute to the Nazi rise to power; at a more general level, fascism grew out of the dynamics and antagonisms of Western capitalism in which also those who were its victims fully participated.) These revisionists also try to balance responsibility in a pseudo-Hegelian way: were Hitler's crimes not mirrored in the one-sidedness of the Jewish position (their exclusive stance, their unwillingness to integrate themselves into the German nation)? While we should totally reject this line of reasoning, the solution is definitely not to draw a line between sins that could be recollectively forgiven and those that are too strong and cannot be—such a procedure introduces a duality that is totally at odds with Hegel's approach. What one should do is to change the very notion of recollective forgiving: to deprive this notion of any echoes of "you are now forgiven, you are no longer really bad." Brandom, of course, raises this problem:

> Some things people have done strike us, even upon due reflection, as simply unforgivable. In these cases, though we might try to mitigate the consequences of evil doings, we have no idea at all how to go about discerning the emergence of a governing norm we could ourselves endorse. (716)

His answer is:

> But now we must ask: Whose fault is it that the doing, or some aspect of it, is unforgivable—the doer or the forgiver? Is the failure that of the bad agent or of the bad recollector? Is whose fault it is a matter of how things anyway just are? Or is it at least partly reflective of the recollector's failure to come up with a more norm-responsive narrative? (716)

But, again, should we in the case of the Holocaust also "acknowledge at least equal responsibility on the part of the unsuccessful forgiver" (717)? And should we also claim that "one must trust that this recollective-recognitive failure, too—like the failure of the original, inadequately forgiven doer—will be more successfully forgiven by future assessors (who know more and are better at it)" (718)? Furthermore, what about the cases like cliterodectomy (or torture, or slavery in general), which we today experience as horror but for which it is easy to reconstruct the normative background that makes them acceptable not only for those who perform it but even for their victims? What about such cases where the retroactive view makes them more unacceptable than they were in their original context? Here also we are dealing with the unity of making and finding: if we sternly judge and reject such cases, we do not only make new norms and impose them onto the past acts, we, in some sense, also find that such acts were always inacceptable even if they appeared acceptable to the agents.

The way to deal with this problem is perhaps indicated by the biblical story of Habbakuk's complaint, the most poignant expression of what one might call "the silence of gods," of the big question addressed at god from Job onward: "Where were you when that horror/Holocaust, etc./happened? Why were you silent, why didn't you intervene?"—here are the words of this complaint:

> How long, Lord, must I call for help, but you do not listen? Or cry out to you, "Violence!" but you do not save? Why do you make me look at injustice? Why do you tolerate wrongdoing? Destruction and violence are before me; there is strife, and conflict abounds. Therefore the law is paralyzed, and justice never prevails. The wicked hem in the righteous, so that justice is perverted.[2]

So how does god answer it? One should read this reply very carefully: "Look at the nations and watch—and be utterly amazed. For I am going to do something in your days that you would not believe, even if you were told." There is no simple teleological justification here in the style of: "Be patient, strange are the ways of the lord, your suffering serves a purpose in the wider divine plan that you cannot grasp from your narrow finite standpoint…"—to say that the Holocaust (or anything similar to it) serves some higher purpose unknown to us is an anti-Christian obscenity since the whole point of Christ's compassion is the unconditionally solidary with those who suffer. To use yet again Agamben's expression, one should gather here full courage of hopelessness.

Back to the Holocaust, what does it mean that we should be "utterly amazed," and that something will happen that we "would not believe, even if we were told"? While utter amazement can be read as referring to the incomprehensible horror of the Holocaust, the unbelievable thing that happened later was the founding of the state of Israel, which, one might surmise, would not have happened without the Holocaust, and only in this sense could Hitler be retroactively "forgiven" by the existence of Israel, which his crimes contributed to. But, again, one has to be very precise here: this in no way justifies the Holocaust as the sacrifice Jews were ready to pay for the return to their land (the thesis of some anti-Semites) or the claim that the Holocaust was part of a secret divine plan to make possible the return of Jews to their homeland (also the thesis of some anti-Semites)—it just means that the founding of Israel was an unexpected and unplanned consequence of the Holocaust. And it also says nothing about other injustices that resulted from this set of acts: the land to which Jews returned was for long time inhabited by other people and cannot be simply designated as "theirs."

The main trap to be avoided here is the one of holistic teleology: something that appears to us as horror can be, from a larger perspective, an element that contributes to global harmony, in the same way that a tiny stain in a large painting contributes to its beauty if we look at the painting from a proper distance. The legacy of Job prohibits us such a gesture of taking a refuge in the standard transcendent figure of God as a secret Master who knows the meaning of what appears to us as a meaningless catastrophe, the God who sees the entire picture in which what we perceive as a stain contributes to global harmony. When confronted with an event like the Holocaust or the death of millions in Congo in the last years, is it not obscene to claim that these stains have a deeper meaning in that they contribute to the harmony of the Whole? Is there a Whole that can teleologically justify and thus redeem/sublate an event like the Holocaust? Christ's death on the cross thus means that one should drop without restraint the notion of God as a transcendent caretaker who guarantees the happy outcome of our acts, the guarantee of historical teleology—Christ's death on the cross is the death of *this* God, it repeats Job's stance, and it refuses any "deeper meaning" that obfuscates the brutal real of historical catastrophes. Even a strong version of this logic—forgiving does not mean not the sacrifice/erasure of the particular content but the recognition that particular content is necessary for the actualization of the universal Good—is not strong enough: recollective forgiving remains an ambiguous notion. In ethical sphere, it can be read as "trying to understand what appears to us as evil," reconstructing a hidden positive motivation that just got expressed in a perverted way. However, retroactivity implies a much more radical dimension of contingency—things are not what they are, they "will have been"; their truth is decided retroactively.

At the level of immediate facts, things are what they are—in the Holocaust millions died; nothing can retroactively change this, and the past can only be changed at the level of its symbolic mediation. But here, things get complicated: what about the opposite case (evoked by Hegel himself): an agent acts with best intentions but unpredictable consequences of this act are catastrophic—how does recollective forgiving work here? Can the judge construct a partial forgiving by way of proving that the most probable consequence would have been benevolent and that the catastrophe was due to a contingent unpredictable accident? And what if we introduce a third level on top of the duality of my subjective intention in performing an act and the actual outcome of my act: the unconscious motivations? This third level should in no way be limited to "base" motifs as the concealed truth of the publicly professed "noble" motifs (a person who claims to perform an act out of the sense of duty was effectively motivated by personal revenge)—it should also include the opposite case (while I thought I acted out of some private "pathological" inclination, a deeper sense of justice actually motivated me).

If we concede that the actual significance of an act "will have been," we touch here the paradoxical nerve of morality baptized by Bernard Williams' "moral luck."[3] Williams evokes the case of a painter ironically called "Gauguin," who left his wife and children and moved to Tahiti in order to fully develop there his artistic genius—was he morally justified in doing this or not? Williams' answer is that we can only answer this question *in retrospect*, after we learn the final outcome of his risky decision: did he develop into a painting genius or not? Exactly the same holds for the legal status of the rebellion against a (legal) power in Kant: the proposition "what the rebels are doing is a crime which deserves to be punished" is true if pronounced when the rebellion is still going on; however, once the rebellion wins and establishes a new legal order, this statement about the legal status of the same past acts no longer holds. Here is Kant's answer to the question "Is rebellion a legitimate means for a people to employ in throwing off the yoke of an alleged tyrant?":

> The rights of the people have been violated, and there can be no doubt that the tyrant would not be receiving unjust treatment if he were dethroned. Nevertheless, it is in the highest degree wrong if the subjects pursue their rights in this way, and they cannot in the least complain of injustice if they are defeated in the ensuing conflict and subsequently have to endure the most severe penalties.... [I]f the people were to rebel successfully, the head of state would revert to the position of a subject; but he would not be justified in starting a new rebellion to restore his former position, nor should he have to fear being called to account for his previous administration.[4]

Does Kant not offer here his own version of "moral luck" (or, rather, "legal luck")? The (not ethical, but legal) status of rebellion is decided retroactively: if a rebellion succeeds and establishes a new legal order, then it brings about its own *circulus vitiosus*; that is, it erases into ontological void its own illegal origins, and it enacts the paradox of retroactively grounding itself—Kant states this paradox even more clearly a couple of pages earlier: "If a violent revolution, engendered by a bad constitution, introduces by illegal means a more legal constitution, to lead the people back to the earlier constitution would not be permitted; but, while the revolution lasted, each person who openly or covertly shared in it would have justly incurred the punishment due to those who rebel." One cannot be clearer: the legal status of the same act changes with time. What is, while the rebellion goes on, a punishable crime becomes, after a new legal order is established, its own opposite—more precisely, it simply disappears, as a vanishing mediator that retroactively cancels/erases itself in its result.

Here is a recent example of the same parallax shift. The US Republican senator Tom Cotton caused an uproar when he said that the nation's founders viewed slavery as a "necessary evil" needed to build a union, and in this way put slavery itself on a course to extinction.[5] But did Marx not say basically the same in his comments on the British colonization of India? Cruel as it was, it brought India on the path of modernity. The trap to avoid here is that of retroactive justification: in the same way that, as we have already seen, the fact that the Holocaust helped to establish the state of Israel doesn't justify it, the fact that the British colonization of India brought it on the path to modernity in no way justifies its horrors. More precisely, what is impossible to occupy is a neutral place that would allow us to judge "objectively" a historical period and provide a balanced view of it: yes, British colonization did this to India, but the result of it was the rise of Indian anti-colonialist struggle, which allowed all of us to fully perceive the horrors of colonization. In short, the very retroactive "justification" of a horrible event at the same time enables us to see it in all its horror. What is impossible, a total ethical fake and lie, is for some British colonizer to say: yes, we are now doing horrible things in India, but in this way, we are opening the path to the process of decolonization. In a similar way, it's obscene to imagine an Auschwitz executioner who coldly claims: "I am really doing this in order to enable the rise of the State of Israeli." Even if in some sense true, the objective fact of the link between the Holocaust and the emergence of Israel cannot be subjectivized in this way. In short, there is no higher "synthesis" between the objective view of history and ethical judgment—here also, the parallax is irreducible.

Notes

1   Robert Brandom, *The Spirit of Trust* (Cambridge, MA: Harvard University Press, 2019). Numbers in brackets refer to the pages of this book.

2   Prophet Habakkuk 1, 1–4, in: *New International Version of The Holy Bible* (Michigan: Zondervan, 2011), 1565.

3   See Bernard Williams, *Moral Luck* (Cambridge: Cambridge University Press, 1981).

4   Immanuel Kant, "On the Agreement between Politics and Morality according to the Transcendental Concept of Publick Right." In *Kant's Political* Writings, ed. H.S. Reiss (Cambridge: Cambridge University Press, 1991), 125–30, here: 126.

5   Bryan Armen Graham, "Tom Cotton Calls Slavery 'Necessary Evil' in Attack on New York Times' 1619 Project," *The Guardian*, July 26, 2020. Available online: https://www.theguardian.com/world/2020/jul/26/tom-cotton-slavery-necessary-evil-1619-project-new-york-times.

Introduction

Dominik Finkelde

1. Subject Matter

The concept parallax refers to the apparent displacement in the position of an object viewed along two different lines of sight. Yet, more precisely, it includes the assumption that one understands the observable change not simply as a subjective change of focus derived from the viewer's altered standpoint but also as a change in the object on the level of its ontological status. In this case, a shift in the epistemic standpoint of the subject implies an ontological change in the object as well.[1] The concept's origin can be found in astronomy, where parallax helps to measure large distances between stars close to the sun. But the effect is already familiar to children, as Anton F. Koch and Christoph Menke take notice of in their chapters to come. Because, if you hold your thumb in front of your eyes with your arm stretched out and then close your right and left eye alternately, the thumb seems to jump back and forth in the center of the field of vision. However, it is not the object that changes its location but the background against which it stands. The latter shifts by changing the lines of perspective emanating from the subject and lets the object make a jump across an indeterminable gap from right to left and vice versa.

Since 2013, Slavoj Žižek abstracts the term from its astronomical origins to express with it his interpretation of the subject-object dichotomy, which, in various debates of ontology (from Kant via Hegel to Heidegger), remains indeterminate. For him, the above-mentioned gap between two mutually exclusive lines of perspective on one and the same object leads to the very heart of what ontology is about. It shows that there is no place of mediation between the alternating positions of the object in its objectivity as such. The gap within the relationship between subjects and objects apparently excludes a reconciliation of perspectives. It cannot be reduced "to something that could be positively described or explained" (Quadflieg, in this volume). In the context of philosophy, the term thus refers to incommensurable relationships between subjects and objects in historical processes of consciousness, mind, and knowledge. After all, objects of all kinds (abstract, middle-sized, physical) only exist as facts for rational animals within sites of ever-more facts. And this means that objects experience by definition ever-new conditions of their existence since the contexts of what we know change constantly. This affects politics, ontology, and aesthetics alike.

To give an example, one can refer to Galileo's astronomical observations and his conflict with Cardinal Bellarmine, rediscussed by Boghossian (2006) and Kusch

(2017).[2] Galileo's calculations obviously reflected more precisely the celestial objects, even though the subject-object determination of Galileo's antipode, Bellarmine, was epistemically more in accordance with the established web of reasons. Galileo's triumph not only shifted the modern subject in the cosmos but provoked a change in the status of cosmic spheres. Parallax refers to this and other similar shifts between subject and object in historical processes, which cause both entities to circle each other repeatedly due to both their lack of reconciliation and internal antagonism. This is a process that has no end, because, as Hegel says, subject and object are mediated in themselves through time. Jacques Lacan expresses this idea likewise when he shows to what extent the subject's gaze is inscribed in the perceived object in the form of a "blind spot" from which the object can literally (in times of epistemic, political, and psychological crises) return the sight.[3]

Overlaps with intensions of other concepts of the Continental and analytic philosophical traditions inevitably arise: from Kant's "thing in itself," with which parallax has the property of expressing a form of noncoincidence between truth and knowledge, to Frege's distinction between "sense and reference," to Kuhn's, Derrida's, and Foucault's understanding of incommensurable epistemes, and Quine's and Davidson's elaborations on "radical translation" or respectively "interpretation." As different as these concepts are, they stand against a similar background of the classical questions to clarify the noncoincidence between knowledge and truth without sacrificing one of the terms or even both all together.

The contributions collected in this volume often follow Žižek's trails and present parallax as an enlightening figure of thought. In doing so, they prove how the incommensurability between the ontic lifeworld and its transcendental a priori conditions of possibility touch not only on questions of ontology and epistemology but also upon questions of politics and aesthetics. Consequently, the chapters present multiple kinds of parallaxes in different areas of theory: from the gap between the human world of meaning and the idea that "nobody is home" in our heads, to Marx's exposure of the difference between an economic "base" and its political "superstructure," to "sex" and "gender" as transcendental categories of parallax. The concept can furthermore be identified in the struggles for the sovereignty of a naturalistic worldview as opposed to, for example, the life forms intertwined with religion. As such, parallax pays particular attention to what cannot be reconciled, and thus, indirectly, focuses the attention on the lack of identity within the diverse determinations of what human reality is about. German idealism plays an important role in several of the chapters where debates within contemporary philosophy—from New Realism, via critical- and Lacanian theory to Speculative Realism and New Materialism—are often mirrored in the works of Kant, Fichte, and Hegel. The chapters illustrate how questions of ontology impact questions of practical and political philosophy as already the simple question "On What There Is" necessarily causes divergent answers.

Recent scholars, in their dedication to understand ontological incompleteness (from New Realism to critical- and Lacanian theory), have shown that the Kantian split between phenomena and the "thing in itself" arises from within appearance itself. This means that the split between reality and appearance is an a priori illusion of perspective that as such cannot be overcome, neither in ontology (Part 1 "Parallax in Ontology") nor in politics (Part 2 "Parallax in Normative Orders")—with aesthetics, perhaps, as the only way out (Part 3 "Parallax in Aesthetics"). Not only is appearance internally split but this split is itself an appearance. And it is for this reason that the incompleteness of Being is—or, at least, appears to be—the precondition of reality to emerge within new forms of knowledge with truth as that which is found and missed simultaneously.

The editors hope that the volume proves to be an encyclopedic source in the future that is helpful for scholars and students engaged in philosophy when thinking about parallactic logics beyond the so-called analytic-Continental divide. The concept summarizes a long line of development in Slavoj Žižek's thought, but as a figure of non-identity, negativity, and ontological incompleteness, it is (among others via German idealism and especially the philosophy of Hegel in contemporary theory) paramount in multiple debates, which focus on gaps between realism and idealism, questions of free will or free subjectivity in our epoch of naturalism, the ambiguous borderline between things and subjects, and the interrelations of the self with collectives in emancipatory politics of race and gender, to name just a few. It is worth mentioning that the volume combines scholars of the Frankfurt School of Critical Theory and scholars in the tradition of the Ljubljana Lacanian School, but also shows how parallax is of importance within debates of Speculative Realism and Dialectical Materialism.

Many of the papers were presented at the conference "Parallax. The Dependence of Reality on Its Subjective Constitution" at the *Munich School of Philosophy—Faculty of the Society of Jesus* in Germany on November 30 and December 1, 2018. The editors thank everyone involved in making this volume possible.

2. The Parallactic Stance: Background and Context

Are facts of an independent world reflected in our concepts, like a bouquet of flowers in a mirror on the wall? Or does our mind, like a cookie-cutter, press the objects of our propositions as facts into the world like into a formless "dough" (Putnam[4])? Or, maybe, it is all completely different, with mind and world being always already united in a third element too extensive in scope to be conceptualized, be it "substance" or "deus sive natura" (Spinoza), spirit (Hegel), the absolute (Schelling), or the physical (Quine)?

Questions like these have shaped philosophy since antiquity and continue to do so. They also strive for results urgently needed in contemporary debates on knowledge, truth, sense, and meaning. Yet, especially in the seventeenth and eighteenth centuries, they intensified fundamentally. For it is with outstanding subtlety that authors such as Locke, Hume, and Kant postulate new intermediate components in the mind-world relationship and so prove that parallax has its roots far deeper in the history of philosophy than generally imagined. This shall be mentioned briefly. The new intermediate components make the distance between the thinking self and the outside world seem more complex than philosophers had, roughly speaking, experienced in centuries before. This explains why, especially in the seventeenth and eighteenth centuries, theories based on the difference between "thinking" and "sensing" surged. They focus on "impressions of sensation," "sense data," or sensual intuitions and categorical subsumption. This, however, opens up new investigations on the complementary relationship between the content of knowledge and its formal conditions, provoking fierce debates up to the present day on how the form-content dichotomy can be understood at all.[5] And even if this complex relationship of mind and world already has its prehistory in Aristotle's doctrine of hylomorphism, from the seventeenth century onward, the conflict intensified in a manner that antiquity could never have put forward. This becomes especially clear when looking at the idea of "conceptual schemes." For, if Kant, with his doctrine of concepts of understanding (*Verstandesbegriffe*), introduces conceptual schemata in the "Transcendental Deduction" of his *Critique of Pure Reason*, he, allegedly, not only seems to postulate an interface in the mind-world-relationship but also leaves open the question of how two categorically exclusive sources of knowledge (sensibility, which his responsible for intuition, and understanding) can relate at all. A "third" element—the "power of the imagination" (*Einbildungskraft*)—must play the mediating function of both. But exactly how is not clear. Concepts can thus be interpreted as being proto-sensible themselves, or, the other way around—sensations to be equipped with conceptual properties. As far as the latter case is concerned, which is advocated by John McDowell,[6] Hilary Putnam (the "middle" Putnam),[7] and Andrea Kern,[8] among others in contemporary debates on the sources of knowledge, we humans would be in immediate contact with facts and states of affairs "because experience is passive, a case of receptivity in operation."[9] Indeed, what we perceive could potentially not even be wrong anymore, as some defenders of a contemporary "disjunctivism" seem to claim. And this sounds apparently much more satisfying for proponents of ordinary folk psychology than the thesis that there is an insurmountable separation or—as mentioned above—a parallactic gap between mind and world that makes people and facts rotate incessantly around each other. What should such a "gap" be at all, or how exactly should it be defined, since in everyday life we usually have no problems relating to states of affairs and only now and then get stunned by an uncanny "turn of events/things," to borrow the words from the Austrian author Adalbert Stifter.[10]

Due to the lack of an answer as to how such a "gap" is to be understood, let alone be determined in a positivistic way, numerous philosophers reject the concept of a "gap" or parallactic fissure in the mind-world relationship altogether. And since this marks a difference for many authors in this volume fascinated by parallax—a difference which truly makes a difference—a brief elaboration of the reality or irreality of the mentioned "gap" may be helpful to the reader. Especially Richard Rorty,[11] Robert Brandom,[12] John McDowell, and Donald Davidson can be mentioned here, with Davidson as directing probably the most outspoken criticism of the so-called Third Dogma (as being at least co-responsible for "gap"-talk), against his venerated teacher Quine.[13] Davidson's aim is to limit ontological pluralism and skepticism as its twin-brother. McDowell follows Davidson with the help of his version of disjunctivism presented in his book *Mind and World* and in many papers thereafter.[14] In this way, both thinkers and their followers aim with different philosophical approaches, yet with the same firm conviction to avoid the aforementioned "gap," "split," or "fissure," in an exemplary manner that is contaminating, without cause for them, the mind-world relationship. The aim of their efforts is to fend off skepticism and to place the relationship of our mind to factual situations in the world on a solid foundation that is free of "psychologism" and, as mentioned, mediating schemes.[15] The breach between sensitivity and understanding has to be closed, and the belief both in the "thing in itself" and in a conceptual interface has to be overcome. If this succeeds, then, according to Davidson, we "reestablish unmediated touch with the familiar objects whose antics make our sentences and opinions true or false."[16] Davidson spells out such a conviction when he says that only by subtracting the talk of truth relative to a scheme can we rehabilitate the concept of objective truth.[17]

Davidson and McDowell are mentioned here to underline that their outspoken rejection of any kind of gap between mind and world includes as well, at least indirectly, a rejection of what "parallax" stands for. Kant's highly controversial concept of the "thing in itself" does not exist for them any more as an inherent boundary marker of our phenomenal reality, since reality is not "Erscheinung" (phenomenal) in a Kantian sense; that is, it cannot be captured in forms of diverse representations. Nor does Hegel's concept of "spirit" as an excessive commuter between subject and object, or appearance and truth, play an essential role.

These philosophical positions are mentioned here because they are diametrically opposed to traditions of philosophy, which many authors, combined in this volume, follow. Indeed, both the founding fathers of critical theory and their descendants today as well as the founding fathers of contemporary dialectical materialism cannot even share the belief in a reconcilable mind-world relationship. Far too many context-dependent differences, from the social superstructure to the economic substructure, or from the gap between ego and unconscious, are intertwined by a missing link. This makes the refusal of the Third Dogma, as demanded by Davidson, impossible. For this reason, many chapters in this volume are explicitly dedicated to the tradition of philosophers who, in contrast to the previously presented positions, explicitly defend a non-coincidence between mind and world as well as the theorem of some kind of interface mediating mind and world—no matter if this affects epistemology, politics, or aesthetics.

Among other things, they do so by referring back to Hegel, Marx, and Adorno, who were often left unnoticed in certain analytical Anglo-Saxon traditions of philosophical research in the second part of the twentieth century. Especially representatives of the Frankfurt School and the Ljubljana School but also followers of various theories of contemporary realism (known under titles such as New Realism, New Materialism, and Speculative Realism) argue in their numerous publications that cognition is not an asset that can be positivistically determined. It partakes in a process that allows mind and world to miss each other so that people and realities—figuratively speaking—unfold themselves behind their backs, that is, through non-encounters and aberrations. And the aberrations often reveal themselves in a way that people would not have imagined from their view equipped with various scientific findings. However, this does not mean that we should abandon the notions of truth or objectivity altogether, as has been posited repeatedly within certain currents of twentieth-century philosophy.

It is therefore not surprising that the Frankfurt and Ljubljana Schools, for their part, tend to adhere often to what can be called "ontologies of negativity" or "ontologies of incompleteness," respectively. In them, the epistemic revaluation of the non-coincidence of knowledge and truth serves the unfolding of a theory of a rather spectral understanding of what reality is about. It is defended in several chapters of this volume. So, while Davidson defends the refutation of the distinction between form and content of knowledge (dating back to Kant), since an insurmountable gap between two different sources of knowledge is postulated and can no longer be overcome, many of the authors gathered here see precisely in this gap a place of significant surplus or excess that is capable of changing the mind and the world relationship time and again. As such, the gap between form and content cannot be traced back to form or content. It is the incompatibility of the two categories themselves that must theoretically be explored.

According to the authors mentioned above, knowledge and truth miss each other not because facts are not recognized precisely enough but because knowledge (epistemic, political, artistic) parallactically reveals the place of arrival of that which it (knowledge embodied in man or the people) did not even see coming. Or to put it another way: truth and knowledge are mutually exclusive, because knowledge prepares the place where truth, as "aletheia," unconcealment, can only appear through the breaking of knowledge's veil of ignorance. This idea, which is developed by Heidegger in his aletheia theory, is missing on the part of the representatives of a naïve or scientific realism (presented here admittedly along very general lines)—regardless of whether it is a representationalist or anti-representationalist realism.

As these remarks have hopefully made clear, the concept of parallax undermines the belief mentioned above, that is, the Davidsonian and the McDowellian belief in a direct relationship between mind and world. Parallax interprets this relationship against the background of a non-coincidence between subject and object that cannot be positively determined.

3. The Chapters

Part One: Parallax in Ontology. The chapters in the first part present various interpretations of parallax that are intrinsically linked to the respective fields of research of the philosophers assembled here. German idealism is generally, but not exclusively, a point of reference within the investigations, as several authors also consider the issue of parallax with reference to the philosophy of the twentieth century, like Sartre, Adorno, Derrida, and its adaptation in the present era. The authors develop and expose the importance of parallax with reference to "transcendental philosophy" within a Lacanian-Hegelian approach (Žižek), with reference to "hermeneutic realism" (Koch), and with regard to a Lacan-inspired "object-disoriented ontology" (Zupančič), to name just a few.

Dirk Quadflieg, in his chapter "Parallactic Entanglement. On the Subject-Object-Relation in New Materialism and Adorno's Critical Ontology," examines the question of why the relation between subject and object has become problematic and ambiguous, such that the metaphor of parallax could appear as a promising way to grasp this otherwise incomprehensible relation. One important source for the new uncertainty of the subject-object relation lies in what is often referred to as the "material turn." Turning to exemplary authors of New Realism, New Materialism, and from the slightly older field of material culture studies, the chapter shows that—despite different theoretical perspectives—the authors highlighted in the chapter are able to convincingly question the traditional preeminence of the subject over the object. However, the constitutive role of materiality and of objects, which some of the approaches contend for, turns out to be all but easy to conceptualize. Against this backdrop, the last part of the chapter introduces Adorno's claim of a "preponderance of the object" to the line of inquiry and argues that the "critical ontology" he depicts in his *Negative Dialectics* still offers a fruitful figure of thought, which could help to prevent some of the difficulties within the current debate on New Materialism.

Graham Harman introduces the reader to Žižek's book *The Parallax View* in his text "Žižek's Parallax, on The Inherent Stupidity of All Philosophical Positions." He explains how it is especially in this book that Žižek's philosophy proves to be inherently dialectical. What Žižek means by the word "Parallax" cannot be reduced to the apparent difference in position of an object when it is seen from two different viewpoints. Žižek rejects any theory in which one and the same object simply "appears" differently when seen in two different ways. More than this, it is a shift "in the object itself" that is Žižek's concern. As a subject-oriented philosopher, he frames his book as a discussion of the parallax object. Dozens of examples of parallax are therefore given. Harman interprets a few of them. He shows that Žižek is a dialectician primarily because the negativity of the retroactive and the self-reflexive is, for him, the best guarantee against an understanding of philosophy as a discipline that presents the contents and not the movement of thought.

Markus Gabriel presents, in his chapter "How Mind Fits into Nature," aspects of his theory of mental realism in dialogue with Thomas Nagel's *Mind and Cosmos*. Nagel's work tries to grasp the relation between mind and nature but evokes the problem of mind's "placement" in nature. As such, Gabriel argues that it puts the investigation on a wrong track of analysis from the start. Mental realism circumvents the placement problem by characterizing a level of reality, which, in its importance for minds, cannot be meaningfully traced back to those facts that we locate in a mind- and consciousness-free universe by deploying our best empirical reasons. Ontological pluralism comes into play and helps Gabriel prove mental realism to be anti-naturalist. Mental realism recognizes both facts and forms of knowledge that cannot be meaningful objects of any natural scientific investigation.

Anton Friedrich Koch presents, in his chapter "Parallax in Hermeneutic Realism," four doctrines essential for his understanding of hermeneutic realism with reference to Sellars, D. Lewis, and Quine. They concern the "triple structure of truth," the "subjectivity thesis," the "readability thesis," and the "antinomy thesis." Koch shows interrelations between the doctrines to finally examine, for each doctrine, to what extent parallax is not only an appealing theoretical tool for hermeneutic realism but also a hidden figure of thought in certain currents of analytic philosophy of the twentieth century.

Alenka Zupančič critically engages, in her text "Object-Disoriented Ontology. Realism in Psychoanalysis," with Quentin Meillassoux's anti-correlation vision of ontology. Meillassoux diagnosed in certain currents of contemporary philosophy a critical stance on modern science. He posits, for his part, modern science as a continuation of metaphysics by other means, that is, as the discipline that stretches out into the "Real" in an absolute sense. Zupančič follows Meillassoux's arguments but sees in his philosophy the revival of a fundamental fantasy: the great Outside. She confronts this fantasy with Lacan, for whom the fantasy of the great Outside conceals what Lacan calls the Real, which is already *right here*. Modern science starts for Lacan when it produces its object through a discourse that has real consequences, or better: one whose consequences touch upon the Real.

Paul Livingston asks in "Temporal Paradox, Realism, and Subjectivity" about the "quality/composition/nature/features" of the minimal, specifically logical or meta-logical structures, which must be appealed to in order to understand the possibility of something like a subjective perspective on the world. Drawing on arguments by Kant, Heidegger, and Dummett, the author argues that the formal conditions for such a perspective can be found in the combination of the meta-logical features or ideas of totality, reflexivity, and paradox. However, contrary to positions that understand subjectivity as the project of an original scission from objects or their totality, these features are already, Livingston argues, present in the world as soon as there is temporal change or becoming, as can be seen from a consideration of its own internal logic. It follows that the position of subjectivity can be understood as a direct formal outcome of the fact of temporal change or becoming. This line of argument discloses a parallactic gap between, on the one hand, "B-series" accounts of temporality, which maintain realism about objects while sacrificing realism about subjectivity, time, and becoming; and, on the other, phenomenological accounts, which see time (in anti-realist terms) as an outcome or product of subjective consciousness.

G. Anthony Bruno's "The Parallactic Leap. Fichte, Apperception, and the Hard Problem of Consciousness" focuses on the normative turn in Fichte's critique of dogmatism to show how an "inward" shift in perspective changes the meanings of "all of our terms" and, therewith, the nature of objectivity. The world that seems factual and to exclude normativity is displaced by a world constituted by the normative framework of judging and acting subjects. Hence, the world that poses an alleged hard problem of consciousness is displaced by one whose problems are, in the first instance, practical rather than theoretical.

Slavoj Žižek explores, in his chapter "The Parallax of Ontology. Reality and Its Transcendental Supplement," the way in which parallax serves as another name for what Heidegger called ontological difference. It designates the fact that the ontological dimension cannot be reduced to the ontic one. An ontic dimension views reality as a whole whose parts we humans are. In this sense, today's cognitive sciences and evolutionary biology unveil how humanity, including its cognitive capacities that enabled the rise of cognitive and evolutionary sciences, gradually emerged out of the animal kingdom. A transcendental-ontological rejoinder to this explanation is that it is ultimately circular: it has to presuppose the modern scientific approach to reality, since it is only through its lenses that reality appears as an object of scientific explanation. The scientific view of reality thus cannot really account for its own emergence—but, similarly, the transcendental-ontological approach cannot explain the fact of contingent external reality. Thus, the gap between the two is irreducible. Does this mean that the duality of the ontic and the ontological is the final word—a fact that we cannot transcend?

Part Two. Parallax in Normative Orders: The second field of research in the volume is dedicated to parallax within political and practical philosophy. Here, subjectivity is presented repeatedly as a distorting factor in any account of how things really are. Ontological investigations are not left behind, but they now form the background of several papers with regard to subjectivity as a feature of reality. Given that inquiries into what there is affect what there is when subjectivity is more than just a hallmark of the conscious mind, this subjectivity plays a central role with regard to "negativity" (Menke), "irony" (Khurana), and "sex as a transcendental category" (Power).

Christoph Menke, in his chapter "Truth as Subjective Effect. Adorno Against Hegel," develops the argument that subjectivity is (nothing but) negativity for Hegel, insofar as true determination is that which emerges from the negativity of the subject. This is the point of Hegel's theory of determinate negation. The determination expresses the self that produces it; the determination is true (and free) insofar as it "contains" negativity (Hegel). This understanding of subjectivity is rejected by Adorno. According to Adorno, the expressivistic interpretation of the connection between self and truth, negation and determination is Hegel's error. Negativity can never be contained in a determination. Negation "remains" negative (Adorno). Therefore, the true determination only emerges from the negativity of the self in such a way that negativity passes through the subject. There is no "mediation"—of negation and destiny, or of self and truth. Their connection consists in the parallax gap that separates them.

Nina Power reflects, in "Is Sex a Transcendental Category of Parallax?," on the apparently insurmountable differences inherent in current debates, where proposals to change the meaning of sex from a "biological definition" to an act of "self-identification" provoke attacks from one group against the other for considering either biology or society not enough or too much. Power, for her part, then asks, "What happens if we agree that sex 'isn't real', or, in other words, that sex is not how we decide who is a man and who is a woman?" She presents, in passing, several debates within feminist theory from the 1970s to the current era from a personal perspective, to then address two neglected aspects: first, the apparently obvious distinction between "sexuation and sexuality," which focuses on the Lacanian insight that there is no experience that is non-sexed experience, and, second, the role of the mother and of motherhood. The latter topic is not only often neglected also within feminist theory but, as a personal form of pleasure, can also turn the figure of the mother within society into a target of male aggression and disdain.

Thomas Khurana delimits, in his chapter "The Irony of Self-Consciousness. Hegel, Derrida, and the Animal That Therefore I Am," the parallactic gap that separates humanity from the animal kingdom with references to Hegel, Heidegger, Derrida, and Agamben. In a well-known passage from his *Lectures on Aesthetics*, Hegel writes that "precisely because he knows that he is an animal," man "ceases to be an animal and attains knowledge of himself as spirit." As this remark by Hegel suggests, self-consciousness is not self-positing and self-validating in the sense that, by virtue of knowing myself to be a being of a certain type, I actualize myself as this type of being. Instead, self-consciousness is structurally self-negating and self-transgressive. Precisely by knowing myself to be a being of a certain kind, I cease to be that very being; in ceasing to be that being through knowing myself to be that being, I attain knowledge of "myself": my peculiar difference from the thing I know myself to be. In the chapter, Khurana investigates the ironic structure of self-consciousness that comes to the fore in the quote mentioned above and elucidates the parallax perspective that self-consciousness requires to grasp its own reality.

Frank Ruda first presents parallax, in his chapter "A Squinting Gaze on the Parallax between Spirit and Nature," as a "two-dimensional" and "retroactive" concept within contemporary debates of dialectical materialism and then focuses his analysis on the relation between nature and spirit in Hegel's philosophy. He shows how, for Hegel, nature can only be reflected upon by thought after the so-called small Logic (the logic of Hegel's *Encyclopedia*) has laid the ground for this, with having been grounded herself by the *Phenomenology of Spirit* from 1807 and the *Science of Logic*. Nature and thought prove to be tied together, mutually implying the other, yet cancelling each other out as well. No epistemological barrier separates thought/spirit from nature, since both relate to each other through the very inconsistency of their relation. Hegel evades a consistent ontology in the mind-nature dichotomy, since consistency would necessarily be false appearance.

Adrian Johnston compares, in his chapter "*I Am Nothing but I Make Everything*. Marx, Lacan, and the Labor Theory of Suture," different forms of split-subjectivity. He brings them in a relation of a mutual illumination. Starting with Alfred Sohn-Rethel's thesis that the commodity form proves to be the concealed socioeconomic nucleus of Kantian subjectivity, he shows that Jacques-Alain Miller's concept of "suture," adapted by Lacan, exemplifies both the subject's status of being not identical to itself and its zero-point of nudity, which Marx depicts as the proletariat's condition of being in capitalist societies. Whereas money is, according to Marx, the commodity par excellence as object, it is labor-power qua universal exception which is the commodity par excellence as subject. This parallactic split between these two commodities (as object and as subject) is for Marx one of the reasons why the proletariat is defined by its nudity (*Nacktheit*). As such it is "nothing but makes," that is, produces, "everything."

Part Three: Parallax in Aesthetics. The third field of research of the volume is dedicated to modes of parallax within aesthetics. The art work itself can be interpreted as an essential medium of understanding parallax, as it potentially "unconceals" that which in reality is more than reality itself (McGowan). As such, it can also become an ontological category, as Eva Schürmann shows with reference to process ontological arguments as presented by Alfred North Whitehead. No less aesthetic are conscious and unconscious transmissions of enjoyment where one allegedly enjoys his life at the costs of another's lack of enjoyment (Pfaller) or when unconscious objects are transmitted either from one body to another in psychoanalytic sessions (McNulty) or from dreaming to awakening (Finkelde).

Todd McGowan explores, in his chapter "Drama as Philosophy. The Tragedy of the End of Art," Hegel's famous dismissal of art's significance. One reason why the German idealist announces that art is "a thing of the past" is grounded in the conviction that philosophy must become artistic itself. The absolute art form, drama, provides a paradigm for philosophy which Hegel himself adopts. He does so by creating a method in which he dramatizes each theoretical position that he confronts, by showing how drama exposes the internal contradiction of the object in a way that philosophical argumentation obscures.

Robert Pfaller investigates, in "Parallaxes of Sinister Enjoyment. The Lessons of Interpassivity and the Contemporary Troubles with Pleasure," how hitherto innocent pleasures (like drinking, smoking, flirting) have been "breaking bad" in recent years, with radically different social groups (like refugees, old white men, Me-Too activists) appearing as the thieves of our enjoyment. The chapter follows Pfaller's famous study on "interpassivity," since at center stage is the question of the cultural, social, and political conditions that would allow us today to "parallactically" reconquer the pleasures as pleasures and perceive our contemporaries not as threats but as comrades in a solidarity of shared enjoyment.

Eva Schürmann unfolds, in her chapter "Nautical Positioning," parallax with regard to process ontology. The most salient feature of this investigation is the continuous fluctuation of all variables of reference. In Alfred North Whitehead's process ontology, she finds the key witness for her argument, since, according to Whitehead, perceptual and qualitative experience constitute the core of all reality, which transforms aesthetics to become a key issue of ontology beyond a mere subject and object separation.

Tracy McNulty shows, in her chapter "Feeling at a Distance, or the Aesthetics of Unconscious Transmission," how, in the process of psychoanalysis, the analyst can be most impacted or affected not by the narrative or the demands that the analysand addresses to him or her but by unconscious acts that pass through the body whose stakes are linked to an unconscious desire of a specific subject matter. A point of maximum opacity or illegibility may show up, something that is not an object of conscious representation or knowledge but something that can, nevertheless, be transmitted from one subject to another. For McNulty it is especially the impact of this object across multiple subjects that contributes to the problem of parallax within processes of transference. As such, the end of an analysis can be understood as a new openness of an individual to what Lacan calls the object-cause of desire in its properly aesthetic dimension, that is, in the form of its unpresentability.

Dominik Finkelde presents, in his chapter "The Dream That Knew Too Much. On Freud, Lacan, and Philip K. Dick," a mutual permeation of non-wakefulness in everyday life and experiences of awakening through dreaming. He clarifies his theory with reference to two examples: (1) a short story called "Exhibit Piece" by the US-American science fiction author Philip K. Dick turned into the episode "Real Life" of the TV-series *Electric Dreams*, and (2) the much-commented dream of the "burning child" which Freud analyzes in chapter seven of *The Interpretation of Dreams*. The chiastic relationship of non-wakefulness during being awake and of awakening through dreaming is explained by Lacan with the help of the Aristotelian concepts of "tyche" and "automaton" and with reference to the Taoist philosopher Chuang Tzu. Finkelde thereby shows how the psyche in her dream work can encounter truth values which, due to repression mechanisms in the waking state, maintain non-wakefulness in our everyday life.

Notes

1   Slavoj Žižek, *The Parallax View* (Cambridge, MA: MIT Press, 2006), 17.
2   Paul Boghossian, *Fear of Knowledge* (Oxford: Oxford University Press, 2006), 59–69. Martin Kusch, "When Paul Met Ludwig: Wittgensteinian Comments on Boghossian's Antirelativism." In *Realism, Relativism, Constructivism: Proceedings of the 38th International Wittgenstein Symposium in Kirchberg*, ed. Christian Kanzian, Sebastian Kletzl et al. (Berlin: Walter de Gruyter, 2017), 203–14.
3   Žižek, *The Parallax View*, 17.
4   Hilary Putnam, *The Many Faces of Realism* (LaSalle, IL: Open Court, 1987), 32.
5   The "material of knowledge" is often interpreted—so Hegel's critique—"as a ready-made world outside thinking, that thinking is by itself empty, that it comes to this material as a form from outside, fills itself with it, and only then gains a content, thereby becoming real knowledge." G.W.F. Hegel, *The Science of Logic*, ed. and trans. George di Giovanni (Cambridge: Cambridge University Press, 2010), 24.
6   John McDowell, *Mind and World* (Cambridge, MA: Harvard University Press, 1996).
7   Hilary Putnam, "Sense, Nonsense, and the Senses. An Inquiry Into the Powers of the Human Mind," *The Journal of Philosophy* 91, no. 9 (1994): 445–517.
8   Andrea Kern, *Sources of Knowledge* (Cambridge, MA: Harvard University Press, 2017).
9   McDowell, *Mind and World*, 10.
10   Adalbert Stifter, *Der Waldgänger* (Stuttgart: Kohlhammer, 1978), vol. 3:1, 101.
11   Richard Rorty, *The Mirror of Nature* (Princeton: Princeton University Press, 1979).
12   Robert Brandom, *Making It Explicit* (Cambridge, MA: Harvard University Press, 1994).
13   Donald Davidson, "On the Very Idea of a Conceptual Scheme," *Proceedings and Addresses of the American Philosophical Association* 57 (1973–4): 5–20.
14   See for example John McDowell, "Avoiding the Myth of the Given." In *John McDowell: Experience, Norm, and Nature*, ed. Jakob Lindgaard (Oxford: Blackwell Publishing, 2008), 1–14; See also Charles Travis, "The Silence of the Senses," *Mind* 113, no. 449 (2004): 57–94; "Reason's Reach," *European Journal of Philosophy* 15, no. 4 (2007): 225–48.
15   Also anti-realists like Michael Dummett, Martin Kusch, Bas van Fraassen, and Maria Baghramian would probably not subscribe to the concept of parallax, at least not within the limits of the Hegelian interpretation which is dear to Žižek: that within an epistemic shift "the object itself returns the gaze" (Žižek, *The Parallax View*, 17) in such a way that subjects themselves change their way of being.
16   Davidson, "On the Very Idea of a Conceptual Scheme," 20.
17   See also Donald Davidson, "A Coherence Theory of Truth and Knowledge." In *Subjective, Intersubjective, Objective* (Oxford: Clarendon Press, 2001), 137–54.

Part One

Parallax in Ontology

1

Parallactic Entanglement

On the Subject-Object-Relation in New Materialism and Adorno's Critical Ontology

Dirk Quadflieg

The optical phenomenon of a parallax usually designates a mismatch of perspectives caused by different points of view. Due to a change of perspectives, the background of a perceived object is changing and thus the object, too, seems to alter its position in space. But the cause for this alteration is, in fact, the different viewpoints of the observer. Taken as a metaphor, a parallax could stand for a twist in the relation of subject and object, such that a transformation, which seems to happen on the side of the object, actually results from a movement of the subject. Since there is no third standpoint which allows for overviewing the whole situation, the term "parallax" rather hints at a blind spot or a gap within the relation of a subject and an object than something that could be positively described or explained. Speaking of a parallactic entanglement of a subject and an object therefore means not only that the relation of object and subject is twisted but also that it is extremely difficult for the subject to locate the reason for these shifting perspectives because they lie within its own movement. For this reason, Slavoj Žižek introduces the term "parallax" to designate most generally "the gap which separates the One from itself."[1]

Nevertheless, the question can be raised, why in recent philosophical debates, the relation of subject and object has become problematic and ambiguous in the first place, such that the metaphor of the parallax appears as a promising way to grasp their incomprehensible relation. Or to put it slightly differently: "What is the problem, a parallax is supposed to give an answer to?" One author who immediately comes to mind, because he so vigorously criticized the modern distinction of subject and object, is, of course, Bruno Latour. His 1991 essay "We Have Never Been Modern" starts with the assumption that modernity is constituted by an asymmetrical division between culture and nature, human beings und nonhuman beings, which has been put into question by many postmodern accounts. Yet, for Latour these dichotomies have never existed as such. According to him, they are the result of a process of separation and purification, intervening in a preexisting network of hybrids and mixed beings.[2] Without the existence of hybrids and the ongoing processes of mixing between the two spheres, there would have been no need for purification. Hence, as Latour argues, although hybridization is usually associated with the era of postmodernity, it is not a completely new phenomenon; it only brings (back) to light what was, in fact, always already happening underneath and prior to the modern separation of humans and nonhumans, subjects and objects. From such a perspective, it is possible to say not only that the clear historic difference between the premodern age and modernity breaks down—and thus that we have never been really modern—but also that the subject-object-distinction is no longer plausible and actually has never been real. As a result, Latour suggests to trace back our knowledge to the interaction of human and nonhuman "actors," acting together in a network of collectives and through controversial relations, which could become the new empirical subject of a new form of sociological research.[3]

It is not my aim here to contest Latour's rather bold hypotheses about modernity; I just want to mention his "actor-network-theory" for reasons of contrast. Compared to the parallactic entanglement of subject and object, which Slavoj Žižek depicts in his book *The Parallactic View*, Latour's critique of the modern subject-object-division nevertheless follows quite a modern narrative of enlightenment: since we are trapped in our own ontological categories, which appear to be universal and ahistorical, we have to radically change our perspective and analyze the historical and material preconditions of our knowledge. For Latour, this kind of analysis can be achieved by an examination of actors and networks, which are accessible through empirical insight. Such an inquiry not only will lead to a better understanding of ourselves and increase our scientific knowledge but could finally ground a more inclusive form of democracy, which would be able to take into account nonhuman beings within a "parliament of things."[4]

By contrast, a parallactic relation of subject and object has a very different impact on the knowing subject. Since a parallax designates a gap or a blind spot, the relation of subject and object cannot be fully grasped and transformed into positive knowledge about ourselves, the essence of things, or new forms of political action. Quite on the contrary, one could say that a parallax is exactly that what makes a stable and lasting form of knowledge impossible, for every "insight" into the blind spot elucidates the general uncertainty of the subject's capacities of knowing. Though it is still an open question whether the notion of parallax points at an ontological or a historic status, it "enlightens" the subject-object-relation only negatively, namely insofar as it puts into question the subject of knowing—in every sense. Still, the question remains, why we should think of the subject-object-relation in such purely negative terms?

Apart from Latour's actor-network-theory we are currently witnessing a broad, new interest in materiality, objects and artifacts, both in philosophy and the social sciences, which is often referred to as "material turn." In the first part of my chapter I want to take a closer look at two recent philosophical debates, in order to elaborate on a basic problem many of these approaches are facing. Against the dominance of linguistic models in philosophy and the social sciences, both "New Realism" and "New Materialism" want to go back to some kind of reality or the outer world of objects to avoid extreme forms of social constructivism and relativism. Yet, as I want to show, in doing so they paradoxically run the risk of losing contact to the side of the object. Thus, in the second part I would like to introduce a slightly older version of the contemporary concern for materiality from the field of material culture studies. Already in the early 1980s, theorists like Daniel Miller had the idea that certain forms of consumer practices had to be described as both a process of objectification and that of self-realization. To elaborate this idea a bit further, the third part of my chapter will go back to Adorno's critical ontology, which he developed in his 1966 *Negative Dialectics*. His claim of a "preponderance of the object" (*Vorrang des Objekts*) still offers a fruitful figure of thought which can not only help to prevent some of the difficulties the current debate on new materialism is struggling with but moreover give a convincing explanation of why the negative model of parallax reveals a promising way to rethink the traditional subject-object-relation.

1. The Disappearance of the Object in New Realism and New Materialism

Within contemporary philosophy and the social sciences, at least two quite different discussions about the role of materiality, the world of outer objects, and reality can be differentiated: one of the most recent, but maybe lesser-known philosophical positions is labeled "New Realism." Maurizio Ferraris and Markus Gabriel are two representatives of this mainly epistemological approach. Though for slightly different reasons, both want to reject a philosophical skepticism, which holds that the world is a mere construct of our concepts. Against such a constructivism, associated mainly with the Kantian tradition and poststructuralism, they argue for the necessity of a grounding of our cognitive capacity in some kind of reality, providing a certainty beyond doubt.[5] Reality or realism here stands for a source of such an undeniable certainty, which in turn is a prerequisite of any possible knowledge, even a skeptic one. Though the reality, this new realism is seeking for, is often tied to a concept of the world, it does not necessarily refer to an outer world of objects and artifacts but could also mean the reality of thoughts or the reality of conditions which have to be fulfilled by judgments to be true.[6] Such a more epistemological version of new realism, represented among others by Markus Gabriel, has no intention to question the relation of subject and object or change their hierarchical order. Quite on the contrary, this approach wants to secure a concept of reason, located in the intellectual capacities of the mind, and thus holds on to the traditional primacy of the subject.

Likewise, more object-oriented forms of New Realism, like the one Mauricio Ferraris argues for, are only interested in the resistance and unchangeability of the outer world of objects insofar as they restrict our concepts and make sure "the world is not a dream."[7] As a result, Ferraris' "positive realism" comes quite close to a naïve positivism by taking the self-identity of subject and object as well as their clear distinction for granted. Although both versions of New Realism refer to a reality as the necessary condition of subjective knowledge, they do not have the intention of conceding objects a new position in philosophical reflection beyond that of a passive and unchangeable ground. They neither want to give up the subject-object-distinction, like Latour's Actor-Network-Theory, nor do they put into question the position of the knowing subject, as indicated by the notion of parallax. New Realism could therefore be characterized as a subject-centered epistemology that is interested in reality only insofar as it helps to secure the position of the knowing subject against the threat of relativism.

By contrast, a second set of recent approaches from the social sciences, known under the umbrella term "New Materialism," seems more promising when it comes to the significance of external objects and artifacts. In contrast to the diverse positions of a new philosophical realism, New Materialism is genuinely interested in the multiple ways matter interferes in processes of signification and the genesis of social and cultural meaning. Though highly influenced by poststructuralist theories of language, many of its exponents, as for example Karen Barad, criticize the predominance of language in political and social theory.[8] Their critique, however, notably differs from that of New Realism. Whereas Markus Gabriel accuses theories of discourse (in the tradition of Foucault and others) of erasing consciousness and human beings from philosophy, Barad is in general sympathetic with the critical analysis of discursive practices like the one Judith Butler outlined in "Bodies that matter."

In her book *Meeting the Universe Halfway*, Barad stresses that Butler already provides a concept of materialization to explain how things, bodies, and persons become real through discursive practices. Yet, from Barad's point of view, Butler's concept of materialization is still too closely tied to practices of meaning and signification and is thus unable to give a more detailed account of how matter and things themselves take part in the formation of social and political power-knowledge relations.[9] In order to do so, she—like many other exponents of New Materialism—refers to Bruno Latour's actor-network-theory and holds that knowledge is produced through an association or "intra-action," as she calls it, of matter and discourse, human and nonhuman agents. Taking up an example mentioned very briefly by Butler, Barad focuses on the role of sonography, more precisely the piezoelectric crystal or transducer at the heart of the ultra-sound technology, to demonstrate how matter is essentially involved in the emergence of a gendered fetus.[10] However, by stressing the physical-technical functioning of the ultrasound machine as a constitutive part for the discursive perception of the fetus as an object, Barad does not really exceed Butler's approach; she just gives a more detailed and complex description of the discursive materialization of a body. Butler's main assumption, that the gendered body is nothing naturally given but becomes real through numerous reiterated discursive practices, is neither contested nor enhanced by the functioning of the piezoelectric crystal or the apparatus it forms together with other parts of the ultrasound machine, doctors, and medical routines during pregnancy.[11]

A more convincing way of challenging theories of discourse would certainly be to claim that the role of matter in or for discursive practices differs essentially from that of other "agents" like human beings or concepts. But with Latour's actor-network-theory in the background, this is exactly what Barad and other authors of New Materialism do not want. Therefore, the more general problem of these approaches could be formulated as a paradox: On the one hand, New Materialism wants to give a new account of matter playing a constitutive role within the formation of social and cultural phenomena. On the other hand, however, they follow Latour's often problematized strategy of undermining the traditional subject-object-division and instead want to speak of interwoven agents—with the result that they tend to lose the reference for the word "matter" again. Or, to put it more succinctly: it seems as if

New Materialism wants to stress the importance of material objects and at the same time has to deny their distinct existence.

2. Objectification as Self-realization.
Material Culture Studies' Original Insight

Starting in the early 1980s, the material culture approach had a slightly different point of departure than the two more-recent theoretical movements mentioned before. At that time, it was not the predominance of linguistic models in the field of humanities that the emerging material culture studies wanted to overcome by turning to material practices but mainly the reductive tendency in Marxist and especially vulgar Marxist notions of commodity fetishism and alienation. The problem that Daniel Miller, Arjun Appadurai, and Igor Kopytoff—just to mention a few names—were facing was that from a Marxist point of view, almost any object of everyday life in Western consumer societies appeared as a mere commodity and thus as an expression of alienation.[12] But criticizing the growing mass of goods just for being objects of trade turned out to be too general and unable to give a more detailed picture of the numerous different forms of our everyday use of objects. From the perspective of early cultural studies, there was a need for more differentiated descriptions of these practices instead of accusing them all equally for being alienated.

Daniel Miller, whose 1987 book *Material Culture and Mass Consumption* still is one of the milestones for material culture studies, is well aware of the philosophical difficulties that a naïve return to materiality as a simply given would imply. Nevertheless, he does not want to put into question the everyday experience of a clear difference between objects and subjects. Instead, he suggests to look at artifacts as products of a process of "objectification," a concept he finds in Hegel, Marx, and Simmel and anthropological research alike.[13] Following this larger tradition, Miller understands objectification as a general process of externalization through which all kinds of cultural phenomena emerge and come about. Hence, culture has to be understood as an ongoing process of externalization of human spirit in the outer world of things. As Georg Simmel already argued, this process implies a necessary moment of alienation, since individuals in societies with a rapidly growing material culture are no longer capable of appropriating the cultural knowledge and potentialities, which are objectified in the mass of worldly objects surrounding them. Alienation is thus not limited to a certain historical division of labor or form of production but necessarily comes along with the development of culture, though it increases with the expansion of the world of objects.[14]

Without following Simmel's pessimistic view on this "tragedy of culture," Miller takes up his notion of alienation and draws a slightly different conclusion. Like authors from the Frankfurt School, Miller believes that it is impossible for modern societies to give up a certain state of division of labor without at the same time losing the very basis for individual freedom and self-realization. Thus, the growing alienation within societies of mass consumption cannot be overcome on the side of production only. One rather has to consider the side of consumption, too, and look for practices that allow individuals or social groups to re-appropriate commodified goods and artifacts.[15]

Now, it might seem as if Miller's interpretation of the necessary moment of alienation in objectification amounts to a simplistic narrative of alienation and re-appropriation. The starting point of such a simplistic account would be a self-identical and powerful subject, externalizing its intellectual capacities in outer objects, thereby distancing itself from its own ideas, so that it has to re-appropriate its own potential through these outer objects, in order to finally find a way back to its true inner self. The reason, why this well-known narrative of the subject and its self-alienation does not apply here, was already given by my short remarks on the modern division of labor and the fact that this division is essential for the flourishing of individual freedom. The very fact that objects of everyday life are indeed produced by unknown others and are thus products of a more and more obscure intentionality has an impact on the process of re-appropriation, since that what is appropriated in consumption is not and cannot be the same as that what had to be invested to form these goods and make them come about. There is a gap between the estrangement in the process of production and the re-appropriation through practices of consumption; this gap could be described as a gap between the universal and the particular. Consumer goods are never just an expression of the state of mind or the physical skills of their particular producers. Rather, they integrate within themselves the general state of a society's technical development and the general form of knowledge, exceeding both producer and consumer. As a result, artifacts are neither a box, wherein the producing subject places a message for later use, nor does the "re"- in re-appropriation mean a complete return to a primordial state of completeness.

In a certain way, it is impossible to appropriate the universality objectified in artifacts and goods of everyday use, since we can never fully grasp all historic aspects and cultural preconditions gathered in an object. From Simmel's point of view, the opening gap between the universality of human spirit realized in the object and the particularity of the subject's use of it is the very reason why under the condition of mass-production subjects are more and more alienated from the growing quantity of objects surrounding them. But one could also argue that without such an opening between the universal and the particular, it would be impossible to use things for different purposes and in other ways than those they were initially made for. In this respect, the gap between the universality objectified within things of our lifeworld and the particularity of use we make of them represents nothing less than a precondition for acting differently or, in other words, a fundamental form of freedom.

Miller, however, does not go all the way to these philosophical reflections about the relation of subject and object but finds another way of putting the problem, which I find also convincing though not easy to grasp. Wanting to escape both, a reductive critique of commodity fetishism and a common sociological explanation, he rejects the widespread tendency to look at things as a mere "mirror" of social relations.[16] Artifacts are more than just an expression of a mode of production and also more than the significance they have in certain social contexts. The question, however, what exactly this "more" stands in for, is all but easy to answer. Miller eventually finds a formula that is rather a new way of phrasing the problem than its solution: he suggests to understand objects as a constitutive part of those contexts that are giving meaning to them.[17] This formula certainly has the advantage of not reducing the object to a mere mirror of social relations, since it allows for conceiving objects as internally integrated in the very production of meaning, instead of just being given meaning from outside, as it were. But even if one sets aside the problematic concept of context, which has been compellingly criticized by Derrida and others, it still remains unclear how objects can participate in the process of signification.

Despite these open questions, Miller's account might be helpful for avoiding the paradox of New Materialism. As indicated before, New Materialism, on the one hand, wants to undermine the traditional subject-object-distinction and, on the other hand, has to stress the particularity of objects and matter in order to distinguish this dimension from mere discourse. Material culture studies, by contrast, do not have the intention to tear down the boundary between subject and object but want to overcome a shortened notion of materialism in the social sciences that interprets objects as a mirror or mere representation of originally social relations. Promising, though not always quite clear, is Miller's conception of objectification, which could be spelled out as an at-once alienating and liberating process of actualization: all products of human spirit have to go through in order to become real. Yet, Miller's insight remains inconsistent as long as the side of the subject is left unaltered. The moment of estrangement in cultural objectification, which Simmel's "tragedy of culture" refers to, implies another perspective on the subject: it is never fully one with itself because it is a being that is essentially both particular and universal, and as universal always already outside itself.

To sum up: New Materialism as well as material culture studies rightly point out that the side of materiality and the object have been neglected in the field of critical theories of society for a long time. But the answers that they offer to bring the object back into the scope of social theory amount to the same problem, namely that none of these theoretical approaches is able to really articulate the shift within the relation between subject and object. The crucial point here is, of course, that the shift itself is inconceivable and ineffable, since there is no third position, which would allow perceiving and describing the affected relation of subject and object from the outside, as it were. With such a result, we finally reach the point where the concept of the parallax becomes visible as a circumscription of the lack that escapes any attempt of conceptualization. And exactly here, Adorno's claim of a preponderance of the object comes into play as a still contemporary attempt of shifting the traditional perspective on the subject-object-relation in order to cast a glance at this lack, which he calls the "non-identical."

3. Adorno's Critical Ontology and the Object's Preponderance

Since the phrase "preponderance of the object" (*Vorrang des Objekts*) is all but self-explaining, it might be helpful to first of all very briefly sketch the basic theoretical framework of Adorno's "Negative Dialectic," within which this idea is developed. What is at stake here is nothing less than a fundamental critique of ontology and transcendental philosophy, in fact, of Western philosophy as such, which from Adorno's point of view relies on a contradictory principle of identity. Identity in the sense of absolute self-sameness is the universal norm of certainty and truth; it characterizes all grounding principles in philosophy, such as being, the subject, and the concept as such. For Adorno, however, this claimed absolute self-identity of these principles is at the same time in need of the other, the non-identical, factual, or non-conceptual; otherwise, it would have no meaning at all. The transcendental subject in Kant, for example, does not exist as a pure form of apperception alone; it depends on sensations and this means on some kind of matter.[18] Kant, who clearly saw the necessity of these "two pillars of knowledge," as he called it, was yet unable to draw the conclusion that the ephemeral and finite sensations themselves do belong to the conditions of the possibility of knowledge. Within the project of transcendental philosophy, such a conclusion remains impossible, for it would ruin the attempt to ground philosophy in the self-sameness of the transcendental subject.

Two crucial aspects of Adorno's critique of identity are worth noting before moving on to the dialectical relation of subject and object he suggests. The first aspect concerns the aim of his critique. When Adorno is speaking in favor of the excluded other of the identity principle, what he calls the non-identical, he neither argues for an integration of this excluded other nor does he want to just replace one foundational concept with another. Far from being a new grounding principle, the non-identical, which appears in or as the parallactic relation of the subject to the object, destabilizes the traditional idea of philosophical grounding. Like Derrida, Adorno wants to deconstruct identity thinking by first of all holding on to the criticized dualism in order to dismantle its exclusionary force and its implicit power-relation. By contrast, giving up the difference of subject and object too fast runs the risk of perpetuating these power-relations without noticing—or produces unintended paradoxes like in New Materialism.

The second important aspect is closely related to the first and concerns the subject of Adorno's critical efforts. Other than in the more object-oriented version of New Realism, his critical analysis of the subject-object-relation is not meant to amount to a better or more stable conjunction of epistemology and ontology. Although he reflects on the ontological status of the subject-object-relation, the main purpose of his argument is to demonstrate that ontology is unavoidably entangled with a sociohistoric reality. This is why Adorno is able to link the ontological principle of identity to a historical form of society, based on the principle of exchange of equivalents. In other words, to challenge the principle of identity via a reformulation of the subject-object-relation affects much more than philosophical issues; over and above, it is a fundamental critique of capitalist societies. For Adorno, thus, "critique of society is critique of epistemology—and vice versa."[19]

Against the backdrop of Adorno's critique of the identity principle, the idea of a "preponderance of the object" certainly becomes more accessible. With respect to the current debates on materiality and the social life of things, some of which were presented in the first part of the chapter, a preponderance of the object might appear modest and as a mere shift of perspectives: the traditional focus on the intentionality and actions of the subject, dominant in philosophy and social theory alike, should be replaced by a new attention for the social meaning or even the agency of objects and things. For Adorno, however, such a shift of perspective has far more consequences, at least if it is not just an expression of changing theoretical interests but motivated by the insight that the subject is dependent on the object. Taking into account the principle of identity, which subjectivity is essentially based on, a preponderance of the object necessarily disempowers the subject's claim for absoluteness.[20] As a result, it is impossible to think of an equilibrium of both sides without destroying the primacy of the subject and that means by the same token it's essence. In this respect, the rather odd expression "preponderance" (the same goes for the German word *Vorrang*) could already be read as an indication for the impossibility of simply reversing the order of primacy. To put it differently, primacy as a logical form is itself already an essential part of the identity principle. Speaking of a "primacy of the object" would thus be just a change of concepts without touching the principle as such.

But apart from this rather grammatical reflection on the use of the word "preponderance" instead of primacy, what does preponderance mean if it is supposed to be more than a simple inversion of the positions of subject and object? Like contemporary theories of materiality, Adorno, too, certainly does not want to fall back into naïve realism. Still, as indicated before, the claim of the object's preponderance has an ontological foundation, laid down and hidden in the material relation, as it were, of subject and object. Adorno's explanation for this is as convincing as it is astonishing in its simplicity: his basic idea is that the relation between subject and object is fundamentally asymmetrical because subjectivity always already implies being part of the world of objects, whereas the reverse connection does not apply for the object. Adorno turns this simple insight, which used to be taken as an evidence for the primacy of the subject, in the opposite direction by interpreting the relation of the two sides in terms of dependency: As idea as well as in reality the subject needs objectivity to become real and thus depends on the object. But this is not in the same way true for the object. Certainly, for the object to be thought, there has to be a subject, but this kind of mediation differs from that of the subject. In Adorno's own words: "The object is not to be thought out of existence from the subject, even as an idea; but the subject, from the object. In the meaning of subjectivity is also the reckoning of being an object; but not so in the meaning of objectivity, to be a subject."[21]

It is important to notice that the asymmetrical or parallactic entanglement of subject and object, expressed in this quote, is situated in between epistemology and ontology, meaning and being. Adorno's emphasis on the dialectical mediation thus has to be taken seriously in any possible respect. Parallax as preponderance of the object makes it impossible to either hold on to some form of an undeniably given reality or to claim that reality is a mere construct of the mind. However, there is no third position in which the two contradictory extremes resolve, and this is also the reason why this dialectic can be called a negative one.

Other than Latour's actor-network-theory, the preponderance of the object does not offer a solution; it is rather a critical intervention in the history of subjectivity and its dominant position. Consequently, the asymmetrical mediation, that the parallactic preponderance of the object stands in for, is, in fact, more about the subject than the object. Even though the object, far from being a pure and unmediated given, needs to be mediated by cognition to be known, this does by no means imply that it is fully constituted or produced through thinking. Objectivity is never completely absorbed by the knowing subject but remains non-identical, which nevertheless appears only within the identical. Due to the asymmetrical dependency of the subject on the object, the non-identical has far more consequences for the former. The fact that the subject is always already in need of some kind of matter or objectivity in order to come about is not exhausted by acknowledging that as an embodied being, it is also part of the empirical and finite world of things. Moreover, if the object appears as non-identical, then the subject as mediated by the object is itself based on such a negative moment of the non-identical. But such a foundation in negativity or in the object as non-identical must be eliminated from the subject's becoming in order to appear as self-sameness and under the rule of the identity principle. Therefore, the historical primacy of the subject could have only come about by systematically blocking out its mediation through the object. Or as Adorno puts it: "Subjective mediation is the block before objectivity."[22]

The term "block" marks the point where Adorno's analysis of the relation of subject and object turns into, what he calls, a critical ontology.[23] For him, ontology is critical in a double sense: First, only on an ontological level, the object's preponderance is able to properly challenge the primacy of the subject. Second, the ontological reflection nevertheless has to start from and is mediated by the subject. Whereas the first aspect interferes into ontology in the traditional sense, the second renders possible to reject the traditional notion of ontology as such. Adorno's term "block," with which he characterizes the parallactic mediation of subject and object, at the same time opens the ontological claim for a historical reflection. In contrast to expressions such as "constitutive blind spot," the notion of "blockage" indicates that something was established through a certain process and therefore, in principle, can be broken open again. The parallactic entanglement of subject and object is ontological only inasmuch as the primacy of the subject and the identity principle determine the existence of this relation. But this ontological status is itself a product of historic mediation; it is nothing naturally given but second nature.

In contrast to Latour's critique of modernity, it is much more difficult for such a critical ontology to see the origin of the block, since it is caused by subjective mediation—that is, the categories of the perceiving and knowing subject—itself. Again, this limitation is a result of Adorno's negative dialectics trying to take into account also the objective mediation of subjective consciousness—and this, of course, includes also the thinking subject of philosophy. For Adorno, the asymmetrical division of subject and object is still powerful, and the block not yet resolved. The reason for this lies in the fact that the blockage is much more than a certain philosophical or scientific way of thinking. It is so deeply rooted within Western late capitalist societies that society itself becomes the "universal block."[24] Such a transmittance might seem premature, but it follows inevitably from Adorno's identification of a critique of epistemology with a critique of society, clearly a heritage of Marxist tradition. In other words, a critical analysis of our categories of thinking necessarily has to take into account the social conditions in which this kind of thinking historically emerged.

An important consequence of Adorno's critical ontology lies in the possibility to decipher philosophical categories as forms of society.[25] By doing so, the blockage or parallectic entanglement is certainly not dismantled and resolved. At best, a small gap is opened for liberating practices, which brings us back to material culture studies and the moment of liberation within objectification. Taking up a Hegelian-Marxist tradition, in material culture studies freedom appears as essentially related to a necessary process of externalization and alienation. Against the backdrop of Adorno's reflection on the preponderance of the object, freedom in or as a relation to the object could now be spelled out more precisely as non-identity, which insists due to the parallax in objective mediation. In this respect, the block is never absolute; in our relation to the object, something non-identical remains, and that reveals a way for liberation. At least in some passages, Adorno seems to take this possibility literally, when he pleas for a new relation between human beings and things: "The things harden themselves as fragments of what was subjugated; the latter's rescue means the love for things."[26]

Despite all romantic misunderstandings that the formula "love for things" bears for obvious reasons, additional clues can be found in Adorno's other works that might help to clarify the meaning of this enigmatic loving stance toward things. I would like to conclude by briefly pointing toward a piece from *Minima Moralia*, which unfolds a remarkable dialectics between an exclusive aesthetic choice of a single object and the potential to do "justice to what exists."[27] Following Adorno, it is precisely the obsession for a particular object that can reveal the universality of beauty. The reason for that is the enormous and infinitely growing mass of objects in late capitalist societies, impossible for the subject to embrace and to appropriate. At the same time, through the universality of the exchange principle, all things become exchangeable and in so far indifferent. Therefore, the "love for things" in Adorno does not mean to embrace all things equally, since this would at the same time mean to address no (particular) thing at all. The only hope lies in an itself arbitrary and obsessive limitation to a particular object, chosen from the mass of indifferent others for no particular reason. This unjust and one-sided gesture of contemplating on one particular object treats all other objects with indifference and by that does justice to their actual being:

> And it is solely through bedazzlement [Verblendung], the unjust closure of the gaze vis-a-vis the claim raised by everything which exists, that justice is done to what exists. By being accepted in its one-sidedness, for what it is, its one-sidedness is understood as its essence and reconciled. The gaze which loses itself in something which is beautiful, is one of the Sabbath. It rescues in the object something of the peacefulness of its day of creation.[28]

Notes

1   Slavoj Žižek, *The Parallax View* (Cambridge, MA: The MIT Press, 2006), 7.
2   Bruno Latour, *We Have Never Been Modern*, trans. Catherine Porter (Cambridge, MA: Harvard University Press, 1993), 10–12.
3   Bruno Latour, *Reassembling the Social. An Introduction to Actor-Network-Theory* (Oxford/New York: Oxford University Press, 2005), 161.
4   Latour, *We Have Never Been Modern*, 142–5.
5   Markus Gabriel, "Existenz, realistisch gedacht." In *Der Neue Realismus*, ed. Markus Gabriel (Berlin: Suhrkamp, 2014), 183–91.

6   Markus Gabriel, "Einleitung." In *Der Neue Realismus*, ed. Markus Gabriel, 8–16, here: 9.
7   Maurizio Ferraris, "Was ist der neue Realismus?" In *Der Neue Realismus*, ed. Markus Gabriel, 52–75.
8   "Language has been granted too much power. The linguistic turn, the semiotic turn, the interpretative turn, the cultural turn: it seems that at every turn lately every 'thing'—even materiality—is turned into a matter of language or some other form of cultural representation." Karen Barad, "Posthumanist Performativity: Towards an Understanding of How Matter Comes to Matter," *Signs: Journal of Women in Culture and Society* 28, no. 3 (2003): 801–31, 801.
9   Karen Barad, *Meeting the Universe Halfway. Quantum Physics and the Entanglement of Matter and Meaning* (Durham: Duke University Press, 2007), 209.
10   Barad, *Meeting the Universe Halfway*, 201–4.
11   Judith Butler, *Bodies that Matter. On the Discursive Limits of "Sex"* (New York: Routledge, 1993), 7–10.
12   See Daniel Miller, *Material Culture and Mass Consumption* (Oxford: Blackwell, 1987); Arjun Appadurai (ed.), *The Social Life of Things* (Cambridge: Cambridge University Press, 1986); Igor Kopytoff, "The Cultural Biography of Things: Commoditization as Process." In *The Social Life of Things*, ed. Arjun Appadurai, 64–91.
13   Miller, *Material Culture*, chap. 1.
14   Georg Simmel, "Der Begriff und die Tragödie der Kultur." In *Hauptprobleme der Philosophie/Philosophische Kultur* (Frankfurt am Main: Suhrkamp, 1996), 385–416.
15   Miller, *Material Culture*, 192.
16   Miller, *Material Culture*, 112.
17   Miller, *Material Culture*, chap. 7.
18   Theodor W. Adorno, *Negative Dialektik* (Frankfurt am Main: Suhrkamp, 1970), 141.
19   Theodor W. Adorno, "Zu Subjekt und Objekt." In *Kulturkritik und Gesellschaft II* (Frankfurt am Main: Suhrkamp, 1977), 741–58, here: 748.
20   Adorno, *Negative Dialektik*, 184.
21   Adorno, *Negative Dialektik*, 184 (trans. Dennis Redmond).
22   Adorno, *Negative Dialektik*, 186 (trans. Dennis Redmond).
23   Adorno, *Negative Dialektik*, 186.
24   Theodor W. Adorno, "Gesellschaft." In *Soziologische Schriften I* (Frankfurt am Main: Suhrkamp, 1977), 9–19, here: 19.
25   Adorno, *Negative Dialektik*, 198.
26   Adorno, *Negative Dialektik*, 191 (trans. Dennis Redmond).
27   Theodor W. Adorno, *Minima Moralia. Reflexionen aus dem beschädigten Leben* (Frankfurt am Main: Suhrkamp, 1951), 94.
28   Adorno, *Minima Moralia*, 94 (trans. Dennis Redmond). I would like to thank Philipp Linstädter for pointing out to me the importance of the sabbathical in Adorno.

2

Žižek's Parallax, or The Inherent Stupidity of All Philosophical Positions

Graham Harman

1. The Escape from Content

The term "parallax" refers to the apparent difference in position of an object when it is seen from two different viewpoints; for obvious reasons, it has played an important role in the history of astronomy. What Žižek means by the word in *The Parallax View* is different, since he rejects outright any theory in which one and the same object simply "appears" differently when seen in two different ways.[1] More than this, "an 'epistemological' shift in the subject's point of view always reflects an 'ontological' shift in the object itself" (17). Subject-oriented philosopher though he is, Žižek frames his book as a discussion of the parallax *object* (17). Dozens of examples of parallax are given in the book, though we will only be able to sample a few of them. The first that concerns us here relates to Žižek's interpretation of Søren Kierkegaard. He begins by using his concept of parallax to explain the Danish philosopher's notion of the "teleological suspension of the ethical" in favor of the religious, as when Abraham was prepared to sacrifice Isaac in accordance with God's deeply "unethical" command[2] (104). He then adds an unexpected twist, inscribing this basic Kierkegaardian parallax on the inside of a larger one. In Žižek's own words: "This parallax split, however, is [itself] caught up in a parallax: it can be viewed as condemning us to permanent anxiety, but also as something that is inherently *comical*" (105). In this spirit, he muses that there is an undeniably ridiculous side to Christianity, in the sense that God is supposed to have become incarnated in a miserable man flogged and crucified; the fact that Mel Gibson's *Passion* has nothing humorous about it is the surest proof that it is no Christian film.

More generally, we have all experienced the often undetectable "parallax gap" between any statement and the exact same statement made "ironically." This is precisely the meaning of "Poe's Law" in social media: no matter how sarcastically any statement is meant, there will always be someone who takes it literally in the absence of any winking emoticon or other index of ironical intent.[3] Although this law might seem at first like just an amusing internet trifle, it speaks to an issue of profound philosophical importance, one that lies close to the heart of Žižek's thinking. Deep down, what Poe's Law really teaches is that *content alone* is never enough to give us the full meaning of a statement. We know this from speech act theory, where the difference between "constative" statements that merely describe and "performative" ones that commit us to something implies that one and the same content can be interpreted in at least two ways.[4] Consider the well-known academic phenomenon of a speaker who summarizes a controversial new philosophy, and when challenged on one of its tenets, responds defensively that they were "merely describing" that philosophy and not defending it. It is a timid action of the sort that could not possibly be performed by Žižek, who accurately states of himself that "I hate the position of [the] 'beautiful soul,' which is 'I remain outside, in a safe place; I don't want to dirty my hands.'"[5] A reader might now ask: if Žižek hates the beautiful soul and wants to dirty his hands by taking adamant positions on issues, how is this compatible with his frequently joking manner? The answer is that the key distinction is not between serious and humorous but between (merely) literal and engaged. The beautiful soul attempts to judge content from a dispassionate distance—though often enough with staged moral theatrics—while failing to see that he or she is also entangled in what they claim simply to observe. In Žižek's case, his jocularity and his hatred of the beautiful soul go hand in hand, though there are many possible ways of rejecting the beautiful soul.

As another example, imagine that I engage in performative speech by promising someone to help them with a task, and when I fail to show up, I give the defense that I meant the promise "ironically." Although it is possible to retaliate in various ways against such breaches of human trust, there is no way to "prove" in rationalist fashion that a statement was meant one way or the other. A further case arises when we consider the philosophy of Nietzsche. If we look him up in any encyclopedia or history of the discipline, we will find more or less accurate statements about his views: "Nietzsche believed that humans should work to create a superman beyond themselves"; "Nietzsche believed that everything that happens will recur again an infinite number of times in the future"; and "contrary to popular belief, Nietzsche was not an anti-Semite but despised anti-Semitism." Although correct enough, notice that none of these literal statements sounds the least bit like Nietzsche himself. In short, he cannot be reconstructed as a series of literal views on various topics. Anyone reading enough of these summaries could pass a comprehensive examination in graduate school, but they would be left with no idea about what makes Nietzsche such a powerful writer. One way to get closer to such an experience would be to read a parody of Nietzsche that expertly mimicked his style but which said *the exact opposite* of everything Nietzsche really thought. Even if such a work defended egalitarian social democracy and argued for the view that everything happens only once rather than recurring, there is a sense in which this work would be *more Nietzschean* than a literal summary of his thought.

Two more related examples are in order before returning to Žižek. Everyone is familiar with Karl Popper's falsificationist theory of science: the scientist is supposed to make bold hypotheses and subject them to risky experiments, all the while prepared to abandon their theories if these experiments yield falsifying evidence.[6] But at one point, Popper adds the qualification that the effort to falsify one's theories must be "sincere"; we cannot just go through the motions with feigned rigors while secretly planning to maintain our hypothesis no matter what happens. But as Popper memorably puts it, "the requirement of sincerity cannot be formalized."[7] In other words, a form of "Poe's Law" applies to the Popperian scientist. While it is highly unlikely that any scientist does experiments "ironically," they may well do them in a less-than-risky spirit. Is it not the case that the philosophy of Žižek's close colleague, Alain Badiou, plows a similar field? Alongside his ultra-idealist ontology of sets, Badiou also develops a quasi-Kierkegaardian theory of events, with the requirement that nothing counts as an event except insofar as a subject remains faithful to it.[8] For instance, the series of incidents that we call the Egyptian Revolution are exactly the same for (a) the conservative television pundit who dismisses it as a temporary uprising with mostly bad effects, and (b) the street activist who was wounded in the fighting and honors the memory of friends cut down by snipers. Only the latter attitude *names* it the Egyptian Revolution in a faithful sense, and thus it is only from that perspective that the revolution really happened. Badiouian events cannot be reduced to *content*, to a list of factual details unfolding from January–February 2011, but require that the crucial ingredient be added from outside.

It seems to me that *The Parallax View*—and Žižek's thinking more generally—should be understood along this same path. Early in the book, we find a series of amusing remarks on the impossibility of literally paraphrasing the works of Shakespeare or Hölderlin without ruining them (11–12). Hölderlin's piously intoned line "Wo aber Gefahr ist, wächst das Rettende auch" might actually *mean* "when you're in deep trouble, don't despair too quickly, look around carefully, the solution may be just around the corner" (12), but in that case it needs something more than its literal meaning if it wants to avoid being a mere platitude. Elsewhere, I have discussed an even more important passage from Žižek's *The Abyss of Freedom* that discusses what he calls "the inherent stupidity of proverbs."[9] It is worth quoting in full again, since it goes well beyond a mere joke—as do most of Žižek's jokes—and sheds considerable light on the core of his philosophical method. I have added the numbers in parentheses myself, as an aid to comprehension:

> Let us engage in a mental experiment by way of trying to construct proverbial wisdom out of the relationship between terrestrial life, its pleasures, and its Beyond. If one says [1] "Forget about the afterlife, about the Elsewhere, seize the day, enjoy life fully here and now, it's the only life you've got!" it sounds deep. If one says exactly the opposite [2] ("Do not get trapped in the illusory and vain pleasures of earthly life; money, power, and passions are all destined to vanish into thin air—think about eternity!"), it also sounds deep. If one combines the two sides [3] ("Bring eternity into your everyday life, live your life on this earth as if it is already permeated by Eternity!"), we get another profound thought. Needless to say, the same goes for its inversion: [4] "Do not try in vain to bring together eternity and your terrestrial life, accept humbly that you are forever split between Heaven and Earth!" If, finally, one simply gets perplexed by all these reversals and claims: [5] "Life is an enigma, do not try to penetrate its secrets, accept the beauty of its unfathomable mystery!" the result is no less profound than its reversal: [6] "Do not allow yourself to be distracted by false mysteries that just dissimulate the fact that, ultimately, life is very simple—it is what it is, it is simply here without

reason and rhyme!" Needless to add that, by uniting mystery and simplicity, one again obtains a wisdom: [7] "The ultimate, unfathomable mystery of life resides in its very simplicity, in the simple fact that there is life."[10]

Whereas Kant caused a firestorm by merely allowing for two sides of each story in his Antinomies, Žižek's virtuoso performance gives us no less than seven. As suggested in my earlier discussion of this passage, it destroys a great deal more than proverbial wisdom: instead, it works equally well against all forms of discursive content, since there is no statement we can make that cannot be thrown into a similar soup of inversions and subtler variants. At least one critic has claimed that this is an exaggeration, that Žižek only meant to expose the futility of the limited case of corny maxims. I do not think so. After all, does the passage above not give us Žižek's most characteristic philosophical method?

In almost any intellectual situation, the first thing Žižek does is identify a series of platitudes that secretly structure all of the positions in a debate, leaving us initially with nowhere to stand without occupying a position of banality. This occurs along a sliding scale of harshness dependent on Žižek's degree of sympathy—or lack thereof—with those who have fallen into whatever deadlock he is considering. At his most critical, he speaks with open annoyance of what seem to be merely trite statements masquerading as insight. For example, he remarks disdainfully on "the two clichés that pervade the European public space with regard to the Israeli-Palestinian conflict" (259). The first is the one that treats Islam as the dangerous Other of the West, unable to adjust to the conditions of globalization, democracy, and feminism, so that any anti-Zionist critique of good, enlightened Israel can only be a form of disguised anti-Semitism. The second, opposite cliché treats Israel as just another instance of Western imperialism and complains that the Holocaust is merely deployed as cynical justification for an essentially neocolonial enterprise. "Where, in this opposition," Žižek asks, "is the truth? Definitely not in any middle ground, of avoiding the two extremes" (258). We will see shortly where he tries to find it.

Slightly higher in Žižek's hierarchy of clichés is when he says that four basically respectable positions have arranged themselves into a "Greimasian semiotic square." This generally means that while the thinkers in question are not entirely stupid, they have each unwittingly adopted one of four possible positions dictated by a hidden structural logic rather than finding a novel way out. In *The Parallax View* he does this to the differing positions in the philosophy of mind taken by the Churchlands, David Chalmers, Colin McGinn, and Daniel Dennett (177–8), and several years later he does the same thing to the four Speculative Realists in *Less Than Nothing*.[11] At the top level of avoided clichés, we usually find three figures to whom Žižek is basically friendly, arranged in a "triad" of views that he still somehow finds unacceptable. An example from *The Parallax View* concerns the respective Leftisms offered by (a) Michael Hardt and Antonio Negri, (b) Ernesto Laclau and Chantal Mouffe, and (c) Giorgio Agamben (264–7). Of these three groupings, Laclau and Mouffe fall into self-contradiction by opposing essentialism in a utopian/essentialist way, Agamben is so paralyzed by the horrors of biopolitics that he becomes a political quietest awaiting an explosion of liberating violence, while Hardt and Negri fall into the easy modern trope that history is on their side (266). Never does Žižek inscribe his own position on any topic into one of these deadlocks of antinomic views, triads of contradictions, or tranquillizing semiotic squares; nor could he possibly offer a proverb to anyone in search of advice. It is only others who fall into such traps, while Žižek flees the scene in a kind of intellectual disaster. I say this without a trace of sarcasm, since it is not a question of hypocrisy, but of method. The primal philosophical scene for Žižek is his—perfectly legitimate—fear of ever uttering a cliché, and his entire philosophy is structured by the methodological need to avoid such a horror. This goes a long way toward explaining his inveterate contrarianism and the often dizzying speed of his dialectical reversals of common wisdom. The avoidance of banality is for Žižek the very business of philosophy, and this is what motivates the presence of every device in his toolbox. One of those tools is called "parallax," and it is the one that concerns us here.

2. Parallax Itself

After beginning *The Parallax View* with two news stories of the time that seemed to embody an impossible conjunction between avant-garde thought and political violence, Žižek draws a more general lesson:

> The illusion on which these two stories rely, that of putting two incompatible phenomena on the same level, is strictly analogous to what Kant called "transcendental illusion," the illusion of being able to use the same language for phenomena which are mutually untranslatable and can be grasped only in a kind of parallax view, constantly shifting perspective between two points between which no synthesis or mediation is possible. Thus there is no rapport between the two levels, no shared space—although they are closely connected, even identical in a way, they are, as it were, on the opposed sides of a Moebius strip. (4)

And soon thereafter: "In short, what both these anecdotes share is the occurrence of an insurmountable *parallax gap*, the confrontation of two closely linked perspectives between which no neutral common ground is possible" (4). He adds the important claim that while such a parallax might seem like a Kantian regression into a basic antinomy that cannot be sublated into a higher third term, this is, in fact, the truth of the Hegelian dialectic itself. After giving a long list of examples of parallax effects, Žižek outlines the structure of his book as follows: "It would be easy to get lost in a nonsystematic deployment of the multitude of parallax gaps; my aim here is to introduce a minimum of conceptual order into this multitude by focusing on its three main modes: philosophical, scientific, and political" (10). Since his parallax always concerns *two* irreducible views of an object, his threefold distinction between philosophy, science, and politics cannot itself be a parallax, and must come from somewhere else, but this topic must be left for another occasion.

Rather than a passive object viewed in two different ways by an active subject, "the subject is defined by a fundamental passivity, and it is the object from which movement comes… But, again, *what* object is this? The answer is: the parallax object" (17). A parallax object is certainly twofold, but not in the manner of phenomenon and noumenon, a distinction that Žižek always treats with scorn. Instead, we are speaking of "a minimal difference which divides one and the same object from itself" (18). For "there is no 'primordial duality' of poles in the first place, only the inherent gap of the One" (36; emph. removed). This gap is something we cross not in gradual fashion but by way of an instantaneous jump, like "that of the well-known visual paradox of 'two faces or a vase': one sees either two faces or a vase, never both—one has to choose" (56).

There is no question of a duel between a thing and its appearances, since what is more important is that objects "can also appear just to appear, concealing the fact that they are what they appear to be" (30). Or stated differently: "the tension between the Same and the Other is secondary with regard to the noncoincidence of the Same with itself" (36). Yet this noncoincidence in the Same does not give us two equally weighted dimensions in the parallax object. For "there is no 'neutral' reality within which gaps occur…" (29). Rather, "there is an irreducible asymmetry between the two perspectives, a minimal reflexive twist. We do not have two perspectives, we have a perspective and what eludes it, and the other perspective fills in this void of what we could not see from the first perspective" (29). This is the point where Žižek takes his usual turn toward "materialism," though it would not be considered materialism under any previous definition of the term. For as he defines it, "[m]aterialism means that the reality I see is never 'whole'—not because a large part of it eludes me, but because it contains a stain, a blind spot, which indicates my inclusion in it" (17). In other words, despite his apparent reversal of focus from the passive object of different perspectives to the passive subject confronting a fractured parallax object, it is the subject that continues to do all the interesting philosophical work for Žižek. After all, what "eludes me" in the object is not something hidden in the object itself but only the stain or blind spot that comes from *my* inclusion as subject *in* the object. Whenever possible, now as ever, Žižek quickly shifts all discussion of the autonomous *object* into an *objet petit a*, which for Lacanians means an object characterized as a *je ne sais quoi* of "my libidinal investment" (18). There is something in the object that makes it a cathected object for me in a way that it may not be for you, and this extra something "can never be pinned down to any of its particular properties" (18). In short, the libidinal parallax happens on the "subject" side of the equation, even if its target is the object. Here as with the faces/vase visual paradox, the radical jump between the two possible perspectives is possible only because both are held together by the viewer. David Hume famously denied the existence of the object in favor of a "bundle of qualities," thereby shifting the principle of unification from an object to the mind itself.[12] In slightly more complex fashion, Žižek treats the object as a "bundle of desires" in some cases (those where it is elevated to the unattainable object of my desire) and a mere "bundle of qualities" in others (those in which it is not thus elevated).

One of the most memorable arguments in *The Parallax View* is the author's claim that Kant's conception of freedom cannot be located in the noumenal sphere any more than in the phenomenal realm where everything is governed by cause and effect. For if we actually did inhabit the noumenal realm, we would be so awestruck by the resulting knowledge that there would be no choice but to obey the divine commands of duty. As he puts it: "[T]he inescapable conclusion is that, at the level of phenomena as well as at the noumenal level, we—humans—are 'mere mechanisms' with no autonomy and no freedom" (23). Hence, "the only place of freedom is thus the gap between these two levels in which appearance as such emerges" (107). Where is this non-phenomenal and non-noumenal "gap" to be located? This is where Žižek's originality appears. The I, he tells us, "is a purely formal function" (21). Whereas the transcendental object is a void *beyond appearances*, "the transcendental subject *already appears as a void*"[13] (21). This becomes more vivid when Žižek links this "purely formal I" to the madness of the "Night of the World" (21), or the "traumatic kernel of animality" (21) in humans. Nonetheless, he tells us with disappointment, Kant drew back from this radical insight and eventually settled for a noumenal "I" in opposition to a phenomenal or empirical one; for Žižek, this is a much weaker version of parallax, if it counts as parallax at all. This brings us directly to Hegel. Whereas Kant's antinomies provide us with four traditional philosophical questions having two undecidedably opposite solutions, "the basic Hegelian correction of Kant" (50) is to treat the doubleness of things themselves as a positive ontological fact rather than just an epistemologically unanswerable question. From a Hegelian standpoint, the "antinomies should not be reified," since they "emerge from shifts in the subject's attitude" (50). Stated differently, "far from overcoming the parallax logic, Hegel shifts it from the Kantian 'in itself' to 'for itself.' It is only Hegel who can think the parallax in its radicality, as the priority of the inherent antagonism" (25). But when he argues later for the superiority of Hegel to Spinoza, we find that Žižek misses something important:

> Does Spinoza not formulate the highest paradox? The substance is One, and the difference between mind and body, its two [attributes], is purely that of parallax: 'body' or 'mind' are the same substance perceived in a different [attribute]. There is nonetheless a key difference between Spinoza and Hegel here: for Spinoza, the parallax is symmetric (there is no point of contact between the two [attributes], each of them merely reveals the same network in a different mode), while for Hegel, the two levels involved in a parallax shift are radically asymmetric: one of the two levels appears to be able to stand on its own, while the other stands for the shift as such, for the gap between the two. (42)

The one that stands for "the shift as such" is, of course, the subject: which is not just the subject but also the subject in its minimal difference from the object. While this certainly provides a "point of contact" between the two terms, it does so precisely by eliminating the object as anything more than a stain or blind spot in the subject. No matter how loudly we call this "materialism," it would have been known as full-blown immaterialist idealism in most periods of the history of philosophy. However rigorous Žižek may think this standpoint is, it radically deflates the world of objects by eliminating object-object relations from the picture as a topic of direct discourse. There is also the fact that like most Hegelians, he misportrays Spinoza as saying that mind and body are the "two [attributes]" of substance, when, in fact, there are *infinitely* many such attributes despite only two of them being discernible to human beings. In this respect, Spinoza is actually an important forerunner of Kant, not a proto-Hegelian.

We now arrive at the true apple of Žižek's eye: Jacques Lacan. Once again we find that there seem to be two nested parallaxes at work, although Žižek expresses surprising disagreement with Lacan on both. The first concerns the status of the Real in Lacanian psychoanalysis. Here, Žižek begins with Claude Lévi-Strauss's account of how various members of the Winnebago tribe draw the disposition of huts in their village differently, depending on whether they belonged to the upper or lower class of the village. Žižek notes that, far from trying to teach a viewer-dependent social relativism, Lévi-Strauss is actually making the more radical claim that there is no objective disposition of buildings in the first place but only a "traumatic kernel" (25) of primal conflict. While there must be literal physical positions for all of the huts that could be photographed from a satellite, this would be just as fruitless as photographing someone's love interest and trying to convince them that this person is not very desirable; in both cases, we would have failed to cross the parallax gap. From here Žižek pivots into a debate about Lacan's own meaning: "[t]he parallax Real is thus opposed to the standard (Lacanian) notion of the Real as that which 'always returns to its place'—as that which remains the same in all possible (symbolic universes)" (26). Rather, it is "the hard bone of contention which pulverizes the sameness into the multitude of appearances" (26). But while this sounds like a clear statement of preference between two options, it is only a sentence more before Žižek redescribes this opposition as a parallax rather than a mutually exclusive choice:

> *In a first move*, the Real is the impossible hard core which we cannot confront directly, but only through the lenses of a multitude of symbolic fictions, virtual formations. *In a second move*, this very hard core is purely virtual, actually non-existent, an X which can be reconstructed only retroactively, from the multitude of symbolic fictions that are "all that there actually is." (26)

The scare quotes around "all that there actually is" suggest some discomfort on Žižek's part with the full-blown idealism suggested by the words themselves. Nonetheless, the terms of this parallax Real are at least clear enough. To give a philosophical analogy here, whereas Hume denies objects in favor of bundles of qualities and Husserl inverts it so that the objects come first, a "parallax" reading would tell us that both are right. However, it would do so only with the proviso that the subject has the last word.

But let's turn to a second parallax in the Lacanian universe, one that Žižek handles well: that between desire and the drive, as embodied in the *objet petit a*. As Jacques-Alain Miller has it, desire is connected with *lack*, while the drive is connected instead with a *hole*. Žižek comments as follows:

> That is the difference between desire and drive: desire is grounded in its constitutive lack, while drive circulates around a hole, a gap in the order of being. In other words, the circular movement of drive obeys the weird logic of the curved space in which the shortest distance between the two points is not a straight line, but a curve. (61)

Whereas desire pursues an (ultimately impossible) object that is merely a transient stand-in for "The Thing," drive wants nothing more than its own continuation as drive. And this is where Žižek thinks Miller misses something important: namely, the Lacanian *objet petit a* pertains not only to desire but to drive as well: "in the shift from desire to drive, we pass from the *lost object* to *loss itself as an object*" (62).

Turning to Marx, Žižek finds parallax again. He asks as follows: "[i]s not the ultimate Marxist parallax… the one between economy and politics—between the 'critique of political economy,' with its logic of commodities, and the political struggle, with its logic of antagonism? Both logics are 'transcendental,' not merely ontico-empirical; and they are both irreducible to each other" (55). One way to see this play out is simply to ask whether the purported contradictions of capitalism will lead automatically to its collapse; if so, then why the need for organized and lengthy political struggle? It is the same sort of perennial question that arises in the draft of Quentin Meillassoux's *The Divine Inexistence*: if the emergence or nonemergence of the virtual God happens purely contingently, irrespective of human activity, then why should this notion affect our actions at all?[14] In any case, Žižek has long been alarmed by the anti-economic leanings of three of his prominent communist colleagues in France: "The 'pure politics' of Alain Badiou, Jacques Rancière, and Étienne Balibar, more Jacobin than Marxist, shares with its great opponent, Anglo-Saxon Cultural Studies and their focus on struggles for recognition, the degradation of the sphere of economy" (55). Žižek accuses them of reducing economics to a lower, more "ontic" level by contrast with politics. With time running short, let's move toward a conclusion.

3. Originary Cliché

We have seen that for Badiou, a truth is constituted by the subject's fidelity to it rather than through the content of the truth itself. This is one of his strongest philosophical links with his friend Žižek, who says much the same: "the paradox of the authority of Truth [is that] Truth is characterized not by the inherent features of true propositions, but by the mere formal fact that these propositions were spoken from the *position* of Truth… Truth itself is not a property of statements, but [is] *that which makes them true*" (150). This will come as no surprise to any Hegelian, given that the *Phenomenology of Spirit* gets underway with the pages on "sense certainty," which turn on the fact that no literal content is inherently true[15] (224). This is echoed again in Žižek's positive remarks on metaphor, which is often despised by such ultra-rationalist enterprises as analytic philosophy: "the meaning of metaphor cannot be reduced to its 'true' referent: it is not enough to point out the *reality* to which a metaphor refers; once the metaphorical substitution is accomplished, this reality itself is forever haunted by the spectral *real* of the metaphorical content" (169).

Of course, object-oriented ontology (OOO) takes metaphor to be excellent evidence for a *realist* ontology: the excess of the real beyond literal language is precisely what makes metaphor possible in the first place.[16] Not so for Žižek, for whom the distinction between noumenal real and phenomenal appearance is already a difference in literal content. All roads away from the banality of content lead for him to the subject, which is inscribed everywhere. The only object is *obejt petit a*, and this "is the paradoxical object which directly *is* the subject" (213). This is not idealism for idealism's sake but idealism for the sake of subverting the platitudes of literal statement, which always fall too quickly into some false opposition, rigid triad, or "Greimasian semiotic square." The way out is always to find the *position* of Truth which alone rescues any content from itself, and which is every bit as operative for Žižek as for Badiou.

The first symptom of this idealist pathway is its fondness for retroactivity over any pre-given real. Of the childhood friends Hölderlin and Hegel, the former fails to become fully a philosopher because he fails to realize that the Ground of being is only retroactively posited rather than something that exists beforehand. That is to say, "what eludes Hölderlin is the true nature of Hegelian Universality as the site of the structural deadlock, of an impasse which particular formations endeavor to resolve" (157). Having already interpreted freedom as the very *gap* between noumenal and phenomenal, Žižek fills out the picture by treating freedom too as a retroactive embrace of antecedent causes: "'Freedom' is thus inherently retroactive: at its most elementary, it is not simply a free act which, out of nowhere, starts a new causal link, but a retroactive act of endorsing which link/sequence of necessities will determine me" (204). He even sees this sort of structure at work in the nonhuman realm: "The excess of the effect over its causes thus also means that the effect is retroactively the cause of its cause" (204). This feeds in nicely to his idealist interpretation of quantum theory, which, despite its claim that the action really happens on the side of the object, refers to "object" in the sense of *objet petit a*. In Žižek's words: "in quantum physics, the 'appearance' (perception) of a particle determines its reality. The very emergence of 'hard reality' out of the quantum fluctuation through the collapse of the wave function is the outcome of observation, that is, of the intervention of consciousness" (172).

The second symptom is self-reflexivity. Less important for Žižek than the traditional subject's relation to the world—which would merely yield the literal content of sense-certainty—is the self-reflexive structure highlighted by German Idealism and the Lacan of the mirror stage. Against theories such as Heidegger's that locate human freedom in transcendental openness, Žižek finds that the closed circle of fate can be broken not because it is not entirely closed "but, on the contrary, because it is overclosed, that is, because the subject's very endeavor to break out of it is included in it in advance" (207). He speaks elsewhere of the "short-circuiting of self-relation" (212) and even "the magic trick of self-relating" (213). But perhaps the most crucial passage is the following one: "there is no 'true substance' of the Self beneath its self-appearance (parallel to the 'real' Sun out there as opposed to the way the Sun appears to us as a yellow ball in the sky), the Self 'is' its own appearing to itself" (217). Aside from the fact that there is little evidence that Žižek thinks there is a real Sun beyond its appearance as anything more than *objet petit a*, we should note that Žižek is more aware than anyone of the turbulent paradoxes of appearance-to-oneself. Whereas some neuroscientific approaches try to undercut the self by replacing it with a mere physical brain, Žižek contends that this is less threatening than the fact that—thanks to Freud—"the subject is 'no longer a master in his own house'—in the house of his (self-)appearances themselves" (172). There is no "true core" of subjectivity (207).

Among other things, this puts Žižek on the opposite side of the fence from phenomenology, with its far less troubled relation to subjectivity than we find in psychoanalysis, or even in German Idealism, with its Hegelian "Night of the World" and Schellingian "blind rotary drives." In fact, Žižek's strong preference for dialectics over phenomenology allows us to end on the same note with which we began. For phenomenology, philosophy is grounded in the fresh and original presence of things before the mind, no longer subjected to mere "empty intentions." Clichés arise only when we lose this primordial experience of the things themselves. But here Žižek gives an important rejoinder: "for phenomenology… 'dead metaphors' are always 'sedimentations' or 'ossifications' of what was once a direct lived experience… what is unthinkable for phenomenology is that something *directly emerges* as a cliché, that it was never meant seriously" (233). Žižek is a dialectician primarily because the negativity of the retroactive and the self-reflexive is, for him, the best guarantee against the originary cliché of philosophical content.

Notes

1   Slavoj Žižek, *The Parallax View* (Cambridge, MA: MIT Press, 2006). Throughout this chapter, all page numbers contained in parentheses refer to this book.

2   Søren Kierkegaard, *Fear and Trembling*, ed. C.S. Evans and S. Walsh (Cambridge, UK: Cambridge University Press, 2006).

3   The law was formulated in 2005 by one Nathan Poe and has no connection with the writer Edgar Allan Poe.

4   See J.L. Austin, *How to Do Things with Words*, second edition (Cambridge, MA: Harvard University Press, 1975).

5   Jonathan Derbyshire and Slavoj Žižek, "Interview with Slavoj Žižek," *New Statesman*, October 29, 2009. Available online: https://www.newstatesman.com/ideas/2009/10/today-interview-capitalism.

6   Karl Popper, *The Logic of Scientific Discovery* (London: Routledge, 1992).

7   Popper, *The Logic of Scientific Discovery*, 418. For a more extensive discussion of this issue, see Graham Harman, "On Progressive and Degenerating Research Programs with Respect to Philosophy," *Revista Portuguesa de Filosofia* 75, no. 4 (2019): 2067–102.

8   For his ontology of sets, see Alain Badiou, *Being and Event*, trans. O. Feltham (London: Continuum, 2005). For his fully developed theory of events, see Alain Badiou, *Logics of Worlds: Being and Event II*, trans. A. Toscano (London: Continuum, 2009).

9   For a fuller discussion, see Graham Harman, *Weird Realism: Lovecraft and Philosophy* (Winchester, UK: Zero Book, 2012), 11ff.

10 Slavoj Žižek and F.W.J. Schelling, *The Abyss of Freedom/Ages of the World*, Schelling trans. J. Norman (Ann Arbor, MI: University of Michigan Press, 1997), 71–2.

11 Slavoj Žižek, *Less Than Nothing: Hegel and the Shadow of Dialectical Materialism* (London: Verso, 2012), 640.

12 David Hume, *A Treatise of Human Nature* (Oxford: Oxford University Press, 1978).

13 Here it seems that Žižek is conflating the transcendental object with the thing-in-itself, though Kant himself is careful to distinguish them. In OOO terms, the

thing-in-itself corresponds to the "real object," while the transcendental object = x
has more in common with the "sensual object." But this topic can be left for another
occasion.

14   Quentin Meillassoux, "Excerpts from *L'Inexistence divine*." In *Quentin Meillassoux:
     Philosophy in the Making*, trans. Graham Harman, second edition (Edinburgh:
     Edinburgh University Press, 2015), 224–87.

15   G.W.F. Hegel, *Phenomenology of Spirit*, trans. A.V. Miller (Oxford: Oxford University
     Press, 1976).

16   See Graham Harman, *Object-Oriented Ontology: A New Theory of Everything*
     (London: Pelican, 2018), chapter 2.

3

How Mind Fits into Nature
Mental Realism after Nagel

Markus Gabriel

We are clearly able to know what is the case without therefore knowing all those things we *don't* know. Epistemically, the domain comprising those things we don't know is infinitely large. If we know that something determinate (let's say: p) is the case, then we think that things are as we say them to be; whenever we express what is the case in any comprehensible language, a given thought ought to be true. If the thought, expressed in English, that it's raining in Hamburg is true, then things are as they're said to be: it's raining in Hamburg. It isn't raining in Hamburg because we say it is. Moreover, we don't say it simply because it happens to be raining in Hamburg: the meaningful use of language is not exhausted by the proclamation of banal facts.

A fact is something that is true. A fact is a truth. Because we know many things, we know many truths. There is no sufficient general reason to succumb to doubts concerning the question of whether the epistemological—and associated ontological— trivialities with which I began for their part correspond to the facts. Let's call this the *argument from facticity*. Its details, to be sure, involve various ramifications bearing on the burden of proof. For present purposes I would like to set these aside.[1] The result of this argument is a position I call "neutral realism." It is realist because it (a) assumes that there is a categorial distinction between truth and holding true and thus assigns justificatory maneuvers (i.e., the concept of justification) to holding true and not to truth, and because it (b) sees no room to doubt that we grasp indefinitely many truths exactly as they are. Typical among these are, for example, that we can express them in a linguistic code. That we can pursue illocutionary goals in stating facts does nothing to change the fact that there are statements of fact and that they are frequently successful.

This contribution began its life as the Fleck Lecture given at the Collegium Helveticum in Zürich. I would like to thank Hartmut von Sass for the kind invitation as well as Joachim Bihmann and Harald Atmanspacher for the subsequent discussion of the considerations that I here present in a revised form. I am also grateful to Thomas Nagel for the many conversations we have had in New York since 2005, which have motivated me to work out the relation between his views and my own. In addition, I would like to thank the team at my chair for helpful comments, whereby Philipp Bohlen, Jens Rometsch, and Jan Voosholz merit particular mention.

Neutral realism is neutral because it does not regard any specific kind of fact, and thus any specific kind of truth, as metaphysically generalizable: no knowable kind of fact to which we might avert is an ontologically legitimate foundation for all other facts. From here, a commitment to a variant of *ontological pluralism* follows in a few steps: there is no ground level of facts composed of a specific kind of fact, such that all other facts (insofar as they obtain) rest upon this ground level of fundamental facts and can be reduced to them, be it conceptually, empirically or metaphysically. Truths are thus irreducibly plural, because there are no metaphysically fundamental facts.[2]

Yet ontological pluralism by itself is not yet sufficient to exclude local ontological reductions. One will not dispose of the general problem of mind's relation to nature, together with its host of specific variants (e.g., the body-soul, brain-consciousness, or mental state-neural correlate problem) merely by recognizing that no one kind of fact is the ground of all other kinds of fact.

The question of mind's relation to nature is usually formulated within the framework of a *placement problem*: in light of how natural processes are devoid of mind and consciousness in every relevant respect, there seems to be no theoretical space for locating mind in the universe. In this context, *mental realism* maintains the following: the expressions with which we refer to the mental characterize a level of reality that cannot be meaningfully traced back to those facts that we locate in the mind- and consciousness-free universe by deploying our best empirical reasons.

In what follows I would like to present and defend the basic tenets of a mental realism that exploits a pluralistic philosophy of nature and thereby avoids having to grapple with the placement problem. I thus want to differentiate my position especially from the neighboring theory of Thomas Nagel, who put forward a hotly debated suggestion as to how mind fits into nature in his *Mind and Cosmos*.

In the first part of my contribution (1) I address the question of how mind and nature should generally be differentiated. By "nature" I will at first understand the object domain of the so-called natural sciences. I also call this *the universe*. The concept of the universe here is thus epistemic insofar as the natural sciences can, in principle, make discoveries only about those existing systems in which natural scientists can intervene. Mind grants us the capacity to form a picture of how we can know the reality of the universe, and this picture cannot sensibly be located in the universe itself without remainder. For, in contrast to natural kinds, it essentially depends upon how we understand our epistemic and evaluative activities.

In the second part (2) I go on to extend the concept of nature in order to show how the way in which the universe appears to us from the standpoint of mind is essential to nature itself. Consciousness, thought, and other aspects of our mental life do not fall outside of nature but have to be taken into account if we so much as want to understand how the natural sciences can deliver knowledge of natural processes that play out in the universe (which *are* devoid of mind or consciousness).

This position, to be sure, is anti-naturalist: it recognizes both facts and forms of knowledge that cannot be meaningful objects of any natural scientific investigation. Ontological pluralism thus comes into play, because the idea that we can take the diachronically and synchronically plural differentiation of truths and the forms of knowledge they concern and simply remove them from the natural scientific worldview is just so much wishful thinking. This can be shown both empirically and a priori. Finally, in the third part (3), I will suggest a conceptual architecture for solving (or dissolving) the mind-nature problem, which might be called a *neo-existentialist conditionalism*. This position develops a series of ideas based on the assumption that every actually occurring event is unique and unrepeatable.

1. Nature and Spirit

A *thought* is a mental state of a living organism—in what follows, paradigmatically of a human being—which is true or false. Thoughts are fact-like: something is true of them. Moreover, they are about something in a specific manner. Thoughts refer to so-and-so and to this and that. Whoever has a thought (that is, thinks) finds herself either in a condition which has the property of being true or in a condition which has the property of being false, *tertiur non datum*. For any actually occurring thought either corresponds to the facts it's about or it doesn't.

Thoughts are about what they're about in a specific way. What a thought is about is its *object*; how it is about it is its *content*. Some thoughts are about objects that are not themselves thoughts, examples being the Earth's moon, fingernails, the number 7, the big bang, bosons, fermions, and so on. A subset of those objects that aren't thoughts are the objects of the natural sciences—whereby psychology might appear to be a problem case insofar as we can both class it among the natural sciences and regard it as concerned with thoughts, which is no easy matter. But be that as it may, one can construct an object domain on this foundation, which I'll designate as *anonymous nature* or *the universe*.

Here, it is important to avoid the pitfalls lurking in the idea that the universe is metaphysically independent of mental life, of the mental representations of living beings. For biochemical organic process, physical measuring procedures, artifacts like tables, chairs, and buildings, and so on also belong to anonymous nature. The universe is not in every conceivable respect as it is because it is metaphysically independent of us. Nature is not independent of consciousness, but this by no means entails that it is dependent on consciousness. Indeed, we might well suspect that this distinction is nonsensical. In any case, it is of no use for discussion the issue of realism.

Yet thoughts are also about thoughts. Thus, the thought to the effect that some thoughts are about objects that aren't thoughts is itself about thoughts. Thoughts of this kind are objects of philosophy. No other science deals systematically with thoughts as thoughts—which is not to say that the question of what thoughts are (e.g., mental states of an animal) is thus answered automatically. There is nothing especially shocking about this, and it is no cause for valorizing or deprecating any particular discipline. It is simply a fact that there is some form of knowledge or science that deals with thoughts as thoughts, and it has proved useful over the centuries to call it by its Greek proper name (philosophy).

The thesis that the universe exists is justified in the philosophy of nature. If the universe exists, we can designate the objects that appear within it as natural kinds. Natural kinds are objects that are not thoughts. In what follows, I also call them non-thoughts. Physics, then, delivers us examples solely of natural kinds (bosons, galaxies, black holes, spin, etc.)—that is, of objects that belong to the universe—if it is correct that there are objects that are dealt with by thoughts without being thoughts themselves. The assertion that the universe does not exist comes in many variants. A contemporary variant is *panintentionalism* or *panpsychism*, which holds that all objects that exist are about something. This is an option entertained implicitly or explicitly by those—like Max Tegmark or *cum grano salis* Luciano Floridi—who believe that the universe consists of information, and thus that all objects of the natural sciences are about something.[3]

I take panintentionalism to be false. It owes its sheen of plausibility to the desperate attempt to locate mind in nature by conceiving of the latter on the model of the former. This is, to be sure, certainly a way of overcoming the mystery of how there can be mind in a seemingly mindless universe; but it comes at the price of offering a monadology hidden in the language of computer science, quantum theory, or neuroscience, without providing adequate justification for any such metaphysics. We can make things easier for ourselves, however, and assume that the impression that not everything has the form of a thought is not deceptive after all. In any case, nothing we actually know about the universe is incompatible with this assumption. There are thus non-thoughts. Some non-thoughts are thinkable and knowable, though we don't know quite how many there are. The universe is not empirically knowable as a whole.

Thoughts that are about thoughts refer to our status as thinkers of various kinds of thoughts. The thinker of thoughts is an animal. Among the necessary conditions of animals' existence are anonymous natural processes. The physical constants have to be constituted in a certain way, the universe has to have developed in a certain way, and so on, so that we find ourselves here today. This is not a surprise, but simply what is the case.

Yet thoughts are not objects that feature in the universe, for the concept of the universe is the concept of an object domain of objects that are not thoughts. Neither bosons nor fermions nor neurons investigate themselves when we direct our thoughts at them.

At this point one could certainly adapt the concept of nature to our status as minded animals and say that nature comprises all the facts known to us, which include the fact that there are thoughts that are about thoughts and thoughts that are about non-thoughts. Since this fact is an object of philosophical enquiry, philosophy would ipso facto be a natural science. Yet all other sciences or forms of knowledge in any way concerned with objects would thereby find themselves in the catchment area of the concept of the natural sciences, which could clearly be a case of overreach in the pre-Socratic style. The assumption that the universe exists— that there is thus a domain of non-thoughts which, within the standard division of academic labor, are the concern of the natural sciences—is philosophically attractive for at least the following reason: it explains a conception of objectivity, which I'll call the *natural conception of objectivity* for short. On this conception, the objectivity of our thinking (our having thoughts) consists in the independence of the objects of our holding true from our holding true. How they are is not identical with our thinking that they are thus and so. I label this potential divergence between truth and holding true *the contrast of objectivity*. Accordingly, neither truth nor holding true by themselves bear the status of objectivity, which instead pertains to their interface, as it were. Which theory of gravitation is the right one is not identical with, say, the advocate of loop quantum gravitation holding her preferred option to be true. Therefore, physics is objective on account of the constitution of its interface, the interface at which the scientist confronts the target system with which she interacts.

Objectivity and fallibility hang together. Whoever has objective attitudes can be in error and is thus corrigible. A good reason for the natural conception of objectivity is the actual constitution of non-thoughts. What itself is not a thought seems to be a good foundation for the reference of thoughts that are objective. This is the logical deep structure of the superficial, widespread belief that the world is independent of our opinions about it in such a way that those forms of knowledge that concern themselves with the universe, with the world that enjoys objective existence independently of our opining, enjoy a privileged status.

The standard issue metaphysics that Thomas Nagel designates with the classical expression "materialism" is the identification of nature with the universe qua domain of non-thoughts. It is therefore unsurprising that standard issue materialism either reduces mind to something mindless or eliminates it, that is, has to contest its existence. Whoever is of the view that all that (really) exists is what occurs in the universe and is objectively measurable cannot do justice to how the apparatus with which they undertake their measurements has to appear to their consciousness—whatever we make of the Copenhagen interpretation of quantum physics. On a side note, Schrödinger saw this especially clearly, even though the insight unfortunately led him toward his philosophically lamentable (because ultimately incoherent) drift into the far-Eastern mysticism of *Mind and Matter*.[4] But that's a topic for another time. I only mention the measurement problem of quantum theory in order to point out the following: the assumption that consciousness as a faculty of mind interacts with the micro-domain of the universe in the form of an essential causal contribution to the collapse of the wave function is just a further far-fetched attempt to squeeze mind into the mindless universe.

It is a constitutive feature of the natural sciences' investigation of the universe that they have no thoughts in view. This is not a critique in the sense of a reproach but an epistemological remark about the architecture of human knowledge. To forestall any misunderstandings, I hasten to add that it is indeed possible to research the natural conditions necessary for the presence of mental states (such as consciousness) with the aid of the natural sciences.

Let us suppose that the search for the minimal neural correlate of consciousness is, firstly, a coherent one and, secondly, successful. The most impressive neuroscientific and philosophical attempt to pin down the minimal neuronal correlate of consciousness is the integrated information theory (IIT) elaborated by Giulio Tononi and Christoph Koch.[5] Their suggestion amounts to the idea that there are neuronal structures with processual properties that allow probabilistic modelling, and these correspond to the purely intrinsic properties of consciousness that are accessible to the standpoint of the experiencing subject in such a way that they have to be their support.

That the support of consciousness is in actual fact neuronal can be ascertained from the neurophysiology of neuronal support cells, that is, from the investigation of the unconscious nature without which there would be no consciousness to begin with. That the person who researches consciousness is conscious of doing so needs to be taken into account. Tononi himself is committed to a revision of the natural conception and to a modified philosophy of nature. His project thus points in the right direction, and I shall take it up again in the third part of this chapter.

There is no mind without thoughts about thoughts. In the case of both the minded animals of our species and many other animals (if not perhaps all animals), these thoughts about thoughts are essentially social insofar as our first thoughts directed at thoughts aime at the thoughts of others. Contrary to the view paradigmatically represented by Johann Gottlieb Fichte, Edmund Husserl, and many others, the newborn I, or the I *in statu nascendi*, has to yield to the insight that there are both others Is and, in addition, the non-I as well. We do not begin alone by ourselves, but in the midst of the non-I, which at first remains unknown to us. Following Wolfram Hogrebe, we can call this the "dark you."[6] "Mind is external, but penetrates into the interior."[7]

Within this framework the *irreducibility thesis* holds: as our synchronically and diachronically variable capacity for forming self-images, mind cannot intelligibly be reduced if we want to understand that our thoughts can be directed both toward themselves and toward non-thoughts. Because we are thinkers of thoughts and thus able to take up truth-apt attitudes, nothing stands in the way of recognizing that we can know reality at some level or other as it truly is. In other words, mind is the "hard core of self-evidence"[8] that cannot be intelligibly contested; it is what we make use of when we—as is currently en vogue—undertake to reveal it as an illusion generated, in some as yet undiscovered way, by the brain.

Let's summarize where we have got to thus far: there are non-thoughts, which can be fused epistemically into a field, the universe. By means of appropriate methods of scaling, we can subdivide this field into various levels, and this division is epistemically accessible within the framework of the natural sciences' division of labor. By contrast, mind as such is not knowable in this way; it recedes into the background as a structure of epistemic capacities without which the natural scientist could not acquire knowledge about the universe. Mind therefore has no place in nature understood as the universe. And to many, this seems deeply mysterious.

2. The Nature of Mind

Mind has no place in nature so long as the latter is defined as the mindless universe of non-thoughts. This shouldn't be surprising. Yet the fact that we cannot locate mind in nature as thus defined represents the metaphysical collateral damage of a certain highly regrettable theoretical setup, that is, a logical deficit. At least two options thus come into view for getting around the problems that arise if we persist in trying to find a place for mind in the realm of mindless happenings.

One can (a) hold on to the concept of the mindless universe as the object of the natural sciences and opt for a more or less refined version of *dualism*. Among the less refined is the variant often ascribed to Descartes, who posited a mental substance besides mindless substance, whereby both are somehow meant to interact. These days, this option is largely the target of polemics; yet it is much superior than its battered reputation would suggest. For on the one hand, it rests on a recognition of the obvious—the existence of mind—and on the other hand, we cannot exclude the possibility that two kinds of substance might interact with one another provided we have an appropriate concept of causality, one that avoids conceiving causality as the "push and pull" system of "microbangings" that James Ladyman rightly mocks.[9]

Moreover, it is also thoroughly implausible on physical grounds to think that the universe is a causally closed space into which mind is precluded from making causal interventions. In his book *How Can Physics Underlie the Mind*, the cosmologist George Ellis, for example, has developed a philosophy of nature that posits strong emergence even at the microlevel of the universe.[10] What thus emerges are new kinds of "levels" of the universe, which causally intervene "top-down" into the order from which they unpredictably emerged. Here, however, I do not wish to advocate any such theory; I merely wish to point out that this territory is still far from having been adequately mapped and thus in no way became obsolete as early modern metaphysics progressed. Dualism is an option to be taken seriously, not some outmoded error.

Another option (b) is to extend nature and see it as an object domain—in my theoretical language: as a field of sense—of processes, some of which are "mental." On this option, mind is fundamentally to be understood in terms of its maximal form. The maximal form of mind is our capacity to lead a life in light of an idea of how we and others fit into an environment that transcends us. We are capable of forming self-images and act in light of a representation of what kind of being the human is as a minded animal. This fundamental anthropological fact is the reason for the unsurveyable, synchronically and diachronically differentiated vocabulary with which humans characterize their spiritual and intellectual situation. I call this vocabulary *mentalistic*. As Charles Taylor already pointed out in his early work *The Explanation of Behaviour*, an important function of mentalistic vocabulary is action explanation.[11] Taylor reiterates this position in a recent exchange of ours: we cannot succeed in explaining actions if we do not understand the sense in light of which they are carried out.[12] The vocabulary expressed in such explanations encompasses such prominent terms as "consciousness," "self-consciousness," "attention," "emotion," and so on. It does not, however, constitute an invariant core that can be equated with the much-discussed phenomenon of "folk psychology." This is merely a specter invoked by those whose intention is really mind's self-elimination. There is no simple language of action explanation that remains constant throughout all natural languages. So much can be ascertained from historically informed research in the humanities (one need only think of Bruno Snell's *The Discovery of the Mind*).[13] Even the term "consciousness" tends to lead many astray, inviting them to believe that it has a natural meaning that can be traced back to some kind of pre-scientific superstition. So much is suspected by Stanislas Dehaene and others.[14] Yet scientific evidence for the existence of this supposed folk psychology is rarely forthcoming. The semantic and intellectual history of the word "consciousness" is usually ignored together with the fact that the very idea that we possess a "consciousness" rests upon a highly complex and variable history.

My favored version of extending the concept of nature so as to encompass the dimension of mind is based on the following conception, which I have called "conditionalism."[15] The starting point is a commitment to a version of the principle of sufficient reason, which I take to be almost analytically true. (I say "almost" on account of certain reservations concerning analyticity.) This, I should emphasize, applies only to events and not to objects; it is thus not a metaphysical theory about everything there is whatsoever (I take such theories to be nonsense). The *principle of sufficient reason for events* states: *everything (knowable) that occurs can be analyzed into necessary and jointly sufficient conditions.* This does not mean that there are universally necessary conditions (like natural laws), which channel all events like a gigantic river bed. The genealogy of this questionable notion and its supersession in modern natural science has been described by Hampe.[16] The necessity of a condition for a given event simply consists in how precisely this event, in its uniqueness, would not be as it is if *this* condition had not been fulfilled.

In this context, the idea that the necessary conditions are jointly sufficient merely excludes the assumption that, besides the necessary conditions, there needs to be some kind of specific catalyst or trigger. An event, in other words, is identical with its occurrence. In order to explain this occurrence, one must naturally adduce everything that has made some contribution to the occurrence and unfolding of this event.

From this perspective, the capacity of certain scientific models to generate prognoses is not based on the universe's being a gigantic bundle of events subject to merciless universal laws—laws which, given the measurable "material" present since the big bang, could not have manifested in any other way. There are no all-embracing chains of events, no mega-event called "nature," in which we find ourselves trapped as some poor pile of particles, potentially deprived of any freedom whatsoever. If *that* is "determinism," then determinism is false. That predictions with high degrees of statistical probability are possible for some kinds of events, while other kinds— paradigmatically individual actions—take place with much lower probability is due to how different events occur in different fields of sense. Actions are of an ontologically different kind to the spin of elementary particles, the rotation of a galaxy around its black hole, or the kinetics of a tumor.

The principle of sufficient reason is both compatible with the objective contingency of quantum theory and with free will, correctly understood.[17] For it rules out there being anything like all-encompassing natural laws that have been present since the big bang, and it therefore precludes an idealized observer like "Laplace's demon," who could predict every future occurrence if it knows both all the natural laws and the original state of nature. Laplace's demon is not epistemically but ontologically impossible. Nature is simply not constituted as a naïve determinist believes it to be. And the simplest proof of this is the "hard core of self-evidence" that is the form of our mental life. That, say, the discovery of the Planck constant could, in principle, have been predicted at the time of the big bang is simply not an intelligible assumption. And just as little could one have predicted that I would now raise my left hand and how precisely this hand-raising would be implemented. It is for these reasons, I maintain, that we should extend the concept of nature and thus leave sufficient room for a nature that is effective within us as minded animals. Taking up the mantra of Gernot Böhmes, we might call this "the nature that we are ourselves."[18]

The nature that we are ourselves, however, does not consist in our belonging to nature. For as minded animals, we are thinkers of thoughts who can become conscious of this fact in a way that I call "*Geist*." On this level of analysis, *Geist* is the capacity to lead a life in light of a conception of "the position of man in the cosmos." Every actualization of this capacity is based upon how a given minded animal finds itself in a dynamic overall state. Qua event, this overall state can be decomposed into necessary conditions of various kinds. In order to conceptually individuate the conditions that make us "minded," I have put forward the following suggestion, which I call *neo-existentialism*.

We can distinguish at least two kinds of error. The first kind consists in giving a false determination of the properties a natural kind—say the mass of the Higgs-Boson. An error concerning a natural kind or a complex structure that involves natural kinds does not change anything about the properties themselves. These are part of the explanation of the error: because certain facts obtain, someone can err without thereby altering these facts.

Things are different when we are mistaken about ourselves. Self-deception provides a paradigmatic illustration: if I begin to believe that I'm a talented Tango dancer and orient my life around this error, I not only will hold a false proposition to be true but might well lead a false life, which could, in turn, have significant consequences were my self-deception to further entrench itself. This idea is even easier to understand when it comes to conflicting conceptions of the human: Consider the prevailing caricatures of the religious and the scientific man, both of which have unfortunately penetrated deeply into philosophy of mind and, in any event, into the popular perception of the "scientific." According to this caricature, we have, on the one hand, people who act in light of the idea that they have an immortal soul, which steers their mental life, and thus their body, like a "ghost in the machine." On the other hand, we have "Brights," who believe they know that the universe is causally closed and that they are identical with their brain, and who therefore dismiss the ideas of the religious as so much superstition and illusion. Neither base their viewpoints on, say, a complete decoding of the human being; given the current state of our knowledge (including medical science), there can be no talk of such a thing. Both images of the human are scientifically underdetermined exercises in pseudo-metaphysics. More important for my considerations here is the fact that the religious person and the scientific person lead different lives because they have different attitudes toward life. Whether one believes that our moral worth is continually being tested by God or the gods or whether one believes that we are advanced killer-apes whose primary goal is spreading our genes by means of suitably developed, culturally encoded methods has consequences for how one lives.

How we understand our status as humans partly determines who or what we are. Let's call this our project. To have a project, however, does not mean being immune to error. The process of self-determination of our life-form does not consist in an ability to change it ad libitum. We either have, for example, an immortal soul (as Plato described it, say) or we don't. Our mental life is either the flickering of neurons or something else: say, perhaps, the mental course taken by the life of a whole organism. Given the normative dimensions of our selfhood, who we want and ought to be also depends on who or what we are as natural beings. We can be wrong about ourselves, including on the level of the general question of who or what the human being is.

Self-deception modifies our status. In this sense, our thinking and judging makes a contribution to how things are with us, whereas our thinking and judging makes no contribution to determining the mass of the Higgs-Boson or the black hole in the middle of the Milky Way.

Let's take stock once again. Mind and nature meet in such a way in minded animals that, if we're to avoid conceiving this meeting in terms of a dualistic interaction, we have to extend our concept of nature. Nature reaches further than the mindless universe. We know it from the inner viewpoint of a minded life-form, the necessary existential conditions of which include natural processes; and we contribute to these processes in a "top-down" manner, through the exercise of our mental capacities. What we think, be it true or false, essentially codetermines how things are with us, and thus with the natural structure that we are.

3. Mental Realism after Nagel

In order to solve, or dissolve, the body-soul and mind-brain problems (which in any case lack precise formulations), the ontology of neo-existentialism appeals to conditionalism. There is simply no general metaphysical problem of the type: "how does mind fit into nature?"—that can take on the concrete form of how a physical event precisely correlates with a psychological event. That such a problem has an intelligible formulation is the shared presupposition behind identity theories, dualisms, epiphenomenalisms, supervenience theories, idealisms, and so on and so on. Yet considered in light of neo-existentialism, these theories stand revealed as specific forms of self-deception, which stem from taking elements of a given mentalistic vocabulary (these days, usually an academically disseminated idiolect of English) as a mirror of nature in which a part of the mind grasps itself.

A famous example of this is the theoretical approach of Thomas Nagel, who coined the concise term "what-is-it-likeness" in order to pin down the difference between subjective and objective in terms of how a state feels a certain way for a person from within. This what-it-is-likeness, he claims, throws up hitherto unresolved metaphysical difficulties, and many have followed him in this regard. Think of David Chalmers' conceptually precise formulation of the suspicion that there is a "hard problem of consciousness," or Joseph Levine's postulate of an "explanatory gap" between the phenomenal inner perspective of our lives and the external perspective of natural science.[19]

In this concluding part of my remarks, I would like to show that Nagel's sketch of a future speculative physics is the cosmological projection of a self-deception, which stems from how, ever since "What Is It Like to Be a Bat?," he has worked on the assumption that an *objective phenomenology*—that is, a conception that allows us to assign mind a causally but not physically explicable role in nature—is impossible.[20]

The project of *Mind and Cosmos* is driven by a metaphysical need that finds articulation in which Huw Price has called a *placement issue*[21]:

> [T]he exclusion of everything mental from the scope of modern physical science was bound to be challenged eventually. We humans are part of the world, and the desire for a unified world picture is irrepressible. It seems natural to pursue that unity by extending the reach of physics and chemistry, in light of their great successes in explaining so much of the natural order.[22]

What is sought is "an account of how mind and everything that goes with it is inherent in the universe."[23] Nagel's placement issue results from the concept of the "natural order," which here—as elsewhere—receives not so much as an attempted explanation. We learn neither what the naturalness of this order is supposed to consist in nor what we are meant to distinguish it from. And we find out just as little about what confers the status of being an "order." I suspect that the expression "natural order," so prominent in the naturalism discourse, is semantically empty, that it merely lends a linguistic form to the oceanic feeling that there is one great whole, in which we are potentially carried along, and which is distinguished from a supernatural dimension whose ontic status (does it exist or not?) remains a matter of debate. Yet this metaphysical constellation is an historical accident of modernity with a somewhat well-researched theological prehistory. Max Weber famously described this with his (usually misunderstood) theory of the "disenchantment of the world." The "natural order" is what remains of reality if one starts by seeing mind as something transcendent, which interferes with nature, in order to then subtract it from nature. Retrospective attempts to haul mind back into the nature it left behind will then, of course, not be all that successful. Nagel considers only one alternative to this constellation, which he dismisses as undesirable without argument. As he laconically states:

> Perhaps the natural order is not exclusively physical; or perhaps, in the worst case, there is no comprehensive natural order in which everything hangs together—only disconnected forms of understanding.[24]

Ontological pluralism suggests Nagel's "worst case" option in the philosophy of nature. If there are facts of different kinds—objects in different fields of sense, without there being a field of sense of all fields of sense (the all-encompassing totality of objects or facts)—why then should the "natural order" have to suffer being identified with the miserable pseudo-reality of the nonexistent world? Put less metaphorically, the argument is as follows: the world does not exist. There is a multitude of fields of sense in which facts of various kinds (mathematical, moral, physical, historical, aesthetic, etc.) obtain. Not all truths hang together in a single world. This raises the question of whether those facts investigated by the natural sciences form an overall domain, the universe. This strikes me as correct, although it remains a contested matter in the philosophy of science. In any case, I have no horse in that particular race. Yet this is not yet to establish whether there is an order in which all mental facts, the obtaining of which essentially requires mind, hang together with the facts of the universe in such a way that there could be an as yet undeveloped science, in the sense of an explanatorily and methodologically stable discipline, that researches this order. Nagel believes that this is the case and so recommends a speculative extension of our current physics. Yet if we apply ontological pluralism in the philosophy of nature, then the option abominated by Nagel comes to seem fairly obvious. We do not have to compel the sciences of nature and man onto the (in any case fictional) procrustean bed of a future natural science. Nature and mind do not belong to a natural order that has yet to be properly investigated.

To be sure, this cannot be the end of the story, for the combination of conditionalism and neo-existentialism suggests a mereology that Nagel considers—albeit in a distorted naturalistic form—only to hastily dismiss.[25] The epistemic and ontological irreducibility of mind resides in our ability to lend categorial structure to that which we can know. On this basis, we can distinguish the conditions of our own existence into the natural and the mental. The mental dimensions of our existence consist in how they would not be as we find them to be if we had not taken up those attitudes toward them through which we find them to be as they are.

Heidegger developed a series of fitting formulations for this, writing, for example: "Das Selbst-sein ist der schon *im* Suchen liegende Fund."[26] (Self-Being is the trove already discovered through searching.)[27] In the reflexive articulation of the structure of our mental capacities (reason, consciousness, thought, emotions, self-consciousness, etc.), we encounter a series of structures, and these are available to our investigations essentially because we ascribe states to ourselves and others. We are thereby entitled to ask of certain types of state, such as consciousness, whether and in what sense they are natural kinds.

The nature-mind distinction is not a priori. Which elements of the human self-portrait depend upon how we relate to them is an open question, and we can hardly foresee what its ultimate answer might be. In everyday life, we find this question existentially pressing on the level of nourishment, health, bodily hygiene, movement, and so on. The way in which we behave in light of our self-conceptions is obviously reflected in the domain of nature, such that the boundary between the psychosomatic and the purely biochemical processes of autopoietic regulation becomes blurred at the ontologically hybrid interface of our minded life-form.

That whole on the basis of which we can divide up our life into processes of various kinds is mental. Ontological classification does not occur by itself; it is not a natural process, the structure of which might be researched with recourse to models that abstract from the fact that we raise knowledge claims, claims subject to conceptually and normatively controlled criteria of self-discovery.

Mind is a whole within which that part of nature with which we are interwoven is embedded as a part. This mereology, to be sure, obtains only from the standpoint of mind; that is, the existence of mind cannot be intelligibly explained on the basis of the presence of parts that are not yet of its kind. In my view, this excludes the *emergentism* favored both by the so-called speculative realists like Quentin Meillassoux and by certain so-called new realists like Maurizio Ferraris, a position which, to put it simply, maintains that mind is a diachronically strongly emergent phenomenon.[28]

A phenomenon is diachronically strongly emergent when what is true of it cannot be derived from that which is true of its parts, where these parts already existed at a prior point in time in the development of the universe. Thus, the elementary particles of which neurons consist already existed before neurons. If neuronal activity is to be identical with mind without the latter being explanatorily redundant, it would then be the case that mind diachronically strongly emerges.

Emergentism is a way of making more precise the impression that mind is a relative latecomer in the emergence of the universe, appearing at the earliest after the emergence of life. Yet this perspective presupposes an entire metaphysical worldview, which postulates an all-encompassing natural process that somehow runs in a linear fashion from the big bang, via the formation of planets and galaxies, through to the evolutionary emergence of species, before nature opens our eyes, as Nagel says, echoing (while misconstruing) Schelling.[29]

The ontological theory I am proposing instead does not, I should stress, falsify any temporal statements concerning the stages of the planet that diachronically preceded us. So far as we know, mind was not always already there. However, we do not know enough about the universe on all its scales in order to develop a definitive metaphysics of nature which might serve as the foundation of an explanation of the emergence of elementary mental states.

Within the framework of my own research, the strength of mental realism remains an open question. I am confident, however, that it is tenable as an *ontological* thesis, which can be justified and technically elaborated with recourse to the irreducibility of mind and ontological pluralism. Recent projects in natural philosophy, such as Nagel's or the impressive conception elaborated by George Ellis, suggest that mental realism is ontologically measurable, so to speak, because—as Ellis has set out in his recent essay with the theoretical physicist Barara Drossel—it can be translated into a plausible, realistic solution to the measurement problem of quantum theory.[30]

Be that as it may, I conclude by noting that ontological pluralism, paired with a recognition of our own existence as minded beings, leads to the insight that nature is not a unity devoid of mind and consciousness, from which mind has to emerge or into which it needs to be resolved. Rather, we ought to start from an irreducible mental realism and infer to nature's real constitution on that basis—provided it is actually knowable. Nagel—who at least begins to contemplate this option— overlooks how there are by now a number of scientifically supported variants of ontological pluralism, which allow us to restrict the mindless levels of the universe in such a way that they need not present any threat to our self-knowledge as minded animals.

The philosophy of mind thus proves to be the starting point of any philosophy of nature that wishes to avoid running into conflict with its own knowability. Mind accordingly enjoys an explanatory primacy in the philosophy of nature, which is demonstrably compatible with our knowledge of fundamentally mindless natural processes. We must thus learn to recognize how we are not strangers within nature, and neither are we tools of a "mouldy film" that has "produced living and knowing beings," as Schopenhauer put it, lending colorful expression to his own self-contempt. As minded beings, we are an especially bothersome species for our fellow animals. In my view, this is because the human is the animal that doesn't want to be one and who is thus inclined to acts of desperation, acts which currently assume the form of an ongoing process of self-eradication. But that is a topic for another occasion.[31]

Notes

1   For further details, see Markus Gabriel, "Neutraler Realismus." In *Jahrbuch Kontroversen 2. Markus Gabriel: Neutraler Realismus*, ed. Thomas Buchheim (Freiburg/München: Karl Alber, 2016), 11–31; Markus Gabriel, *Sinn und Existenz. Eine realistische Ontologie* (Berlin: Suhrkamp, 2016).

2   For a discussion of the extent to which such a position requires defending a genuine ontological relativism, which would go beyond Quine's concept of ontological relativity, see Dorothee Schmitt, *Das Selbstaufhebungsargument. Der Relativismus in der gegenwärtigen philosophischen Debatte* (Berlin/Boston: De Gruyter, 2018).

3   Max Tegmark, *Life 3.0: Being Human in the Age of Artificial Intelligence* (New York: Alfred A. Knopf, 2017); Luciano Floridi, *The 4th Revolution. How the Infosphere Is Reshaping Human Reality* (Oxford: Oxford University Press, 2014). On the current state of the discussion surrounding panpsychism, see William E. Seager (ed.), *The Routledge Handbook of Panpsychism* (London: Routledge, 2019).

4   Erwin Schrödinger, *Geist und Materie* (Braunschweig: Friedrich Vieweg & Sohn, 1959). For a balanced assessment of the relation between physics and the philosophy of mind, see, for example, Michel Bitbol, *Physique et philosophie de l'esprit* (Paris: Flammarion, 2000); and Michael Bitbol, *Hat das Bewusstsein einen Ursprung? Für eine achtsame Neurowissenschaft* (Paderborn: Wilhelm Fink, 2019). A precise presentation of the relation of mind, computers, and quantum mechanics (upon which, moreover, Thomas Nagel relies) can be found in Michael Lockwood, *Mind, Brain and the Quantum. The Compound "I"* (Cambridge, MA/Oxford: Oxford University Press, 1989).

5   The *spiritus rector* here is certainly Tononi. See Giulio Tononi and Christof Koch, "Consciousness, Here, There, but Not Everywhere." Available online: https://arxiv. org/ftp/arxiv/papers/1405/1405.7089.pdf; and the introductory Giulio Tononi, *Phi. A Voyage from the Brain to the Soul* (New York: Pantheon, 2012); and Marcello Massimini and Giulio Tononi, *Sizing Up Consciousness. Towards an Objective Measure of the Capacity for Experience* (Oxford: Oxford University Press, 2018). See to the recent Christof Koch, *The Feeling of Life Itself. Why Consciousness Is Widespread but Can't Be Computed* (Cambridge, MA: MIT Press, 2019).

6   Wolfram Hogrebe, "Das Dunkle Du." In *Die Wirklichkeit des Denkens. Vorträge der Gadamerprofessur*, ed. Markus Gabriel and Jens Halfwassen (Heidelberg: Winter, 2007), 11–36.

7   Wolfram Hogrebe, *Riskante Lebensnähe. Die szenische Existenz des Menschen* (Berlin: De Gruyter, 2009), 17.

8   Thomas Nagel, *Mind and Cosmos. Why the Materialist Neo-Darwinian Conception of Nature Is Almost Certainly False* (Oxford/New York: Oxford University Press, 2012), 83.

9   See James Ladyman, Don Ross, David Spurett, John Collier, *Every Thing Must Go. Metaphysics Naturalized* (Oxford/New York: Oxford University Press, 2007).

10   George Ellis, *How Can Physics Underlie the Mind? Top-Down Causation in the Human Context* (Berlin/Heidelberg: Springer, 2016).

11   Charles Taylor, *The Explanation of Behaviour* (London: Routledge & Kegan Paul, 1964).

12   See Charles Taylor, "Gabriel's Refutation." In *Neo-Existentialism. How to Conceive of the Human Mind after Naturalism's Failure,* ed. Markus Gabriel (Cambridge: Polity, 2018), 46–52.

13   Bruno Snell, *The Discovery of the Mind,* trans. T.G. Rosenmeyer (Oxford: Blackwell, 1953). I have pursued this point in my *I Am Not a Brain* (Cambridge: Polity, 2017), and *Neo-Existentialism.*

14   Stanislas Dehaene, Hakwan Lau, Sid Kouider, "What Is Consciousness, and Could Machines Have It?" *Science* 358 (2017): 486–92. For an extensive counterargument, see Markus Gabriel, *Fiktionen* (Berlin: Suhrkamp, 2020), §§6–11, 15. I

15   Gabriel, *Neo-Existentialism,* 75.

16   See Michael Hampe, *Eine kleine Geschichte des Naturgesetzbegriffs* (Berlin: Suhrkamp, 2007); Michael Hampe, *Tunguska oder Das Ende der Natur* (München: Carl Hanser Verlag, 2011).

17   Gabriel, *I Am Not a Brain.*

18   Gernot Böhme, *Leib. Die Natur, die wir selbst sind* (Berlin: Suhrkamp, 2019).

19   See, of course, David Chalmers, *The Conscious Mind. In Search of a Fundamental Theory* (Oxford/New York: Oxford University Press, 1997); Joseph Levine, *Purple Haze. The Puzzle of Consciousness* (Oxford: Oxford University Press, 2001).

20   Thomas Nagel, "What Is It Like to Be a Bat?" In *Mortal Questions* (Cambridge/New York: Cambridge University Press, 1979), 165–80, 178–80. On the concept of objective phenomenology, see Gabriel, *Fiktionen,* §9.

21   Huw Price, *Naturalism without Mirrors* (Oxford: Oxford University Press, 2011), 253–97.

22   Nagel, *Mind and Cosmos,* 36.

23   Nagel, *Mind and Cosmos,* 15.

24   Nagel, *Mind and Cosmos,* 15f.

25   Nagel, *Mind and Cosmos,* 57.

26   "Self-Being is what is already discovered in searching." Martin Heidegger, *Beiträge zur Philosophie (Vom Ereignis). Gesamtausgabe Band 65* (Frankfurt a. M.: Vittorio Klostermann, 2003), 398. On this, see Wolfram Hogrebe, "Riskante Lebensnähe." In *Lebenswelt und Wissenschaft. XXI. Deutscher Kongress für Philosophie 15.—19. September 2008 an der Universität Duisburg-Essen,* ed. Carl Friedrich Gethmann (Hamburg: Felix Meiner, 2011), 40–62, esp., 52–5 and, for a detailed account: Jaroslaw Bledowski, *Zugang und Fraktur. Heideggers Subjektivitätstheorie in* Sein und Zeit (Tübingen, forthcoming).

27   Translation Dominik Finkelde.

28   Maurizio Ferraris, *Emergenza* (Turin: Einaudi, 2016).

29   Nagel, *Mind and Cosmos,* 85, 117, 124.

30   See Barbara Drossel/George Ellis, "Contextual Wavefunction Collapse: An Integrated Theory of Quantum Measurement," *New Journal of Physics* 20, no. 113025 (2018).

31   See Markus Gabriel, *Moralischer Fortschritt in dunklen Zeiten. Universale Werte für das 21. Jahrhundert* (Berlin: Ullstein, 2020).

4

Parallax in Hermeneutic Realism

Anton Friedrich Koch

Look at a door handle fifteen feet in front of you. Close your left eye and cover the area of the handle with your outstretched thumb. Then (variant one) close your right eye and open your left. Now the handle is visible and the thumb appears to the right of it. Switch back and forth between closing and opening your right and your left eye. Accordingly, the thumb will one time cover the handle and will appear to the right of it the other time. Now try something different (variant two): open your left eye and leave the right eye open, while focusing the handle in a stereoscopic view. This time you will be under the impression of two vagabond thumb guises, one covering the handle, which, strangely enough, remains visible, while the other thumb guise appears somewhat further to the right.

These are two cases of parallax, the first one confronting us with an apparent contradiction, for it is impossible for our thumb to cover and not to cover an object if the thumb and the object do not move relative to each other in the meantime, while the second seems to confront us with *shine* in the triple German sense of the word: light, certificate, and illusion: We have an optical experience (Schein$_1$) that certifies (Schein$_2$) the presence of one or two thumb-like guises, but must in some way be illusory (Schein$_3$). Of course, the appearance of a contradiction can easily be resolved and the nature of the relevant shine (or *Schein*, for that matter) can easily be understood by recourse to parallax, given the two spatially distinct viewpoints of our eyes, and so no mystery remains. In fact, parallax is what makes stereoscopic vision possible.

By extrapolation and analogy, we can (and do) extend the notion of parallax in philosophy from vision to perception and even further to knowledge and belief in general, provided we have a suitable variety of perceptual, epistemic, or doxastic standpoints and perspectives available, and we can then study the theoretical effects of our respective extensions.[1] If this is a common philosophical habit, then the position labelled *hermeneutic realism* (and defended in a booklet of this title)[2] is no exception, but can rather be seen as an invitation to grant the phenomenon of parallax various interesting roles in philosophical theory building. In what follows, hermeneutic realism is first (partially) characterized by four of its doctrines, then some interrelations between those doctrines are sketched, and finally it is examined for each doctrine to what extent it could be interpreted as a recourse to parallax.

1. Four Doctrines of Hermeneutic Realism

1. The triple structure of truth. We human beings raise objective truth claims, thereby positing something to be the case independently of our positing it, that is, presupposing it in the technical Hegelian sense of *positing as not posited* (but as being the case in and by itself). This basic *fact of truth* (or *of truth claims*, more cautiously spoken, but some of the claims will actually be true, or else dissent would not occur) lies at the heart of the tantalizing dialectic between metaphysical realism and pragmatic antirealism. The realists emphasize the independence of the real, the pragmatists our discursive positing. To the realists truth appears as some surd, matter-of-factual correspondence between thinking and being, to the pragmatists as assertability according to intersubjective rules of verification. The realists stay in line with logic; the pragmatists have to accept truth value gaps and to abandon logic, especially the principle of the excluded middle, as their spokesman Michael Dummett has forcefully argued, who advocated recourse to an intuitionist ersatz logic. But there is no such thing as a deviant logic proper. Thus pragmatic antirealism falls into absurdity, as does metaphysical realism in its own different way, because the real, to the realists, turns into an unknowable thing in itself, and the concept of truth dissolves into indeterminacy for lack of conditions of reliable application. The gigantomachia of realism and pragmatism over truth and logic therefore leads to an impasse and to exhaustion on both sides. The way out, of course, is offered by the familiar interface between human discursive spontaneity and the independently real, which we call sensible intuition or perception. Thereby, a third candidate for a rough and nominal explication of truth comes into sight after correspondence and assertability, the one Heidegger associated with pre-Socratic conceptions of truth: unconcealment.

Now hermeneutic realism teaches that truth has a threefold structure or three essential aspects, a realistic (or objective), a pragmatic (or normative), and a phenomenal (or epistemic) aspect, which together make up the concept of truth. These aspects, though, are no independent conceptual elements or modules, but rather encompassing conceptions under which truth can appear as such. Otherwise, metaphysical realists would never have mistaken truth as mere correspondence, nor pragmatists as mere assertability, nor pre-Socratics as mere unconcealment. The disagreement between any two proponents of this or that particular aspect of truth testifies to the prima facie incompatibility of the aspects and invites one to resort to parallax to alleviate truth-theoretical conflicts.

2. The subjectivity thesis and the theory of a priori spatiotemporal self-orientation. To the extent that the real is objective, we are fallible with respect to it. Fallibility, in other words, is the epistemic reverse of ontic objectivity. A necessary condition of fallibility, as Plato showed in the *Sophist*, is that our "shortest," that is, elementary truth claims are already compositional or synthetic. Moreover, they are synthetic in an asymmetric, viz., predicative way, containing a subject and a predicate (a name and a verb). Predication thus is the basic alethic combination, and with predication come the interrelated logical, ontological, epistemological, and semantic dualities of subjects and predicates, individuals and general traits, intuitions and concepts, designators and predicative terms, respectively. Now if thinking is essentially predicative, that is, conceptual, that is, general, then there is no epistemic individuation by (general) thought alone, just as there is no ontic individuation by general traits alone. Epistemic individuation in its most fundamental form requires also spatiotemporal intuition, and ontic individuation at its basis requires as well a pre-conceptual sphere of individuality and plurality, that is, something like space and time. But space and time by themselves are not yet sufficient to complement general traits in grounding ontic individuation, as the following little bit of reasoning shows: things are not individuated by their general traits, but, given these, by their positional characteristics in space and time. How then are spatiotemporal positions individuated? Not by the things occupying them, on pain of vicious circularity. Nor can they be individuated all by themselves, that is, by sheer magic, on pain of violation of the weak, purely logical version of the principle of the identity of indiscernibles, which is a truth of second order logic. According to this weak principle, if x is not identical to y, something must nontrivially be true of x that is not true of y. Of course, the trivial fact, that if $x \neq y$, then "( ) = x" is true of x but not of y, will not suffice to ground the non-identity of x and y. On the other hand, the strong metaphysical version of principle of the identity of indiscernibles as appealed to by Leibniz is much too strong and out of the question here, because general traits, being general, cannot individuate things.

If ontic individuation thus seems to lead us into an antinomy—things are, but cannot be, individuated by sheer magic—epistemic individuation shows the way out. Sensible intuition, informed by indexical modes of intentional consciousness and ultimately by an egocentric indexical coordinate system, is what makes epistemic individuation possible even under unfavorable conditions, such as, for instance, global symmetries as in Peter Strawson's (unrealistically simple) chess board universe or Max Black's (unrealistically simple) two-sphere world or such endless repetitions as in David Lewis's worlds with two-way eternal recurrence.[3] A coordinate system must, of course, be anchored in a real frame of reference in order to fulfil its function as a means of epistemic individuation, and an indexical coordinate system that has to compensate for the deficits of general descriptions in epistemic individuation can be anchored neither by general description nor indexically by itself. It must be anchored pre-indexically and pre-descriptively by an original a priori self-individuation and self-localization of subjects who know a priori that they are asymmetric corporeal subjects and who can distinguish a priori eight basic directions in one temporal and three spatial dimensions: future and past, up and down, back and forth, right and left—always relative to their respective *me here now*.

We have arrived at the threshold of the subjectivity thesis, a crucial point of which is that the ontic and epistemic order converge in those very special corporeal things who think and perceive. Their a priori epistemic self-individuation achieves their ontic individuation, and relative to them all other spatiotemporal items, far and near, past, present and future, are individuated ontically by indexical relational properties such as *being over there to the right* or *having happened a million years ago*. The subjectivity thesis states that it is logically necessary (for resolving the antinomy of individuation) that thinkers (1a) are, and (1b) know themselves a priori to be, asymmetric corporeal subjects and that (2a) the spatiotemporal universe contains some of them at some places and times and that (2b) they know a priori that the universe must contain some of them. But we tend to forget or suppress most of this a priori knowledge when we do philosophy (Descartes, for instance, suppressed his a priori knowledge that he was a corporeal subject) and then painstakingly have to restore it by inquiring into the presuppositions of the fact of truth. This is what is done in hermeneutic realism. With the subjectivity thesis, parallax turns ontological, because the ontic individuation of things (or of spatiotemporal positions, for that matter) requires that they have irreducibly indexical properties, which they can only have relative to perceiving and thinking subjects. Parallax, that is, the different spatiotemporal viewpoints of subjects, thus inscribed into the ontological structure of things is their unconcealment, their epistemic accessibility via phenomenal indexical characteristics.

3. *The readability thesis.* Things do not have indexical properties relative to animals, because animals cannot read them. Sapience is the capacity for reading things as ur-tokens of their names and as ur-tokens of elementary sentences about them. Qua ur-tokens or, as we might as well call them, Lagadonian tokens of their proper names, things are objects; qua Lagadonian tokens of sentences about them, they are (bundles of) elementary objective facts; qua Lagadonian tokens of phenomenal indexical designators, Sellarsian *this-suches*, that is, qua perceived in sensible intuition, they are objective phenomena (or phenomenal objects). "Lagadonian" is David Lewis's term, alluding to Gulliver's travel to Lagadonia, for languages in which things serve as their own proper names.[4] The readability thesis states that language as such, any full-fledged empirically meaningful language, has Lagadonian aspects, because it invariably has us treat things (a) as objects, that is, as Lagadonian tokens of their names; (b) as objective phenomena, that is, Lagadonian tokens of indexical designators of them; and (c) as facts, that is, Lagadonian tokens of elementary sentences about them. Parallax comes into play here by way of seemingly competing, but in fact compatible ontological standpoints, the standpoint of an ontology of objects and the standpoint of an ontology of objective facts and a standpoint of an ontology of phenomenal objects presenting themselves in perception.

Of course, the thesis of this threefold readability of things has laboriously to be defended and is defended in hermeneutic realism by selective recourse to the early Wittgenstein's theory of elementary sentences as logico-semantic pictures of facts and to Sellars's theory of elementary sentences as representational, proto-semantic pictures of objects. These differing picture theories agree in their diagnoses that the respective logical form each of them assigns to elementary sentences is the same as the (onto-) logical form of facts or objects respectively. So things, be they facts or objects, can be understood as we understand sentences, and then, of course, as written sentences, because they are not like vocal utterances that immediately fade away, but remain like inscriptions. The details must be left for other occasions. Suffice it here to give some hints with reference to Sellars.[5] In his picture theory of elementary sentences, he takes the grammar of predicate logic as basic. An elementary sentence thus consists of n designators modified by being juxtaposed to an n-place predicate. Then he points out that predicates, though certainly indispensable for thinking and speaking, are, in principle, dispensable for picturing things. Instead of modifying the name "Socrates" by placing the predicate "is sitting" to the right of it, one could as well write "Socrates" in a certain style, e.g., in italics, thus "*Socrates*," and instead of placing "is singing" to the right of it, one could write it in capitals, thus "SOCRATES." Moreover, one could fuse these one-word sentences into one, thus "*SOCRATES*," in order to picture Socrates as sitting and as singing. This is what happens on maps, where a cartographic designator, say a dot, may represent a city and picture it as a city by being red and as being a city of a certain size by having itself a certain size, etc. But if we can read maps and translate them into word language in this way, why not say that by the same token, that is, by very similar—Lagadonian—tokens, we can read things and translate them into word language? This, in fact, is the basic idea in the argument for the readability thesis, according to which we treat and read things (a) as objects: Lagadonian name tokens, (b) as Sellarsian *this-suches*: Lagadonian tokens of indexical designators, and (c) as facts: Lagadonian tokens of elementary sentences. Reading things is only possible against the background and with the help of a public language, and there is a two-sided pressure between things and language or being and thinking. In perception, things exert an epistemic pressure on language and theory, which is basically a logical pressure of Lagadonian tokens of observation sentences on our web of belief. Due to this pressure, the meanings of our words evolve, and due to this evolution, meanings exert a semantic counter-pressure on the correct readings of the Lagadonian tokens of observation sentences that things are. In this way, the readability thesis avoids any semblance of the myth of the given. Yes, Lagadonian sentence tokens are true, paradigmatically true, but their exact meanings and their correct translations vary with the development of our language.

One nice feature of the readability thesis, which again and in a different way points to parallax, deserves an extra mention at the end. Sellars developed his inferentialist semantics in the wake of Carnap's temporary syntacticism. According to both theorists, Sellars and the Carnap of the *Logische Syntax der Sprache* (Vienna 1934), there are no semantical relations. Meaning and reference are "syntactical," more specifically, inferential roles. Thus,

"Sokrates" in German refers to Socrates

says in first approximation that the German word "Sokrates" is materially equivalent to "Socrates." Of course, it must then be explained independently what material equivalence is, but let us grant that it can be done. Sellars gives an additional twist to the syntacticist or inferentialist analysis by introducing dots as interlingual quotation marks:

"Sokrates" in German is materially equivalent to ·Socrates·
where ·Socrates· is the role that "Socrates" plays in the target language, here English.

It has seemed counterintuitive, to say the least, to many authors who otherwise sympathize with Sellars's positions and arguments that he denies reference the status of a word-world relation. But the readability thesis mends the harm. According to it, the assertion that "Socrates" refers to Socrates is both an intralingual and an extralingual claim, for it states that the word type "Socrates" has as its intralingual Lagadonian ur-token Socrates, the extralingual Athenian philosopher. Closely related to this problematic is the syntacticist or inferentialist claim that categorial contexts like "( ) is a thing," "( ) is an object," "( ) is a fact," etc. are, at root, metalinguistic or are formulated in what Carnap called the material mode of speech (in which we talk about language in a deferred way by apparently talking about objects). Here the readability thesis dispels the haze by expressly allowing, indeed requiring, us to speak about worldly things in the metalanguage: things are Lagadonian tokens of designators or sentences after all. That the moon is an object just means that the moon is the Lagadonian token of a name. That it is a fact that the moon is shining just means that the moon right now (as she happens to be shining) is a Lagadonian token of the true sentence "The moon in shining." Since things can be read, we can look at them with both an object language eye and a metalanguage eye: another case of parallax. Given these virtues of the readability thesis, it seems a great mystery that Sellars did not advance the thesis himself.

    4. *The antinomy thesis.* Set theorists discuss whether they should countenance non-well-founded sets, e.g., the unit set Ω the only member of which is Ω itself. If we try to explain what Ω is, we get:

$$\Omega = \{\Omega\} = \{\{\Omega\}\} = \{\{\{\Omega\}\}\} = \ldots = \{\{\{ \ldots \}\}\}$$

Set theorists, familiar with set formation and identity, understand well what they are talking about when they argue for or against the acceptance of Ω and its ilk. By parity of reasoning, we may conclude that logicians, familiar with negation and the biconditional, understand well what they are talking about, when (or rather if) they argue for or against the acceptance of the non-well-founded negation v (and its ilk), the negated counterclaim of which is v itself. Thus, if we try to explain what v says, we get:

$$v \leftrightarrow \sim(v) \leftrightarrow \sim(\sim(v)) \leftrightarrow \sim(\sim(\sim(v))) \leftrightarrow \ldots \leftrightarrow \sim(\sim(\sim(\ldots)))$$

To accept the set theoretic candidate object Ω is to acknowledge its existence; to accept the logical candidate truth (truth claim) v is to acknowledge its truth. Irrespective of the analogy, this makes a considerable difference. We may or may not acknowledge the existence of Ω without contradiction. But to acknowledge the truth of v means confirming its negation and declaring it false, while to declare it false means negating it and thus acknowledging its truth: a contradiction with no way out, thus an antinomy, the antinomy of negation also known as the Liar, which in Quine's unsurpassable formulation reads:

> "Yields a falsehood when appended to its own quotation" yields a falsehood when appended to its own quotation.[6]

Liar sentences thus turn out to be ordinary language formulations, by way of semantic ascent, of the genuinely logical antinomy of negation, and it is only the technical device of semantic ascent that creates the impression of a semantic antinomy instead. The logical antinomy of negation, by the way, is what made Parmenides shy away from negation and what serves as the exclusive textual basis of Hegel's *Logic*, which reports the evolution of logical space, starting from the incoherent logical big bang of *becoming* and driven by classical logic to ever-new interim forms of the logical antinomy, until the process comes to a halt in an allegedly coherent fixed point called *absolute idea*. Anyway, to make a long story short, thinking and being, according to the antinomy thesis, are essentially contaminated, even informed by the antinomy of negation, but nevertheless stand under the strict rule of classical logic with its laws of non-contradiction, "~(p∧~p)," and identity, "x=x," and its law of the excluded middle, "p∨~p." This very peculiar situation, that thinking is, but cannot be, inconsistent and that being accordingly is, but cannot be, incoherent, is an invitation to invoke parallax again.

2. A Sketch of Some Interrelations between the Doctrines

The doctrines outlined are interrelated in multifarious ways that deserve and have received a book-length development, but shall only be indicated here selectively in a brief and possibly puzzling overview. Evidently, the realistic, phenomenal, and pragmatic aspects of truth are intertwined with the corresponding modes of time: past, present, and future, and thus with our a priori spatiotemporal self-orientation. What we know a priori is what is presupposed in our capacity to raise truth claims; we therefore have an implicit a priori knowledge of the aspects of truth and consequently of the three modes of time. With regard to the three dimensions of space, we can first point out that raising truth claims is an activity of discursive and, in the final analysis, predicative thinking. The aspects of truth will therefore essentially inform discourse, and they do so by creating the basis for three discursive proto-dimensions. Things are phenomenally unconcealed to the extent that we see or, more generally, perceive them fall under general concepts, which marks a fundamental discursive up/down-dimension. Our discursive acts are judgmental and qua judgments ought to be right according to the realistic aspect of truth, but might as well be wrong. This marks a fundamental right/left-dimension whose normativity refers us to a third, pragmatic dimension in which we move from premises to conclusions according to the pragmatic or normative aspect of truth: the discursive back/front-dimension of rule-guided inferential activity. Concept, judgment, and inference are thus three logical vectors that correspond to the epistemic (phenomenal), to the objective (realistic), and to the normative (pragmatic) aspect of truth and define three discursive proto-dimensions, which, in turn, provide a priori clues for distinguishing three basic spatial dimensions with six directions in egocentrically structured space. This distinguishing is achieved by combining the alethic-discursive clues with our a priori knowledge that we are corporeal thinkers who qua corporeal are subject to natural acceleration (empirically fleshed out by gravitation), and qua thinking subjects can move freely with self-induced acceleration which, because it is free, is normatively forked between right and wrong or right and left. Natural acceleration pulls us down to the ground, while in free acceleration, we can move forward on and over that same ground, choosing between right and wrong or, spatially conceived, right and left.

Moreover, we must distinguish between space as such and time as such in the first place, always with reference to the aspects of truth, and we do so through mediation of the logical modalities. Space, in comparison with time, is the sphere of the phenomenal aspect, contingency, and presence, while time is the Janus-faced dimension of (1) the pragmatic aspect, possibility, and future and (2) the realistic aspect, necessity, and past. Due to this double character, time is the axis of determination according to natural law as well as the axis of freedom—a clash of roles that points ahead to an incompatibilism of determinism and freedom and, once more, makes a recourse to parallax look appealing. Time appears open and free, when we look forward in it to the future, and fixed by nomological necessity, when we look back in it to the past. But it is one singular timeline that presents us with this double view. The particular antinomy of time, diagnosed by Hegel and worked out by the Hegel scholar J.M.E. McTaggart, gains additional momentum here. Not only do the opposite modes—future and past, with the present in between—coincide in one, in time, so that one and the same event, one and the same moment is future, present, and past.[7] But beyond that, one and the same event, if it happens to be an action, is free as a future event and nomologically determined as a past event, and it seems that it cannot be both.

This riddle again requires a parallactic solution, viz., a meta-compatibilist, libertarian theory of time's arrow on the basis of a two-dimensional stereoscopic view of time as developed and defended elsewhere.[8] The theory makes use of the antirealist idea of truth value gaps and corresponding ontic gaps and of the fact that natural laws have conditional form. Time, insofar as it is the axis of nomological determinism, leaves no room for freedom in the lawful connections between antecedent and consequent states of the world. But if antirealism is right, there are ontic gaps in the antecedent states themselves that are transferred to the consequent states by natural laws, unless the animal who owns the *logos* and can verify truth claims intervenes. In the context of such interventions, according to antirealism, truths can get lost and new ontic gaps can arise, when, for example, eyewitnesses die before having reported, while on the other hand, truths can arise and ontic gaps can be closed, when new verifications come about that were previously impossible. Let me skip the details and focus on the antirealist idea of alethic and ontic gaps; and let us be clear from the outset that we must not tinker with logic, as antirealists do in response to their recognition of alethic and ontic gaps. The animal who owns the *logos* owes solidarity to logic at its points of weakness, where it seems to turn against itself, and so the law of the excluded middle is not up for grabs, nor is the law of non-contradiction—alethic gaps and the antinomy of negation notwithstanding. But remember that we had to cut back on metaphysical realism anyway and make some concessions to antirealism in order to find a way out of their aporetic dialectic, regardless of theoretical considerations about freedom. So why not concede that there may be alethic and ontic gaps but insist that it is, in principle, impossible to identify one of them with certainty? And why not deny that truths can get lost and new ontic gaps can open up but insist that we can close alethic and ontic gaps in free actions? Whenever we plan and decide, we conceive macroscopic gaps in the future to close them. Perhaps a certain gap that we wanted to close was no real gap; then the intended state of affairs would have occurred anyway. Perhaps we will never know. But in willing and acting we will undoubtedly close some macroscopic future gaps—with consequences for unspecifiable microscopic gaps in the past that will then be closed retroactively according to natural laws. Time, the whole of it, becomes more and more determinate in time, or as we usually say: time passes, that is, time itself and within time (this is the two-dimensional view).

In this emancipatory, anti-bourgeois way, alethic gaps and the antinomy of negation teach us that there is no effective procedure, that is, no *law and order* procedure, to safeguard logic against its self-critical, seemingly auto-aggressive tendencies. We must care for it with *phronêsis*, hermeneutic skill. We must, for example, take an antinomy into inferential quarantine or treat a candidate of an alethic gap as a mere epistemic gap, etc. Deviant logics are of no help, because we cannot think according to them, and logic cannot be completely formalized anyway. The antinomy thesis and the theory of our a priori self-orientation, in particular the libertarian theory of time's arrow, unite to illuminate this important point.

Finally, as regards the readability thesis, its relationship to the aspects of truth is not hard to discern, at least in outline. When we treat things as objects, that is, read them as Lagadonian name tokens, we are under the guidance of the objective aspect; when we perceive them intuitively, that is, read them as Lagadonian *this-suches*, we are under the guidance of the phenomenal aspect; and when we treat them as states or episodes, that is, read them as Lagadonian sentence tokens, we are under the guidance of the pragmatic aspect. As objects, they are truth-makers, which is what remains of correspondence; as intuitively perceived, they are paradigmatically unconcealed; and as states or episodes, they are tokens of facts and, so to speak, warrantedly self-asserting.

3. Parallax in the Doctrines of Hermeneutic Realism

1. Truth and parallax. Imaginary knowers in possession of Leibnizian individual concepts of things or of a true Carnapian state description or a Sellarsian world story would look at the world not in particular lines of sight or perspectives but in a universal view from nowhere and would not receive any additional information by explicit identifications. Omniscience, if it were possible, would thus be beyond parallax and identity. That, for example, the brightest planet in the evening sky is identical to the brightest planet in the morning sky would already be entailed in the complete individual concept of Venus. It is only to finite, embodied knowers in their midst that things present themselves in the usual incomplete and multiply shadowed ways, not to an omniscient God or super-scientist (which is why only finite knowers can individuate things, according to the subjectivity thesis). Identifications, that is, fusions of modes of presentation, when made transparent theoretically or phenomenally, thus become inessential, in principle, redundant, as all true identifications would be for omniscient knowers. Identity like parallax, where it is essential, is essentially opaque; and essential parallax will not allow a transparent fusion of modes of presentation in a true stereoscopic view. A physical example of essential parallax and opaque identity can arguably be found in quantum mechanical wave-particle duality. Here, one and the same underlying reality presents itself in two modes that cannot be consistently and transparently fused into one description. Light is waves, not particles, seen from "here," and particles, not waves, seen from "there." But the operative cases of "here" and "there" do not fit together, as, by contrast, they do in special relativity, where an observer "here," in one inertial system, can calculate by means of Lorentz's transformation equations the outcomes of measurements an observer "there," in a different frame of reference, will perform. Now as far as truth is concerned, its concept is primitive and indefinable. Truth can only be partially defined with reference to Tarski's Convention T (i.e., Tarski's criterion of adequate definitions of the truth predicates of certain formal languages) and must besides be explained and learned with regard to paradigmatic cases of truth, just as basic color concepts are explained and learned with regard to paradigmatic instances of them. But as we have seen, truth will appear as correspondence in the perspective of its realistic or objective aspect, as unconcealment in the perspective of its phenomenal aspect, and as assertability in the perspective of its paradigmatic aspect. These perspectives cannot be fused transparently, which means that their identity as the singular underlying fact of truth is nonredundant, essential, and opaque and that truth itself is inherently oriented toward the diverging perspectives associated with the aspects. The perspectives on truth are thus built into the very thing we call truth, and truth-theoretic parallax is essential and material. Yet the unity of truth or veridical being is undeniable and has as its model and paradigm the peculiar unity of time across the three divergent temporal modes. This seems to be part of what Heidegger means when he says that time is the "sense" or the horizon of (veridical) being.

2. Subjectivity and parallax. In an intriguing discussion and critique of the subjectivity thesis, Thomas Hofweber argues that the thesis would be committed to an untenable solipsism due to its ontological perspectivalism, if the latter were not strengthened to a more radical position, fragmentalism, according to which

> [n]ot only is there no God's eye point of view on all of reality, there is no coherent whole of reality. Fragmentalism goes beyond perspectivalism in that it rejects the God's eye point of view not simply because any description of reality from the outside must be incomplete, but because any description of all reality must be incoherent and contradictory. Fragmentalism maintains that there is no coherent whole of reality that could be described from any point of view.[9]

In fact, the subjectivity thesis entails a kind of fragmentalism or, as I would like to put it, a thesis of multiple essential and ontological parallax. The identity or coherence of the whole of reality is analogically opaque as the identity of light is according to quantum mechanics, although not only in a double way but in a multiple way, which means that in analogy to the *wave-particle duality*, we have here a *many-subjects plurality*. Hofweber critically asks, why reality must "fragment in a way tied to subjects, rather than some other ways."[10] The answer, according to the subjectivity thesis and the theory of the a priori spatiotemporal self-orientation, of course, is: because only subjects are capable of epistemic self-individuation, and only in embodied subjects do epistemic and ontic self-individuation converge. Moreover, only subjects can overcome the fragmentation of reality up to a certain, important degree, by being able to read the details of an intersubjective spatiotemporal perceptual field and translate them into a shared language that makes reading things possible in the first place. Certainly, the subjectivity thesis of hermeneutic realism, in contrast to macrophysics, is not a relativity theory, itself formulated mathematically in an absolute, standpoint-neutral style and offering precise transformation equations for transparent fusions of standpoints, but an essentially standpoint-centric theory. Nevertheless, hermeneutic realism not only recognizes but also aspires to a specifically hermeneutic, opaque "fusion of horizons"[11] and a specifically hermeneutic universality. Leibniz's motto— "Calculemus!"—is suitable for the exact, narrowly theoretical sciences, but not for the hermeneutic sciences and not for philosophy, the hermeneutic science a priori. Hermeneutics is not an ensemble of effective procedures but the laborious craft of giving reasons and of understanding, always subject to the indeterminacies of translation and interpretation to which Quine and Davidson have emphatically referred. Still the hermeneutic sciences within these limitations are actual sciences and geared to universal validity under the regulative ideal of a great, albeit opaque and always imperfect, fusion of all possible subjective horizons. If this fusion could be achieved and made transparent, incoherence would be the result. Completeness and consistency do not fit together, not only in the axiomatization of mathematics but also in general. Reality, Heraclitus's *physis*, loves to hide: *kryptesthai philei*, which means that it presents itself in hiding and hides itself in being present, because its identity and coherence are essentially opaque and permeated by ontological parallax.

What about the mathematical, narrowly theoretical sciences of nature? Mathematical language essentially abstracts from indexical forms of expression, and mathematical theory essentially abstracts from the antinomy of negation. Both abstractions result in a considerable loss of expressive power and concrete content and on the other hand in a considerable gain in obvious universality and in security against hidden antinomies. Although mathematics cannot be formalized or axiomatized completely and consistently and its consistency cannot be proved, as Gödel showed, it is a great scientific success story and an offer to other sciences to use mathematical language as much as possible. In particular, modern physics has benefited enormously from mathematization and paid the price of irretrievably abstracting from certain basic traits of reality, not only from its mental traits but also from important "physical," completely natural traits such as the modes (and arguably as well the arrow) of time and the phenomenal qualities of things, not to mention basic ontological parallax. This is why physics is essentially limited to the status of *physica militans*, that is, to a potentially endless series of physical successor theories, never terminating in a final theory of everything or a world formula.

So here we meet a new form of theoretical parallax again. We can view reality through our manifest image of ourselves and the world and through our abstract and mathematical natural sciences. In none of the cases do we get a complete and consistent picture, but one time a concrete, standpoint-centric picture and in the other case an abstract, standpoint-neutral one, in one case a full, but always controversial approach to what it means to be a human being in the world and in the other case computable knowledge of physical events. The most basic and most general science in the first case is philosophy and in the second case theoretical physics. (As far as the science of logic is concerned, it also exists in two styles: as rich, concrete, not fully formalizable logic here and as sparse, abstract, formal, and mathematical logic there.)

Earlier, the two-dimensional stereoscopic view of time and the meta-compatibilist libertarian theory of time's arrow were mentioned. This turns out to be a case in point. On the one hand there is the parameter t of fundamental physics, along which all events, including unspecifiable alethic-ontic gaps, are nomologically determined in both temporal directions (according to the Schrödinger equation, let us say). Call this *physical time*. On the other hand, we live and act in *concrete time*, which is directed toward the future and modified by the temporal modes; and we can do so, because we are free agents who understand the temporal modes on the basis of the aspects of truth and actualize the arrow of time on the basis of our willing and acting. Thus, physical time can be regarded as orthogonal to directed concrete time, where concrete time is the dimension in which the determinacy of physical time, that is, successive physical timelines, increases (and the sum total of ontic gaps decreases) *symmetrically* in both directions. In concrete time, by contrast, determinacy increases *asymmetrically* with free actions and ontic gaps are closed in one direction only: toward the future. Symmetrical physical time, all of it, gets more and more determinate in ways not detectable by physics, while concrete time in its directedness passes, that is, consumes the inexhaustible leeway of freedom.

3. Readability and parallax. As mentioned above, Sellars takes the grammar of predicate logic as basic in his picture theory (as well as in general). But, of course, in a further development of the readability thesis, we could free ourselves from this restricted grammar, which Frege designed for the specific purposes of mathematics, and for example distinguish between different logical types of predicates such as qualitative and dispositional predicates, specific and generic common names, etc. Accordingly, we could treat and read our dog Fido first as a Lagadonian token of his proper name, second as a Lagadonian token of the specific common name "dog," and third as a Lagadonian token of the generic common name "animal" and say, echoing Hegel, that Fido, like all things, is a judgment and also, like all things, a syllogism.[12] He is a judgment, because we can read him as "Fido is a dog," and a syllogism, because we can read him as "Fido, being a dog, is an animal." This nicely demonstrates the great parallactic flexibility of the readability thesis. We already saw that readability grounds two closely related forms of parallax. (1) We can view things from (at least) three linguistic perspectives: (a) treat them as objects; that is, read them as Lagadonian name tokens, (b) perceive them as *this-suches*; that is, read them as Lagadonian tokens of indexical designators, and (c) be convinced of them as of facts; that is, read them as Lagadonian sentence tokens. (2) We can look at things with a metalanguage eye, as in (1), or with an object language eye, as we think and speak empirically about them. Now (3) it dawns on us that we could also choose to read them with Frege according to modern predicate logic (as in (1)) or with Aristotle according to traditional formal logic or with Hegel according to speculative logic.—And that is certainly not all there is to say here about parallax, but it may be enough for our current objectives.

4. Antinomy and parallax. Those who understand negation and the biconditional understand non-well-founded negation or self-negation and thus are caught in the purely logical antinomy of negation that fuels Hegelian speculative logic. There, self-negation appears as the other-of-itself in the doctrine of being, as absolute shine or reflection in the doctrine of essence, and as the concept in the doctrine of the concept. In each case, the antinomy is temporarily treated by parallax, but the success of the treatment is not permanent. To see how it works, remember that one way to represent self-negation was by an infinite sequence of negation signs (plus brackets):

$$\sim(\sim(\sim(\ldots)))$$

Now if we take the negation signs pairwise, we seem to get an infinite sequence of double negations, that is, affirmations, and thus non-well-founded affirmation or self-affirmation. We can formulate it in ordinary language by way of semantic ascent as the *Truth Teller*:

> (TT) "Yields a truth when appended to its own quotation" yields a truth when appended to its own quotation.

The truth value of (TT) may be hard to decide: if we take (TT) as true, it comes out true, and if we take it as false, it comes out false. But this reassures us that at least it is not obviously self-contradictory. Of course, (TT) is only one "half" of the Liar. Biased against inconsistency (as, of course, thinkers ought to be) we abstracted from it by ignoring that infinitely many negation sings are not even-numbered infinitely many negation signs. Therefore, we must be aware that a further, outer negation sign may remain on the left-hand side of our formula:

$$\sim[\sim\sim(\sim\sim(\sim\sim(\ldots)))]$$

In ordinary language this comes to a negation of the Truth Teller, which may be true or false, but again seems to be consistent:

> Non-(TT) It is not the case that "yields a truth when appended to its own quotation" yields a truth when appended to its own quotation.

Thus, logical parallax yields two internally consistent products of self-negation that together form a contradictory pair. In the doctrine of being, they turn out to be the *something-identical-to-itself* and its *other*; in the doctrine of essence, *identity* and *difference*; and in the doctrine of the concept, the *universal* and the *particular*. But cheating by way of a one-sided abstraction cannot be cured by way of an equally one-sided counter-abstraction, or so Hegel's science of logic shows in its respective progress. Something and its other come together again in a logically stereoscopic view as the self-contradictory finite; identity and difference as the contradiction as such; and the universal and the particular return to the unified concept as the Janus-faced singular, which is at the same time the self-loss of the concept and its original division into judgment. These are Gestalten of the Hegelian rhombus, with self-negation on top, then self-affirmation and its negation in the second row, and self-negation again at bottom. In this way, the antinomy is first alleviated by parallactic abstraction; then parallax logically develops and leads us back to a stereoscopic view of the antinomy; and this view, being antinomic, turns into a squint that requires further logical treatment and progression. It remains a mystery not only to the present author but to Hegel scholarship, in general, how the antinomy of negation can be finally and definitely overcome in what Hegel calls the *absolute idea*.

But that was parallax in speculative logic, not so much in hermeneutic realism. The latter tries to cope with the antinomy not systematically, but through hermeneutic craftsmanship. Here, too, parallax can play important roles in varying forms, for example, by opening a small gap between thinking and being, which serves both realism and logic. In the realm of thinking, or so one might say, logic—classical Aristotelian, Fregean, Hegelian, everyday logic—is constitutive, while in the realm of being, it is regulative only, leaving room for undetectable ontic under-determinacies, which ought to be closed by free agents according to the law of the autonomy of the will. Logic might as well leave room for undetectable ontic over-determinacies, that is, ontic correlates of contradictions, as hidden marks of the finitude of being. But this is a long and winding story, mostly untold, which would be far too much on this occasion.

Notes

1   In this vein, Wilfrid Sellars tried to show how the manifest image of man-in-the-world and a future scientific image "blend together in a true stereoscopic view," cf. Wilfrid Sellars, "Philosophy and the Scientific Image of Man." In *Science, Perception and Reality* (London: Routledge & Kegan Paul, 1963), 1–40, here: 9.

2   Anton Friedrich Koch, *Hermeneutischer Realismus* (Tübingen: Mohr Siebeck, 2016).

3   See P.F. Strawson, *Individuals. An Essay in Descriptive Metaphysics* (London: Methuen, 1959), 123; Max Black, "The Identity of Indiscernibles," *Mind* 61 (1952): 153–64; David Lewis, *On the Plurality of Worlds* (Oxford and New York: Blackwell, 1986), 157.

4   Lewis, *On the Plurality of Worlds*, 145.

5   Cf. Wilfrid Sellars, *Naturalism and Ontology* (Reseda, CA: Ridgeview Publishing Company, 1979), chapters 3 and 5.

6   W.V. Quine, "The Ways of Paradox." In *The Ways of Paradox and Other Essays. Revised and Enlarged Edition* (Cambridge, MA and London: Harvard University Press, 1976), 1–21, here: 7.

7   Cf. G.W.F. Hegel, *Enzyklopädie der philosophischen Wissenschaften im Grundrisse* (Berlin 1830) (Heidelberg: Osswald'scher Verlag. C.F. Winter, 1830), §260; J.M.E. McTaggart, "The Unreality of Time," *Mind* 17 (1908): 457–73.

8   Anton Friedrich Koch, "Die Zeit in zweidimensionaler Betrachtung," *Deutsche Zeitschrift für Philosophie* 64 (2016): 879–93.

9   Thomas Hofweber, "The Place of Subjects in the Metaphysics of Material Objects," *dialectica* 69 (2015): 473–90, 488.

10   Hofweber, "The Place of Subjects in the Metaphysics of Material Objects," 489.

11   Gadamer's term ("Horizontverschmelzung"). See Hans-Georg Gadamer, *Wahrheit und Methode* (Tübingen: Mohr Siebeck, 1975), 290.

12   Hegel, *Enzyklopädie der philosophischen Wissenschaften im Grundrisse*, §§167, 181.

5

Object-Disoriented Ontology
Realism in Psychoanalysis

Alenka Zupančič

Many recent philosophical discussions have been marked, in one way or another, by the rather spectacular relaunching of the question of realism, triggered by Quentin Meillassoux's book *Après la finitude* (2006), and followed by a broader, albeit much less homogeneous, movement of "speculative realism." We are witnessing a powerful revival of the issue of realism, with new conceptualizations or definitions of the latter, as well as of its adversary ("correlationism" in place of the traditional nominalism). "Realist ontologies" are emerging faster than one can keep track of them, and we can take this acceleration of realism as an opportunity to raise the question of whether—and how— the conceptual field of Lacanian psychoanalysis is concerned in this debate, considering that the concept of the Real is one of the central concepts of Lacanian theory.

As a quick general mapping of the parameters of this discussion, let me just very briefly recall Meillassoux's basic argument. It consists in showing how post-Cartesian philosophy (starting with Kant) rejected or disqualified the possibility for us to have any access to being outside of its correlation to thinking. Not only are we never dealing with an object in itself, separately from its relationship to the subject, there is also no subject that is not always-already in a relationship with an object. The relation thus precedes any object or subject; the relation is prior to the terms it relates and becomes itself the principal object of philosophical investigation. All contemporary (post-Cartesian) philosophies are variations on philosophies of correlation. As Meillassoux puts it:

> Generally speaking, the modern philosopher's "two-step" consists in this belief in the primacy of the relation over the related terms; a belief in the constitutive power of reciprocal relation. The "co-" (of co-givenness, of co-relation, of the co-originary, of co-presence, etc.) is the grammatical particle that dominates modern philosophy, its veritable "chemical formula." Thus, one could say that up until Kant, one of the principal problems of philosophy was to think substance, while ever since Kant, it has consisted in trying to think the correlation. Prior to the advent

This chapter is a reprint from: Alenka Zupančič, *What IS Sex?* (Cambridge, MA: MIT Press, 2017), 73–84 © 2017 Massachusetts Institute of Technology, by permission of The MIT Press.

of transcendentalism, one of the questions that divided rival philosophers most decisively was "Who grasps the true nature of substance? He who thinks the Idea, the individual, the atom, the God? Which God?" But ever since Kant, to discover what divides rival philosophers is no longer to ask who has grasped the true nature of substantiality, but rather to ask who has grasped the true nature of correlation: is it the thinker of the subject–object correlation, the noetico–noematic correlation, or the language–referent correlation?[1]

The inadequacy of this position is revealed, according to Meillassoux, when it is confronted with "ancestral statements" or "arche-fossils": statements produced today by experimental science concerning events that occurred prior to the emergence of life and of consciousness (e.g., "The earth was formed 4.56 billion years ago"). They raise a simple and still, according to Meillassoux, insoluble problem for a correlationist: How are we to grasp the meaning of scientific statements bearing explicitly upon a manifestation of the world that is posited as anterior to the emergence of thought, and even of life—posited, that is, as anterior to every form of human *relation* to that world? From the correlationist point of view these statements are, strictly speaking, meaningless.

One of the great merits of Meillassoux's book is that it has (re)opened not so much the question of the relationship between philosophy and science as the question of *whether they are speaking about the same world.* Alain Badiou has recently raised—or, rather, answered—a similar question in the context of politics: "There is only one world." Yet this question is also pertinent to the issue of epistemology's, or science's, relation to ontology. It may seem, in fact, as if science and philosophy have been developing for some time now in parallel worlds: in one it is possible to speak of the Real in itself, independently of its relation to the subject, whereas in the other this kind of discourse is meaningless. So, what do we get if we apply the axiom "There is only one world" to this situation? Instead of taking the—on the side of philosophy—more common path, criticizing science for its lack of reflection upon its own discourse, Meillassoux takes another path: the fact that certain scientific statements escape its "horizon of sense" indicates that there is something wrong with philosophy. It indicates that, in order to ensure its own survival as a discursive practice (one could also say: in order to ensure the continuation of metaphysics by other means), it has sacrificed far too much, namely, the Real in its absolute sense.

One should perhaps stress, nevertheless, that this less common path is becoming a kind of trend in contemporary philosophy, and Meillassoux shares it with several authors, authors who are very different in terms of theory. Let us take as an example Catherine Malabou and her philosophical materialism, which—at the time she wrote her book *Les nouveaux blessés*—aimed to develop a new theory of subjectivity based on cognitive sciences. In her polemics with Freudian and Lacanian psychoanalysis, she opposes to the "libidinal unconscious," as always-already discursively mediated, the "cerebral unconscious" (autoaffection of the brain) as the true, materialist unconscious.[2] Yet if Malabou's materialism moves in the direction of a "naturalization of the discursive," or, more precisely, if it represents an attempt to reduce the gap between the organic and the subject via finding the organic causes of the subject,[3]

Meillassoux takes the same path (of reducing this gap) in the opposite direction, via the discursiveness of nature, although he does not go all the way. His realist ontology, differentiating between primary and secondary qualities of being, does not claim that being is inherently mathematical; it claims that it is absolute, that it is independent of any relation to the subject, although only in the segment that can be mathematically formulated. Meillassoux thus preserves a certain gap or leap (between being and its mathematization), without addressing it. The susceptibility of certain qualities to being mathematically formulated is the guarantee of their absolute character (of their being "real" in the strong sense of the term). Meillassoux's realism is thus not the realism of the universals but—and paradoxically—the realism of the *correlate* of the universals, which he also calls the referent:

> Generally speaking, statements are ideal insofar as their reality is one with signification. But their referents, for their part, are not necessarily ideal (the cat on the mat is real, although the statement "the cat is on the mat" is ideal). In this particular instance, it would be necessary to specify: the *referents* of the statements about dates, volumes etc., existed 4.56 billion years ago, as described by these statements—but not these statements themselves, which are contemporaneous with us.[4]

There seems to be no way around the fact that the criterion of the absolute is nothing but its correlation with mathematics. Not that this implies something necessarily subjective or subjectively mediated, but it surely implies something discursive. And here we come to the core problem of Meillassoux's conceptualizations, which is at the same time what is most interesting about them. I emphasize this as opposed to another dimension of his approach, a dimension enthusiastically embraced by our *Zeitgeist*, even though it has little philosophical (or scientific) value and is, rather, based on free associations related to some more or less obscure feelings of the present "discontent in civilization," to use the Freudian term. Let us call it the psychological dimension, summed up by the following narrative: Since Descartes we have lost the *great Outside*, the absolute outside, the Real, and have become prisoners of our own subjective or *discursive cage*. The only outside we are dealing with is the outside posited or constituted by ourselves or different discursive practices. And there is a growing discomfort, claustrophobia, in this imprisonment, this constant obsession with ourselves, this inability to ever get out of the external inside that we have thus constructed. There is also a political discontent that is put into play here: that feeling of frustrating impotence, the impossibility of really changing anything, of absorbing the small and big disappointments of recent and not-so-recent history. Hence the certain additional redemptive charm of a project that promises again to break out into the great Outside, to reinstate the Real in its absolute dimension, and to ontologically ground the possibility of radical change.

One should insist, however, that the crucial aspect of Meillassoux lies entirely elsewhere than in this narrative, which has detected in him (perhaps not completely without his complicity) the support of a certain fantasy, namely and precisely the fantasy of the "great Outside" which will save us—from what, finally? From that little yet annoying bit of the outside which is at work here and now, persistently nagging, preventing any kind of "discursive cage" from safely closing upon itself. In other words, to say that the great Outside is a fantasy does not imply that it is a fantasy of a Real that does not really exist; rather, it implies that it is a fantasy in the strict psychoanalytic sense: a screen that conceals the fact that the discursive reality is itself leaking, contradictory, and entangled with the Real as its irreducible other side. That is to say: the great Outside is the fantasy that conceals the Real that is already *right here*.

The philosophical core of Meillassoux's project, however, does not consist in opposing the real to the discursive, and dreaming of the breakthrough beyond the discursive; on the contrary, the core of his project is their joint articulation, which would escape the logic of transcendental constitution, and hence of their co-dependence. This joint articulation relies on two fundamental claims: the thesis (mentioned above) about the possible mathematization of primary qualities and the thesis about the absolute necessity of the contingent. Needless to say, both of these theses are *philosophical* and aim at laying the foundations for what modern science seems to simply presuppose: namely, and precisely, a shared articulation of the discursive and the real. It would thus seem that they try to adjust the naïve realism of science, replacing it with a reflective, philosophically grounded "speculative" realism.

Yet the first really interesting question is already apparent here: What, in fact, is the status of the realism which science's operations presuppose? Is it simply a form of naïve realism, a straightforward belief that the nature which it describes is absolute and exists "out there," independently of us? Meillassoux's inaugural presupposition indeed seems to be that science operates in the right way, yet lacks its own ontological theory that would correspond to its praxis. Considering the framework of his project, it is, in fact, rather astonishing how little time Meillassoux devotes to the discussion of modern science, its fundamental or inaugural gesture, its presuppositions and consequences—that is to say, to the discussion of what science is actually doing. Contrary to this, we can say that Lacan has an extraordinarily well-elaborated theory of modern science and of its inaugural gesture (to some extent this theory is part of a broader structuralist theory of science), in relation to which he situates his own, psychoanalytic discourse. And this is where one needs to start. The relationship between psychoanalytic discourse and science is a crucial question for Lacan throughout his *œuvre*, even though it is by no means simple. For on the one hand it presupposes their absolute kinship and co-temporality (marked by countless explicit statements like "the subject of the unconscious is the subject of modern science," "psychoanalysis is possible only after the same break that inaugurates modern science," etc.). On the other hand, there is also the no-less remarkable difference and dissonance between psychoanalysis and science, with the concept of truth as its most salient marker, which involves the difference in their respective "objects." In short: the common ground shared by psychoanalysis and science is nothing other than the Real in its absolute dimension, but they have different ways of pursuing this Real.

What is the Lacanian theory of science? In the context of a similar debate, and drawing on the work of Jean-Claude Milner, this question has been recently reopened, and given its full significance, by Lorenzo Chiesa,[5] to whom I owe this part of the discussion. According to this theory, Galileanism replaced the ancient notion of nature with the modern notion, according to which nature is nothing other than the empirical object of science. The formal precondition of this change lies in the complete mathematization of science. In other words, after Galileo, "nature does not have any other sensible substance than that which is necessary to the right functioning of science's mathematical formulas."[6] To put it even more strongly: the revolution of Galilean science consists in producing its object ("nature") as its own *objective* correlate. In Lacan's work we find a whole series of such very strong statements, for example: "Energy is not a substance…, it's a numerical constant that a physicist has to find in his calculations, so as to be able to work."[7] The fact that science speaks about this or that law of nature, and about the universe, does not mean that it maintains the perspective of the great Outside (as not discursively constituted in any way), rather the opposite. Modern science starts when it produces its object. This is not to be understood in the Kantian sense of the transcendental constitution of phenomena, but in a slightly different, and stronger, sense. Modern science literally creates a new real(ity): it is not that the object of science is "mediated" by its formulas; rather, it is indistinguishable from them, it does not exist outside them, *yet it is real*. It has real consequences or consequences in the Real. More precisely: the new Real that emerges with the Galilean scientific revolution (the complete mathematization of science) is a Real in which—and this is decisive—(the scientific) *discourse has consequences*. Such as, for example, landing on the moon. For the fact that this discourse has consequences in the Real does not hold for nature in the broad sense of the word, it holds only for nature as physics or for physical nature. But, of course, there is always, says Lacan,

> the realist argument. We cannot resist the idea that nature is always there, whether we are there or not, we and our science, as if science were indeed ours and we weren't determined by it. Of course I won't dispute this. Nature is there. But what distinguishes it from physics is that it is worth saying something about physics, and that discourse has consequences in it, whereas everybody knows that no discourse has any consequences in nature, which is why we tend to love it so much. To be a philosopher of nature has never been considered as a proof of materialism, nor of scientific quality.[8]

Three things are crucial in this dense and decisive quote. (1) The shift of emphasis from a discursive study of the Real to the *consequences* of discourse in the Real, related to this (2) the definition of the newly emerged reality, and (3) the problem of materialism. Let us first briefly stop at the third point, which we have already touched upon in passing with the question of the "cerebral unconscious." At stake is a key dimension of a possible definition of materialism, which one could formulate as follows: Materialism is not guaranteed by any matter. It is not the reference to matter as the ultimate substance from which all emerges (and which, in this conceptual perspective, is often highly spiritualized) that leads to true materialism. The true materialism—which, as Lacan puts it with trenchant directness in another significant passage, can only be a dialectical materialism[9]—is not grounded in the primacy of matter nor in matter as first principle but in the notion of conflict or contradiction, of split, and of the "parallax of the Real" produced in it. In other words, the fundamental axiom of materialism is not "matter is all" or "matter is primary" but relates rather to the primacy of a cut. And, of course, this is not without consequences for the kind of realism that pertains to this materialism.

This brings us to points (1) and (2) of the quote above, which we can take together since they refer to two aspects of this new, "dialectically materialist," realism. The distinction between nature and physics established by Lacan does not follow the logic of distinguishing between nature as an inaccessible thing in itself and physics as transcendentally structured nature, accessible to our knowledge. The thesis is different, and somehow more radical. Modern science—which is, after all, a historically assignable event—creates a new space of the Real or the Real as a new dimension of ("natural") space. Physics does not "cover" nature (or reduplicate it symbolically), but is added to it, with nature continuing to stay where it has always been. "Physics is not something extending, like God's goodness, across all nature."[10] Nature keeps standing there not as an impenetrable Real in itself but as the Imaginary, which we can see, like, and love, but which is, at the same time, somewhat irrelevant. There is an amusing story about how some of his friends dragged Hegel to the Alps, in order for him to become aware of, and to admire, the stunning beauty of the scenery there. All Hegel said about the sublime spectacle that was revealed to him is reported to have been: *Es ist so* (It is so; it is what it is). Lacan would have appreciated this very much. *Es ist so*; there is nothing more to say about these beautiful mountains. This is not because we cannot really know them but because there is nothing to know. (If we say that a stone we see is of this or that age, we are talking about another reality—one in which consequences of discourse exist.)

Lacan's definition of this difference is indeed extremely concise and precise. What is at stake is not that nature as scientific object (that is, as physics) is only an effect of discourse, its consequence—and that in this sense physics does not actually deal with the Real, but only with its own constructions. What is at stake is, rather, that the discourse of science creates, opens up, a space in which this discourse has (real) consequences. And this is far from being the same thing. We are dealing with something that most literally, and from the inside, splits the world in two.

The fact that the discourse of science creates, opens up, a space in which this discourse has (real) consequences also means that it can produce something that not only becomes a part of reality but can also change it. "Scientific discourse was able to bring about the moon landing, where thought becomes witness to an eruption of a real, and with mathematics using no apparatus other than a form of language."[11] To this Lacan adds that the aforementioned eruption of a real took place "without the philosopher caring about it." Perhaps we can see in this remark a problematization of a certain aspect of modern (continental) philosophy, which tends to miss a crucial dimension of science at precisely this point of the Real and keeps reducing it to the logic of "instrumental reason," "technicism," and so on. We could also see in it a hint at the contemporary coupling of philosophy and "university discourse," the minimal definition of which would be precisely: the social link in which discourse has no consequences.

To return to the starting point of this digression: with regard to the question of realism in science, Lacan's diagnosis could be summed up as follows: although it may be true that naïve realism constitutes the spontaneous ideology of many scientists, it is utterly irrelevant for the constitution of scientific discourse, its efficiency, and its mode of operation. As we have already seen, this means: modern science did not arrive at the absolute character of its referent by relying on the presuppositions of naïve realism, that is, by naïvely assuming the existence of its referent "in nature," but by reducing it to a letter, which alone opens up the space of the real consequences of (scientific) discourse. And the word "reducing" is not to be taken in the sense of reducing the richness of sensible qualities to an absolute minimum, yet a minimum in which we would be dealing with the continuation of the same substance; it should be taken in the sense of a cut, and of substitution. What is at stake also is not the classical logic of representation: the letter does not represent some aspects of sensible nature, but literally replaces it. It replaces it with something that belongs to discourse (to the semblance), yet something that can be—precisely because it belongs to discourse— formulated in the direction of the Real. This brings us back to the point formulated earlier: "It is not worth talking about anything except the real in which discourse itself has consequences."[12] This is not an argument about the Real being merely the effect of discourse. The link between discursivity and the Real (which is, after all, also what Meillassoux tackles in his polemics with contemporary obscurantism)[13] finds here a much firmer foundation than in the case of simply stating that the referent (a "natural object") is absolute in, and only in, its mathematizable aspect. Meillassoux (and this is a weak point of his argument) does not see the mathematization of science as a cut in reality that (only) produces the dimension of the Real, but as the furthest point of a continuum, of a continuous sharpening of the ways in which scientists speak about reality; and the Real refers to the purely formal/formalizable segment of a thing remaining, in the end, in the net of this sharpened form of scientific speech. Let us recall: "the referents of the statements about dates, volumes etc., existed 4.56 billion years ago, as described by these statements—but not these statements themselves, which are contemporaneous with us." The ideal character of a scientific formula catches in its net, here and now, a fragment of the thing that is in itself absolute (that is to say, which existed as such, and independently of this net, 4.5 billion years ago). Or, to put it another way: the Real is that portion of a substance that does not slip through the net of mathematizable science but remains caught in it. Lacan's metaphor, and with it his entire perspective, is quite different in this respect: the Real is guaranteed not by the consistency of numbers (or letters) but by the "impossible," that is, by the limit of their consistency. If it is not worth talking about the Real (or Nature) *outside* of discourse, the reason is that we necessarily stay on the level of semblance, which means that we can say whatever we like. The Real, on the other hand, is indicated by the fact that not all is possible. Here we come to the other crucial component of the Lacanian Real, binding the realism of consequences to the modality of the impossible. Together, they could be articulated as follows: something has consequences if it cannot be anything (i.e., if it is impossible in one of its own segments).

> The articulation, and I mean algebraic articulation, of the semblance—which, as such, only involves letters—and its effects, this is the only apparatus by means of which we designate what is real. What is real is what makes/constitutes a hole [*fait trou*] in this semblance, in this articulated semblance that is scientific discourse. Scientific discourse advances without even worrying whether it is a semblance

or not. What is at stake is simply that its network, its net, its *lattice*, as we call it, makes the right holes appear in the right places. It has no other reference but the impossible at which its deductions arrive. This impossible is the real. In physics we only aim at something which is the real by means of a discursive apparatus, insofar as the latter, in its very rigor, encounters the limits of its consistency.

But what interests *us*, is the field of truth.[14]

Before addressing this last question of truth, and of what it implies for the relationship between psychoanalysis and science, let us return to the beginning of our considerations. It would not be appropriate to conclude without accepting the challenge of Meillassoux's initial question, in all its estimable directness and simplicity. That is, what does the Lacanian realism of consequences, combined with the impossible, imply for the status of so-called ancestral statements? Does the statement "the earth was formed 4.5 billion years ago" make any sense independently of us; that is, does it refer to a specific *object* which did in fact (albeit according to our way of counting, and based on radiometric dating) exist 4.5 billion years ago?

Why not venture an answer? In order to formulate it I will draw on a very fascinating story, which revolves precisely around fossils and which—if taken in *its* speculative dimension—can give to the notion of arche-fossil a very intriguing Lacanian twist. In his book, Meillassoux does, in fact, at some point hint at this story—but it remains a completely cursory hint, serving only as a rhetorical argument for mocking the absurdities with which correlationism would seem to be compatible, and it misses precisely the speculative potential of the story in question.

In one of his superb essays, entitled "Adam's Navel," Stephen Jay Gould draws our attention to a most astonishing, "ridiculous," yet extremely elegant theory suggested by the renowned British naturalist Philip Henry Gosse.[15] Gosse was Darwin's contemporary, and he published the work that interests us (*Omphalos*) in 1857, that is, only two years before the publication of Darwin's *On the Origin of Species*. He was a most passionate naturalist, and one of his greatest passions was fossils, which he studied and described with particular devotion. At that time the nascent science of geology had already gathered evidence for the earth's enormous antiquity, which bluntly contradicted its age according to Genesis (6,000 years). And this was Gosse's principal dilemma—for he was not only a dedicated naturalist but also a deeply religious man. The core of his theory thus consisted of an attempt to resolve the contradiction between the (relatively recent, according to the Bible) creation ab nihilo and the real existence of fossils of a much more venerable age. He came up with a rather ingenious theory according to which God did indeed create the earth about 6,000 years ago, but he did not create it only for the time to come, for the future, but also retroactively, "for the past"—at the moment of creating the earth, he also put the fossils in it. We should not miss the beauty of this self-effacing gesture: God creates the world by effacing the traces of his own creation, and hence of his own existence, to the benefit of scientific exploration. And it is probably no coincidence that the theological world rejected this theory even more passionately than the scientific world did. The Reverend Charles Kingsley, author of *The Water-Babies* and a friend of Gosse, was asked to review Gosse's book. Refusing, he wrote to Gosse:

Shall I tell you the truth? It is best. Your book is the first that ever made me doubt, and I fear it will make hundreds do so. Your book tends to prove this—that if we accept the fact of absolute creation, God becomes *Deus quidam deceptor* ["God who is sometimes a deceiver"]. I do not mean merely in the case of fossils which *pretend* to be the bones of dead animals; but in the one single case of your newly created scars on the pandanus trunk, your newly created Adam's navel, you make God tell a lie. It is not my reason, but my *conscience* which revolts here.... I cannot... believe that God has written on the rocks one enormous and superfluous lie for all mankind.[16]

Indeed, the consensus opined that God could not have "written on the rocks one enormous and superfluous lie." According to Gould, modern American creationists also mostly, and vehemently, reject this theory for "imputing a dubious moral character to God."

The interest of Gosse's theory for our discussion consists above all in pointing out the insufficiency of a simply linear theory of time with respect to the question of the Real. Also, the patina of bizarreness that surrounds Gosse's story should not blind us to the fact that, structurally speaking, his dilemma is exactly Meillassoux's. We have only to replace God's creation with human creation (nature as subjectively/ discursively constituted), and we get a strangely similar question: does science study only something which we have ourselves constituted as such, posited (as external), or is this exteriority independent of us, and has it existed exactly as it is since long before us? The Lacanian answer would be: it is independent, yet it *becomes* such only at the very moment of its discursive "creation." That is to say, with the emergence—ex nihilo, why not?—of the pure signifier, and with it of the reality in which discourse has consequences, we get a physical reality independent of ourselves. (This, to be sure, is not to say that we do not have any influence on it.) And, of course, this independence is also gained for the time "before us." The reality of arche-fossils or objects of ancestral statements is no different from the reality of objects contemporary with us—and this is because neither the former nor the latter are correlates of our thinking but are instead *objective correlates of the emergence of a break in reality as a homogeneous continuum* (which is precisely the break of modern science, as well as the break of the emergence of the signifier as such). This is the very reason why Lacan's theory is indeed "dialectically materialist": the break implies nothing other than a speculative identity of the absolute and of becoming. They are not opposed, but they need to be thought together. Something can (in time) *become absolute* (i.e., timeless). The absolute is *at the same time* both necessary and contingent: there is no absolute without a break/cut in which it is constituted as absolute (that is to say, as "necessarily necessary"—whereby this redoubling is precisely the space in which discourse has consequences), yet this break itself is contingent.

Meillassoux's gesture, on the other hand, consists in absolutizing contingency as the only necessity. In this way he ultimately subscribes to the logic of constitutive exception which totalizes some "all": all is contingent, all but the necessity of this contingency. Unlike this logic of constitutive exception, Lacan's axiom could be written as "the necessary is not-all." It does not absolutize contingency but suggests that contradiction is the point of *truth* of the absolute necessity: the absolute is at the same time both necessary and contingent.

And this finally brings us to the crucial difference that nonetheless exists between psychoanalysis and science, and which Lacan keeps relating to the question of truth, staring from his famous 1965 essay "Science and Truth," where we read:

> The fact is that science, if one looks at it closely, has no memory. Once constituted, it forgets the circuitous path by which it came into being; otherwise stated, it forgets a dimension of truth that psychoanalysis seriously puts to work.[17]

As he further specifies, this is not simply about past structures, accidents, or even mistakes that often pave the way for huge scientific breakthroughs (resolving a "crisis"); it is about the subjective toll (*le drame subjectif*) that each of these crises takes (Lacan mentions J.R. Mayer and Cantor). However, the subject here is not simply the one who comes up with this or that new idea; it is what emerges in the *discontinuity* that defines scientific advances. If science has no memory, it has no memory of that out of which emerges the objective status of its enunciations. Once again, this is not about scientific truths being necessarily subjective (or about going against the claim that scientific statements hold regardless of by whom, why, or how they are enunciated): this "subjective toll" is not something that—had it not been forgotten—would have in any way changed or influenced the *objective* status of the claims. What falls out (of memory) is simply this: at the core of every significant scientific breakthrough, there is a radical *discontinuity* which establishes the absolute ("eternal" or timeless) status of its objects; and subject is the name of this discontinuity. As Lacan put it in the same essay, "the subject is, as it were, internally excluded from its object."[18] This is precisely the subject that carries the dimension of truth that psychoanalysis "puts to work."

And this is what is nicely captured in Gosse's story if we shift the picture just a little bit: science is the God who, in creating reality, cannot but efface the traces of his own creation, the God who "has no memory." This is what "the subject of the unconscious is the subject of modern science" means. Written on the rocks is not one enormous lie; that science creates its object does not mean that this object did not exist before this creation, and that hence the "ancestral statements" or "arche-fossils" are simply meaningless; it means that the absolute character of the existence of "arche-fossils" is the *very form* of absolute contingency. Psychoanalysis claims that the reality of (signifying) creation comes with an unexpected addition: the unconscious. The unconscious is proof of the existence of the contingent; it is where something of which we have no memory continues to work as truth. What this truth testifies to first and foremost is the *cut* through which all that is "meaningful," or that is said to be "true" or "false," is created. For example—and if we jump back to science—this also implies that no amount of "plasticity of the brain" can smooth out, or avoid the cut involved in, the signifiers capable of producing a plausible scientific theory of this same "plasticity." It cannot do away with this cut without losing its own *real* and falling instead straight into yet another *Weltanschauung* or "world-view." For the brain, as a meaningful referent of science, is not the piece of meat in our heads but an object such that scientific apparatus has consequences for it (and in it). This is what "brain sciences" often tend to forget, and what the subjects of the unconscious remind us of.

Notes

1   Quentin Meillassoux, *After Finitude* (London: Continuum, 2008), 5–6.

2   Catherine Malabou, *Les nouveaux blessés* (Paris: Bayard, 2007).

3   This is why Slavoj Žižek is right to point out that the cost of this kind of material ism might well be a re-spiritualization of matter (see Slavoj Žižek, *Living in the End of Times* (London: Verso, 2010), 303), as is the case of Jane Bennett's notion of "vibrant matter." Needless to say, however, my cursory reference to Malabou here fails to do justice to her argument in its entirety, as well as to some very valuable points that she makes in presenting it.

4   Meillassoux, *After Finitude*, 12.

5   See Lorenzo Chiesa, "Hyperstructuralism's Necessity of Contingency," *S: Journal of the Jan van Eyck Circle for Lacanian Ideology Critique* 3 (2010): 159–77.

6   Jean-Claude Milner, *Le Périple structural* (Lagrasse: Verdier, 2008), 287–8.

7   Jacques Lacan, *Television: A Challenge to the Psychoanalytic Establishment* (New York: W. W. Norton, 1990), 18.

8   Jacques Lacan, *Le Séminaire, livre XVI. D'un autre à l'Autre* (Paris: Seuil, 2006), 33.

9   "If I am anything, it is clear that I'm not a nominalist. I mean that my starting point is not that the name is something that one sticks, like this, on the real. And one must choose. If we are nominalists, we must completely renounce dialectical materialism, so that, in short, the nominalist tradition, which is strictly speaking the only danger of idealism that can occur in a discourse like mine, is quite obviously ruled out. This is not about being realist in the sense one was realist in the Middle Ages, that is in the sense of the realism of the universals; what is at stake is to mark off the fact that our discourse, our scientific discourse, finds the real only in that it depends on the function of the semblance" Lacan, *Le Séminaire, livre XVIII*, 28.

10   Lacan, *Le Séminaire, livre XVI*, 34.

11   Lacan, *Television*, 36.

12   Lacan, *Le Séminaire, livre XVI*, 31.

13   His argument in this respect is that correlationist philosophy, precisely since it claims that we can know nothing about things in themselves, forces us to admit that even the most irrational obscurantist nonsense talked about things in themselves is at least possible.

14   Lacan, *Le Séminaire, livre XVIII*, 28.

15   Stephen Jay Gould, "Adam's Navel." In *The Flamingo's Smile: Reflections in Natural History* (Harmondsworth, UK: Penguin, 1985), 99–113.

16   Quoted from Garrett Hardin, *Naked Emperors: Essays of a Taboo-Stalker* (Los Altos, CA: William Kaufmann, 1982).

17   Jacques Lacan, *Écrits* (New York: W. W. Norton, 2006), 738.

18   Lacan, *Écrits*, 731.

6

Temporal Paradox, Realism, and Subjectivity

Paul M. Livingston

One aim of this chapter is to suggest that central logical and positional features of subjectivity can plausibly be seen as resulting from the structure of *time as given*, rather than conversely. By "time as given," I shall mean whatever underlies such facts as that what is now present will later be past, that objects may enjoy contradictory determinations at different times, and that temporally indexical facts (such as the fact that it is 9:58 AM now) are irreducibly tensed. It is plausible that these facts, and the formal structures they exemplify, obtain prior to and independently of any activity or process of human thinking, perception, consciousness, or representation. Accordingly, it should be possible, as I argue here, to understand the temporally positional and perspectival structure of these activities or processes on the basis of the prior structure of given time. Such an understanding produces a position according to which tense, change, and becoming are real but are not dependent on the processes or activities of a subject. As I shall argue, this provides a realist alternative to both of two seemingly opposed traditions of thinking about time: first, the long tradition, characteristic of Kant's idealism and culminating in Husserl's phenomenology, of thinking about time as constitutively dependent on subjectivity; and second, the objectivist naturalism, typical of the analytic tradition, according to which tense, change, and becoming play no part in reality as it is in itself.

1.

Much discussion about time has begun with the observation that we describe and experience events from the perspective of the present: that is, we understand events as happening *now*, or in *the past*, or *in the future*. Famously, J.M.E. McTaggart made this observation the center of his idealist argument against the reality of time: the placement of temporal events in "B-series" relationships (timeless relations of events standing before, at the same time as, or after other events) requires their prior placement in "A-series" relationships (those, rather, oriented from the perspective of the "now"). The placement of events in the "A-series" is, however, contradictory, for it involves ascribing to one and the same event mutually incompatible determinations. And it is no help to describe the different determinations (e.g., as (now) "future," and (later) "present," and (still later) "past") as themselves ascribed at different times, since the question of the compatibility of *these* descriptions then arises again and has the same form.

In response to the argument, many philosophers have argued that the temporal indexicals evidently involved in all such determinations might be seen rather as innocuous within the framework of a broader account of the linguistic functioning of indexicals in general, as "token-reflexive" expressions, or as determining functions from "character" to "content" (in the manner of Kaplan).[1] On this kind of analysis, the temporal indexicality of the determination of an event as "present," "past," or "future" is analogous (for example) to that of the spatial indexicals "here" and "there," or (again) to the egocentric indexicals "I" and "you." This analogy is thought to suggest that all of the facts that are meant to be accommodated within the (putatively basic) A-series relationships can, in fact, be captured, without contradiction, in an indexical-free and non-perspectival objective framework. Just as there is no real contradiction between something's being "here" (for me) and simultaneously "there" (for you) or between some fact being a fact about "me" (for you) while it is about "you" (for me), so too, on this suggestion, the temporal facts that are expressed by A-series placements are to be understood simply as objective ones free of temporal indexicality or tense, essentially those expressed by the statements of their B-series locations. This approach, then, dissolves the putative contradiction; but as many have noted, it does so only at the cost of rejecting a basic kind of realism about tense, change, and becoming. For in the envisaged objective framework, there are in an evident sense no really tensed facts: no facts, that is, that are *irreducibly* characterized as past, present, and future. There is no fact, for example, that is irreducibly the fact that *I am (now) sitting* (as opposed to the fact that *I am sitting at 11:49 AM on December 23*); and there is no fact that is (irreducibly) the fact that *it is 3:50 PM now*.

Given this, we can ask what an alternative treatment that is, instead, realist about tense, change, and becoming might look like. This question will point, as well, to essential respects in which closer attention to the logical structure of specifically *temporal* indexicality (as opposed to the spatial and egocentric cases) can, in that context, serve to indicate special grounds for its irreducibility. In his 1960 article, "A Defence of McTaggart's Proof of the Unreality of Time," Michael Dummett distinguishes the two parts of McTaggart's argument.[2] In the first part, McTaggart argues that there will be no time if there are no irreducibly tensed (or A-series) facts; in the second, he states (as we have seen) that the existence of such facts implies a contradiction. If we are to understand the real structure of the argument, we should not pass over part one too quickly by assimilating the temporal cases to those of other indexicals. For, Dummett argues, the application of part one to part two depends on special features of temporal indexicality that do *not* hold with respect to spatial or ego-centric indexicals. In particular, Dummett argues, while the use of indexicals is not plausibly essential to the expression of any real facts in the spatial or egocentric cases, temporal indexicals *do*, by contrast, enter essentially into the expression of at least some facts which they are used to express (in particular, the A-series ones).

Briefly, Dummett's argument for this is as follows. In the case of the description of an arrangement of objects in space, I can readily envision as determinate such an arrangement in a particular space while I do not, myself, stand anywhere in particular within, or in relation to, the space in question. Dummett here gives the example of the space of my visual field: "In that space [i.e., that of the visual field as presented to me] there is no here or there, no near or far: I am not in that space."[3] On the strength of this analogy, Dummett suggests, we might conceive of a being who could sufficiently perceive objects in our three-dimensional space along with their spatial relations while herself occupying no position in that space. Such a being would apparently have no need for indexical expressions in describing correctly even the totality of the three-dimensional universe, and it follows from this that indexicality does not enter essentially into such a description. Something similar, indeed, seems to be the case with respect to the kinds of facts that we may express using personal pronouns. Barring *essentially* private mental events, at any rate, any fact that I can express in the first person using "I" can also be known and expressed in the second person by you as a fact about me, or equally from an indifferent third-person perspective as a fact about "P.L."[4]

By contrast with these cases, however, the complete description of events and relations in time *does* essentially require indexical (or, as Dummett says, "token-reflexive") expressions. For:

> Suppose someone who can observe all events which take place in our universe, or some region of it, during some period of time. We may first suppose that he observes them successively, that he cannot choose which events he will next observe but can observe them only in the order in which they take place. Then even if he knows both what he has observed and what he is going to observe, he cannot give a complete description of his observations without the use of temporally token-reflexive expressions. He can give a complete narration of the sequence of events, but there would remain to be answered the question, "And which of these events is happening *now*?" We can indeed avoid this by putting the observer's thoughts and utterances into the description, but now we have merely made the original observer part of the region observed, and the point may be made again for an observer who gives a description of this enlarged region.[5]

Further, as Dummett goes on to say, if we now envision an observer able to survey the whole sequential course of temporal events simultaneously (or at any rate, in any order she chooses), we may envision her in a familiar way as observing a four-dimensional configuration, one dimension of which represents time. But this would no longer evidently be an observation of that sequence itself but rather only of a (static) *model* of it: not of the events themselves but only of a possible form of representation of them. To mistake the observation of such a model for the observation of the facts modeled would be like, Dummett suggests, mistaking the observation of a path for the observation of the traveler who moves along it. In this way, we would miss the reality of the genuine phenomena of change, tense, and becoming, and thereby exclude from our model what are, in fact, essential features of the facts and relations purportedly modeled.

The observation of the temporal facts thus requires essentially a position that cannot be characterized as external to those facts themselves, and this feature—what we may call the positional *non-externality* of the temporal facts *as observed*—appears to characterize their logic essentially, and by contrast with the spatial or personal cases.

"As observed," *not* "as described." For it is evidently quite coherently possible for a *description*, for example, in writing, of any specific course of events to be given at a time which is unrelated to the time of the events described. We might imagine, for example, a narrative of a course of events as written down in a book, where it is not stated whether the course of events described has already taken place or is just being predicted in the future tense. However, what is not coherent, in view of Dummett's reconstruction of McTaggart's argument, is to suppose such a course of events to be *observed* at no time in particular: to come to be fully and completely known by a knower, that is, without the knower knowing whether they have already taken place, are now taking place, or are only predicted to take place in the future (with respect to that knower's temporal position in making the observation itself). Even if, for example, we were to envision such a knower as observing, in advance, a certain course of events as fore-ordained (so to speak), we could only envision that knower as observing the ordination, not the course of events itself: what would be left out of what such an observer observes would be the *actual* unfolding of those events in time, their actual happening itself.[6]

We may put this in more general terms, and switch to (more revealing) phenomenological language, by describing this phenomenon of *non-externality* as characterizing an essential aspect of the *givenness* of temporal facts: of the temporal facts, that is, *as* they are provided to any possible knower or observer who is envisioned as knowing or observing them, themselves. The advantage of this formulation, over formulations in terms of the possible *description* of such facts, is that it brings out the sense in which the temporal facts are themselves irreducibly "given": available, that is, only to or from a *position* which itself has an essential temporal form.[7] Here, the crucial underlying consideration is that any determination of temporal relations is itself something that *happens*, and thus something that happens *at a time*; whereas in the analogous spatial case, there is no necessity for the spatial relations to be determined *from* a particular position in space. The requirement, in the temporal case, suffices to determine with respect to any specification of temporal relationships a present *now*, and thus to orient the facts as determined with respect to it. It follows that, as Dummett argues, temporal facts are plausibly, if real, irreducibly indexical: essentially, and as a matter of their underlying form, they are not to be characterized as such and in general without referring to irreducibly indexical facts.

What consequences follow from this, with respect to the reality or unreality of tense, change, and becoming, and (as a consequence) of time itself? In the last part of the chapter, Dummett returns to the question how the essential indexicality of the specification of temporal facts and relations is supposed to establish that time is unreal. Might one not take the first part of the argument rather to establish that time cannot be reduced to anything else, and thus is, far from being an illusion, in a strong sense irreducibly basic and real? However, as Dummett notes, a further premise that is at least implicitly operative in McTaggart's move from the first to the second part of the argument is that there can be a *complete* description of reality: one, that is, that includes everything that is the case, and can be given from *no* particular point of view. If part one of the argument (the part establishing the irreducibility of indexicality for temporal facts) is granted, then it will follow that if time is real, there can be no such complete and perspective-independent description. Nevertheless, this leaves open, as

Dummett briefly notes, the possibility of a radical alternative that upholds temporal realism while denying the "prejudice" of such a complete description of reality.[8] On this alternative, there will be no such thing as a single, complete (and coherent) description of reality. Instead, owing to the irreducible indexicality of the temporal facts, there will only be a number of perspective-dependent distinct "maximal" descriptions, in one of which (for example) "the event M is happening" figures, while in another, "the event M happened" does, and in still another, "the event M is going to happen."[9]

2.

As Dummett's considerations already begin to indicate, the affirmation of temporal realism, in the sense of an irreducibly tensed reality, has important consequences for our understanding of the overall form of reality; further, these consequences extend to the structure and situation of (what are called) "subjects" within it. In "Tense and Reality," Kit Fine argues that an accurate assessment of the space of options for the theorization of time requires that we consider closely the bearing of the various possible views on the question of what "overall concept of reality" we should adopt.[10] As with other kinds of cases involving the use of indexical terms (including spatial, personal, and modal ones), the issues that arise on analysis of temporal indexicality and tense require us to determine whether and to what extent we must see reality itself as "aspectual" (e.g., irreducibly tensed, or centered, or actual) rather than treating it as non-aspectual in itself but merely accessed or described from a particular point of view.[11] As we have already seen, in the temporal case, the second option produces a familiar kind of objectivist anti-realism. On this view, all that is truly included in reality are four-dimensional positions in spacetime, but there is no possibility of reflecting tense, change, and becoming as real features of things or of the world as a whole. Temporal realism, on the other hand, appears here to require (as we have seen) some sense in which temporal indexicality figures *essentially*—and not merely as a matter of our own point of view—in the givenness of time and the constitution of temporal facts themselves.

For each of the cases, one kind of realist view—what Fine calls "standard" realism—simply maintains that one *single* position is privileged in the constitution of reality.[12] Thus, for example, the "standard" realist about modality maintains that the *actual* world is the only real one, and the "standard" realist about egocentric position maintains solipsism: reality is constituted from a *particular* egocentric point of view. In the temporal case, the "standard" realist view is presentism: the view that the present plays a privileged role in the constitution of reality, so that all other temporal moments enjoy, at most, a secondary status, or are not real at all. Each of these configurations of "standard" realism thereby uphold the claim that reality is *essentially* aspectual (tensed, first-personal, etc.). But as Fine notes, they combine this with the claim that a certain *particular* aspect or position (the present, the self, etc.) is to be privileged. The two claims, however, can be separated, and varieties of what Fine calls "non-standard" realism will uphold the first while denying the second. In particular, on either of the two varieties of non-standard realism that Fine explores, the irreducibly aspectual or perspectival character of reality is affirmed, while, nevertheless, an assumption of *neutrality* is maintained. No particular position is privileged, and the facts that ultimately constitute reality are not uniformly oriented toward one position rather than any other.

Given the conjunction of aspectual realism with *neutrality*, there are, Fine argues, two possible "non-standard" realist options. The first of these is a *relativist* one: reality is constituted by facts that are themselves relative to positions, so that (in the temporal case) it is true at a time *t* that reality is constituted by (tensed) facts that are present at time *t*, and at any other time that it is constituted by facts that are present at that time.[13] On this sort of view, the irreducibly indexical and positional character of time is thus affirmed. But what is denied is the claim that there is any "absolute" and non-relative overall constitution of reality at all: what constitutes reality, in the most ultimate sense, changes from moment to moment. Finally, however, there is the possibility of affirming what Fine calls a "fragmentalist" view.[14] On this kind of view, by contrast with the "relativist" one, reality *does* have an absolute constitution: there is a single way that reality is, as such and in general. However, since reality is also constituted by irreducibly aspectual facts, it is not, overall, coherent. Instead, it includes, at a basic level, facts that are (logically) inconsistent with one another. In the temporal case, for example, it will include such mutually incompatible (tensed) facts as that *I am sitting* and *I am standing* (as well as similarly incompatible ones in the past and future tenses).

Given this framework, there are various considerations that favor non-standard varieties of realism over the standard variety and, further, favor the fragmentalist variant over the relativist one. Most broadly, the standard realist in each case has difficulties in accounting for the evident reality of other indexical positions, beyond that of the first person present. It is evidently problematic to argue, in accordance with solipsism, that only I exist, or, with presentism, that the present moment is somehow to be privileged beyond all others. By maintaining neutrality with respect to the possible positions, the relativist overcomes this objection. But she faces further difficulties in accounting for the way in which the constitution of reality is relative, since it is apparently incumbent upon her to explain how the facts to which it is relative in each case obtain, themselves. For example, the relativist in the temporal case holds that the constitution of reality is relative to times; but what are "times," and how do *they* figure in reality itself? Here, moreover, any coherent account would seem to reinstate times themselves as essential constituents of an *absolute* reality; and, once this is acknowledged, it is difficult to avoid the conclusion that, since times differ but are all included, this reality will after all include constituent facts that are inconsistent with one another.[15] But this is then just the fragmentalist conclusion, once again, on which there is no overall view of reality that is consistent as a whole.

In considering the advantages of the fragmentalist view over the relativist one in the egocentric case, Fine notes that the relativist view is, here, essentially the view that reality is irreducibly relative to a plurality of (what we may call) "metaphysical" subjects: that is, to a plurality of distinct positions from which the world, as a whole, appears or to which it is presented. Such a "metaphysical subject," as a bare position of being-appeared-to, is to be distinguished from the "empirical" subject which is the subject of facts about (for example) the psychological continuity and personal identity of individuals over time.[16] The view of the relativist with respect to egocentricity is then, essentially, that each subjective reality is given or constituted only relative to a metaphysical subject, in this sense. However, it is difficult to see that there *are*, internal to reality, any such metaphysical subjects, once we clearly disjoin the facts about them from facts about empirical subjects or persons. And at any rate, in requiring the various metaphysical perspectives, the relativist view again threatens to make them part of what is, anyway, an absolute conception of reality in itself. This situation is what has led philosophers, Fine suggests, to locate "the" metaphysical subject, in the singular, outside the world; but such a conception is not obviously coherent.[17] This leaves standing only the fragmentalist view, on which there are a variety of mutually inconsistent sets of perspectival facts: facts capturing (as we may put it) how the world is presented from differing points of view or at different moments.

3.

Throughout his chapter, Fine treats the temporal and other cases largely in parallel, arguing that the evident structural analogies between the distinct domains of irreducible indexicality motivate the fragmentalist variety of non-standard realism overall. In the remainder of this chapter, however, I will argue for a further and stronger conclusion: that the structure of given time may itself be seen as *logically founding* that of (what has been called) subjectivity, whereas the converse is not the case. That is, it is sufficient, in accounting for the logical possibility and metaphysical reality of subjectivity, to assume the real existence of irreducibly basic facts of the passage of time, while, on the other hand, it is not possible to account for the reality of temporal facts in general as a product, an outcome, or an aspect of subjectivity or any kind of subjective activity.

As we have seen, the fragmentalist conclusion with respect to time appears to follow, on natural assumptions, from the combination of temporal realism with the further assumptions that the overall character of reality is *neutral*—it does not privilege any one temporal perspective over any others—and that it is *absolute*; that is, not fundamentally relative to anything within it. Any viewpoint that combines these assumptions with respect to aspectual reality will yield a total picture of reality that is logically inconsistent overall. Rather than dismissing them just for that reason, however, it is worthwhile, in view of the positive argument for them, to examine whether they may be seen as illuminating the structure of given time itself. The relationship between temporality and contradiction is, of course, a central theme of Western philosophical thinking about time since (at least) Parmenides. In particular, it is possible to see a wide variety of philosophical theories about time as, essentially, ways of defusing the contradictions that otherwise threaten to arise in our analyses of the phenomena of change and becoming.[18] Given this, these approaches then yield a familiar and problematic kind of oscillation. This is an oscillation between positions that are anti-realist about time, while maintaining the reality of those objects and relations which figure in a tenseless description of the world (today, the objectivist "B-series" theories) and those that see time or its appearance as having a basis in subjective consciousness or activity, while treating the objects of the world as constructions or productions of this subjectivity (the varieties of idealism).

Without following any of these strategies, however, it is also possible to describe temporal change positively as a contradictory structure grounded in (what can be understood as) the contradictory structure of given time itself.[19] On this analysis, the contradictoriness involved on a basic level in something's being one way (at one time) and also another (at another) is to be understood as itself arising from the more basic paradox of the givenness of the *now* as a temporal perspective of presentation: that is, as a point from which the *totality* of facts of reality is, in each case, presented. Under this interpretation, temporal *paradox* emerges as a dynamic structure, and a basic one in the real constitution of all temporal becoming.[20] Most centrally, this paradoxical structure is that of the temporal *now* or present: the temporal perspective from which the objects and facts of the world, as a whole and as such, are presented or given. The paradox follows from the fact that, at each moment, this *now* is *already* becoming other, so that whatever facts it comprehends are *already* (now) becoming different. From this there follows the contradiction that the temporal *now*, along with all it comprehends, is both fully present and not, both unitary and essentially divided from itself.

Crucially, the structure of given time underlying this paradox is not one of incommensurability or inconsistency "between" a "subjective" and an "objective" view of reality.[21] The challenge of temporal realism, to which the analysis of the paradox responds, is not that of combining or fitting together a "view from nowhere" with a "view from somewhere." It is rather of recognizing that, while the idea of a temporal "view from nowhere" is incoherent (Dummett's point), none of the situated "views from somewhere" are to be privileged in a neutral overall description of reality. This implies a basic inconsistency, but it is not the inconsistency between a subjective and an objective view. Rather, as I have suggested, it is intelligibly grounded in the structure of given time itself: that of the "now" as it gives itself in temporal reality. Since this structure is the most basic structure of temporal reality, it is not, itself, produced by or founded on temporal perspectives. Rather, as I shall briefly argue, it is only because of it that such perspectives exist at all.

As we have seen, the challenge of realism in any of the aspectual cases is essentially that of accommodating within an overall conception of reality as a whole the variable and aspectual facts that appear to be understandable only as given from a particular perspective *within* that whole. In the temporal case in particular, the challenge of maintaining an overall neutral realism is that of finding a way to accommodate, within such a neutral overall conception of reality, the facts of temporal position and becoming: that (for example), it can be the case that *it is* 5:13 PM, and that objects may enjoy contradictory but uniformly correct determinations ("sitting"; "standing"). Given this, as we have seen, the only way to accommodate all of the relevant determinations is to suppose that temporal reality is itself fragmented into an irreducible variety of perspectives, each one of which can reflect *all* of the world. But now, switching to the question of subjective perspectives, we may ask: what was meant to be explained, on a realist view, by the introduction of subjective perspectives into reality itself? If we put aside the various facts about the historical and factual constitution of empirical subjects, it is clear that what was supposed to be accounted for *just was* this fragmentation of reality into mutually incompatible perspectives, each of which reflects the *whole* of reality—the totality of the facts. Indeed, as we saw above in connection with the initially parallel considerations about egocentricity, the temptation to introduce a "metaphysical" subject as an element of reality is, at bottom, rooted in the desire to accommodate the variety of possible, but jointly incoherent, positions from which reality *as a whole* can be viewed.

As we saw, once the idea of irreducible subjective perspectives is introduced, there is a further temptation to reflect the totality of *one* such position—its ability to present the facts of the world as a whole—by locating that position as a "transcendental" one situated *outside* the totality of the world itself. But it is evidently then not coherent to suppose that the occupant of such a position could (so much as) be described: since it is now located outside the world of facts, there can be (for example) no facts about it, nothing that is true of it. And in any case, if we now apply the temporal consideration of *non-externality* that we derived from Dummett's argument, it is clear that the idea of a constitutive exterior subjectivity is, anyway, incoherent in itself. For such a subjectivity would then have to be able to observe or present to itself the temporal facts, as such and as a whole; and as we saw, this is not possible, without distortion, from a position outside temporal relations themselves. But to introduce, in the face of these difficulties, the position of (now) plural "metaphysical" subjectivities back into the world of temporal facts just *is* to introduce into the world an irreducible plurality of temporally oriented perspectives. And since it is inherent to the structure of given time *itself* that it already produces the plural reality of such contradictory positions, the *further* introduction of the subjective positions now falls away as unnecessary.[22]

4.

At *Physics* IV, 219a21–219b1, just after considering the apparent contradiction that the "now" which divides between past and future must be both again and again different and yet always the same, Aristotle appeals to what he sees as the essential link between time and motion that is established by facts about our *apprehension* of a continuous motion:

> But we apprehend time only when we have marked motion, marking it by before and after; and it is only when we have perceived before and after in motion that we say that time has elapsed.... When we think of the extremes as different from the middle and the mind pronounces that the "nows" are two, one before and one after, it is then that we say that there is time, and this that we say is time. For what is bounded by the "now" is thought to be time—we may assume this.[23]

With this, Aristotle exemplifies an understanding of the logical form of time that continues through much of Western philosophy and yields a variety of familiar conceptions of the form of given time. On this understanding, the *aporia* or contradiction of temporal becoming in itself—the structure which makes it possible that the "now" is again and again both the same and different, and that an identical object may undergo contradictory determinations—is to be resolved by time's referral to *thought*: that is, to the forms in which we can think, measure, or make determinations about it. It is, then, the capacity of thought to render non-contradictory judgment that allows for the thinkability of temporal relations and determinations in general; and it is in relation to this capacity that whatever is real, as opposed to merely apparent, about temporal becoming is to be understood.

This understanding of the basis of given time is not simply, or only, idealist, since it may also (as it does in Aristotle) function in tandem with the recognition of *substance* as a substrate of identity in the real: what is supposed to remain the same through the progression of temporal differentiations.[24] Nevertheless, it is clear that it underwrites a variety of idealist positions in a familiar way. One leading example is the position of Kant in the *Critique of Pure Reason*, according to which the appearance of causality, temporal change, and becoming are to be referred to the prior framework of the categories of pure understanding in their synthesis with the fluid deliverances of the sensibility, of which time and space are forms. Kant theorizes this synthesis, problematically, by appealing to the standing structure of the transcendental unity of apperception, or the capacity of a transcendental subjectivity to unify a given manifold under concepts by means of the imaginative activity of the schematism. This resolves for thought the apparent problem that is posed for it by the fluidity of the sensory and its consequent lack of ability to provide stable identities and non-contradictory categories from itself. But in a broader view, the purported solution only displaces the problem elsewhere. For we can now ask about the time in which the synthetic activity of the transcendental subject takes place: does that activity itself take place within, or outside, the time that is thus constituted? Evidently, once the problem is posed in this way, it replicates the originally aporeatic structure we have discussed above. This points, once again, to the essentially contradictory structure at the basis of given time and to the unavailability of any noncontradictory solution to the problem of becoming it poses.

More generally, if idealism can be defined as the strategy of ensuring the consistency of being, in reaction to temporal contradiction, by identifying *thought* as the region in which this contradiction can be overcome, then it is clear that Aristotle's gesture already instantiates a strategy that will be practiced repeatedly, and up to the present, by philosophers committed to the noncontradictory unity of thinking and being (or of the rational and the real).[25] For any position of this sort, this noncontradictory unity is assured only by the possibility that thought can occupy a stable overall position, outside the reality of temporal relations, from which it can assess these relations as such. But as we have seen here on the basis of considerations of the structure of given time, there is no such position. Temporal determination is always, just as such, something that happens *in* time, and the temporal relations constitutive of reality and marked in our tensed and indexical language cannot be adequately determined, in their totality, from *any* noncontradictory position. Moreover, and for the same reason, the position of any total determination of the temporal facts—that of the giving of time that is the "present" itself—will be inherently and irreducibly contradictory. If, then, we are to retain as a basic referent the schema of the relationship of thinking and being which has oriented Western philosophy since Parmenides, it is clear that the reality of time itself witnesses its irreducible complication, or even the possibility of its supersession within a still more thoughtfully oriented learning.[26]

Notes

1   David Kaplan, "Demonstratives." In *Themes from Kaplan*, ed. Almog Perry and Wettstein (Oxford: Oxford University Press, 1989).

2   Michael Dummett, "A Defense of McTaggart's Proof of the Unreality of Time." In *Truth and Other Enigmas* (London: Duckworth, 1978), 351–7

3   Dummett, *Truth and Other Enigmas*, 354.

4   I leave it open here whether this holds also for the relevantly parallel modal case, that is, whether it is coherent to suppose that any fact about the actual world could be given from a (modal) perspective that is exterior to it.

5   Dummett, *Truth and Other Enigmas*, 354–5.

6   As Dummett suggests, this would be the case, plausibly, even if it were known *with complete certainty* that the fore-ordained events would (in the future) occur exactly as predicted.

7   More generally, recent analytic discussions of the form and implications of "realist" and "anti-realist" positions have suffered from an overemphasis on the question of the possibility of a complete *description* of the facts; as we see in this and other cases, this has tended, in particular, to obscure the equally relevant question of the actual *givenness* of the (possibly) described facts themselves.

8   Dummett, *Truth and Other Enigmas*, 357.

9   Dummett, *Truth and Other Enigmas*, 356.

10 Kit Fine, "Tense and Reality" (2009), 2. Available online: https://as.nyu.edu/content/dam/nyu-as/philosophy/documents/faculty-documents/fine/Fine-Kit-tenseandreality.pdf; see also Kit Fine, "The Reality of Tense," *Synthese* 150, no. 3 (2006): 399–414.

11 Fine, "Tense and Reality," 1.

12 Fine, "Tense and Reality," 25–8.

13 Fine, "Tense and Reality," 28–32.

14 Fine, "Tense and Reality," 32–7.

15 Fine, "Tense and Reality," 20.

16 Fine, "Tense and Reality," 80–3.

17 Fine, "Tense and Reality," 84.

18 See, e.g., Paul M. Livingston, *The Logic of Being: Realism, Truth, and Time* (Evanston, IL: Northwestern University Press, 2017), chapters 1 and 6.

19 For a fuller version of this argument, see Livingston, *The Logic of Being*, 161–7.

20 This is the structure of what I called the "kairological paradox of passage" or of "becoming in the now" in Livingston, *The Logic of Being*, 165–7.

21 And thus the current claim is not that temporality is underlain by something like a "parallax view" (in the sense of the incommensurability between different subjective perspectives: Slavoj Žižek, *The Parallax View* (Cambridge, MA: MIT Press, 2006)).

22 There are further questions, of course, about the empirical conditions for the constitution of persons as identical over time and (perhaps) as bearers of agency. But these are questions about (what Fine calls) "empirical" rather than "metaphysical" subjectivity; and at any rate the present considerations seem sufficient to me to account for any features of subjects or subjectivity that may reasonably be thought to play a *constitutive* role in reality as such.

23 Aristotle, *Complete Works of Aristotle: The Revised Oxford Translation*, ed. J. Barnes (Princeton, NJ: Princeton University Press, 1983), *Physics* IV, 219a21-219b1.

24 Compare the argument that immediately follows, at 219b13-33, according to which the "now" is analogous to a body which remains the same while being moved.

25 For example, it is the strategy of Sebastian Rödl's perceptive *Categories of the Temporal*, which aims to identify and describe a number of such categories by developing a "transcendental logic" of the essential forms of temporal thought. The project is a chapter of what Rödl calls "critical metaphysics," where the latter is guided by the insight that "the order of being is nothing other than the order of the thinking, judging, experiencing subject" (Sebastian Rödl, *Categories of the Temporal: An Inquiry into the Forms of the Finite Intellect*, trans. Sibylle Salewski (Cambridge, MA: Harvard University Press, 2012, p. 40). [orig. published as *Kategorien des Zeitlichen: Eine Untersuchung der Formen des endlichen Verstandes* (Frankfurt am Main: Suhrkamp Verlag, 2005)]). But this makes evident the specific limitation of the deduction which follows: that what is deduced cannot be categories of time as it is in itself, or (at any rate) as having a structural order—a way of being—that is wholly independent of that of "the" subject, in this sense.

26 "Each individual and each object in this whole Universe should be glimpsed as individual moments of Time. Object does not hinder object in the same way that moment of Time does not hinder moment of Time. For this reason, there are minds which are made up in the same moment of Time, and there are moments of time in which the same mind is made up. Practice, and realization of truth, are also like this. Putting the self in order, we see what it is. The truth that self is Time is like this. We should learn in practice that, because of this truth, the whole Earth includes myriad phenomena and hundreds of things, and each phenomenon and each thing exists in the whole Earth. Such toing-and-froing is the first step [on the way] of practice. When we arrive in the field of the ineffable, there is just one [concrete] thing and one [concrete] phenomenon, here and now, [beyond] understanding of phenomena and non-understanding of phenomena, and [beyond] understanding of things and non-understanding of things. Because [real existence] is only this exact moment, all moments of Existence-Time are the whole of Time, and all Existent things and all Existent phenomena are Time" (Dōgen, "Uji (Existence-Time)." In *Shobogenzo*, book 1, trans. Gudo Nishijima and Chodo Cross (Bristol: Windbell Publications, 1994), 92).

7

The Parallactic Leap

Fichte, Apperception, and the Hard Problem of Consciousness

G. Anthony Bruno

In *The Phenomenon of Life*, Hans Jonas defines a problem as a "collision between a comprehensive view" and "a particular fact which will not fit into it."[1] Part of Jonas' concern is how death and life pose problems for views that explain the world as vital and mechanical, respectively. While vitalist and mechanistic views face the easy problem of accommodating facts amenable to their explanatory methods, they face the hard problem of facts that resist these methods. Thus, vitalism collides with the fact that life expires for no apparent purpose and mechanism collides with the fact that death elicits outrage and hope. Vitalism and mechanism accordingly face the hard problem of mortality.

A more recently formulated hard problem confronts physicalism: the hard problem of consciousness. In "Facing Up to the Problem of Consciousness," David Chalmers argues that physicalism cannot show why scientifically explicable phenomena like perception and action are "*accompanied by experience*,"[2] by the fact that there is something it is like to perceive and act—a fact that Chalmers attributes to subjectivity.[3] This fact is absurd insofar as it is neither amenable to the explanatory methods of science nor entailed by phenomena so amenable. Absent a supplementary principle of explanation, the "rich inner life" or phenomenal character of experience is "objectively unreasonable" for physicalism, which must behold this first-personal fact across an explanatory gap.[4]

A precursor to the hard problem of consciousness confronts nihilism, which denies that anything exists without an external condition. Jacobi coins this term in a 1799 open letter to Fichte to signify the loss of faith in the immediacy of experience, in the fact that the reality of what we perceive and the value of what we do—"*the true*"—is manifest without mediation by or inference from external conditions. This fact collides with the nihilism of rational "science," which abstracts from the true by reflecting endlessly on its conditions. Nihilism "ceases to feel its pressure," becoming lost in a "game" of reflection.[5] Nihilism thus disavows our pre-reflective experience of directly perceiving and acting in the world. Jacobi's reply is that the true gives reason its "value": faithless reason, numb to the true, lacks purpose. He accordingly appeals to what it is like to perceive and act, stating that perception is marked by a "feeling" or "*intimation* of the true" and that one "feels" that one is free and has "inner *certitude*" of the reality of one's actions.[6] As he says in his *Spinoza Letters*: "I have... no conviction more vital than that *I do what I think*."[7]

Jacobi traces nihilism to "the ancient *a nihilo fit*," the principle that nothing exists without a condition, and regards Spinoza as its exemplar, for his fidelity to this principle entails that nature is a machine whose parts have infinite causal conditions and in which direct perception and free action are "mere illusion."[8] Jacobi must locate "the *wonder* of perception and the unfathomable *mystery* of freedom… outside the mechanism of nature," since nihilism denies that we feel the true in perceiving and acting, that "[i]n our consciousness… reason and freedom are found inseparably connected."[9] Like physicalism, nihilism collides with the first-personal fact of what perception and action are like. Unless this problem is solved, nature's inclusion of conscious experience will remain, as Chalmers warns the physicalist, an "unanswered question" and, as Jacobi chides the nihilist, "completely inexplicable."[10]

One advantage of Kant's Copernican turn is to dismiss the question that imposes this hard problem. We need not ask how nature is accompanied by the first-person standpoint because "I think" is a form of thinking that must be able to accompany any cognition of nature.[11] The first person is neither the illusion that Jacobi dreads nor the absurdity that concerns Chalmers, but a condition of the possibility of cognizable nature. Kant's term for this condition in the *Critique of Pure Reason* is "apperception," which denotes the self-consciousness that unifies our consciousness of nature qua sum of appearances under universal and necessary laws, viz., the categories of the understanding.[12] If cognizing nature assumes the first-person standpoint as its ground, that standpoint poses no hard problem. No view that conflicts with the first person collides with an inexplicable fact, but only collides with itself.

Fichte inherits the Kantian insight that a Copernican turn is parallactic: we see that nature depends for its lawful unity on apperception precisely by marking a reorientation in objects that arises from a reorientation toward ourselves. As Kant says in the B-Preface, just as Copernicus' success in astronomy requires registering a shift in the motion of celestial bodies given our revolving position, success in metaphysics requires registering a shift in the position of empirical objects given our peculiar constitution. Objects' *a priori* spatiotemporality arises when we see that they must conform to our forms of cognition.[13] In *Attempt at a New Presentation of the Wissenschaftslehre*, Fichte embraces this parallax, pursuing "a complete revolution in the way we think" such that "the object will be posited and determined by our power of cognition, and not vice versa."[14]

Yet Kant's formal conception of apperception worries Fichte in his *Nova Methodo* lectures. This conception cannot exhaust the ground of experience, for it does not show why we posit objects "*at all.*" For Fichte, it is our agency that first opens a world of objects, viz., as ends and obstacles: "it is by means of such acting—and, moreover, only insofar as it is a hindered or arrested activity—that we obtain any consciousness whatsoever of what is actual." The apperceptive I "catches sight" of objects because it originally discovers itself "*as acting*" among, toward, and away from them. As Fichte says: "[e]xperience refers to acting. Concepts originate through acting and exist for the sake of acting; only acting is absolute." Apperception, then, is not a form of thinking but a real activity. Indeed, it is only by affirming the I's real activity that transcendental idealism can establish "the primacy of practical reason,"[15] *contra* nihilism.

Fichte adapts Kant's idea of apperception in order to refute Spinozism's nihilistic corollary.[16] Whereas Kant holds that the "I think" is "a thinking, not an intuiting," Fichte argues in his *Aenesidemus* review that apperception must be "realized through intellectual intuition" if transcendental idealism is to exhibit the "existence and autonomy of the I."[17] As he explains in the *New Presentation*, apperception is an intellectual intuition insofar as it grasps the I as "an acting."[18] Fichte addresses his argument to those with a "lively zeal" for "science," i.e., for an idealism whose absolute ground is "faith in oneself... in one's own self-sufficiency and freedom." He disregards "those who, as a result of protracted spiritual servitude, have lost their own selves... yanked back and forth by the secret fury pent up within them."[19] Theirs is a faithless reason, one in thrall to external conditions, committed to a nihilistic view that contradicts their I-hood.

In what follows, I argue that, for Fichte, the I poses no hard problem because it collides exclusively with nihilistic views like Spinozism, which are refuted by a properly idealist conception of apperception, according to which the first-person standpoint is the absolute ground of our experience of nature. If idealism refutes nihilism, nature is no more explicable than that there is something it is like for me to perceive and act. In Section 1, I show why Kantian apperception is necessary for possible experience. In Section 2, I reconstruct Fichte's argument that a modified conception of apperception refutes guises of nihilism, thereby solving the hard problem of consciousness. In Section 3, I suggest that transcendental idealism undermines Chalmers' proposed solution to and Daniel Dennett's dismissal of this problem.

1. What-It-Is, What-It-Is-Like, For-Whom-It-Is-Like

To grasp the necessity of apperception for possible experience, consider two explanatory gaps. An empirical gap separates scientifically explicable physical facts from directly accessible phenomenal qualities in that the latter neither are nor follow from what is so explicable. This gap is empirical because it lies between scientific and ordinary experience, between *a posteriori* encounters with the objectively physical—what-it-is—and subjectively phenomenal—what-it-is-like. As Chalmers argues, physicalism cannot close this gap.

A further, non-empirical gap separates the phenomenal character of experience from its subjective character in that experience's involving something it is like, which varies across conscious episodes, cannot explain its involving something it is like for me, which abides across conscious episodes *qua* mine. This gap is non-empirical because it lies between experiential states and an experiential standpoint, between episodes in a heap and their belonging to a unity: my perspective.[20] Whereas particular experiences have phenomenal character—a what-it-is-like—the whole of experience has subjective character—a for-whom-it-is-like. As Kant shows, only a transcendental idealist conception of apperception can close this gap.

In the A-Deduction, Kant says:

> consciousness of oneself in accordance with the determinations of our state in internal perception is merely empirical, forever variable; it can provide no standing or abiding self in this stream of inner appearances, and is customarily called inner sense or empirical apperception. That which should necessarily be represented

as numerically identical cannot be thought of as such through empirical data. There must be a condition that precedes all experience and makes the latter itself possible, which should make such a transcendental presupposition valid.[21]

This passage shows why an account of experience that fixates on the empirical gap rises to the level of empirical apperception, the "inner sense" of "determinations of our state," and why this is insufficient. As "consciousness of oneself," inner sense exhibits the phenomenal character that collides with physicalism and nihilism.[22] But since empirical data are contingent, the content of inner sense is "forever variable." It yields nothing necessary, no "abiding self" whose identity can unify the "stream of inner appearances."[23] By itself, then, empirical apperception is blind to its own "condition." This condition, Kant says, is a "transcendental presupposition" and, just before this passage, he says it is "nothing other than transcendental apperception."[24] Hence, we must turn from the empirical gap between physicality and phenomenality to the non-empirical gap between phenomenality and subjectivity; that is, an account of experience must rise to the level of transcendental apperception. Crucially, this indicates that the hard problem of consciousness ultimately requires filling the transcendental gap.

Kant elucidates transcendental apperception in §16 of the B-Deduction:

> The I think must be able to accompany all my representations; for otherwise something would be represented in me that could not be thought at all, which is as much as to say that the representation would either be impossible or else at least would be nothing for me... I call [the I think] pure apperception, in order to distinguish it from the empirical one... I also call its unity the transcendental unity of self-consciousness in order to designate the possibility of *a priori* cognition from it. For the manifold representations that are given in a certain intuition would not all together be my representations if they did not all together belong to a self-consciousness; i.e., as my representations (even if I am not conscious of them as such) they must yet necessarily be in accord with the condition under which alone they can stand together in a universal self-consciousness, because otherwise they would not throughout belong to me.[25]

Empirical apperception by itself is a phenomenal flow with no abiding self, "dispersed and without relation to the subject's identity."[26] Since empirical data are contingent, their necessary condition of unity differs in kind: it must be "transcendental." Kant ascribes transcendental unity to "a universal self-consciousness" in which I can regard determinations of my state as mine. Whereas inner sense arises *a posteriori*, self-consciousness "precedes" representations as the *a priori* condition of their unity, the lawful structure of which unity is provided by the categories.[27] Hence Kant calls transcendental apperception the "supreme" principle of cognition, without which "I would have as multicoloured, diverse a self as I have representations of which I am conscious."[28] Since inner sense affords merely a contingent unity of phenomenal consciousness, it cannot be mistaken for transcendental apperception.[29]

The relevant gap for an account of experience is thus non-empirical. Experience's involving a what-it-is-like cannot explain its involving a for-whom-it-is-like; that is, phenomenal consciousness cannot explain its own unity. We fill this gap if we see that consciousness presupposes self-consciousness as its transcendental condition. As Kant says: "only because I ascribe all perceptions to one consciousness (of original apperception) can I say of all perceptions that I am conscious of them."[30] We cannot simply aggregate outer sense of physical objects and inner sense of determinations of our state. This would yield a heap of episodes lacking the lawful unity of a self-conscious perspective, which is why the hard problem ultimately confronts us with the transcendental gap. A representation is "nothing for us" unless it can belong to the "standing and lasting I" that is the "transcendental ground" of the "lawfulness of all appearances," that is, of "the formal unity of nature."[31]

If there is something it is like to perceive and act in nature, it is something for us. It belongs to the first-person standpoint of transcendental apperception, which functions to unify nature under laws. This standpoint poses a hard problem only for views that nihilistically evade the fact of phenomenality or inadequately explain that fact by halting at the level of empirical apperception.[32] This is to say that the I poses no hard problem for any truly comprehensive view. Consciousness presupposes self-consciousness.[33]

A manifold of representations is only mine if it can belong to the "thoroughgoing identity" of apperception—if, Kant says, I can "combine" it in "one consciousness" in "an act of spontaneity." Yet apperception, for Kant, is a "simple representation" in which "nothing manifold is given," a form of thinking whose manifold depends on sensation.[34] For Jacobi, apperception annihilates perception of the true insofar as it "add[s]" the object to a sensory manifold by combining the latter in consciousness, as he says in *David Hume on Faith*.[35] Kant thus seems to indulge a nihilistic game of reflecting on mediating external conditions—here, subjective rather than causal.[36] For Fichte, however, we refute nihilism if we regard apperception as an immediate consciousness or intellectual intuition of the I's real spontaneity. I will now reconstruct Fichte's refutation and show how it solves the hard problem of consciousness.[37]

2. The Primacy of Practical Reason

In §6 of the Second Introduction to the *New Presentation*, Fichte announces the "gist" of his philosophy: "[r]eason is absolutely self-sufficient... It follows that everything reason is must have its foundation within reason itself... In short, the *Wissenschaftslehre* is transcendental idealism."[38] Although the "*letter*" of Kant's idealism leaves the apperceptive I dependent on sensibility for a manifold, its "*spirit*" seeks to show that experience is absolutely grounded on reason, or "the *pure* I."[39] Fichte's textual support for transcendental idealism's identity with the *Wissenschaftslehre* is Kant's claim in §16 that apperception is the supreme principle of cognition.[40] Fichte describes apperception as consciousness that is "the same in all consciousness," "not determinable by anything contingent within consciousness," "determined by nothing but itself," and "determined absolutely."[41] We saw that, for Kant, since contingent inner states yield no I, the latter must determine itself spontaneously. Fichte now adds that the I must determine itself "absolutely" on pain of "dogmatism," his term for nihilistic views like Spinozism for which "everything that occurs within consciousness is a product of a thing in itself," including consciousness "allegedly produced by freedom."[42] Unless the I absolutely determines itself—unless its spontaneity unconditionally grounds experience—dogmatism is possibly true.[43] The letter of Kant's idealism tolerates this possibility by restricting the I to a form of thinking dependent on sensibility.[44]

If consciousness is a mere product, as Jacobi fears, spontaneity is illusory.[45] We would then deny subjectivity and the phenomenality that it conditions, trading the for-whom-it-is-like and what-it-is-like of experience for the what-it-is of existence. But we avoid this nihilistic result if we prove that apperceptive spontaneity practically grounds all consciousness. In *Foundations of the Entire Wissenschaftslehre*, Fichte says that this proof requires positing the I as a first principle, positing its "activity" as a ground from which to derive the forms of cognition, including those of sensibility. He charges that Kant "points" to this activity but provides no derivation,[46] clarifying his charge in the *New Presentation*: if, as Kant holds, consciousness is "conditioned" by the I, its content arises outside the I, limiting (if conforming to) the latter; but if consciousness is "determined" by the I, its content is derivable from the I's spontaneity alone.[47] This content includes the forms of sensibility, on which the I would not be dependent.[48] Only by showing that practical reason is, in this sense, "the source of the theoretical" can an idealist consistently affirm the former's primacy.[49] But how precisely can idealism prove the primacy of practical reason?

Fichte credits Kant with directing our gaze away from objects toward ourselves, a parallactic turn he identifies with the "spirit" of idealism.[50] As he says in §1 of the First Introduction, philosophy's "first demand" is to "look within [one]self," as this alone draws attention to the system of representations that are "accompanied by a feeling of necessity" and the question of its "basis." Since Fichte's synonym for this system is "'experience'—whether inner or outer,"[51] it follows that it includes inner sense of phenomenal states and outer sense of physical facts and that the question of its basis concerns the apperceptive I. Since the I must determine itself absolutely on pain of dogmatism, it follows, moreover, that this question specifically concerns the apperceptive I's unconditional spontaneity, that is, the primacy of practical reason. Fichte proves the latter by contrasting two responses to philosophy's first demand.

Just as the condition of empirical apperception differs from the latter in kind, the basis or first principle of experience is non-empirical. A dogmatist posits as its principle the thing in itself, while an idealist posits the I.[52] Like Jacobi, Fichte identifies consistent dogmatism with Spinozism, which nihilistically renders the I "an accident of the Not-I," a product of mechanical nature. Idealism instead views the Not-I as a "way of looking at the I," a limitation of its activity.[53] A dogmatist requires the Not-I to ground our representations: the latter must be effects in a system of conditions to preserve nature's causal closure. Fichte replies in §6 of the First Introduction that no one, not even a dogmatist, can "deny the testimony of immediate consciousness," which "everyone who has taken a hard look within themselves must long since have discovered," viz., that the I is an "*immediate* unity of being and seeing." The I is not simply conscious of objects of possible experience but is conscious of this consciousness, that is, is self-conscious. An object "exists *for*" the apperceptive I in this sense: its "being" is unified by my "seeing" it. To ask "*[f]or whom*" an object exists, then, is to invoke the I as the unity or "double series" of being and seeing.[54]

Fichte indicates why dogmatism's nihilistic corollary raises the hard problem that confronts physicalism. Dogmatism neglects the "ideal" series of apperceptive seeing, limiting its inquiry to the "real" series of objective being in which each member is the effect of another "lying outside" it. This series yields nothing that "exist[s] for itself," specifically, nothing that "*observes itself*," like the apperceptive I.[55] It therefore cannot explain consciousness, for it excludes the latter's condition. As we saw, the hard problem of consciousness ultimately confronts the transcendental gap and is solved only if we rise beyond empirical apperception to transcendental apperception: a what-it-is cannot explain a what-it-is-like precisely because it cannot explain a for-whom-it-is-like. Dogmatism's limited inquiry generates the hard problem by tracing causal conditions in a real series that lacks the transcendental condition of an ideal series. Hence Fichte infers that dogmatism cannot "transition" from being to seeing. Indeed, he says, "in all the various guises in which it appears," dogmatism "leaves an enormous gap" between being and seeing.[56] Like dogmatism, physicalism leaves the same—transcendental—gap because physicality's inability to explain phenomenality is essentially its inability to explain subjectivity.

Dogmatists and physicalists do not rise above empirical apperception. As Fichte says: "[m]any people have simply not progressed in their own thinking past the point of being able to grasp the single series constituted by the mechanism of nature… For such people, a representation becomes a particular sort of thing."[57] As we saw, mere empirical apperception is blind to its own condition, viz., the spontaneity of combining representations in one consciousness. Only transcendental apperception closes the gap between the what-it-is-like and for-whom-it-is-like of experience. It is the "self-sufficiency and spiritual freedom"[58] by which idealism can prove the primacy of practical reason and refute dogmatism.

Nevertheless, theoretical reasoning cannot settle the dispute between idealism and dogmatism:

> Neither of these two systems can directly refute the opposing one; for the dispute between them is a dispute concerning the first principle, i.e., concerning a principle that cannot be derived from any higher principle. If the first principle of either system is conceded, then it is able to refute the first principle of the other. Each denies everything included within the opposite system. They do not have a single point in common on the basis of which they might be able to achieve mutual understanding and be united with one another. Even when they appear to be in agreement concerning the words of some proposition, they understand these same words to mean two different things.[59]

A clash of first principles is theoretically insoluble. First, each is a derivational ground and so underivable. Second, each supports rigorous, thoroughgoing explanation, producing a system as plausible as its contrary. Third, each renders a contrary system incoherent, lacking common ground with the same and yielding a stalemate. As Fichte elsewhere explains, "[e]very philosophy presupposes something that it does not demonstrate on the basis of which it explains and demonstrates everything else."[60] A dogmatist can by "a correct inference" from her principle discredit the alleged "fact" of spontaneity as "an illusion," thereby colliding with no hard problem.[61] And one is "unable to refute a dogmatist" by positing the I's spontaneity, since her principle entails spontaneity's incoherence. Katalin Balog identifies the same theoretical insolubility between physicalism and anti-physicalism:

> [e]ach side can unseat the other side's core assumption if they are permitted to make their own core assumption. The anti-physicalist appeals to the anti-physicalist principles, the physicalist appeals to the conceivability of a purely physical world with phenomenality. Both can show that, once granted that one core assumption, their view is consistent and can rebut challenges from the other side. Neither side can, without begging the question against the opponent, show that the other's position is untenable.[62]

Positing subjectivity as the principle on which phenomenality depends begs the question against a physicalist, for whom there is neither the empirical nor the transcendental gap whose closure requires subjectivity. She is free to posit physicality as her first principle, produce a consistent and complete system, and talk past her disputant. But then her core assumption, like her disputant's, is a bare assurance.[63]

The dispute must therefore be resolved practically. For an idealist, this requires grasping the primacy of practical reason, viz., by grasping one's apperceptive spontaneity. One cannot be compelled to do so, Fichte says: "self-consciousness does not impose itself upon anyone, and it does not simply occur without any assistance from us. One must actually act in a free manner."[64] The primacy of practical reason must therefore be proven first-personally. Likewise, denying its primacy must be refuted first-personally: its denial must be self-refuting. Hence, although Fichte cannot refute the dogmatist with theoretical reasoning,[65] he can show that she practically refutes herself.

Positing a first principle in response to philosophy's first demand is done, Fichte says, "by means of a free act of thinking."[66] This is because a response is normative. I hold myself as responsible for it and regard it as correct.[67] A dogmatist's "inner self" agrees in this respect with her disputant: her capacity to posit a principle is inescapably normative and thus spontaneous. As Fichte puts it, "a philosophical system is not a lifeless household item" but "is animated by the very soul of the person who adopts it."[68] No response, then, is compatible with dogmatism's nihilistic corollary. Positing the Not-I is accordingly a performative contradiction, since its corollary precludes its possibility. In placing my response in the real series of mechanical nature, I belie it *qua* response.[69] I refute myself. As Fichte infers, a dogmatist's denial of the primacy of practical reason is her "antidote" to her own position, her "cure."[70]

In the Paralogisms, Kant says that if we abstract from the I, we "turn in a constant circle, since we must always already avail ourselves of the representation of it at all times."[71] Fichte agrees in the *Foundations*, stating that a dogmatist positing the Not-I must "think unawares of the *absolute subject as well*, as contemplating this substrate," and so must "unwittingly subjoin in thought the very thing from which they have allegedly abstracted, and contradict themselves."[72] But Fichte denies Kant's claim that apperception merely thinks the I, arguing that it must intellectually intuit the I if we are to prove the primacy of practical reason. Fichte clarifies that intellectual intuition does not grasp a "being," which Kant prohibits,[73] but rather "an acting—and this is something that Kant does not even mention (except, perhaps, under the name 'pure apperception')."[74] Of course, when Kant mentions "apperception," he means a mere representation. For Fichte, however, the I's spontaneity must, on pain of dogmatism, be intuitably real. Intellectual intuition is accordingly the immediate awareness of the I's reality. It apprehends the "I do" that must be able to accompany my representations, the "acting" that grounds "the encountered object of this acting"[75]—the primacy of practical reason.

Proving this primacy is first-personal. I discover that I am "active" and "cannot be driven from this position."[76] Fichte invokes Jacobi against complaints that this discovery is indemonstrable.[77] Jacobi's rhetorical point in charging that nihilism leaves perception and action "inexplicable" is that it offers third-personal explanations, whereas the true is not explicable by external conditions, but is simply a matter of faith. Intellectual intuition of spontaneity is indemonstrable because it is unconditioned, attained "not through a *transition,* but by means of a *leap.*"[78] Nihilistic views refute themselves by resisting this leap. Like dogmatism, physicalism fails to rise to the apperceptive standpoint that closes the transcendental (hence also the empirical) gap. If we want to avoid nihilism and any hard problem that confronts its various guises, we must, Fichte says, "elevate ourselves."[79]

3. Transcendental Realism's Waver

Consciousness poses a genuine problem for Fichte, one that is insoluble absent a practical stand. An idealist takes this stand by demonstrating that subjectivity collides with no comprehensive view because it conditions any view's being comprehensive. I conclude by briefly suggesting that transcendental idealism undermines Chalmers' and Dennett's responses to the hard problem of consciousness.

A transcendental realist treats appearances as things in themselves lying beyond our sensibility. In the Paralogisms, Kant argues that since her representations nevertheless rely on sensibility, they are "insufficient to make their reality certain." She "can never be fully certain of reality from any possible experience" and so she "plays the empirical idealist." Hence her position wavers between casting reality beyond her standpoint and acknowledging features of that standpoint from which she cannot infer that reality. By contrast, a transcendental idealist treats appearances as representations and so need not doubt their reality: they exist "on the immediate testimony of [her] self-consciousness." She is thus "an empirical realist," for she grants appearances "a reality which need not be inferred."[80] She achieves a stable position, unlike her wavering counterpart.

Dennett's response to the hard problem exhibits a transcendental realist's waver. In "Quining Qualia," he acknowledges such a problem's nihilistic threat by observing that many insist on qualia—on experience involving a what-it-is-like—as a "bulwark against creeping mechanism." However, on the assumption of "third-person objective science," he argues that qualia cannot exist because their inversion is neither introspectively detectable nor intersubjectively comparable.[81] In "A History of Qualia," he explicitly infers the dissolution of the hard problem from qualia's non-existence: if consciousness is a "user-illusion" as real as El Dorado,[82] there is no empirical gap, but only physical facts. Yet Dennett cannot infer such—or any—facts from within his own user-illusion.

As a transcendental realist, he cannot cognize reality on the basis of representations that he himself discredits.[83] Hence, he plays the empirical idealist.

Chalmers fares no better. Affirming qualia *contra* Dennett, he supplements physical principles with psychophysical principles, raising consciousness from *explanandum* to *explanans* in order to render perception and action explicable.[84] But expanding one's metaphysical principles does not entail a principled metaphysics. That requires proof of our right to the concepts on which such principles rest. In the Deduction, Kant observes concepts that "circulate with almost universal indulgence, but that are occasionally called upon to establish their claim by the question *quid juris*, and then there is not a little embarrassment about their deduction because one can adduce no clear legal ground for an entitlement to their use either from experience or from reason."[85] A transcendental deduction proves our right to the categories as concepts that universally and necessarily condition the possibility of experience. As Chalmers offers no such deduction, his principles risk the "embarrassment" of conceptual grounds to which we lack right, the fate of a transcendental realist's disregard for experiential conditions.[86] Worse yet, he says that his principles need only appeal to "non-empirical constraints such as simplicity and homogeneity."[87] But these are constraints to which physicalism can equally appeal, mere theoretical concerns that we saw guarantee an insoluble dispute. Worse still, raising consciousness to a principle presupposes self-consciousness as its supreme principle.

Given the nature of the disputed datum—what it is like for me to perceive and move through the world—a practical stand is needed. According to Fichte, transcendental idealism serves this end by inviting us to view the concept of apperceptive activity as "*primary*" and that of being as "*derivative*."[88] This involves the parallax of shifting from a world that poses a hard problem of consciousness to one whose problems are primarily, familiarly practical. Such is the resolve necessary for overcoming the various guises of nihilism.[89]

Notes

1   Hans Jonas, *The Phenomenon of Life: Toward a Philosophical Biology* (Evanston: Northwestern University Press, 2001), 9.

2   David J. Chalmers, "Facing Up to the Problem of Consciousness." In *The Character of Consciousness* (New York: Oxford University Press, 2010), 8.

3   Chalmers, "Facing Up to the Problem of Consciousness," 5.

4   Chalmers, "Facing Up to the Problem of Consciousness," 5. Cf. Thomas Nagel, "What Is It Like to Be a Bat?" *Philosophical Review* 83, no. 4 (1974): 435–50; Frank Jackson, "Epiphenomenal Qualia," *Philosophical Quarterly* 32, no. 127 (1982): 127–36; Joseph Levine, "Materialism and Qualia: The Explanatory Gap," *Pacific Philosophical Quarterly* 64 (1983): 354–61.

5   F.H. Jacobi, *The Main Philosophical Writings and the Novel Allwill*, trans. G. di Giovanni (Quebec: McGill-Queen's University Press, 1994), 511–12.

6   Jacobi, *The Main Philosophical Writings*, 513–14, 529–30.

7   Jacobi, *The Main Philosophical Writings*, 193.

8   Jacobi, *The Main Philosophical Writings*, 187–8, 530–1.

9   Jacobi, *The Main Philosophical Writings*, 519, 530. Cf. G.W. Leibniz, *Philosophical Texts*, trans. and ed. R.S. Woolhouse and R. Francks (Oxford: Oxford University Press, 1998), 270: "*perception*, and everything that depends on it, is *inexplicable by mechanical principles*, by shapes and motions."

10   Chalmers, "Facing Up to the Problem of Consciousness," 8; Jacobi, *The Main Philosophical Writings*, 193.

11   Immanuel Kant, *Kants gesammelte Schriften* (Berlin: de Gruyter, 1900), B131–2; cf. A383.

12   Kant, *Kants gesammelte Schriften*, A126–7, B136–7, A401–2.

13   Kant, *Kants gesammelte Schriften*, Bxvi-i.

14   J.G. Fichte, *Sämmtliche Werke*, ed. I.H. Fichte (Berlin: de Gruyter, 1965), I:421.

15   J.G. Fichte, *Gesamtausgabe der Bayerischen Akademie der Wissenschaften*, ed. R. Lauth, H. Jacobs, and H. Gliwitzky (Stuttgart-Bad Cannstatt: Frommann-holzboog, 1962–2012), IV/2:61. Cf. Kant, *Kants gesammelte Schriften*, 5:30, 121; 8:13–14.

16   Although Jacobi charges Fichte with nihilism in the open letter, depicting the *Wissenschaftslehre* as an "*inverted* Spinozism" that reduces objects to moments of "pure and empty consciousness" (502), we will see that, in texts that provoke Jacobi's charge, Fichte argues that his idealism refutes Spinozism's nihilistic corollary.

17   Kant, *Kants gesammelte Schriften*, B157; Fichte, *Sämmtliche Werke*, I:16. On nihilism's role in German idealism's formation, see Frederick Beiser, *German Idealism: The Struggle against Subjectivism, 1781–1801*. (Cambridge, MA: Harvard University Press, 2002); Paul Franks, *All or Nothing: Systematicity, Transcendental Arguments, and Skepticism in German Idealism*. (Cambridge, MA: Harvard University Press, 2005).

18   Fichte, *Sämmtliche Werke*, I:472.

19   Fichte, *Sämmtliche Werke*, I:421–2; Fichte, *Gesamtausgabe*, IV/2:17.

20   This unity is presupposed by experience, *a fortiori* scientific experience of the brain; cf. Dan Zahavi, "Brain, Mind, World: Predictive Coding, Neo-Kantianism, and Transcendental Idealism," *Husserl Studies* 34, no. 1 (2018): 47–61.

21   Kant, *Kants gesammelte Schriften*, A107.

22   On discontinuities between Kantian and contemporary theories of consciousness, see Thomas Sturm and Falk Wunderlich, "Kant and the Scientific Study of Consciousness," *History of the Human Sciences* 23, no. 3 (2010): 48–71.

23   Cf. David Hume, *A Treatise of Human Nature*, ed. D.F. Norton and M.J. Norton (Oxford: Clarendon Press, 2007), 162.

24   Kant, *Kants gesammelte Schriften*, A106–7.

25   Kant, *Kants gesammelte Schriften*, B131–2.

26   Kant, *Kants gesammelte Schriften*, B133.

27   On the inner sense/apperception distinction, see Henry Allison, *Kant's Transcendental Idealism* (New Haven: Yale University Press, 2004), 277–9; Karl Ameriks, *Interpreting Kant's Critiques* (Oxford: Oxford University Press, 2003), 62; Béatrice Longuenesse, *Kant and the Capacity to Judge* (Princeton: Princeton University Press, 1998), 239n.

28   Kant, *Kants gesammelte Schriften*, B134–5.

29   As Kitcher (Patricia Kitcher, "The Unity of Kant's Active Thinker." In *Transcendental Philosophy and Naturalism*, ed. J. Smith and P. Sullivan (Oxford: Oxford University Press, 2011), 55–73) observes, Tetens' conception of inner sense as the record of an act of thinking fails to secure the apperceptive ground of cognition. Recording acts of thinking, even associating different feelings with different acts, e.g., assumptions

as opposed to inferences, is insufficient for apperception, for the latter requires a single consciousness to unify the acts of thinking that rationally constitute cognition, e.g., the assumptions that support the inference to a conclusion (62–6). For criticism of Kitcher's account of apperception, see Sebastian Rödl, "The Single Act of Combining," *Philosophy and Phenomenological Research* 87, no. 1 (2013): 213–20.

30   Kant, *Kants gesammelte Schriften*, A122. Cf. Dan Zahavi, "Intentionality and Phenomenality: A Phenomenological Take on the Hard Problem," *Canadian Journal of Philosophy* 29 (2003): 63–92; Dan Zahavi and Uriah Kriegel, "For-Me-Ness: What It Is and What It Is Not." In *Philosophy of Mind and Phenomenology: Conceptual and Empirical Approaches*, ed. D. Dahlstrom, A. Elpidorou, and W. Hopp (New York: Routledge, 2015), 36–53.

31   Kant, *Kants gesammelte Schriften*, A116, A123, A127. Cf. Gottlob Frege, *The Frege Reader*, ed. M. Beaney (Oxford: Blackwell, 1997), 339: "If there is no owner of ideas then there are also no ideas, for ideas need an owner and without one they cannot exist."

32   Cf. Kitcher, "The Unity of Kant's Active Thinker," 70–1.

33   One may wonder if apperception explains how phenomenality arises. But Kant need only explain how it composes a unity of consciousness. Whereas physicalism's causal explanation of how things arise renders phenomenality absurd, Kant's formal explanation of what unifies consciousness renders it intelligible.

34   Kant, *Kants gesammelte Schriften*, B132–3, B135.

35   Jacobi, *The Main Philosophical Writings*, 335.

36   Jacobi, *The Main Philosophical Writings*, 337, cf. 335n45.

37   Martin, Pippin, Hickey, and Breazeale observe the merits of Fichte's idealism as an alternative to naturalism but overlook its ability to solve the hard problem of consciousness. Wayne Martin, *Idealism and Objectivity: Understanding Fichte's Jena Project* (Stanford: Stanford University Press, 1997); Robert Pippin, "Fichte's Alleged Subjective, Psychological, One-Sided Idealism." In *The Reception of Kant's Critical Philosophy: Fichte, Schelling and Hegel*, ed. Sally Sedgwick (Cambridge: Cambridge University Press, 2000), 147–70; Lance P. Hickey, "Fichte's Critique of Dogmatism: The Modern Parallel," *The Philosophical Forum* 35, no. 1 (2004): 65–80; Daniel Breazeale, *Thinking Through the Wissenschaftslehre* (Oxford: Oxford University Press, 2013). Tse articulates a Fichtean critique of physicalism but does not offer a refutation of nihilism (Plato Tse, "Fichte's Critique of Physicalism: Towards an Idealist Alternative," *Inquiry* 62, no. 5 (2019): 527–45, 532).

38   Fichte, *Sämmtliche Werke,* I:474; cf. 462–3, Fichte, *Gesamtausgabe*, IV/2:25.

39   Fichte, *Sämmtliche Werke,* I:477, 479n; cf. 478. For Fichte's distinction between I-hood and selfhood, see Fichte, *Sämmtliche Werke,* I:255–7, 476, 501–4, 530n, III:57.

40   Kant, *Kants gesammelte Schriften*, B136, 132; corrected citations from Fichte, *Sämmtliche Werke,* I:475, 476.

41   Fichte, *Sämmtliche Werke,* I:476.

42   Fichte, *Sämmtliche Werke,* SW I:430.

43   See Fichte, *Sämmtliche Werke,* I:443.

44   Fichte acknowledges that Kant posits a thing in itself, but claims that it functions as a noumenon, whose concept enables thought to delimit appearances and thus depends solely on the I's thinking (Fichte, *Sämmtliche Werke,* I:482–3); cf. Fichte, *Sämmtliche Werke,* I:491, 514.

45   Jacobi, *The Main Philosophical Writings*, 189; cf. Fichte, *Sämmtliche Werke,* I:100.

46   Fichte, *Sämmtliche Werke,* I:96, 100; cf. Kant, *Kants gesammelte Schriften*, B145–6.

47 Fichte, *Sämmtliche Werke*, I:477.

48 See Fichte, *Sämmtliche Werke*, I:488.

49 Fichte, *Gesamtausgabe*, IV/2:61; see Matthew C. Altman, "Idealism Is the Only Possible Philosophy: Systematicity and the Fichtean Fact of Reason," *Idealistic Studies* 31, no. 1 (2001): 1–30.

50 Fichte, *Sämmtliche Werke*, I:479.

51 Fichte, *Sämmtliche Werke*, I:422–3.

52 Fichte, *Sämmtliche Werke*, I:424–5.

53 Fichte, *Sämmtliche Werke*, I:119–20; Fichte, *Gesamtausgabe*, IV/2:43–4; cf. Fichte, *Sämmtliche Werke*, I:499.

54 Fichte, *Sämmtliche Werke*, I:435–6.

55 Fichte, *Sämmtliche Werke*, I:435–7.

56 Fichte, *Sämmtliche Werke*, I:438. Fichte also describes this as a gap between "things" and "representations."

57 Fichte, *Sämmtliche Werke*, I:439.

58 Fichte, *Sämmtliche Werke*, I:439.

59 Fichte, *Sämmtliche Werke*, I, 429; cf. 499, 509-n.

60 Fichte, *Gesamtausgabe*, IV/2:17.

61 Fichte, *Sämmtliche Werke*, I:430, 439; cf. Fichte, *Gesamtausgabe*, IV/2:15–16.

62 Katalin Balog, "In Defense of the Phenomenal Concept Strategy," *Philosophy and Phenomenological Research* 84, no. 1 (2012): 1–23, here: 20. Cf. Martin Heidegger, *Schelling's Treatise on the Essence of Human Freedom*, trans. J. Stambaugh (Ohio: Ohio University Press, 1985): "[t]he truth of a principle can in general never be demonstrated by success. For the *interpretation* of a success *as* a success is, after all, accomplished with the help of the presupposed but unfounded principle" (138).

63 Balog (Balog, "In Defense of the Phenomenal Concept Strategy," 21) claims that the dispute can be settled by comparing "the overall simplicity and explanatoriness of the respective metaphysical frameworks." But these are only further theoretical concerns in a theoretically insoluble dispute. Each system boasts the simplicity of a first principle. And each boasts the explanatoriness of derivations grounded on that principle.

64 Fichte, *Sämmtliche Werke*, I:429; cf. 499.

65 See Fichte: "We certainly can refute [dogmatists'] system *for us*; indeed, it must be refuted, and this is something that can be accomplished quite easily […] But we cannot refute it *for them*" (Fichte, *Sämmtliche Werke*, I:510). Cf. Daniel Breazeale, "Fichte's Spinoza: 'Common Standpoint', 'Essential Opposition', and 'Hidden Treasure'," *International Yearbook of German Idealism* 14 (2018): 103–38.

66 Fichte, *Sämmtliche Werke*, I:425.

67 See Pippin, "Fichte's Alleged Subjective, Psychological, One-Sided Idealism," 158: "[t]o assume [dogmatism] would still be to determine oneself to act as if determinism were true. But that would make it a norm for action and so to refute oneself." Cf. Jonas, *The Phenomenon of Life*, 129–30; Allen Wood, "Fichte on Freedom: The Spinozistic Background." In *Spinoza and German Idealism*, ed. E. Förster and Y.Y. Melamed (Cambridge: Cambridge University Press, 2012), 132.

68 Fichte, *Sämmtliche Werke*, I:434; cf. 505.

69 See Fichte: "in presupposing the thoroughgoing validity of the mechanism of cause and effect, [dogmatists] directly contradict themselves. What they say stands in contradiction with what they do; for, to the extent that they presuppose mechanism, they at the same time elevate themselves above it. Their own act of thinking of this

relationship is an act that lies outside the realm of mechanical determinism" (Fichte, *Sämmtliche Werke,* I:509–10); Cf. F.W.J. Schelling, *Ideas for a Philosophy of Nature,* trans. E.E. Harris and P. Heath (Cambridge: Cambridge University Press, 1988), 30.

70   Fichte, *Gesamtausgabe,* IV/2:16.

71   Kant, *Kants gesammelte Schriften,* A346/B404.

72   Fichte, *Sämmtliche Werke,* I:97; cf. 500–1.

73   See Kant, *Kants gesammelte Schriften,* B148, B307.

74   Fichte, *Sämmtliche Werke,* I:472.

75   Fichte, *Sämmtliche Werke,* I:463. Failing to intuit one's spontaneity, Fichte says, is a weakness of character, not intellect (505).

76   Fichte, *Sämmtliche Werke,* I:467.

77   Fichte, *Sämmtliche Werke,* I:508.

78   Fichte, *Sämmtliche Werke,* I:298.

79   Fichte, *Sämmtliche Werke,* I:503–6. Cf.: "There is… nothing demeaning about [the dogmatist's] situation *per se.* Anyone who today accuses his brother of this sort of incapacity was necessarily once in this same condition himself; for this is the condition into which we were all born, and it takes time to raise oneself above this condition" (511).

80   Kant, *Kants gesammelte Schriften,* A368-72.

81   Daniel Dennett, "Quining Qualia." In *Mind and Cognition: A Reader,* ed. W. Lycan (Cambridge, MA: MIT Press, 1993), 392.

82   Daniel Dennett, "A History of Qualia," *Topoi* 39, no. 1 (2017): 5–12, 3b–4b.

83   Dennett's deference to cognitive science cannot survive this discrediting, for scientific objectivity is bound by the conditions of experience. Science cannot dispense with the apperceptive standpoint because it is an experience differing only in degree from ordinary experience. See Zahavi, "Brain, Mind, World."

84   Chalmers, "Facing Up to the Problem of Consciousness," 17.

85   Kant, *Kants gesammelte Schriften,* A84-5/B117. While Blamauer (Michael Blamauer, "Is the Panpsychist Better Off as an Idealist? Some Leibnizian Remarks on Consciousness and Composition," *Eidos* 15 (2011): 48–75) detects an idealist solution to the hard problem of consciousness in Leibniz, the latter's silence on the question *quid juris* bespeaks a transcendental realism.

86   Although Chalmers' empirical idealism is less obvious, he arguably attempts to infer from experience's what-it-is-like to its transcendentally real principles of explanation.

87   Chalmers "Facing Up to the Problem of Consciousness," 19.

88   Fichte, *Sämmtliche Werke,* I:499.

89   For helpful comments, I thank Martijn Buijs, Addison Ellis, Gabriel Gottlieb, Matt Habermehl, Colin McLear, Kevin Temple, and Plato Tse. This chapter develops my 2017 CPA commentary on David Suarez (manuscript), "Why Subjectivity Can't Be an Object."

8

The Parallax of Ontology
Reality and Its Transcendental Supplement

Slavoj Žižek

In the history of philosophy, the gap that thwarts every ontological positivity acquires many forms, and insofar as philosophy is its time conceived in notions, we have to begin with the gap that determines our historical moment. Today, its predominant form is undoubtedly the gap, parallax, between reality in a naïve positive sense of "all that exists" and the transcendental horizon within which reality appears to us. From its very inception, philosophy seems to oscillate between two approaches: the transcendental and the ontological or ontic. The first concerns the universal structure of how reality appears to us: which conditions must be met for us to perceive something as really existing? "Transcendental" is the philosopher's technical term for such a frame as defines the coordinates of reality; for example, the transcendental approach makes us aware that, for a scientific naturalist, only spatiotemporal material phenomena regulated by natural laws really exist, while for a premodern traditionalist, spirits and meanings are also part of reality, not only our human projections. The ontic approach, on the other hand, is concerned with reality itself, in its emergence and deployment: How did the universe come to be? Does it have a beginning and an end? What is our place in it? In the twentieth century, the gap between these two methods of thinking became most extreme: the transcendental approach reached its apogee with Heidegger, while the ontological one today seems kidnapped by the natural sciences: we expect the answer to the question of the origins of our universe to come from quantum cosmology, the brain sciences, evolutionism. At the very beginning of his bestseller, *The Grand Design*, Stephen Hawking triumphantly proclaims that "philosophy is dead"[1]: metaphysical questions about the origin of the universe, etc., which were once the topic of philosophical speculations, can now be answered through experimental science and thus empirically tested.

Upon a closer look, of course, we soon discover that we are not quite there yet—almost, but not quite. Furthermore, it would be easy to reject this claim by demonstrating the continuing pertinence of philosophy for Hawking himself (not to

This chapter is a reprint from: Slavoj Žižek, *Sex and the Failed Absolute* (London: Bloomsbury, 2020), 27–41. © Slavoj Žižek, 2020, *Sex and the Failed Absolute*, Bloomsbury Academic, an imprint of Bloomsbury Publishing Plc.

mention the fact that his own book is definitely not science, but a very problematic popular generalization): Hawking relies on a series of methodological and ontological presuppositions which he takes for granted. Science remains caught in the hermeneutic circle; that is, the space of what it discovers remains predetermined by its approach.

But if the transcendental dimension is the irreducible frame or horizon through which we perceive (and, in a strict Kantian sense which has nothing to do with ontic creation, constitute reality), why reduce it to a supplement of reality? Therein resides yet another dialectical coincidence of the opposites: the all-encompassing frame is simultaneously a mere supplement of what it enframes. Reality deprived of its transcendental frame is an inconsistent mess of the Real, and its consistency relies on a supplement which constitutes it as a Whole. We encounter here again an example of the paranoiac motif, from science-fiction stories, of the "wrong button"—a small, supplementary, disturbing even, element in a scene of reality, which, if we accidentally press it, triggers the disintegration of reality. What we (mis)took for a tiny part of reality is what was holding it together.

The predominant view today is somewhere along the lines of Sellars and McDowell, best exemplified by the title of McDowell's book *Mind and World*, what one is tempted to call a dynamized Kantianism: one insists on realism, there is some impenetrable real out there, our mind does not just move in its own circle, but our access to this real is always mediated by the symbolic practices of our life-world. The problem we are dealing with is therefore: How to move beyond (or beneath) the couple of reality and its transcendental horizon? Is there a zero-level where these two dimensions overlap? The search for this level is the big topic of German Idealism: Fichte found it in the self-positing of the absolute I (transcendental Self), while Schelling found it in the intellectual intuition in which subject and object, activity and passivity, intellect and intuition immediately coincide. Following the failure of these attempts, our starting point should be that the zero-level of reality and its transcendental horizon is not to be sought in some kind of synthesis of the two but in the very gesture of the rupture between the two. Since today scientific realism is the hegemonic view, the question to be raised is: can the transcendental dimension be accounted for in these terms? That is, how can the transcendental dimension arise/explode in the real? The reply is not a direct realist reduction, but another question: what has to be constitutively excluded (primordially repressed) from our notion of reality? In short, what if the transcendental dimension is the "return of the repressed" of our notion of reality?

What eludes this transcendental approach is not reality itself but the primordial gap that cuts from within into the order of being making it non-all and inconsistent—a difference which is not yet a difference between two positive terms but difference "as such," a pure difference between something(s) and Void, a difference which coincides with this Void and is in this sense itself one of the terms of what it differentiates (so that we have Something and its Difference). (Heidegger aimed at the same paradox with his "ontological difference" which is not a difference between entities, not even the difference between beings and Being as different entities: Being *is* difference itself.) This crack in the ontological edifice opens up the space for the so-called deontological dimension, for the order/level of what Ought-to-Be in contrast to what simply is, for the normative in contrast to the factual. The old question "How to derive Ought from

Is?" (or: Meaning from Reality) can only be answered by way of locating an original cleft in the midst of the order of Being itself.

With regard to this cleft, all today's attempts to combine analytic thought with the Continental tradition remain caught in the Kantian split between brute positive reality and the normative domain of meanings, argumentation, and validity; any attempt to overcome this duality is considered an illegitimate overstepping of the boundaries of our reason. (There are some evolutionary positivists—Dennett, Pinker, etc.—who try to overcome the split by providing an evolutionary account of the rise of our normative abilities out of natural evolution, but there are no direct idealists who would take the risk of accounting for the order of reality itself out of the self-deployment of Reason.) The paradigm was established by Habermas, for whom rules of communicative action function as a pragmatic a priori which cannot be reduced to the positive content (natural or social reality) since they are always-already presupposed in any approach to reality. Within this paradigm, Pippin and Brandom also assert the space of normative reason (argumentation, justification of validity) as irreducible to any positivist scientific explanation. Even Lacan (in most of his teaching, at least) rigidly opposes the positive real of natural objects where "nothing is lacking" and the symbolic order grounded in lack and negativity; and, in the most traditional transcendental way, he insists that the transcendental circle is unsurpassable—we are caught in it; whatever we perceive as its outside is already overdetermined by the symbolic totality (in the same way that, for Western Marxists, whatever we know about nonhuman external nature is already overdetermined by the totality of social praxis, or, as Lukács put it, nature is always a social category).

All these authors concede, of course, that humanity emerged on a tiny planet in our universe, that we are part of global natural processes, but they insist on how, in our approach to reality, we are caught in the circle of socio-symbolic praxis. They are thus caught in a version of what Foucault called the empirico-transcendental doublet: empirically, we are part of nature, natural reality, but transcendentally, our ultimate horizon is that of symbolic praxis—which means that some version of the Kantian inaccessible nature-*an-sich* always lurks in the background. But is this the last word to be said on this topic? Is it possible to enact here the passage from Kant to Hegel? Brandom is the one who goes farthest in this direction with his version of the "semantic idealism," which asserts the identity of subjective and objective, that is, the conceptual identity of our reason and of objective reality, which means the conceptual structure of reality itself—but, again, with an essential proviso: this identity is only semantic, not ontological:

> Talk of "idealism" is talk about a conception of how the subjective is related to the objective. As I understand Hegel, the view I call his "objective idealism" is the view that the concepts and categories we use to understand the objective world and the concepts and categories we use to understand the discursive practices in virtue of which we are subjects are *reciprocally sense-dependent*. That is, one cannot grasp or understand objective categories such as *object*, *fact*, and *law of nature* except insofar as one also understands what it is to use an expression as a singular term (that is, as purporting to refer to or pick out an object), to assert a sentence (that is, to purport to state a fact), and to reason counterfactually (about

what *must* be the case). The great misunderstanding of idealism (responsible for its contemporary philosophical status as "the love that dare not say its name") is to mistake this *sense*-dependence for a *reference*-dependence—to mistake dependence in the order of *understanding* for dependence in the order of *existence*. For it is *not* a consequence of this view that there were no objects, facts, or laws before there were people to use singular terms, sentences, and modal vocabulary such as "necessary." Objective idealism is a thesis about *meanings*. It is a kind of holism relating concepts of objective relations to concepts of subjective processes or practices—the ability to use various sorts of words. In this sense, the semantic pragmatism I am recommending is a kind of semantic idealism.[2]

Brandom is careful to point out that his semantic idealism, that is, his version of the Hegelian identity of subjective and objective, in no way implies that "there were no objects, facts, or laws before there were people to use singular terms, sentences, and modal vocabulary such as 'necessary.' Objective idealism is a thesis about *meanings*. It is a kind of holism relating concepts of objective relations to concepts of subjective processes or practices." What restrains him from taking the fateful step into full ontological idealism is, of course, the fear that, in this case, he would end up in a simple idealist conclusion that objects in our reality are somehow in themselves dependent on our reasoning. This is why, when he is compelled to provide some ontological foundation for his semantic idealism, he takes recourse not to reality itself but to its segment that provides the base of our normative reasoning, the symbolically structured social practices:

> Normative pragmatism about ontology transposes questions about the fundamental categories of *things* into questions about *authority*, and then understands those questions in terms of *social practices*.[3]

However, from our standpoint, Brandom's position remains all too Kantian since it leaves open the question: If there *were* "objects, facts, or laws before there were people to use singular terms, sentences, and modal vocabulary such as 'necessary,'" that is, if they exist independently of our reasoning (of our social practice), can we somehow conceive them in *that* state, or are they Kantian "things in themselves"? The full step from Kant to Hegel goes beyond Fichte's or Schelling's direct identity of the real and the ideal, objective and subjective; it rather focuses on the question of how reality has to be structured so that symbolic order can emerge in it. Consequently, it posits that positive reality prior to the explosion of the Symbolic is not just that (a positive reality), that there is a crack in it, a proto-deontological tension or cleft: at its most basic, reality is not what it is but what fails to be what it is, whose facticity is traversed by an impossibility. Things "become what they are" because they cannot directly be what they are. The materialist common sense imposes as the ultimate feature of reality as it is "in itself" that of radical indifference: "nature in itself" is a chaotic non-All in which all tension and differences, all our struggles, do not disappear but persist as indifferent—from the global standpoint, they do not matter. From the Hegelian view, however, the Real "in-itself" as the not-One is not simply beyond (or, rather, beneath) any form of One-ness but is not-One in an active sense of "non" as a negation which presupposes a reference to the One. The One is here from the beginning—as thwarted, traversed by an impossibility of being what it is, which means that, even at the most basic level, there is no indifference.

Transcendental stance is usually linked to subjectivity, but today we also get transcendental positions which present themselves as anti-subjectivist—for example, Claude Lévi-Strauss designated structuralism as transcendentalism without subject. (While Lévi-Strauss characterized his structuralism as transcendentalism without subject, what we should aim at is exactly the opposite: the notion of a non-transcendental subject, of subjectivity that precedes the transcendental dimension.) In a unique case of self-reference, the ultimate case of a symbolic event of something emerging all of a sudden and creating its own past is the emergence of the symbolic order itself. The structuralist idea is that one cannot think the genesis of the symbolic (order): once it is here, this order is always-already here, and one cannot step outside it; all one can do is to tell myths about its genesis (which Lacan engages in occasionally). Like the inversion of the wonderful title of Alexei Yurchak's book about the last Soviet generation, *Everything Was Forever, Until It Was No More*, nothing of it (the symbolic order) was here, until all of it was all of a sudden *always-already* here. The problem is here the emergence of a self-relating "closed" system that has no outside: it cannot be explained from outside because its constitutive act is self-relating; that is, the system fully emerges once it starts to cause itself, to posit its presuppositions in a closed loop. So it's not just that the symbolic order is all of a sudden fully here—there was nothing, and a moment later it is all here—but that there is nothing, and then, all of a sudden, it is as if the symbolic order was always-already here, as if there was never a time without it. The supreme irony here is that Louis Althusser himself, the ultimate theorist of subjectivity as an ideological illusory effect, remains transcendental: when he talks about overdetermined structure, he emphasizes how structure is always-already here, how it cannot be accounted for in genetic-historicist terms. (To avoid a misunderstanding, let me repeat: our position is not that we should counter transcendentalism by deploying the evolutionary genesis of the synchronous structure: the [much more difficult] task is to indicate the "missing link" between before and after, what had to be "primordially repressed" so that a synchronous structure can emerge. A synchronous structure always emerges "out of nothing"; it cannot be reduced to its genetic predisposition, but this "nothing" can be specified.)

This brings us to the classical topic of the relationship between eternity and historical cuts. The obvious way to undermine the metaphysical duality of ever-changing (natural or historical) reality and the higher eternal order is, of course, to claim that there is no higher eternal order, that everything is caught in the constant change which is our only eternity. Then comes the more elaborate Derridean version, that of "always-already" (which should not be confused with the transcendental always-already): there is the Fall—a gap, the violent cut of Difference which disturbs the eternal peace, the sinful act which ruins innocence, etc.—but this Fall or gap always-already happened, nothing precedes it, the preceding Peace or Innocence is a retroactive illusion, and so on. Then, there is a fourth (properly Hegelian) move: the "always-already" transposition of the cut (or Fall) doesn't suffice; there are cuts, but they are not just temporal cuts; they are in some sense cuts in eternity itself: at a certain temporal (historical) moment, something New emerges that changes not only the present and the future but the past itself; things become what they eternally were/are. As we have just seen, this temporality characterizes structuralism—but is this all? Is the proper historicity (as opposed to evolutionary historicism) that of a succession of cuts each of which retroactively changes the past and creates its own eternity? This is not enough since it just brings the transcendental logic to the end—in order to make the crucial step further, one should turn around the standard perspective: not "what is nature for language? Can we grasp nature adequately in/through language?" but "what language is for nature? How does its emergence affect nature?" Far from belonging to logo-centrism, such a reversal is the strongest suspension of logo-centrism and teleology, in the same way that Marx's thesis on the anatomy of man as the key to the anatomy of ape subverts any teleological evolutionism. Or, in Hegelese, instead of asking what is Substance for Subject, how can Subject grasp the Substance, one should ask the obverse question: what is (the rise of the) Subject for (pre-subjective) Substance? G.K. Chesterton proposed such a Hegelian reversal precisely apropos man and animals: instead of asking what are animals for humans, for our experience, one should ask what man is for animals—in his less-known *Everlasting Man*, Chesterton makes a wonderful mental experiment along these lines, imagining the monster that man might have seemed at first to the merely natural animals around him:

> The simplest truth about man is that he is a very strange being; almost in the sense of being a stranger on the earth. In all sobriety, he has much more of the external appearance of one bringing alien habits from another land than of a mere growth of this one. He has an unfair advantage and an unfair disadvantage. He cannot sleep in his own skin; he cannot trust his own instincts. He is at once a creator moving miraculous hands and fingers and a kind of cripple. He is wrapped in artificial bandages called clothes; he is propped on artificial crutches called furniture. His mind has the same doubtful liberties and the same wild limitations. Alone among the animals, he is shaken with the beautiful madness called laughter; as if he had caught sight of some secret in the very shape of the universe hidden from the universe itself. Alone among the animals he feels the need of averting his thought from the root realities of his own bodily being; of hiding them as in the presence of some higher possibility which creates the mystery of shame. Whether we praise these things as natural to man or abuse them as artificial in nature, they remain in the same sense unique.[4]

This is what Chesterton called "thinking backwards": we have to put ourselves back in time, before the fateful decisions were made or before the accidents occurred that generated the state which now seems normal to us, and the way to do it, to render palpable this open moment of decision, is to imagine how, at that point, history may have taken a different turn. With regard to Christianity, instead of losing time with probing how Christianity related to Judaism, how does it misunderstand the Old Testament when it incorporates it as announcing the arrival of Christ, and trying to reconstruct how Jews were prior to Christianity, unaffected by the retroactive

Christian perspective, one should rather turn the perspective around and "extraneate" Christianity itself, treat it as Christianity-in-becoming, and focus on what a strange beast, what a scandalous monstrosity Christ must have appeared to be in the eyes of the Jewish ideological establishment. The hyperbolic case is here provided by those rare societies that, until now, succeeded avoiding contact with "civilization." On May 2008, media reported on the discovery of an "uncontacted tribe" in the thick rainforest along the Brazilian-Peruvian frontier: they never had any contact with the "outside world" of global civilization; their life was probably unchanged for over 10,000 years. Photos of their village were released, taken from a plane. When anthropologists first overflew the area, they saw women and children in the open and no one appeared to be painted. It was only when the plane returned a few hours later that they saw these individuals covered head-to-toe in red: "Skin painted bright red, heads partially shaved, arrows drawn back in the longbows and aimed square at the aircraft buzzing overhead. The gesture is unmistakable: Stay Away." They are right: contact is usually a disaster for such remote tribes. Even if the loggers do not shoot them or force them off their land, diseases against which these isolated humans have no resistance typically wipe out half an uncontacted tribe's numbers in a year or two. Our civilization is for them literally a melting pot—they melt and disappear in it, like the ancient underground frescoes in *Fellini's Roma*, which were protected as long as they were isolated in the underground vacuum; the moment (very careful and respectful) researchers penetrated their domain, the frescoes got pale and started to disappear. We often ask ourselves how we would react to meeting aliens much more developed than ourselves—in the photos of the uncontacted tribe, we ourselves are their aliens. Therein resides the horror of these pictures: we see the terrified natives observing an inhuman Other, and we ourselves are this Other, and the moment we raise the question in this way, we move beyond (or, rather, beneath) the transcendental dimension.

In a homologous way, the Real in quantum physics is not wave oscillation (as opposed to the reality that emerges through the collapse of the wave function) but this collapse itself "in its becoming," as a movement, before it is stabilized into constituted reality. In the same way that Chesterton challenged us to imagine how a human being appears in the eyes of apes, we should imagine how the constitution of reality takes place within the space of wave oscillations. And the same goes for sexual difference: the Real of sexual difference is not the difference between masculine and feminine identities but this difference "in its becoming," the movement of (self)differentiation which precedes the differentiated terms.

The cut we are aiming at (the break in the Real itself through which subjectivity explodes) is therefore not something that can be described in the terms of evolutionary biology, of the transformation of apes into humans. The empirical way this transformation happened is something ultimately indifferent and totally contingent—there was no teleological urge to pass to a higher level of progress in it. As Stephen Jay Gould repeatedly emphasized, in all probability this passage occurred through the process of what he called "ex-aptation": an organ or ability that originally served a certain evolutionary need lost its function, even became an obstacle, just persisting in our body, a useless remainder like the appendix, and it inadvertently triggers the rise of a new (symbolic) order which emerges not as an element but as a structure. In an aleatory way, all of a sudden, a new Order, a "new harmony," emerges out of (what retroactively appears as) Chaos, and although we can (retroactively) ascertain a long gestation period, one contingent last element triggers the swift shift from chaos to the new order. (Gould even speculates that human speech emerged out of the malfunction of some throat muscles in humanoid apes.) This new Order cannot be accounted for in terms of "adaptation"—a univocal ad quem is missing here (adaptation TO WHAT?). But such a naturalist description cannot account for the explosion of subjectivity in the Real: it remains at the level of (transcendentally constituted) positive reality, while the cut (explosion) we are talking designates the arche-transcendental process of the rise of the very transcendental dimension constitutive of our reality.

What this means is that the true In-itself is not the way things were before the symbolic Cut but this very cut seen from the standpoint of Before, or, to put it in Kierkegaard's terms, in its becoming, not from within its perspective once it is established as the new order. A clarification which draws a line of separation between this position and that of Meillassoux's critique of correlationism might be of some use here. In his rejection of transcendental correlationism (the claim that in order to think reality, there must already be a subject to whom this reality appears), Meillassoux himself remains too much within the confines of the Kantian-transcendental opposition between reality the way it appears to us and the transcendent beyond of reality in itself, independently of us; in a Leninist way (the Lenin of *Materialism and Empiriocriticism*), he then asserts that we can access and think reality in itself. But something is lost in this very field of the transcendental dilemma, something which concerns the very core of the Freudian discovery (the way this discovery was formulated by Lacan): the inherent twist/curvature that is constitutive of the subject itself. That is to say, what Lacan asserts is precisely the irreducible (constitutive) discord, non-correlation, between subject and reality: in order for the subject to emerge, the impossible object-that-is-subject must be excluded from reality, since it is its very exclusion which opens up the space for the subject. The problem is not to think the real outside transcendental correlation, independently of subject; the problem is to think the real *inside* the subject, the hard core of the real in the very heart of the subject, its ex-timate center. The true problem of correlationism is not if we can reach the In-itself the way it is outside correlation to the subject (or the way the Old—"fossils" as remainders of nature the way it was before humanity emerged—is outside its perception from the standpoint of the New) but the New itself "in becoming." Fossil is not the Old the way it was/is in itself; the true fossil is the subject itself in its impossible objectal status—fossil is myself, that is, the way the terrified cat sees me when it looks at me. This is what truly escapes correlation, not the In-itself of the object but the subject as object.

Usually we have the split in object (between for us and the way the object is in itself), but thinking, the subject, is conceived as homogeneous; what Lacan does is to introduce a split also into the subject, between its thinking and its (not actual life-being but its) non-thought thought, its non-non-thought, between discourse and real (not realty). So the point is not only to overcome the inaccessible In-itself by claiming that "there is nothing beyond the veil of semblances except what the subject itself put there" but to relate the In-itself to the split in the subject itself. Meillassoux ironically mentions the ingenious Christian reply to the Darwinist challenge: one of Darwin's contemporaries proposed a ridiculously perspicuous reconciliation between the Bible and the evolutionary theory: the Bible is literally true, the world was created *c.* 4,000 years BC—so how can we explain fossils? They were *directly created by god as fossils*, to give humanity a false sense of opening, of living in an older universe—in short, when god created the universe, he created traces of its imagined past. Meillassoux's point is that the post-Kantian transcendentalism answers the challenge of objective science in a similar way: if, for the theological literalists, god directly created fossils in order to expose men to temptation of denying the divine creation, that is, to test their faith, the post-Kantian transcendentalists conceive the spontaneous everyday "naïve" notion of objective reality existing independently of us as a similar trap, exposing humans to the test, challenging them to see through this "evidence" and grasp how reality is constituted by the transcendental subject.[5] We should nonetheless insist that the Christian solution, meaningless as a scientific theory, of course, contains a grain of truth: what Lacan calls *objet a*, the subject's impossible-real objectal counterpart, is precisely such an "imagined" (fantasmatic, virtual) object which never positively existed in reality—it emerges through its loss; it is directly created as a fossil.

In a different way, object-oriented ontology also remains transcendental: although it presents its vision of reality as "objective," not rooted in any subjective standpoint but encompassing subject as one among objects, this vision is clearly grounded in a certain disclosure of reality (to paraphrase Heidegger) that can only emerge within the horizon of human understanding. My reproach to object-oriented-ontology is thus not that it is too objectivist but that it relies on an anthropomorphic return to the premodern enchanted world. This is how Jane Bennett formulates her "Nicene Creed for would-be materialists":

> I believe in one matter-energy, the maker of things seen and unseen... I believe it is wrong to deny vitality to nonhuman bodies, forces, and forms, and that a careful course of anthropomorphization can help reveal that vitality, even though it resists full translation and exceeds my comprehensive grasp. I believe that encounters with lively matter can chasten my fantasies of human mastery, highlight the common materiality of all that is, expose a wider distribution of agency, and reshape the self and its interests.[6]

What vibrates in vibrant matter is its immanent life force or its soul (in the precise Aristotelian sense of the active principle immanent to the matter), not subjectivity. New Materialism thus refuses the radical divide matter/life and life/thought: selves or multiple agents are everywhere in different guises. A basic ambiguity nonetheless persists here: Are these vital qualities of material bodies the result of our (human observer's) "benign anthropomorphism," so that the vitality of matter means that "everything is, in a sense, alive,"[7] or are we effectively dealing with the strong ontological claim asserting a kind of spiritualism without gods, that is, with a way of restoring sacredness to worldliness? So if "a careful course of anthropomorphism can help reveal that vitality,"[8] it is not clear whether the vitality of material bodies is a result of our perception being animistic or of an actual asubjective vital power—an ambiguity which is deeply Kantian.

Derrida's deconstruction also remains entangled in this deadlock of the transcendental. His famous statement (from his *Grammatology*) "*Il n'y a pas de hors-texte*" ("There is no outside-text") is often mistranslated as "There is nothing outside the text," making it appear that Derrida advocates a kind of linguistic idealism for which nothing exists beyond language. How, then, are we to read it? There is effectively a fundamental ambiguity that sticks to it: it oscillates between a transcendental and an ontological reading. *Il n'y a pas de hors-texte* can mean that all ontological claims are always-already caught in the arche-transcendental dimension of writing: they are never directly about reality out there since they are always overdetermined by a specific texture of traces that form the impenetrable background of all our claims. But it can also be read in a directly ontological way: external reality, life, is already made of traces and differences; that is, the structure of *différance* is the structure of all there is. Derrida came closest to this reading in his unpublished seminar from 1975, *La vie la mort*, the first six sessions of which are devoted to biology (specifically, to François Jacob and his research on DNA structure and the laws of heredity). Notions like "différance," "archi-writing," "trace," and "text" are thus not only the meta-transcendental background of our symbolic universe, they also refer to the basic structure of all living (and putatively also of all there is): "general text" is Derrida's most elementary ontological claim. It is important to note how this ambiguity is connected with another one that concerns the status of the "metaphysics of presence." Derrida abundantly varies the motif of how there is no simple Outside to the metaphysics of Presence: we can only gradually and locally deconstruct it, undermine it, expose its inconsistencies, etc.—to postulate the access to a pure Outside would have meant succumbing to the ultimate trap of Presence. However, insofar as metaphysics of presence equals the history of European philosophy, a naïve but pertinent problem arises: What about, say, ancient China? Were the Chinese also caught in the "metaphysics of presence" (which then elevates "metaphysics of Presence" into a universal feature of humanity), or are they outside European metaphysics? If yes, how can we get in contact with them? (A couple of times, Derrida does touch this status of Chinese language with regard to European logocentrism, but he limits himself to the general statement that Chinese language is not phonocentric since in its writing words do not reproduce phonic letters but directly notions, which is why writing comes first and speech comes second: all Chinese share the same writing which is pronounced differently in different parts of China. However, this does not mean that the general structure of difference [trace] is not at work there also—so the problem with which we are dealing persists.)[9]

The latest ontological turn of so-called Continental thought is marked by the same ambiguity. The widely shared insight today is that "we cannot leave nature to science and study norms of thought or action in philosophy regardless of any conception of the physical universe. As soon as we confront the issue of how to integrate our account of ourselves as knowers and agents of a specific kind with what we know about nature, it should transpire that not all conceptions of nature are compatible without self-description as autonomous agents."[10]

There is nonetheless an ambiguity that pertains to this statement, an ambiguity homologous to the one that characterizes the so-called anthropic principle in (the interpretation of) quantum cosmology: in the same way that we can take the anthropic principle in its "strong" version (our universe was created in order to make the rise of human intelligence possible) or in its "weak" version (human intelligence is not the goal of creation but just a guiding line of our understanding of the universe which has to be structured so that human intelligence could arise in it, albeit in a contingent way), the thesis that our conception of nature should be compatible with our self-description as autonomous agents can be read in a "strong" way and in a "weak" way. It can mean that, in our conception of nature, we are effectively describing the way nature is in itself, independently of our observation and interaction with it, or it can mean that our conception of nature is never truly a neutral view of nature-in-itself but remains embedded in our (human) standpoint, mediated by it.

Notes

1   Stephen Hawking and Leonard Mlodinow, *The Grand Design* (New York: Bantam, 2010), 5.
2   Italo Testa, "Hegelian Pragmatism and Social Emancipation: An Interview with Robert Brandom," *Constellations* 10, no. 4 (2003): 554–70, here: 558. Available online: http://filosofia.fflch.usp.br/sites/filosofia.fflch.usp.br/files/docentes/sites/safatle/2015/posgrad/aulas_FLF5189/Brandom,%20Robert%20-%20Hegelian%20Pragmatism%20and%20social%20emancipation%20-%20an%20interview%20with%20Robert%20Brandom.pdf.
3   Testa, "Hegelian Pragmatism and Social Emancipation," 559.
4   G.K. Chesterton, *The Everlasting Man*. Available online: www.dur.ac.uk/martin.ward/gkc/books/everlasting_man.html#chap-I-i.
5   Quentin Meillassoux, *After Finitude* (New York: Continuum, 2010), 62.
6   Jane Bennett, *Vibrant Matter* (Durham: Duke University Press, 2010), 117.
7   Bennett, *Vibrant Matter*, 117.
8   Bennett, *Vibrant Matter*, 122.
9   It is also possible to read Derrida's notion of trace as "arche-transcendental" in the sense of our attempt to move beyond (or, rather, beneath) the transcendental to the very crack in the Real that opens up the space for the transcendental, but we are entering here an ambiguous sphere open to different interpretations.
10 Markus Gabriel and Anders Moe Rasmussen, *German Idealism Today* (Berlin: De Gruyter, 2017), 10.

Part Two

Parallax in Normative Orders

9

Truth as Subjective Effect
Adorno or Hegel

Christoph Menke

The term "parallax" signifies a specific form of unity: the unity between two elements or determinations that consists in nothing but their gap—in the leap that leads from one to the other, connecting them precisely by separating them. I look along my outstretched arm at my thumb in front of an object in the distance. I look first with one eye, then with the second eye, and this difference—the leap, or bounce, that occurs in the closing of one eye and the opening of the other—forms the unity that constitutes the act of cognition: I thereby calculate how far the object stands from me. The leap between the one gaze and the other thus implies nothing less than the leap from one-sidedness or partiality to objectivity. So, here we have two leaps: from one gaze to the other and from the gaze (as mere sensation) to cognition. The first leap leads from one particular perspective to another particular perspective, while the second leap—which is thereby performed—leads from the particular (that is in itself manifold or plural) to the universal, the one. The double leap that is at stake here thus brings about the unity of cognition at the same time *through* and *beyond* the plurality of one-eyed, half-blinded gazes. It thereby constitutes both the subject and the object of cognition (or subjectivity and objectivity). The unity that subjectivity and objectivity are each for themselves and that they are only together—both the subject and the object of cognition have their respective unity only through their unity with each other: through the unity of cognition—is thus nothing other than a unity constituted by a double leap. But this mutual dependency does not establish a symmetry between them. Because, as the image of the parallax clearly shows, the unity (qua leap) is the effect of a specific gaze, namely, the leap of the gaze that constitutes the unity of cognition. Therefore, the unity of subject and object is itself a subjective effect. It is the subject's gaze. It is the leap that *is* the subject; it is the leap through which it is (or becomes) the subject

The chapter draws on material published in "Yes and No, Adorno or Badiou: The Negativity of the Subject," trans. Roland Végsö. In *Badiou and the German Tradition of Philosophy*, ed. Jan Völker (London: Bloomsbury, 2019), 147–70; revised and expanded German version "Ja und Nein. Die Negativität der Dialektik." In Christoph Menke, *Autonomie und Befreiung* (Berlin: Suhrkamp, 2018), 178–211.

of cognition and hence constitutes objectivity. Objectivity, that is, truth, is the effect of the leap that the subject does not so much perform but that rather constitutes it. Thus understood, the term "parallax" refers to nothing other than the fundamental move of modern philosophy: the subjective constitution of truth as objectivity. The question of the parallax, the question that this term raises, is how to understand that truth is the effect of the leap, the gap or split, which defines the unity of the subject.

I want to take up this question at this point and in the way in which it confronts dialectical thinking. Here, I juxtapose two figures of dialectical thinking: Hegel and Adorno. Both understand the parallax model in such a way that the leap through which the subject brings forth truth is based on its power of negativity. But they each very differently understand the ways by which negativity leads to truth.

1.

In Hegel's work, one way of thinking through the problem is to understand it as the question of freedom. In this perspective, the double leap in which the subject constitutes itself and the object at the same time—the leap from one particularity to the other as the leap into universality—is nothing other than the subject's freedom. For this, however, freedom must be conceived as radically different from the bourgeois conception that has become the basic ideological principle of bourgeois society (and thus of liberalism). Freedom must be thought of as self-determination and free self-determination as the true form of determination as such: free determination is true determination, and true determination is free determination. Hegel's theory of freedom as self-determination is thus his way of conceiving of the unity of subjectivity and objectivity. What interests me in the following is the constitution of this unity by negativity.

a) Self-determination

Hegel develops his concept of freedom as self-determination by a critical discussion of bourgeois freedom. Bourgeois freedom is the natural ability to choose. Choice means selecting from a given set of possibilities. The ability to choose, therefore, presupposes that one has possibilities. This holds true not only in the obvious sense that there must be already given possibilities that are available for the subject so that he or she can choose from them and thereby exercise her freedom. But it also holds true in the more general and basic sense that relating to properties and states *as* possibilities is itself an act of the subject. This means that *having* possibilities is also a subjective capability. The subject is not determined by certain properties, states, or impulses, insofar as she is able to disregard them, to abstract from them, or to negate their power of determination. Only someone who can deny any specific determination, and hence resist her being determined as such, can choose among determinations. The choice of a determination presupposes negation. "Choice," the keyword of bourgeois freedom, is the unity of negation and determination. This is the problem of any concept of freedom, though: how to conceive of the unity of negation and determination.

It is obvious that the bourgeois notion of freedom as the capacity to choose cannot solve this problem. It connects the two sides (the selection of *one* determination under the precondition of abstracting from *all* determinations) only externally, and, as a result, it oscillates between them. Therefore, the free subject of choice is just as empty as she is full. She is empty because nothing carries absolute meaning for her. At the same time, however, she is loaded with all the possibilities that are given to it in a situation from which she cannot escape. The bourgeois subject of choice is always *either* negative *or* determined—but never both in one. In order to think the unity of negation and determination, it is thus necessary to go beyond the freedom of choice. Using the terms in Kant's sense, we can say that we must move from a "negative" to a "positive" conception of freedom.[1] And the positive concept of freedom (which is the true one) conceives of freedom precisely as the unity of negation and determination or position.

The basic idea of the positive concept of freedom is that the unity of negation and determination can only be conceived if this unity is understood as a fundamental, conceptual transformation of determination—of the meaning of "determination." In the bourgeois concept of choice, the determination remains the same before and after the act of freedom. In the act of choosing, the individual abstracts from the fact that she is determined by specific needs and then chooses one of her needs or an ordered series of needs as her determination. But, here, determination remains (unchanged) in kind. In Hegel's language, we could say that determination (*Bestimmung*) remains mere "determinacy" (*Bestimmtheit*). According to Hegel, the freedom of choice is "the transition from undifferentiated indeterminacy to *differentiation, determination*, and the *positing* of a determinacy as a content and object."[2] There is determinacy before and after the act of choice, both of which have the same form (or are ontologically, in terms of their mode of being, the same). Whether pre-given, self-given, "given by nature," or "generated by the concept of spirit,"[3] the determinations of the subject are simply *given*, in that they exist positively as the (abstract) other of negation.

In contrast, the true concept of freedom consists in thinking of the free act as a transformation of determination: by thinking of freedom as "self-determination,"[4] it is at the same time understood as a transformation in the *form* of determination. The fundamental meaning of the term "self-determination" is self-realization; the term which Hegel takes over from Kant has an expressivist meaning.[5] In its act of self-determination the free subject thus not only posits a determination; rather, in each act of positing something as its determination, the subject also posits itself: it expresses itself in giving itself a determination. Determinacy (*Bestimmtheit*) becomes self-determination (*Selbstbestimmung*) when it is not only the effect but the expression, that is, the presentation of the positing *in* the effect. The claim that free determination is the self-determination of the subject means that, as a determination by the self, it is at the same time the self *as* determination. In its determination, the self "remains with itself... and in this determination, it joins together with itself alone."[6]

Only this way can the requirement be fulfilled to grasp the unity of negation and determination—while the freedom of choice is merely the external back and forth *between* negation and determination and remains caught in this dualism. According to the formal structure of this unity, the negation through which the subject first dissolves the determinacies that condition it remains present in the second step of the free positing of a determination. The first step is the negation of givenness or positivity. The second step is the negation of this negation in the positing of determinations: however, not as the abstract other of the (first) negation but in such a way that the self remains with itself as negative *in* its determination.[7] Accordingly, free self-determination is a determination that is *at the same time* negation—the negation of every given determination—and not negation, since in the negation of negation it is at once the overcoming *and* preservation of negation.

b) Determinate Negation: Logical and Ontological

Positive freedom is the unity of negation and determination. As such, positive freedom is nothing other than the truth of determination in general. *Every* determination is in truth (in its true form as determination) a free determination or an act of self-determination. This is the lesson of Hegel's theory of determinate negation, which states that determination is the negation of negation. At the center of this theory, we find "the recognition of the logical principle that negation is equally positive."[8]

On the first level, the concept of determinate negation serves to describe the way by which the operation of negation proceeds in actuality, that is, in the praxis of negation. In this process, the negated "does not resolve itself into a nullity, into abstract nothingness, but essentially only into the negation of its *particular* content; or that such a negation is not just negation, but is *the negation of the determined fact* that is resolved, and is therefore determinate negation."[9] Since negation is always the negation of something, that is, a specific determination, it does not stand in an external opposition to what it negates. Negation is the "nothingness of that *from which it results*."[10] The negation of determination is its "*immanent* movement."[11] Since negation is the result of a determination that it negates (or that negates itself), negation itself *has* a result. "Looked at as a result, what emerges from this process is the *determinate* negative which is consequently a positive content as well."[12] If negation as such is "determinate negation" (if every operation of negation in reality is always determined), then it is a negation *of* a determination and, *consequently*, at the same time the production of another determination.[13]

But this reconstruction describes negation merely as a logical operation— "logical" in the classical and not in the Hegelian sense. The understanding of negation as a logical operation defines it on the basis of its effects on the meaning and, thereby, on the truth-value of a determination. Logically speaking, the negation of a false thought produces its contradictory opposite as true and the negation of a true thought produces its contradictory opposite as false.[14] Logical operations refer to relations among determinations. The dialectical concept of determinate negation, on the contrary, refers to what a determination *is*: it applies to the *form* of determination and not its content. The concept of determinate negation, therefore, is not merely a logical concept but an ontological one. Hence the other side of "the recognition of the logical principle that negation is equally positive" is the insight that "determinateness [*Bestimmtheit*] is negation posited as affirmative."[15] This is why for Hegel, "Spinoza's proposition: *omnis determinatio est negatio*, [is] a proposition of infinite importance": because it offers us another understanding of "determination."[16] Accordingly, being a determination *means* being the result of a negation.

The ontological meaning of determinate negation lies in the concept of the "result." That is, negation is an act directed at a first determination, which then produces a second determination as a result. The second determination "contains" in itself the first determination and its negation, or more precisely: "in the result there is therefore contained in essence that from which the result derives—a tautology indeed, since the result would otherwise be something immediate and not a result."[17] Because it is a result, the second determination is "richer" than the first "because it negates or opposes the preceding and therefore contains it, and it contains even more than that, for it is the unity of itself and its opposite."[18] The second determination, however, is not "richer" than the first in its content but in its form. It is richer precisely because it comes second and, therefore, it has a history, that is, the history of resulting from a negation of a previous determination. Precisely because it has a history and therefore a past, the second determination is a structurally "new" determination: "But when… the result is conceived as it is in truth, namely, as a *determinate* negation, a new form has thereby immediately arisen, and in the negation the transition is made."[19] Every determination that is understood to be a result of a negation, or rather, of its history, is a new determination. To understand determinations, that is to say, determination as such (as a result and, therefore, as a new determination), thus "constitutes the truly dialectical factor."[20]

The thesis of determinate negation claims that every determination is the result of an act of negation directed at another determination. In a logical sense, this means that determinations are bound up with each other through their negations. That is, one determination *is* (nothing other) than the negation of another or the negation of one determination is "immanent" to the other. Although the logical understanding makes it appear as if they were both of the same kind and form as determinations bound by negation, the ontological understanding of determinate negation makes it clear that they are fundamentally different. Thus, determinate negation is the act of their formal differentiation, the production of a "new form," or the production of determination in a new form. Determinate negation is not a relation of "material" (Robert Brandom) but of *formal* incompatibility. Determinate negation produces a form in which determination and negation, the positing of determinations, and the cancellation of mere givenness are thought together.

This unity of negation and determination defines what Hegel calls both *free* and *true* determination. That both expressions are correct here means that the true (form of) determination is posited or produced by the subject. Subjective positing is positing due to negation, and "negation" means abstraction from any pre-given determinacy. But as the critique of the model of choice shows, everything depends on how this is conceived. In choice, negation is followed by the selection of one of the pre-given determinants. The true determination, on the other hand, is free or *self*-determination, because here the determination *contains* the negativity—which constitutes the subject—within itself: it is its expression. In Althusser's words, self-determination is the "determination as self"[21] or the self as present in its determination.

2.

We can distinguish two steps in Hegel's argument. I call the first step Hegel's *thesis*. The thesis claims that true determination *is* self-determination, insofar as it is the identity of truth and freedom or subjectivity. Or in other words, true determination is the determination which expresses the positing subject. I call the second step the *operation* by which Hegel establishes that identity. Hegel does so by defining subjectivity as the force of negativity. That the true determination is the expression of the subject then means nothing other than that it not only presupposes the power of negativity as external but also "contains" it "within itself."

If we now look at Adorno, it is obvious that he rejects Hegel's "thesis", in that true determination is not self-determination. On the contrary: a determination's moment of truth lies precisely where it transcends the subject. I will sketch this claim first (in section a). But what about Hegel's "operation," the grounding of determination in negativity? In taking over the concept of determinate negation, Adorno follows Hegel in the joining of determination and negativity. With this, however, he seems to take over exactly the argument on which Hegel grounds his identity thesis: he seems unable to escape the spell of idealistic dialectic. Or does Adorno conceive of the connection between negativity and determination in such a way as to avoid the consequence that Hegel has drawn from it: namely, that since negativity is the power of the subject, the grounding of true determination in negativity *must* mean that true determination and free self-determination are the same—that truth is the expression of the positing self (section b)?

a) Rescue [*Rettung*]

At first a brief remark on Adorno's rejection of Hegel's thesis, his equation of truth and subjectivity: in his "Meditations on Metaphysics," Adorno calls the "flattening of the intelligible into the imaginary"[22] the fundamental mistake of all "phenomenological" philosophies. Phenomenology reduces the intelligible to acts—that is, subjective acts—of the imagination. Adorno contrasts this reduction with the following provision of the human spirit (*Geist*). He states: "To be a mind at all, it must know that what it touches upon does not exhaust it, that the finiteness that is its like does not exhaust it. The mind thinks what would be beyond it."[23] The mind is only mind, it *thinks* only where it is not equal to itself, that is, where it is more or other than itself. Thinking means: to think more than or differently from what we can think. True thought is not the product of the thinking subject. It is not exhausted by the subjective act of thinking that produced it. Rather, thinking is defined by a "moment of transcendent objectivity."[24] In Adorno's words, it is "the negation of the finite which finiteness requires" that defines the mind: "The concept of the intelligible is the self-negation of the finite mind… In the mind, mere entity becomes aware of its deficiency."[25] That is, the mind or thinking is "the departure from an existence obdurate in itself," in that "in its self-negation, the mind transcends itself."[26]

This self-transcendence through "self-reflection" is the opposite of the self-realization or -expression that, according to Hegel, constitutes the freedom of the subject. The self-negation of the spirit is, therefore, not (positive-) dialectical. It is not sublated by the negation of negation (the negativity of the spirit in its self-determination). Rather, it is the movement in which the spirit transcends itself and its self-determination in the movement of thinking. Adorno calls this movement of the spirit beyond itself the "rescue" (or the "saving": *Rettung*) of that which it thinks:

> Nothing can be saved unchanged, nothing that has not passed through the portal of its death. If rescue is the inmost impulse of any man's spirit, there is no hope but unconditional surrender of that which is to be rescued as well as of the hopeful spirit. The posture of hope is to hold lightly what the subject will hold on to, what the subject expects to endure.[27]

Rescue is the rescue of the matter of thinking, or in other terms, the rescue of its matters by the spirit, from the spirit which flattens matter into mere phenomena, that is, into appearances *for it*. Rescue is the self-movement of the spirit in which it relinquishes itself. It is the relinquishment of the spirit that it alone can accomplish because otherwise it would not be its relinquishment to the intelligible and infinite, but to that which merely exists as positivity; that is, its relinquishment to the spirit that does not rescue phenomena through its own self-relinquishment but accepts them as they perpetuate an "obstinate insistence on existence, forms of a clutching."[28]

"Rescue" is a concept that describes the connection between truth and the subject in terms of an infinite difference. Here, the concept of truth is again, as in Hegel (see above), understood in an ontological sense. Truth means the true form of determination (or of thought). The concept of truth refers to the *way* a determination should *be* in order to be a true determination. It must be understood as unconditioned or transcendent. True determination, therefore, infinitely exceeds anything produced by the subject. Herein Adorno sees his fundamental opposition to Hegel's positive dialectic. Because Hegel's main thesis is that true determination is the self-determination of the subject, Hegel's dialectical account of truth as freedom amounts to "the unrestrained expansion of the subject": the "Hegelian subject-object is subject."[29] In contrast, Adorno aims to think of true determination as a passing *beyond* the self-determination of the subject that is realized precisely and only *by* the subject—in the procedure that the subject is. We encounter truth only where the subject does not "remain with itself," as Hegel put it, but transcends itself, as it goes beyond itself in itself.

b) The Move to Negative Dialectics

The problem of Adorno's argument surfaces where the question of negativity emerges, for Adorno agrees with Hegel's dialectical operation that there is true determination only *through* the negativity of the subject. Contrary to Hegel, however, Adorno does not believe that this means that true determination is (but) the subject's self-determination. According to Adorno, we must distinguish between the idea of self-determination, on the one hand, and the recourse to the negativity of the subject, on the other hand. It is precisely this critical distinction that accounts for Adorno's move to *negative* dialectics. The question is whether there is conceptual room for this distinction and hence for the project of a negative dialectics.

The basic anti-Hegelian claim of negative dialectics can be summarized by the following statement: negative dialectics holds that it is incorrect "[t]o equate the negation of negation with positivity." For when Hegel asserts this (as Adorno claims he does), "[what] thus wins out in the inmost core of dialectics is the anti-dialectical principle."[30] In negative dialectics, on the contrary, the "negation of particularities… *remains* negative."[31] That is, it has no "circumventing result" by which negation via the negation of its self-negation would simultaneously preserve itself.[32] Negativity does not have a result. But this is not the case, because for Adorno there is only (pure or mere) negativity with no true determination or because negativity is everything. Quite the contrary: the claim that negation does not have a determination as its "result" means that such determination would not be true. Contrary to Hegel, for Adorno, the "result" is not the form of truth. This is why negativity has to "remain negative": its result-lessness, or purity, is precisely the condition of true determination. Therefore the "rescue" of truth leads through the "portal of death."[33] Thus, Hegel's figure of self-determination requires that we think negativity and determination "as one [*in einem*],"[34] as two sides of self-determination, on the one hand. Adorno, on the other hand, defines their connection "in the movement of thought" in such a way that, while "the fixed, positive point, just like negation, is a *moment*," these two—the positive and the negative, as moments—do not form a "synthesis."[35] The positive and the negative are joined by their irreducible difference. Or put in terms of process: the act of negation dissolves the false, reified "positivity" of the concept that seeks to identify the thing only in order to thereby reveal, on the other side of negation, that "there is perhaps a so-called positive motive force of thought."[36] This "moment of positivity, which acts as a corollary to negativity," is not cancelled but, on the contrary, *released* by the negativity of thought.[37] Negative dialectics is not the dissolution of the positive in negativity but the rescue of the positive as a moment through the destructive power of negation that acts against the violence "in the act of identification."[38]

Against Hegel, Adorno argues that negativity does not produce a determination as a result and, consequently, determination cannot be the result of the negativity of the subject, hence the term "*negative* dialectics." With Hegel, Adorno argues that, at the same time, there is no true determination without the negativity of the subject and thus negativity precedes truth, hence "negative *dialectics*." Negative dialectics thus dissolves the argumentative connection between what I have called Hegel's "thesis" and Hegel's "operation"; negative dialectics is nothing but the gap between them. For it rejects the claim that to think together negativity and determination *means*, and *must* mean, to think of determination as self-determination.

But this description of *how* negative dialectics understands the connection between true determination and the negativity of the subject differently from Hegel's positive dialectics still seems to leave open the question of *why* the negativity of the subject is necessary at all in order to think true determination as the self-transcendence of the subject. The reason for this lies in the aforementioned fact that, according to Adorno, true positivity cannot be rescued without the critical cancellation and even destruction of false, reified positivity. Its needs negativity for truth because—and as long as—there is positivity.[39] Without the power of negativity, there is no true determination; without negativity, there is only reified positivity, the merely given. This is the way in which determinations exist *by themselves*. To be given (and hence not true) is the natural form of existence of determinations—their second nature. It needs the intervention, and hence the negativity, of the subject in order to overcome such positivity and thus to make truth possible. This is why Hegel's definition of thought as the "enormous power of the negative" is decisive for Adorno.[40] The "energy" and "restlessness" that define thinking is the power to dissolve the natural given positivity from within itself.[41] This is the labor of the negative. It can only become effective as a "moment" in its interplay with the "positive motive force of thought." But it cannot be derived from this positive motive force, in that it is an irreducible force. Without its efficacy, there is no truth.

3.

What does it mean that truth is a subjective effect? The question needs a twofold answer: the answer must tell what "subjective" means and "effect" means.

The answer to the first question is that truth is an effect of negativity. Subjectivity means negativity. The true determination is that which emerges from the negativity of the subject. This is the point of Hegel's theory of determinate negation. In it, the concept of truth refers, first and foremost, to the *form* of a determination. As we have seen, according to Hegel, the true determination is the new determination. And the new determination is that which has arisen from, that is, brought about by, the negation of the pre-given determination.[42]

The second question is about the effect of truth: What does it mean that truth is an effect? And what constitutes the effectiveness or efficacy of the subject (understood as negativity) for truth? Efficacy means bringing forth; truth is brought forth (truth does not exist by itself, as a given). But what does bringing forth mean? I have interpreted Hegel's theory of self-determination to mean that bringing forth is expression, namely, that in Hegel's theory of self-determination the (generative) connection between self *and* determination means "determination *as* self" (Althusser). The determination expresses the self that produces it; the determination is true, and free, insofar as it "contains" negativity (Hegel). This is what Adorno rejects. According to Adorno, the expressivistic interpretation of the connection between self and truth, negation and determination is Hegel's one small but decisive error. Negativity can never be contained in a determination; there is no determination that can contain negativity. Negation "remains" negative (Adorno). Therefore, the true determination only emerges from the negativity of the self in such a way that it passes through it. There is no "mediation"—of negation and determination, of subjectivity and truth. Their connection consists in the leap (or gap) that separates them.

Notes

1   Immanuel Kant, *The Metaphysics of Morals*, ed. Mary J. Gregor (Cambridge: Cambridge University Press, 1996), part I, Introduction, sect. I.

2   Georg Wilhelm Friedrich Hegel, *Elements of a Philosophy of Right*, trans. H. B. Nisbet (Cambridge: Cambridge University Press, 1991), 39.

3   Hegel, *Elements*, 38.

4   Hegel, *Elements*, 41.

5   Christoph Menke, "Autonomy and Liberation: The Historicity of Freedom." In *Hegel on Philosophy in History*, ed. Rachel Zuckert and James Kreines (Cambridge: Cambridge University Press, 2017), 159–76.

6   Hegel, *Elements*, 41.

7   The full definition of self-determination, therefore, is the following: "the self-determination of the 'I', in that it posits itself as the negative of itself, that is, as *determinate* and *limited*, and at the same time remains with itself [*bei sich*], that is, in its *identity with itself* and universality; and in this determination, it joins together with itself alone" (Hegel, *Elements*, 41).

8   G.W.F. Hegel, *The Science of Logic*, trans. George di Giovanni (Cambridge: Cambridge University Press, 2010), 33.

9   Hegel, *Science of Logic*, 33.

10   Hegel, *Phenomenology of Spirit*, trans. A.V. Miller (Oxford: Oxford University Press, 1977), 51.

11   Hegel. *Phenomenology*, 36.

12   Hegel, *Phenomenology*, 36. "Because the result, the negation, is a *determinate* negation, it has a *content*" (Hegel, *Science of Logic*, 49).

13   To put it differently: negation is already negation of negation. For if negation is to be understood as determinate negation (the act of negation of a determination as the expressive realization of its immanent or self-negation), then every act of negation is at the same time an act of determination and, therefore, possesses a positive content since it is the negation of a self-negating determination, and, as such, in the negation of determination, it is at the same time the negation of the (self-negation) of this determination.

14   "Thus for every thought there is a contradictory thought; we acknowledge the falsity of a thought by admitting the truth of its contradictory. The sentence that expresses the contradictory thought is formed from the expression of the original thought by means of a negative word." See Gottlob Frege, "Negation." In *Collected Papers on Mathematics, Logic, and Philosophy*, ed. Brian McGuinness (Oxford: Blackwell, 1984), 385. Robert Brandom's interpretation of determinate negation as "material incompatibility" corresponds to this logical concept of negation. See Robert Brandom, "Holism and Idealism in Hegel's *Phenomenology*." In *Tales of the Mighty Dead: Historical Essays in the Metaphysics of Intentionality* (Cambridge, MA: Harvard University Press, 2002), 178–86, here: 180–2.

15   Hegel, *Science of Logic*, 87.

16   Hegel, *Science of Logic*, 87.

17   Hegel, *Science of Logic*, 33.

18   Hegel, *Science of Logic*, 33.

19   Hegel, *Phenomenology*, 51.

20   Hegel, *Science of Logic*, 34.

21   Louis Althusser, "Du contenu dans la pensée de G.W.F. Hegel." In *Écrits politiques et philosophiques*, vol. 1 (Paris: Stock, 1994), 59–238, especially 123–42: "Le contenu comme Soi."

22   Theodor W. Adorno, *Negative Dialectics*, trans. E.B. Ashton (London: Routledge, 1973), 391. See Christoph Menke, "Metaphysik und Erfahrung. Zu Adornos Begriff der Philosophie." In *Spiegelungen der Gleichheit* (Frankfurt am Main: Suhrkamp 2003), 184–99.

23   Adorno, *Negative Dialectics*, 392.
24   Adorno, *Negative Dialectics*, 392.
25   Adorno, *Negative Dialectics*, 392.
26   Adorno, *Negative Dialectics*, 392.
27   Adorno, *Negative Dialectics*, 391–2.
28   Adorno, *Negative Dialectics*, 391.
29   Theodor W. Adorno, *Hegel: Three Studies*, trans. Shiery Weber Nicholsen (Cambridge, MA: MIT Press, 1993), 5, 13.
30   Adorno, *Negative Dialectics*, 158.
31   Adorno, *Negative Dialectics*, 158. Emphasis added.
32   Adorno, *Negative Dialectics*, 159.
33   As Ansgar Martins insists, this formulation should not be understood in a Christological sense. Martins explains this point with reference to a similar passage from Gershom Scholem's *Major Trends in Jewish Mysticism*: "Unlike the death of Jesus, Sabbatai Zevi does not transmit new, authentic revolutionary values. His apostasy merely destroys the old ones" (Quoted in Ansgar Martins, *Adorno und die Kabbala* [Potsdam: Universitätsverlag, 2016], 88). Therein lies the antinomian motif that brings Adorno and Scholem together: "The path into the abyss precedes the one that leads upwards" (Quoted in Martins, *Adorno und die Kabbala*, 87). See also, Asaf Angermann, "Redemption *ex negativo*: Critical Theory and the History of Mystical Heresy," *Bamidbar* 4, no. 1 (2014): 1–20.
34   Hegel, *Elements,* 41. Translation modified.
35   Theodor W. Adorno, *Lectures on Negative Dialectics: Fragments of a Lecture Course, 1965/1966*, trans. Rodney Livingstone (Cambridge: Polity, 2008), 29, 27. Translation modified. Adorno also calls this "positive moment" the moment of "naïveté" in thinking (Adorno, *Negative Dialectics*, 39).
36   Adorno, *Lectures*, 26.
37   Adorno, *Lectures*, 26.
38   Adorno, *Lectures*, 30.
39   On the question of the how, and why, of being of positivity, see note 43.
40   Adorno, *Negative Dialectics*, 38.
41   Adorno, *Negative Dialectics*, 157.
42   This is the simple version of the theory of determinate negation with which I first worked here. In a more complete way, one would have to say that the pre-given determination itself is (or was) already a negation. And not only the negation of another determination (that is the logical level on which negation refers to the content) but—ontologically understood—the negation of negativity. In Hegel's words: the determination is the "limitation" (*Beschränkung*) of the "identity," as negativity, of the self. Therefore, the negation of a determination is always the negation of the negation that is the true definition or shape of determination. Since the negation which thus constitutes the determination is the negation of negativity, the negation of the negation of determination is nothing other than the repetition of the initial or first negativity. The production of truth as the new is therefore the return to the origin, that is, more precisely, the retroactive production of negativity as origin. "Origin is the goal."

10

Is Sex a Transcendental Category of Parallax?

Revisiting the Feminist Second Wave

Nina Power

There are several conceptual impasses at the heart of contemporary feminist thinking. These arguably stem from unfinished business with second-wave feminism, when central questions of politics, economics, labor, and sexuality were most deeply posed. Today we can observe the negative and positive definitions of the objects of materialist and radical feminist knowledge, and wonder what this means for any feminism today. Where materialist feminism understands women's lot in relation to their historical exploitation in relation to production and reproduction, radical feminism identifies the root of women's struggle in patriarchy. Thus, there are two "negative" objects at the heart of each position: one, the capitalist mode of production and, two, men, or, more specifically, male domination.

In the meantime, questions of "essentialism" have plagued feminist philosophical thinking. As Catherine Malabou puts it in *Changing Difference*: "In the post-feminist age the fact that 'woman' finds herself deprived of her 'essence' only confirms, paradoxically, a very ancient state of affairs: 'woman' has never been able to define herself in any other way than in terms of the violence done to her. Violence alone confers her being— whether it is domestic and social violence or theoretical violence."[1] While this chapter will take issue with Malabou's suggestion that it is "violence" that ontologically defines woman or womanhood, it will, like Malabou, revisit the question of essentialism in relation to debates around sex and gender today in relation to the tensions between materialist and radical feminism and ask whether it is possible to define woman in such a way that does not rely on these hidden negative objects (capitalism or patriarchy).

It is my conviction that the feminisms loosely termed "second-wave" are not yet concluded, which is to say, that the concerns of the feminisms of this period regarding their relation to Marxism, to history, to culture, to ecology, to race, to men, to technology, and so on remain live questions that have not yet been transcended or displaced by any shifts in social, technological, or historical developments, despite the wish, perhaps, that this might be so, for example, in the lineage of technophilic feminisms from Shulamith Firestone to Xenofeminism today. Developments in reproductive technology have not, I suggest, been accompanied by revolution at the level of the sex-class. In other words, techno-feminism has not escaped techno-capitalism.

I wish to remain with the tensions and difficulties of radical, materialist, Marxist, deconstructionist, and psychoanalytic feminisms in light of the ongoing difficulty of defining "woman" and "women" in anything other than negative terms—a feature seemingly inherent to thought, language, and reality—as, for example, "not-men," the "second sex," or, as Malabou puts it in 2011: "That 'woman' finds herself now in the age of post-feminism deprived of her 'essence' only confirms paradoxically a very ancient state of affairs: 'woman' has never been able to define herself other than through the violence done to her."[2]

Malabou's proposal that we define woman as "an empty but resistant essence, an essence that is resistant because empty and a resistance that strikes out the impossibility of its own disappearance once and for all"[3] might remind us, at the outset, of Karl Marx's early formulation of the class with radical chains, an estate which is the dissolution of all estates. Malabou's definition is not a positive identification, just as Marx's definition of the proletariat is not either, but the analogies between women and the proletariat, productive in some respects, are, of course, stretched thin in other ways.

Malabou suggests that feminism today can be seen as a feminism without women. But a paradox remains:

> if we name *it* the feminine, if we incorporate the inviolable [Derrida's name for the feminine] we… run the risk of fixing this fragility, assigning it a residence and making a fetish out of *it*. If we resist it, we refuse to embody the *inviolable* and it becomes anything at all under the pretext of referring to anyone.[4]

What is feminism, she asks, "if it involves eradicating its origin, woman"?[5] And later: "the deconstruction of sexual identities does not imply letting go of the fight for women's liberation."[6] Malabou's reliance on violence to define "woman"—"woman is nothing any more, except the violence through which her 'being nothing' continues to exist"[7]—cannot but seem plaintive, though she suggests it opens a new path for feminism that goes beyond both essentialism and anti-essentialism. But why does any philosophically informed definition of woman have to be negative? Is there no way of escaping the reliance on a positive binary term whose empty opposite pole is labelled "woman"? Why does woman have to be associated with violence, rather than some more positive identifying unifying characteristic?

Here we must turn to the methodology of our approach. Sex would seem, on the face of it, to be an obvious candidate for thinking about parallax, or thinking "parallaxically," if we are talking about ways of seeing, or places, positions to see and think from. I am using parallax here in the sense that when an object appears to change its position, it is because the person or instrument has also changed their position. We could say, very simply, that the world looks differently depending on if you are a man or a woman. *How* it looks different, or how we come to understand these terms "man" or "woman" as positions, whether biological, linguistic, legal, existential, and so on, is a complex matter. Recent years have seen extremely emotional and, at times, violent contestation over what these terms mean and who can claim them.

Debates in the United Kingdom, but elsewhere too, over proposals to change the meaning of sex from "biological definition" to "self-identification" have seen women attacked for wanting to attend meetings to discuss proposed changes to legislation, and many women, and some men, have lost employment after being accused of holding "transphobic" positions (though the people accused of this would not accept this word): that is to say, they have been attacked for saying that sex is real, and that this difference has consequences, and for disputing the idea that being a man or a woman is a matter of a feeling, for criticizing the idea that one can say one is a man or a woman because one *feels* that way. But what happens if we agree that sex "isn't real," or, in other words, that sex is not how we decide who is a man or who is a woman? Among trans activists, sex is postulated as something that can be changed, either through a declaration and/ or through surgical and chemical intervention. So, we have two competing claims here: one, that sex is real, and the other, that sex is not real, or, perhaps, that sex is not as real as *something else that is more important*—whatever that something else is: desire, image, fantasy, feeling.

It is obvious from this brief sketch that there is in contemporary life a serious and deep clash of positions here regarding what it means to be a "man" or a "woman." What role does, and what role can, psychoanalysis play in these turbulent times? Those who hold that male and female are realities that have distinct features are often criticized as holding "essentialist" positions, that is to say, that commitment to the biological existence of two separate sexes brings with it, or threatens to, ideas of how each sex should behave (i.e., men should behave in a "masculine" way, women in a "feminine" way, for example, as some traditionalist religious positions might entail).

It is, however, arguably possible to both be committed to the reality of biological sex but not be committed to the idea that any particular kind of "gendered" behavior follows from this acceptance of reality (the doctor says: "it's a girl!" or "it's a boy!" but does not say how these facts should play out in each individual's lives). "Intersex" individuals are sometimes invoked to complicate the motion of sex, to suggest that sex is a spectrum not a binary, but even in these rare cases, it is evident that there is no third sex, and disorders or sexual development are always disorders of male or female sexual development; that is, they confirm the sex binary.

As second-wave feminisms repeatedly argued, the acceptance of a biological basis to sex does not entail that boys or girls, men or women, should therefore *behave* in particular ways because of the fact that one is born male or female. In fact, we could say, gender roles and stereotypes are precisely that which should be *abolished*, both individually and collectively. This argument historically filtered down in education and broader society for the two or three decades following these ideas of "gender abolition," such that there was a loosening up of gender stereotypes, and more freedom regarding dress, interests, and behavior, including sexual behavior (i.e., just because one was a feminine boy or man and attracted to other boys, for example, did not make that person a girl or a woman).

The psychoanalytic position, particularly in Lacan's work on feminine sexuality, comes at the question from a slightly different angle. As Jacqueline Rose puts it: "Lacan does not refuse difference ('if there was no difference how could I say there was no sexual relation'…), but for him what is to be questioned is the seeming 'consistency' of that difference—of the body or anything else—the division it enjoins, the definitions of the woman it produces."[8] It appears as if there is more mystery in the psychoanalytic position, more flexibility. As Juliet Mitchell puts it:

> [Freud's] account of sexual desire led Lacan, as it led Freud, to his adamant rejection of any theory of the difference between the sexes in terms of pre-given male or female entities which complete and satisfy each other. Sexual difference can only be the consequence of a division; without this division it would cease to exist. But it must exist because no human being can become a subject outside the division into two sexes. One must take up a position as either a man or a woman. Such a position is by no means identical with one's biological sexual characteristics, nor is it a position of which one can be very confident—as the psychoanalytical experience demonstrates.[9]

The profound uncertainty and ongoing ambivalence in relation to the inescapably sexed nature of existence, recognized by psychoanalysis, has nevertheless arguably shifted in the wider culture to a desire to, at times, completely dispense with the recognition of the originary division or difference. Every signifier relating to sexuation seems to just *float*, which makes the question of sex a question of power: who has the power to name. While it may have been expeditious at a certain point to criticize the sexual binary in the name of attacking the hierarchy of this binarism (the idea, longstanding in Western thought, that the male is "better" than the female), the attempt to eradicate the binary now can in many ways be seen as ushering in a new era of anti-feminism, in which women's right to define themselves is once again eradicated.

Here I want to address two neglected aspects of the question of sex. Firstly, the too-quick slide between sexuation and sexuality, as if the problem of sexual difference can be passed over by the invocation of desire (the parallax of sexuation/ sexuality). And, secondly, the relative neglect of the inheritance and history of second-wave feminist theory in contemporary psychoanalysis, particularly in the occlusion of the figure of the mother, both metaphorically and in everyday life (the parallax mother).

1. Sexuation/Sexuality

So, to be clear, in more recent years, a new notion of "gender" has emerged, what we have noted as the "feeling" idea. This idea has no necessary basis in biological sex; that is, one can simply say that one "is" or "identifies" as a woman or a man (or as neither) for it to be "true." What is the role or relation to psychoanalysis in this later notion? This idea of sex as "assertion," where one says one simply "is" a man or a woman, is troubled by the idea that one can never truly assert with such certainty that one is (or is not) anything at all. At the same time, psychoanalysis has troubled the idea of uncritical access to such a thing as biological reality or that there is a pre-linguistic space of bodies or desires that we can access.

Yet, we live in an everyday double-bind when it comes to sexuation. We both believe and do not believe (to some extent) in the reality of sex. We both notice it, and ignore it. Is "sex" therefore a "transcendental" condition for the possibility of knowledge?

Either in the sense that we see the world through the lens of sex, that is, we see sex as if it is *in* the world, or that we see the world in a sexed way, that is, from the standpoint of our own sex, consciously or otherwise. We could say it is a transcendental condition in both of these senses.

We thus both see sex and disavow it. There is no non-sexed experience or knowledge. It is not possible for human beings to understand the world outside of sex, even if there are various knowledges that do not pertain to sex as such (mathematical truths are not "male" or "female," for example, although this too has been contested by thinkers such as Luce Irigaray, for example). It is possible to talk about the ways in which multiple things—language, discourses, disciplines, experience, history—are sexuated, or are lived in a sexed manner, which is something no living human being can exit from entirely, even if "one's sex" is always a problem or a question for everyone.

Psychoanalysis, in its focus on desire, often skips over quickly from sexuation to sexuality, as if the latter realm is the only place in which the former is lived out. But sexuation is much more than how one relates to the other: here we could take a much more existentialist approach, such as that found in the work of Simone de Beauvoir:

> [woman] is the most deeply alienated of all the female mammals, and she is the one that refuses this alienation most violently; in no other is the subordination of the organism to the reproductive function more imperious nor accepted with greater difficulty... These biological data are of extreme importance: they play an all-important role and are an essential element of woman's situation.[10]

If we are to take seriously the idea that sex *is* a transcendental category of parallax, we would mean (a) not only that is sex the condition for the possibility of knowing but also (b) that seeing from these two different perspectives, male and female, might be possible in a fused or disjunct way, that is, to see things from the male *and* female perspective, or the male *or* female perspective. But is sex something that changes how we see everything? We can and do talk about "human" knowledge, knowledge of and for and gained by the species, but is this knowledge truly "without sex"? There is no third-sex position, though there is "neutral" knowledge that does not depend on the sex of the person comprehending it.

At the same time, there is no position outside of sex as such. The androgyne, by combining the desirability of both man and woman, thus appealing to both without being reduced to either, is a powerful alchemical symbol, but ultimately knows what a masculine woman or a feminine man would learn about desire. There are also no true hermaphrodites—that is to say, human beings possessed of two complete working sets of reproductive organs, one male, one female. The so-called intersex cases are disorders of sexual development and do not constitute third sex. So we are left with the binary, no matter how much we play with it.

As Alenka Zupančič puts it in *What Is Sex?*, "if one 'removes sex from sex,' one removes the very thing that has brought to light the problem that sexual difference is all about. One does not remove the problem, but the means of seeing it, and of seeing the way it operates."[11]

When Freud talks about human bisexuality in the 1905 edition of *Three Essays on the Theory of Sexuality* in discussing "male inverts" (that is to say, male homosexuals), Freud writes:

> Expressing the crudest form of the theory of bisexuality, a spokesperson for male inverts described it was a female brain in a male body. But we do not know what characterizes a "female brain." There is neither need nor justification for replacing the psychological problem with the anatomical one.[12]

What Freud identifies is a certain kind of temptation: that it is possible to understand or "be" the opposite sex in relation to sexual object choice. Thus, a homosexual man is "like" a woman because his object choice is the same as a heterosexual woman, and, consequently, there is something "anatomical" that differentiates him from a heterosexual man. But this is too simple, even as we see a resurgence of this kind of thinking today among some proponents of the transgender narrative, namely that it is possible to be born "in the wrong body" or that male or female brains can exist in male or female bodies.

So, what is the psychological—or for the purposes of this chapter—transcendental problem of sex? If we take part of Hegel's criticism of Kant seriously, we should too historicize the question of sex. One of the major problems of today's technologically oriented, transhumanist narrative, in which it is somehow imagined possible, through drugs and/or surgery, to transform material reality into a kind of wish-fulfillment, what is left behind is the incomplete meeting of psychoanalysis and feminism. This can be seen particularly in the figure of the absence of the mother in much contemporary psychoanalytic discourse. Here second-wave feminism figures both as the "maternal" discourse, as in, generationally old enough to be the conceptual mother of today's, arguably infantilized, discussions of sex, and also as the set of questions and thoughts that properly posed the role and significance of the mother, and is now being obscured again.

2. Parallax Mother

We are living through not just a period of extreme real and virtual misogyny but also through yet another backlash against feminism, particularly against the kind of feminism that had something to say about sexual difference, sexual relations, violence, and patriarchy. Seen a certain way, this can be seen as a culturally and historically widespread attack on mothers in general, though we might say too that the history of humanity is nothing other than an endless series of backlashes of one group against one another, usually on the basis of misrepresentation and projection.

I am not here attempting to reduce womanhood to motherhood, nor womanhood nor motherhood to any kind of normative idea of what that would mean, but rather to ask perhaps open and general questions about what the relationship between matricide, feminism, and memory might be. And here I am focusing on second-wave feminism, not as a historical artifact but rather as an approach to the world that has its political emphasis on women's liberation, its theoretical focus on patriarchy as a historical but also a structuring feature of human thought—whether we are talking about philosophy or psychoanalysis or any other academic discipline—but also as a social question about how men and women might live together. The concern with "matricide" here is also that we are in the process both of forgetting and murdering the insights of the so-called second wave. I suspect we may need to come up with a somewhat piecemeal, fragmentary, funny, and unfinished way of addressing the question "how might we live together," and behind all this is what a psychoanalytically feminist theory of humor might be vis-à-vis the question of sexual difference and social relations between men and women (but this is for another time). The "truths" of psychoanalysis and the "truths" of feminism both seem to have suffered a similar fate in recent years—skipped over, ignored, or imagined to be something else, generationally displaced, as if these disciplines did not ask the exact same questions, as humanity does of itself, over and over again.

So, why focus on matricide, feminism, and memory? It strikes me that there are at least three main themes, on different but related levels, that initially came to my mind, and before I outline these, I want to briefly introduce an important distinction between "not-forgetting," on the one hand, and "remembering," on the other. This is a distinction that Alain Badiou brings up in his *Ethics*:

> [T]he concrete circumstances in which someone is seized by a fidelity: an amorous encounter, the sudden feeling that this poem was addressed to you, a scientific theory whose initially obscure beauty overwhelms you, or the active intelligence of a political place... you have to have encountered, at least once in your life, the voice of a Master... if it is true that—as Lacan suggests—all access to the Real is of the order of an encounter. And consistency, which is the content of the ethical maxim "Keep going!" [*Continuer!*], keeps going only by following the thread of this Real. We might put it like this: "Never forget what you have encountered." But we can say this only if we understand that not-forgetting is not a memory.[13]

So I want to try to be faithful to this idea of not-forgetting. But what have we encountered, and what should we not forget, especially when it comes to those things that are structurally forgotten most of all? Which "Master" are we talking about when it comes to mothers, and how can we even use this word in this way? The parallax optics on mastery and mothering cause a short-circuit from the start.

The material circumstances of matricide should be noted. The 2017 Femicide Census noted that 7.1 percent of the 113 women killed in England, Wales, and Northern Ireland in 2016 were killed by a male family member, that is, a son, father, brother, nephew, or grandson.[14] The report noted that some of the contexts for these killings could be contextualized under the heading of "mercy killing" or "domestic child-parent" situations in news reports, for example. While matricide is relatively rare, and certainly only form a small proportion of the total instances of femicide (most women are killed by their current or former partner), we might ask ourselves whether there is a broader culture of animosity toward mothers, without, of course, exempting ourselves from such murderous, or at the least ambivalent, feelings. We are all capable of violence and aggressivity, which is completely forgotten in some of the discourses around "Me Too" or "toxic masculinity," but violence is, in actuality, unevenly distributed when it comes to women and men.

Women are not always, of course, on the side of passivity, nurturing, and so on. The capacity to care is also and always the capacity to harm. But women historically and practically are the most immediate and obvious group targeted whenever resentment is expressed. As Jacqueline Rose puts it in her recent text *Mothers: An Essay on Love and Cruelty*:

> motherhood is, in Western discourse, the place in our culture where we lodge, or rather bury, the reality of our own conflicts, of what it means to be fully human. It is the ultimate scapegoat for our personal and political failings, for everything that is wrong with the world, which it becomes the task—unrealisable, of course—of mothers to repair.[15]

Similarly, in *The Mother in Psychoanalysis and Beyond: Matricide and Maternal Subjectivity*, the editors, Rosalind Mayo and Christina Moutsou, concur with Rose's diagnosis, suggesting that we all hold "mothers responsible for a variety of personal and social ills and problems, in which maternal vulnerability is denied and silenced."[16]

There is more open and public discussion, though perhaps still not enough, of the hardships of motherhood in recent years. In a popular article by Charlotte Naughton entitled "Why Don't We Care about New Mothers Suffering?," she writes,

> For most people who have a baby, it is inconceivably hard. Modern society protects us from most of the ravages of nature—serious illness, cold, discomfort and pain. But in childbirth and looking after a newborn, we experience the harsh realities of our basic existence; we get closer to our primal selves. And we're not used to it. Post-partum depression and psychosis among mothers are on the rise, according to a recent survey of health visitors, and childbirth and infant mortality are still serious problems in many parts of the world.[17]

As Rose comments, "one reason why motherhood is often so disconcerting seems to be its uneasy proximity to death."[18] Rose's project in her essay, and any psychoanalytic account of motherhood that acknowledges its proximity to death, must also therefore be a question of *eros*. Rose writes:

> Above all, whenever any aspect of mothering is vaunted as the emblem of health, love and devotion, you can be sure that a whole complex range of emotions, of what humans are capable of feeling, is being silenced or suppressed. Such injunctions wipe pleasure and pain, eros and death from the slate. Why, French psychoanalyst Jean Laplanche once mused, are there no artistic representations, or any recognition in psychoanalytic writing, of the erotic pleasure that a mother gains in breastfeeding her child? As if to say, breastfeeding is okay (indeed obligatory), but not so okay is its attendant pleasure.[19]

The pleasure of the breast-feeding mother, perhaps represented on occasion only in religious portrayals of the Virgin Mary with Jesus at her breast, points, perhaps, to a deeper question of envy. The envy of women, of motherhood, of female pleasure in general is buried deep within our culture. It relates to the broader crisis of definition relating to the term "woman," identified above, which has implications for how motherhood does and doesn't overlap with this term. Not all women are mothers, but all mothers are women. Mothers are vital but constantly erased. The obscuring of the mother is part and parcel of the floating quality of the signifier "woman."

Many things cause problems here, in an ongoing way. Maintaining the boundary of womanhood has always been difficult—within psychoanalysis, woman is the "not-all," but in broader social life, it seems that womanhood is a more-or-less completely permeable. It is a term "up for grabs," as it were, a series of images and words open to everyone, but also strangely obscured.

In recent years in the UK we have had quite furious public debates over, for example, the use of the term "non-men" by the Green Party in 2016 to include women, trans women, and non-binary people—the term "men" was not changed to become "non-woman"—with the group "Green Party Women" suggesting that "as a whole, women are happy with terms such as 'non-men' to be used."[20] More recently, there has been anger over changes in the language used around the body with Cancer Research UK tweeting that "[c]ervical screening (or the smear test) is relevant for everyone aged 25–64 with a cervix."[21] In March 2017, popular feminist writer Laurie Penny asked on Twitter: "someone tell me, what's a shorter non-essentialist way to refer to "people who have a uterus and all that stuff"?[22] An online forum based in the UK called, not unimportantly, "Mumsnet," with over 12 million visitors per month, has many members who have similarly reacted with intense anger over suggestions that they cannot refer to women using the definition "adult human female."[23]

By merely discussing this question all at the moment, it becomes almost impossible to avoid being positioned on one "side" or the other, but from a psychoanalytical and philosophical point of view, we might well ask some difficult questions regarding how "biological sex" is functioning, or not functioning, in these discussions, and why "woman," rather than "man," has become such a contested term in recent years at the level of the sociopolitical. It is hard to avoid the conclusion that women are being increasingly obscured both conceptually and politically. In his 1938 work on the family, Lacan writes the following:

> Biological kinship: Another completely contingent similarity is the fact that the normal components of the family as they are seen in our contemporary western world—father, mother and children—are the same as those of the biological family. This identity is in fact nothing more than a numerical equality.[24]

We know that emphasis on or rather a reduction to the biological or "biologism" is completely antithetical to an understanding of the symbolic order, of our entry into language, but there is a crisis of identity at the heart of some of these, often extremely fraught, debates. We seem to have moved from an understanding of identity that accepts that all identity is constructed in a complex negotiation with oneself and others and with broader social conditions, to an extreme position on social perception, in which the demand is made of the other that the other recognize the person demanding as whatever they say they are. Recognition at the social and historical level cannot, however, proceed with individual desire and demand as its central feature.

3. Conclusion

Sex (as in sexuation, rather than sexuality) is constitutively a problem, or a question, for *everyone*, man or woman. There is no way out of the hand we are dealt, no matter how we might wish it otherwise. We see the world from the standpoint of being a man, or as a woman, whatever similarities or differences there might be between the sexes, and however much these positions change during the course of history. It is not enough to skip over sexuation in favor of sexuality; even if the sexed body points to deeper questions of difference, it certainly does not permit avoiding the reality of sexed life. Whatever the difference between men and women might be, it is imperative for the collective sanity of humanity that we hold firm to the fact that there *is* a difference, however it is lived. This holding on to a definition of sexual difference has important positive implications for law, history, society, and thought. Life becomes extremely complicated if we do not hold on to the difference between men and women, however we decide to understand these words.

We can hold on to the parallax of sex itself in order to move around this increasingly contested question. But for that to be possible, we cannot begin by giving up the word "woman" to the ether, as if it has no historical or conceptual weight, and no positive meaning for the future. The second wave is, as yet, an unfinished project.

Notes

1   Catherine Malabou, *Changing Difference: The Feminine and the Question of Philosophy*, trans. Carolyn Shread (Cambridge: Polity Press, 2011), "Note," v.
2   Malabou, *Changing Difference*, "Note," v.
3   Malabou, *Changing Difference*, "Note," v.
4   Malabou, *Changing Difference*, 35.
5   Malabou, *Changing Difference*, 36.
6   Malabou, *Changing Difference*, 93.
7   Malabou, *Changing Difference*, 98.
8   Jacqueline Rose, "Introduction—II." In *Feminine Sexuality: Jacques Lacan and the école freudienne*, ed. Juliet Mitchell and Jacqueline Rose, trans. Jacqueline Rose (London, New York: W. W. Norton), 56.
9   Juliet Mitchell, "Introduction—I." In *Feminine Sexuality, Feminine Sexuality: Jacques Lacan and the école freudienne*, ed. Juliet Mitchell and Jacqueline Rose, trans. Jacqueline Rose (London, New York: W. W. Norton), 6.
10 Simone de Beauvoir, *The Second Sex*, trans. Constance Borde and Shelia Malovany-Chevallier (London: Jonathan Cape, 2009), 44.
11 Alenka Zupančič, *What Is Sex?* (London, Cambridge, MA: The MIT Press, 2017), 44.

12   Sigmund Freud, *Three Essays on the Theory of Sexuality: The 1905 Edition*, trans.
     Ulrike Kistner, ed. and introduced by Philippe van Haute and Herman Westernik
     (London: Verso, 2016), 8.

13   Alain Badiou, *Ethics*, trans. Peter Hallward (London: Verso, 2001), 52.

14   Available here: https://www.womensaid.org.uk/wp-content/uploads/2018/12/
     Femicide-Census-of-2017.pdf

15   Jacqueline Rose, *Mothers: An Essay on Love and Cruelty* (London: Faber & Faber),
     "Opening."

16   Rosalind Mayo and Christina Moutsou (eds.), *The Mother in Psychoanalysis and
     Beyond: Matricide and Maternal Subjectivity* (London: Routledge, 2017), 1.

17   Available here: https://www.theguardian.com/commentisfree/2018/jul/02/baby-
     blues-suffering-new-mothers-mental-health

18   Rose, *Mothers*.

19   Rose, *Mothers*.

20   Quoted here: https://medium.com/@julian.vigo/woman-by-proxy-2b42c1572392

21   https://www.telegraph.co.uk/news/2018/06/14/cancer-research-removes-word-
     women-smear-campaign-amid-transgender/

22   Quoted here: https://sisteroutrider.wordpress.com/2017/03/15/the-problem-that-
     has-no-name-because-woman-is-too-essentialist/

23   www.mumsnet.com

24   Available here: https://www.scribd.com/document/73359960/Jacques-Lacan-Family-
     Complexes-in-the-Formation-of-the-Individual

11

The Irony of Self-Consciousness
Hegel, Derrida, and the Animal That Therefore I Am

Thomas Khurana

Spirit is Philosophy of Nature.

—Friedrich Schlegel

If there is one feature of self-consciousness that is commonly associated with German idealism, it is the idea that self-consciousness is self-positing and self-validating. An essentially self-conscious being is one that knows itself to be the very thing it is. What is more, its being what it is depends upon its self-consciousness. To be a knower, an agent, a judger is something we can only be in virtue of knowing and taking ourselves to be a knower, an agent, a judger. The reason for this is not that knowing, acting, or judging is a question of arbitrary discretion (i.e., of simply taking myself to be knowing, acting, or judging), the reason is that it belongs to the very form of knowing, acting, and judging that these operations are enacted self-consciously. Knowing and consciousness of knowing, acting and practical knowledge of our acting, judging and consciousness of judging are, in each case, one and the same act of the mind.[1] In the case of finite knowers, agents, judgers, it is possible that the operation and our consciousness of the operation come apart on the level of content—my consciousness of my action deviates from what I actually do; I take myself to know something that I am not entitled or committed to; I mischaracterize my own judgment. But the operation and our consciousness of that operation cannot come apart on the level of form. If they do, the operation is an act of knowing, acting, or judging in name only. This is precisely what it means to consider these types of operation not only as enacted consciously, but as essentially *self*-conscious: the operation is self-conscious insofar as its consciousness is constitutive of and inseparable from the operation it is conscious of.

As I said, it is common to regard this notion as one of the primary ideas that German idealism has bequeathed to us, an idea that the contemporary Anglo-American scholarship on German idealism in general and on Hegel in particular is clearly attracted to. In what follows, I would like to direct our attention to a different feature of Hegel's conception of human self-knowledge that seems in tension with the idea that it defines the very structure of self-consciousness to be self-validating and self-confirming. This is a feature of Hegel's account that is developed further in various ways in contemporary continental thought. The feature I have in mind becomes explicit in an interesting remark in Hegel's *Aesthetics* in which he develops our self-consciousness out of the knowledge we have of ourselves as animals. It is in knowing ourselves to be animals, Hegel argues, that we cease to be animals. This account points to an inherently ironic structure of human self-consciousness and to a structural dependence of our self-conscious operations on an activity of a different type. Self-consciousness is thus—at least in some essential respect—not (i) self-*positing* and (ii) self-*confirming* but (i) *dependent* on a prior activity and (ii) self-*transgressive* in character. In what follows, I will first trace this idea in Hegel's account of self-consciousness, before connecting it to the way Derrida has deepened our sense for the irony of self-consciousness in his reflections on "the animal that therefore I am."[2]

1. The Irony of Self-Consciousness

In a well-known passage from his *Aesthetics*, Hegel writes that "precisely because he *knows* that he is an animal," man "ceases to be an animal and attains knowledge of himself as spirit."[3] This remark by Hegel seems to suggest that the self-knowledge we have of ourselves as spiritual beings is not self-grounding, self-positing, and self-confirming. It is not the case that by virtue of the very fact that I know myself to be a being of a certain type I actualize myself as this type of being. Instead, spiritual self-knowledge springs from a self-negating and self-transgressive form of self-knowledge: Precisely by knowing myself to be a being of a certain kind, I cease to be that very being. And, what is more, in ceasing to be that being in virtue of my self-undermining knowledge, I attain knowledge of my spiritual existence: knowledge of myself as being different from what I know myself to be. Call this the ironic structure of spiritual self-knowledge. If we take this structure seriously, knowledge of myself as a spiritual being is attained by superseding my existence as a certain type of being by the very act of knowing myself to be that type of being. Spiritual self-knowledge thus ultimately is knowledge of the transgressive and negative force of self-consciousness: knowledge of the way in which knowing myself to be a certain type of being turns me into something else.

If we focus on the merely formal structure of this self-consciousness for a moment, Hegel's account certainly seems paradoxical. By knowing myself to be X, I cease to be X. My knowledge thus seems self-defeating. The knowledge itself affects what is known by it in such a way that the knowledge does not capture the object of knowledge anymore. On the other hand, it is only in virtue of it being true—in virtue of it being knowledge in the full sense of the word—that it attains this transformative effect: only because I am *in fact* an animal, can I cease to be an animal in virtue of my knowing myself to be an animal. It is thus only by being true that this knowledge makes itself untrue. The knowledge is thus not just in tension with itself, it is strictly speaking paradoxical. It is untrue by being true. Concerning the human being, this paradoxical knowledge can be read in both directions: to become and to know ourselves to be human we have to know ourselves as animals and thereby cease to be animals. Failing to realize that we are animals, on the other hand, paradoxically turns us into beasts.[4]

Now, it is through unfolding the paradox of this specific self-knowledge—knowing myself to be an animal and thereby ceasing to be one—that I supposedly attain a higher form of self-knowledge: knowledge of myself as spirit. As it stands, the passage from the *Aesthetics* offers no independent and positive account of what it means to know myself as a spiritual being. It thereby suggests that the higher form of self-knowledge cannot be accessed directly; rather, it can only be accessed through our grasp of the self-undermining character of our immediate self-knowledge. True self-knowledge is attained through our grasp of the very irony of self-consciousness.

It is quite natural to assume that Hegel can't be serious about this. We might think that the quotation I gave is just an odd formulation. After all, it stems from a lecture course, posthumously published and put together by Heinrich Gustav Hotho on the basis of Hegel's own as well as various student notes. Note, however, that the gloss from the *Aesthetics* is in line with two other fundamental characterizations that Hegel gives of the nature of essentially self-conscious, spiritual beings: first, his claim (i) that consciousness is its own concept and thus exceeds *itself*, in contrast to what is limited to a merely natural life and, second, (ii) that the self exists as the "negativity of itself" ("Negativität seiner selbst").[5]

(i) In the introduction to his *Phenomenology*, Hegel writes: "Consciousness is for itself its concept, and as a result it immediately goes beyond the restriction, and, since this restriction belongs to itself, it goes beyond itself too."[6] Consciousness is not just an accompanying awareness of a certain item or content, it is the conceptual grasp of its content and therein conceptual grasp of itself. Consciousness thus does not merely accompany what it is conscious of, it constitutes it. Consciousness of the form that Hegel is trying to account for is in this sense essentially self-conscious. This does not just mean that in being conscious of an item I am at the same time conscious of being aware of it. It means: I constitute the content of my consciousness through my conception of my own consciousness. Consciousness of X and self-consciousness of my being conscious of X are one act of the mind. What Hegel now underlines more specifically, however, is the fact that in being its own concept, consciousness is not tied to any particular content it is aware of but gains a reality and freedom over and above its content. Insofar as we identify consciousness with what it is conscious of, this means that consciousness, in going beyond its limited content, is also going beyond itself. In knowing and conceiving itself, consciousness thus exceeds itself. For consciousness to be essentially self-conscious thus does not mean that consciousness simply confirms and affirms itself in its own self-conscious grasp of itself. Rather, consciousness moves beyond itself as it realizes that it is its own concept.[7] It is this capacity for a distinct type of self-transgression that distinguishes a self-conscious being—a being in which consciousness is its own concept—from what is merely alive: "What is limited to a natural life is *not* capable of going beyond its immediate existence *by virtue of itself*."[8] It is rather driven out of itself by something other than itself. Consciousness, on the other hand, surpasses itself not despite but *by virtue of itself*.

(ii) Another general determination of spiritual beings that is in line with the self-transgressive nature of self-consciousness is the characterization of a self as existing as the "negativity of itself."[9] This is a general characterization that Hegel gives of what he calls "subjectivity." Arguably a subject is a being which is characterized by the fact that it is not just distinct from the objects in the midst of which it may find itself, but distinguishes itself from these objects. If the subject is the capacity for self-distinction, however, it is not simply given as the opposite of what it is not. It is the capacity to define itself by negating its other, an operation that draws the very border of self and other and is thus not only in excess of the other but also of the self. Subjectivity is not just a power to discriminate but a power of self-distinction, not just a power of negation but of self-negation. Subjectivity thus exists as "the negativity of itself."

Obviously, these sparse comments do not show us yet how exactly to defend these ambitious claims and how to demonstrate them to be superior to the self-confirmation view of self-consciousness. I do think, however, that these two instances at least make clear that the paradox we have encountered in the *Aesthetics* is far from being an exceptional formulation; it reflects Hegel's considered view. On Hegel's account self-consciousness has a self-transgressive and self-negating character.

Earlier on, I expressed this by saying self-consciousness has an ironic structure. Now, this is a way of putting things that invites an objection. Isn't Hegel very clear about his deep distaste for irony? How could he possibly entertain an ironic conception of self-consciousness if he at the same time attacks Schlegel repeatedly for his ironic view of subjectivity? I think that in the context of this attack, Hegel uses the term "irony" in a quite different sense than I did when I was speaking of the irony of self-consciousness.

What Hegel is targeting with the term "irony" is actually a variety of the self-positing view of subjectivity. It is the tendency to regard the subject as the sole ground of all reality in such a manner that all reality appears as an effect of the subject's arbitrary positing and a mere means in its endeavor of self-enjoyment. As Hegel writes in the *Aesthetics*, "everything genuinely and independently real becomes only a show, not true and genuine on its own account or through itself, but a mere appearance due to the *ego* in whose power and caprice and at whose free disposal it remains. To admit or cancel it depends wholly on the pleasure of the *ego*, already absolute in itself simply as *ego*."[10] And in his *Philosophy of Right*, Hegel captures the self-understanding of the same attitude in the following terms:

> I go further than you, for I am also beyond this law and can do this or that as I please. It is not the fact of the matter [*Sache*] which is excellent, it is I who am excellent and master of both law and fact; I merely play with them as with my own caprice, and in this ironic consciousness in which I let the highest of things perish, I merely enjoy myself.[11]

To the extent that this consciousness exceeds its own content and thus itself, this seems close to the way in which I have characterized Hegel's position. But the similarity is only apparent. Yes, the ironic subject that Hegel attacks regards itself as beyond the contents of its consciousness. But it completely fails to notice the extent to which it is thereby also dragged beyond *itself*. What Hegel attacks as a merely ironic subject is a self-consciousness that fools itself into thinking that it is the master and the stable owner of its transgressive power, that regards itself as safe from and unscathed by the negativity it unleashes onto its objects. The self-consciousness that I have described and that is much more appropriately called ironic is itself subject to a process of self-transgression. It is not a master of a power to negate and transcend that can sovereignly enjoy its transgression but the self-consciousness of its own shakenness, a consciousness of the work of the negative it enacts upon itself.[12]

2. Animality and Spiritual Self-Knowledge

If you grant me, given the evidence presented thus far, that Hegel seems to attribute an ironic, self-transgressive character to self-consciousness, how do we now render this irony intelligible? How are we to understand that by truly knowing myself to be X, I cease to be X and that to know myself to be a spiritual being means developing this paradoxical self-knowledge? We have to look more closely at what exactly I know myself to be in this case to understand how this can make any sense. Let us return to the passage from his *Aesthetics* once again in a little more detail:

> Man is an animal, but even in his animal functions, he does not remain in them as an in-itself [*bleibt er nicht als in einem Ansich stehen*], as the animal does; he becomes conscious of them, recognizes them, and lifts them… into self-conscious science. In this way man breaks the barrier of his given immediacy [*ansichseienden Unmittelbarkeit*], so that precisely because he *knows* that he is an animal, he ceases to be an animal and attains knowledge of himself as spirit.[13]

Although Hegel holds that a basic form of subjectivity and a certain form of self-feeling already pertain to the animal, Hegel contends that it is characteristic of the animal to expose the very structure of spirit only in itself or as such (*an sich*) but not *for itself*.[14] Animality is thus defined as an *essentially unconscious form of subjectivity*. If it would not sound so weird, one should actually say: an *un-self-conscious* form of subjectivity. This explains why knowing myself to be an animal amounts to ceasing to be an animal: by knowing myself to be an animal—instead of just feeling my vital operations in the process of my life—I lose a defining feature of my animality according to Hegel's conception.

But how then can this self-defeating, self-undermining knowledge lead to knowledge of myself as a spiritual being? Why does this knowing not just cancel itself out? It belongs to Hegel's account of animal life that it does not only preclude self-conscious knowledge of itself but at the same time already exposes the very structure and concept of spirit. In his *Phenomenology*, his *Logic*, and his *Philosophy of Nature* Hegel develops in various ways the notion that animal life amounts to an immediate form of spirit. In knowing myself to be an animal, I thus know myself to have the structure of sprit. In this sense knowing myself to be an animal not only undermines itself such that it falls away, it also gives me a first determination of my spiritual existence.

But how can we negotiate and integrate these two moments in one and the same consciousness? In the first respect, knowledge of myself as an animal undermines itself and thus undoes the self-understanding it had just promised to provide; in the second respect knowledge of myself as an animal gives me a positive, albeit incomplete idea of my existence as something else. What connects these two thoughts is the fact that the structure exposed by the animal already involves a certain negative and self-transgressive character. In going beyond animal life and in ceasing to be an animal, spiritual life in some sense stays true to its animal nature: to a process that exceeds the forms it itself produces. At the same time, it goes beyond animal life, because it develops a form of self-transgression that is distinct from the two forms it takes in animal life: metamorphosis and death. The way Hegel describes it, natural life is not limited to the reproduction of a pre-given form but also involves a process of producing and superseding its form, taking on and exceeding its forms. This productive and transgressive process, however, depends on the continuity of the immediate existence of the living being; where it is pushed to go beyond its immediate existence, the natural living being reaches a true limit: death. As Hegel writes in the introduction of the *Phenomenology*, immediately preceding the passage in which he describes the way consciousness is beyond itself: "What is limited to a natural life is not on its own capable of going beyond its immediate existence. However, it is driven out of itself by something other than itself, and this being torn out of itself is its death."[15]

In a related passage from the *Preface* he writes:

> Death, if that is what we wish to call that non-actuality, is the most fearful thing of all, and to keep and *hold fast to what is dead requires the greatest force*.... [T]he life of spirit is not a life afraid of death and austerely saving itself from devastation; rather, it bears death calmly, *and in death, it sustains itself.*[16]

A spiritual unity, allegedly, can thus sustain itself in death and has the superior force to hold on to what is dead. However, we should not take this to suggest that self-consciousness could, in fact, survive the death of the life it relies on, like a soul separating from the embodied life that once carried it. What this means is rather that self-consciousness has a way of going beyond itself that is neither a change in defining form—*metamorphosis*—nor the interruption of the formative process and the complete dissolution of form—*death*—but rather *irony*: manifesting itself in its lived, past form and going beyond it. Importantly, this means that not only is self-consciousness always already beyond itself but equally that it lags behind itself: it actualizes and grasps itself in a form which it thereby has already superseded. Self-consciousness is consciousness of what it has ceased to be by knowing itself. The general form that this dialectics takes is that self-consciousness takes the shape of a (self-)consciousness of life, consciousness of its lived existence.[17]

The topic that Hegel is most concerned with is how to unfold the dialectical structure of self-consciousness without dissolving it to either side. In the *Phenomenology*, Hegel analyzes this as the problem of how to think the unity of pure self-consciousness—I am I—and objective consciousness. The master and the slave are one-sided models of a self-consciousness in which these two moments come apart: the master misconceives of himself as a pure self-consciousness and delegates the objective consciousness and engagement with the world to the slave. The chapter on the freedom of self-consciousness, in turn, analyzes stoicism, skepticism, and unhappy consciousness as three shapes of interiorizing the dialectic that, however, still remain insufficient. This insufficiency presents itself as a form of *lifelessness*.[18] Where stoicism retreats into pure thinking (in which the in itself and the for itself form an immediate unity)[19] and abstracts from its life, out of which it arises and upon which it remains dependent without acknowledging it, skepticism oscillates between an abstract self and an animal existence that amounts to a loss of self-consciousness. Unhappy consciousness grasps the contradiction but without finding a way to reconcile itself with this contradiction. A true form of self-consciousness would need to find ways of attaining this reconciliation—a reconciliation, to be clear, that is not a closing of the ironic gap of animality and spirituality but a reconciliation *with this gap*.

Such a reconciliation can only be brought about by the transformative work of producing a second nature that Hegel points to in the passage from his *Aesthetics* with which I started: it entails becoming *conscious* of, *recognizing*, and *lifting* this animality into self-conscious science. It is neither enough for a spiritual being to just withdraw from its lived existence, nor to just immerse itself in its living existence. Self-consciousness has to work through and transform its living existence.[20] It is crucial to see that this transformative work cannot consist of just dissolving life into science; rather, it must consciously reproduce the unconscious form of spirit we call life and relate to it in a different manner.[21] That is the reason why producing a second nature is neither a process that turns our nature into a pure expression of spirit nor a process through which our spirit is renaturalized. Producing a second nature transforms our nature and naturalizes our spirit in such a way that their difference is maintained. Only a being with a second nature of this kind has a truly ironic self-consciousness, for irony depends on the unity of its very tension, on holding together its two sides.[22] It maintains the parallax of animality and spirituality that defines the position of the human.[23]

A self-conscious, spiritual being understood in those terms is a being that has not one but two principles of unity: the unity of life and of self-consciousness, to use Hegel's terms; the unity of the unconscious and the conscious, to use a Freudian language;[24] and the unity of force and the unity of capacity, to employ a Herderian scheme.[25] For the human being, to know itself must be a form of knowing this doubleness.

It is an important feature of this type of account in its various instances that it doesn't take this other principle of unity that our self-consciousness both depends upon and supersedes as a given. No matter whether we describe this principle of unity as one of life, of the unconscious, or of force, it stands in an essential relation to the correlative unity of self-consciousness through which it is both known and superseded. This is not to say that life, force, or the unconscious is a mere projection or arbitrary positing of self-consciousness. For self-consciousness can only arise and sustain itself as the cognitive grasp and transgression of a self-active process of a different sort. In the human being, self-consciousness and the unconscious are thus strictly equi-primordial.[26]

3. And Say the Animal Responded?

Obviously, there is a lot more to be said at this point. But instead of remaining with Hegel's further development of the irony of self-consciousness, let me try to sharpen one aspect of this idea by turning to a different elaboration of this problem from Derrida's *L'animal que donc je suis* (*The animal that therefore I am (following)*). The very title of Derrida's work seems to capture the thought that I have tried to develop up to this point in a very economical fashion. The title is referring to a human self-knowledge that is knowledge of the fact that I am an animal—and at the same time or therefore—that I am *following* or *coming after* the animal. Derrida here plays with the ambiguity of the French *suis*, which could be derived from *être* as well as from *suivre*. We can take this title to enact the ironic movement Hegel is interested in: by knowing and acknowledging that I am an animal, I cease to be merely an animal. Rather, I follow or trace the animal that I am and that, by tracing, I supersede. The human being is characterized by Derrida as the *auto-bio-graphical animal* precisely in the sense that it traces and writes its own life. It is an animal that follows—both pursues and survives, both exceeds and returns to—its own animality.[27]

The reason why I want to attend to Derrida's elaboration of the irony of self-consciousness at this point is the specific way in which Derrida dramatizes the character of this self-conscious life by means of a peculiar social scene. Even though we have focused in the above on a Hegelian characterization that seemed to focus on the animality and the self-consciousness of a single subject, it is also true for Hegel's account that self-consciousness is only for another self-consciousness and articulates itself necessarily in terms of a social scene. Famously, the master-slave-dialectic presents us with a social constellation that unfolds the dialectical relation of self-consciousness and life. On the one hand, the social struggle that Hegel describes is dependent on both parties putting their life at stake for their recognition as spiritual beings. It is thus only in proving that we are not "limited to natural life" that we demonstrate our self-conscious existence. At the same time, the dynamic of the conflict ultimately shows us that the self-consciousness of the master that externalizes its own life is a dead end. It transpires that self-conscious liberation depends on the insight that "life is as essential... as is pure self-consciousness."[28] In order to liberate itself and to prove freedom to be its essence, the subject does not only have to stake its own life, it has to re-appropriate its own life at the same time as the mode of existence of its own freedom. It is thus only in knowing ourselves to be animals that we cease to be mere animals, only in holding on to and grasping our animality that we may actually supersede it.

Derrida seems to agree with Hegel that to fully understand the form of the autobiographical animal, the animal that therefore I am and follow, we have to develop this constellation not from a solipsistic scene in which a self-conscious being relates to its own animality but from a social scene. The scene that Derrida is interested in is, however, not a struggle that depicts a self-consciousness trying to exceed the limitation to its animal life by establishing a supra-animal sphere of mutual recognition, failing to do so in two related ways (as master and slave). The scene Derrida is interested in is one in which a self-conscious being is caught by an animal's gaze and shaken in its confident grasp of itself and its own difference from the animal it has presumably ceased to be. Where the Hegelian constellation starts from a self-consciousness that knows itself to be an animal and thereby ceases to be one, the Derridean constellation is one in which a human being is subjectivized anew by being caught by an animal gaze and related back to the animal it has remained. The scene Derrida starts from involves him "caught naked, in silence, by the gaze of an animal, for example, the eyes of a cat." He asks himself "*who I am*," or more precisely: "who I am (following) at [that] moment." And he reports: "I have trouble, yes, a bad time overcoming my embarrassment."[29]

It is tempting to read this scene as a simple reversal of the Hegelian constellation: the animal striking back, the animal capturing and arresting a self-conscious being in its gaze, and thereby turning this self-consciousness into something else again: a mere animal. Being seen naked by his cat, Derrida has, as he lets us know, the impulse to flee; he himself, the self-conscious being, seems to turn into the animal that is being followed and pursued. But to conceive of this as a simple reversal underestimates the intricacy of the scene that Derrida is interested in and the main point of his argument.

It is common to assume that it is Derrida's main point in *The Animal That Therefore I Am* to highlight the fact that various types of animals do have the capacities philosophical discourse has traditionally denied them. In this case, the scene of the cat would serve to show that the cat could objectify us just like the gaze of another subject. His deeper philosophical ambition, however, is, as Derrida makes explicit at various points, to show that what philosophical discourse was aiming to ascribe to human beings by denying it to the animal is, in fact, not present in a pure and undivided way in the human being either.[30] Derrida is thus interested in the effect that the gaze of his cat—not the cat or the animal in general but *"this* irreplaceable living being"[31]—seeing him naked has on his own sense of himself and the way in which this questions the self-assertion of his humanity and the disavowal of his own animality.[32] Attending to his own immediate reaction suggests that the separation between the animal and the human is not as neat as traditionally assumed.

Becoming the perceived object of the gaze of the animal is in this sense described by Derrida as deepening the irony of self-consciousness, not as a simple reactive reduction of self-consciousness to an instance of animality. In this situation, where he is seen by his cat, naked, he feels ashamed in a strange way: he feels both ashamed of being nude in the gaze of an indeterminate other *and* ashamed of being ashamed. This reflexive deepening of shame is tied to a strange "nudity" of self-consciousness in the animal gaze. It is only in being both an animal—a naturally existing living thing—and more than an animal—a self-conscious subject that cannot and should not be reduced to its natural existence—that one is capable of being nude and capable of being ashamed of one's nudity. Neither a *mere* animal—if there is such a thing, which seems doubtful on Derrida's account—nor an angel could be nude and could have reason to be ashamed of their nudity. Being under the gaze of an animal seems to point us to our own animality and hence to a mode of our existence that is shameful for a self-consciousness that is structurally beyond its animal existence. The self-conscious animal might thus feel stripped down under the gaze of an animal: it realizes that it can be seen as any other animal, that it, too, is nothing other than an animal to be followed. Derrida is thus "ashamed of being as naked as a beast."[33] At the same time it is evident that, under the assumed philosophical conception of the animal, our nudity shouldn't, strictly speaking, matter for the animal's gaze, as animals should presumably have no access to nudity. We are ashamed of our animality and ashamed of being ashamed since, on the level of animality itself, there is no reason to be ashamed. Interestingly, both feelings can lead to the same impulse: the impulse to flee on Derrida's part, to avoid this embarrassing gaze or the self-embarrassment of being embarrassed by this gaze.

There is a temptation to simplify this scene in a Sartrian manner: the gaze of the other, the other animal in this case, reduces me to a facticity and reinvigorates my attempt to liberate myself from being reified in this way—I flee in order to distance myself from the animal that I've ceased to be by means of my self-consciousness. The shame at being ashamed reinforces this tendency and documents my rejection of even allowing the mere feeling that an animal gaze could reify me. My reaction seems to ostensibly underline my sense that this form of reification is the privilege of a self-conscious gaze like my own. If it is the case that I must contest the attempt of another subject to reduce me to a facticity, it seems even more urgent to extricate myself out of a situation in which I accord a facticity the ability to reduce me to a facticity.[34]

What makes Derrida's understanding of the scene interesting, however, is that it is not exhausted by this interpretation. Derrida argues that being met by an animal gaze is not merely negatively instructive for our self-conscious existence: it is not just creating a situation we should avoid or reject in our attempt to prove our self-conscious existence once again. As the reflexive experience it involves shows, the gaze of the other animal, in its crucially indeterminate character, is rather positively subjectivizing. In its heterogeneity, the gaze of the other animal does not just reduce us but reconstitutes an open virtuality to our existence, not yet exhausted and arrested by our own knowledge of ourselves, our own keeping track of ourselves. To be truly self-conscious requires being receptive to the way in which our knowledge of ourselves can be challenged by this gaze. As Paul Valéry has put this point: "This gaze of dog, cat, fish conveys to me the notion of a point of view, and of being-viewed-by, and consequently of a private corner… that excludes the things that I know and contains only things that I do not. There is a mode of knowing me there."[35]

The experience of the gaze of the animal thus deepens the irony of self-consciousness. Precisely by my conscious grasp of myself do I become aware of and receptive to other modes of being seen not mastered by my conscious grasp. In my confrontation with an animal gaze that cannot be confined to what I already master, my self-conscious sense of myself is thus challenged, and I am exceeded by possible ways of being "known" beyond my grasp. To be a subject means to be able to be "known" in this way and to be moved by such "knowledge." The respective gaze that challenges my self-understanding and opens up the space for a way of "knowing" me beyond my grasp displays a "too much of address," ("Zu viel von Anspruch"), to use a Freudian expression.[36] The gaze of the animal addresses us in a silent way that exceeds our self-conscious conception of ourselves and provokes the subjectivizing question in us: What is it that you want from me, if you want anything at all? What do you see in me, if you see anything at all?

In Laplanche's classical model, the "too much of address" is constituted by the message of the adult that the child cannot understand and by the excess of excitation produced in the child that leads to the attempt to bind and organize this overflow of excitation through phantasy. The too much of address thus, in Laplanche's scheme of things, produces unconscious formations that manifest and deal with the enigmatic messages of the other. The "other thing in me," the unconscious, is thus inherently connected to, if not produced by, "the other person."[37] In this case, however, the too much of address is produced by an animal gaze that we cannot be certain of being able to place. In this case, it is not the gaze of a being we are sure speaks a higher language that we are not yet in a position to understand. We are rather challenged by the openness of animal existence, a "point of view regarding me," that of an unqualified and in this sense "absolute" "other."[38] Being caught by the gaze of the animal allows me to experience the fact that it is undecidable whether the enigmatic message that haunts me and drives me out of the limitations of my finite form of life challenges me from above or from below.[39]

In this way, Derrida points to a social scene in which the social is not depicted as that which allows us to elevate ourselves above our merely animal existence, as the social force necessary to suppress and supersede our immediate animal desires. It is rather a social scene that discloses the openness of animality itself and that forces us to experience both the inseparability *and* the gulf between our animality and our self-consciousness. Sociality does not appear as a normative realm that elevates us above our animal existence but as a spiritual animal kingdom that reconnects us to our animality in a different manner: as a demand and a potential, as well as a barrier and a limit to its own self-conscious grasp.

4. Conclusion

I have tried to reconstruct an ironic feature of Hegel's conception of human self-consciousness that is often overlooked. As the passage from the *Aesthetics* suggests, self-consciousness is not a simple act of self-agreement and self-confirmation but a self-transgressive process. Precisely by knowing myself to be an animal, I cease to be an animal, and only by enduring this self-undermining process of knowledge do I attain spiritual self-knowledge: knowledge of myself as being different from what I know myself to be. This ironic structure suggests that a self-conscious being can neither leave its animality simply behind nor simply rest content with its own animality. Self-consciousness is tied to a consciousness of my life that it, at the same time, has to supersede. Self-consciousness is, in this sense, neither an immanent nor a transcendent transformation of my life, neither metamorphosis nor death, but an ironic transformation of my mode of living, tied to an irreducibly double perspective self-consciousness gains on itself.

In the final section I have tried to develop some thoughts on what type of social constellation corresponds to such a notion of self-consciousness. It has to be one in which it comes to the fore that we are both animal and self-conscious beings and one in virtue of the other. More precisely, it has to enable a form of social address in which it remains open whether our animality is exceeded by a spiritual address or established spiritual practical identities are challenged by the way our animality looks back at us. We thus need a form of sociality that grasps the precarious intertwinement of our animal existence and our self-conscious self-relation as a source for irony.

Notes

1   For different versions of this idea cf. Sebastian Rödl, *Self-Consciousness* (Cambridge: Harvard University Press, 2007); Robert Pippin, *Hegel's Realm of Shadows: Logic as Metaphysics in "The Science of Logic"* (Chicago: University of Chicago Press, 2018), 131.

2   Jacques Derrida, *The Animal That Therefore I Am* (New York: Fordham University Press, 2008).

3   G.W.F. Hegel, *Aesthetics: Lectures on Fine Art*, trans. T.M. Knox, vol. 1 (Oxford: Clarendon, 1975), 80.

4   In *The Open*, Agamben underlines the other side of the irony of anthropological knowledge by pointing to Linnaeus. According to Linnaeus, the human being is not just the being defined by the fact that it cognizes itself. It is the being that cognizes itself as human by first cognizing itself as nonhuman. Only a human that recognizes that it is an animal and belongs to the *anthropomorpha* like other primates is, by this very fact, more than simply an animal. Those who deny that they belong into the company of primates thereby paradoxically prove to be unworthy of the category of the human: "Homo… must recognize himself in a non-man in order to be human" (Giorgio Agamben, *The Open* (Stanford: Stanford University Press, 2004), 26–7).

5   G.W.F. Hegel, *The Phenomenology of Spirit*, trans. and ed. Terry Pinkard (Cambridge: Cambridge University Press, 2018), §761, §176.

6   Hegel, *Phenomenology*, §80.

7   We see here that Hegel in this regard is not rejecting the thesis about self-consciousness with which we started but qualifying our understanding of it such that it becomes clear that self-positing entails or requires self-transgression.

8   Hegel, *Phenomenology*, §80, emphasis added.

9   Hegel, *Phenomenology*, §176. On the significance of this type of absolute negativity, see T. Khurana et al. (eds.), *Negativität. Kunst—Recht—Politik* (Berlin: Suhrkamp, 2018), 12ff.

10   Hegel, *Aesthetics*, 1:65.

11   G.W.F. Hegel, *Elements of the Philosophy of Right*, ed. A. Wood, trans. H.B. Nisbet (Cambridge: Cambridge University Press, 1991), §140R, trans. modified.

12   Whereas the criticized form of irony is on Hegel's account an instance of evil, the irony of self-consciousness is an instance of virtue: "The evil consists in insisting upon itself against the good; it is positive negativity," whereas virtue is "perfect struggle," "absolute negativity," that is to say: "opposition and struggle in and against itself [*an ihr selbst* Entgegensetzung und Bekämpfung]" (G.W.F. Hegel, *Science of Logic*, trans. George di Giovanni (Cambridge: Cambridge University Press, 2010), 379, trans. modified).

13   Hegel, *Aesthetics*, 1:80.

14   For a detailed elaboration of this notion of animality, see Thomas Khurana, *Das Leben der Freiheit. Form und Wirklichkeit der Autonomie* (Berlin: Suhrkamp, 2017), chapter IV.

15   Hegel, *Phenomenology*, §80.

16   Hegel, *Phenomenology*, §32.

17   Cf. Khurana, *Leben*, 435ff. For the Shakespearean subtext of the idea, especially the connection between the speculative sentence "Das Sein des Geistes [ist] ein Knochen" and Hamlet's meditation on Yorick's skull, see Anselm Haverkamp, "Hegel in the Light of Hamlet." In *Entertaining the Idea*, ed. L. Gallagher, J. Kearney, J. Reinhard Lupton (Toronto: Toronto University Press, 2020).

18   Hegel, *Phenomenology*, §199: "it consists in being free within all the dependencies of his individual existence, whether on the throne or in fetters, and in maintaining the lifelessness which consistently *withdraws* from the movement of existence, *withdraws* from actual activity as well as from suffering, and *withdraws* into *the simple essentiality of thought.*"

19   Hegel, *Phenomenology*, §197.

20 This is what Hegel means, when he requires that the self needs to perform the absolute negation of *Dasein* at or in *Dasein* itself. See his complaint against stoicism that in it self-consciousness "has not achieved itself as the absolute negation of this existence *in this very existence* [*hat... sich nicht als absolute Negation des Daseins an ihm vollbracht*]" (Hegel, *Phenomenology*, §201).

21 This is what Schelling calls "art"; cf. his *System of Transcendental Idealism*, trans. P. Heath, (Charlottesville: University Press of Virginia, 1978), Part VI.

22 Cf. Slavoj Žižek, "Discipline between Two Freedoms." In *Mythology, Madness, and Laughter*, eds. Markus Gabriel and Slavoj Žižek (London: Continuum, 2009), 95–121, 117–18.

23 We are thus concerned here with "a parallax split as immanent to reality itself," as Žižek put it *Incontinence of the Void* (Cambridge: MIT Press, 2017), 52. In our specific case, we are not dealing with the availability of two different standpoints on the same object that produce a parallax that allows us to locate the object. We are rather dealing with a stance that is internally split and grasps reality precisely to the extent that it grasps this very split. Self-consciousness is defined by the parallactic shift that it enacts: by knowing myself to be an animal—seeing myself in a first position—I cease to be one—I inhabit a different position—and attain knowledge of myself as spirit—grasp the nature of my split position.

24 Jonathan Lear, *A Case for Irony* (Cambridge: Harvard University Press, 2014).

25 Christoph Menke, *Force: A Fundamental Concept of Aesthetic Anthropology* (New York: Fordham University Press, 2012).

26 Freud himself has already suggested this by way of his characterization of the primary and the secondary process. Even though these terms seem to suggest that the primary process simply precedes the secondary process, on closer inspection, it is hard to make any sense of the way in which the primary process as characterized by Freud proceeds without presuming its relatedness to the secondary process (cf. Thomas Khurana, *Die Dispersion des Unbewußten* (Gießen: Psychosozial, 2002), 62ff.). There is thus no primary process without a secondary process; the "primary" process "has '*become* primary,'" as Laplanche once put it ("The Unfinished Copernican Revolution." In *Essays on Otherness* [London: Routledge, 1999], 53–85, here: 70). In this sense, there is no way of becoming self-conscious without thereby coming to possess an unconscious as well.

27 It is part of Derrida's critique of the dominant philosophical treatment of animals that he alerts us to the fact that animals, too, are capable of tracing themselves and thus, in some sense, of "autobiographing [themselves] as it were" (Derrida, *Animal*, 50). This is not to deny, however, that between the ipseity of animal auto-affection and self-movement, on the one hand, and the I of the I think, on the other, there remains "an abyss" (ibid, 50). Derrida's project therefore is not to suggest there is a "continuity between what calls *itself* man and what *he* calls the animal" (ibid., 30). Rather than effacing this rupture, Derrida aims at complicating our understanding of the anthropological difference. On his account, the limit between the human and what Derrida terms the *animot* is neither single nor divisible (ibid., 40). We should therefore question the philosophical tendency of reducing the vast multiplicity of creatures to the fiction of "*the* animal"; and we should rethink the nature of the limit itself. While Hegel does not seem particularly attentive to the first issue, he clearly paves the way for the second investigation.

28 Hegel, *Phenomenology*, §189.

29 Derrida, *Animal*, 3.

30 Derrida, *Animal*, 135: "It is *not just* a matter of whether one has the right to refuse the animal such and such a power (speech, reason, experience of death, mourning, culture, institution, technics, clothing, lying, pretense of pretense, covering of tracks, gift, laughter, crying, respect etc....). It *also* means asking whether what calls itself human has the right to rigorously attribute to man... what he refuses the animal, and whether he can ever possess the *pure, rigorous, indivisible* concept, as such, of that attribution." (cf. also 31, 95, 133, 173.) cf. Michael Naas' instructive reconstruction in "Derrida's Flair," *Research in Phenomenology* 40 (2010), 219–42, 231ff.

31 Derrida, *Animal*, 9.

32 In Derrida's whole treatment of the scene, he obviously seems less concerned with what it tells us about his cat than what it demonstrates regarding the one seeing himself being seen naked by an animal.

33 Derrida, *Animal*, 4.

34 On Sartre's account I recover myself by "apprehending as an object the one who apprehended my own objecthood," "for I cannot be an object for an object" (Jean-Paul Sartre, *Being and Nothingness* [New York: Washington Square Press, 1992], 289, trans. modified).

35 And he continues: "The gaze of creature at creature is the strangest of encounters. To exchange contemplations. This convergence, mutual alignment, virtual double negation!" (P. Valéry, "Animal's Gaze." In *Poems in the Rough*, trans. H. Corke [Princeton: Princeton University Press, 1969], 82f., trans. modified).

36 Sigmund Freud, *Der Mann Moses und die monotheistische Religion*. In *Gesammelte Werke XVI* (Frankfurt am Main: Fischer, 1999), 101–246, here: 178; Eric Santner, *On the Psychotheology of Everyday Life* (Chicago: University of Chicago Press, 2001), 32; Jean Laplanche, *New Foundations for Psychoanalysis* (Oxford: Basil Blackwell, 1989), 126.

37 Jean Laplanche, "Seduction, Persecution, Revelation." In *Essays on Otherness* (London: Routledge, 1999), 166–96, here: 169–70.

38 Derrida, *Animal*, 11.

39 Cf. Lear, *Irony*, 44ff.; Menke, *Force*, 50ff.; Derrida, *Animal*, 18.

A Squinting Gaze on the Parallax between Spirit and Nature

Frank Ruda

1.

A parallax names "the apparent displacement of an object (the shift of its position against a background), caused by a change in observational position that provides a new line of sight."[1] If I close my right eye and look at something I hold in front of me and then repeat the same with my left eye closed, what the respective eyes see differs. Even though I hold in my hand one and the same thing and may not have moved it at all, the thing seems to have changed its position. This is almost too trivial an observation: there can be a difference in and to a thing that appears to be externally caused by the different perspectives from which I look at it. It is spontaneously tempting to understand this as a simple effect of changing our subjective perspective. A parallax would then amount to a subjective change (of perspectives) alone.

2.

This spontaneous understanding is problematic, because it misses a crucial component without which the concept of the parallax loses its determinacy (and hence its status as concept). Slavoj Žižek has systematically argued for as to why the parallax should be elevated into the ranks of philosophical concepts: with it, we are not only dealing with a transformation of a subjective epistemological position, but what is at stake is ultimately the object in question. The epistemic shift of subjective perspectives enables an insight into the ontological rift determining the constitution of the object. With the squint of an eye, I am confronted with an inconsistency in the perceived object: an inconsistency that is not externally caused by me but rather points to a different kind of subjective involvement. Being a peculiar convergent squint, a parallax view can make intelligible that and how the very inconsistency of an object or of objectivity is linked to my distorted relation to it. This distortion springs from "a redoubling of myself as standing outside and inside my picture," which is why "the reality I see is never 'whole'... it contains a blind spot, which signals my inclusion in it."[2] Including my gaze into the picture that I look at from the outside changes the whole picture. It pierces a hole into it, as much as it displaces me. The subject is not an object among objects but some- (strange-) thing that is integrated into the domain of objectivity, precisely in the place where the latter is itself not fully constituted and coherent. The relation between subjectivity and objectivity is a parallax one.

3.

Does this mean that every subject-object-relation is parallactic in the very same sense? It seems rather obvious that convergent parallax squintings will look different, depending on the domain or specific relation in and onto which one looks awry. When, for example, the object in question is not a physical object but something political or the whole of (or the transcendental structure of) reality, what the specific parallax means (as there can be multiple types of parallax: ontological, political, economic, ecological, etc.)[3] needs elucidation. One must add specificity to the singular, theoretical, and practical shapes, to use Hegel's term, of the parallax. This implies more than just inscribing my own position of perceiving reality into reality—since, this could still be rendered as a (more or less sophisticated) form of subjective perspectivism. The determinateness of the parallax must come from somewhere else, too. One must account for the fact that the objective rift that emerges due to the subjective shift must be regarded also as an enabling condition for the very movement through which it appears.

4.

With such a reading of the parallax, we leave subjective perspectivism behind and move to a peculiar form of (a parallax) objective-subjective/subjective-objective materialism. Žižek calls this materialism dialectical, "adopting what is arguably the most stupid philosophical system of the twentieth century,"[4] "imbecility incarnate."[5] It is dialectical because it does not only emphasize a subjective impact on objectivity but also the entanglement of the objective constitution of subjectivity a retroactive precondition produced by subjectivity. So, with the insight into the objective inconsistency brought about by the subjective change of perspective, it becomes clear that the subjective transformation is conditioned by an objective inconsistency[6]—"the cause is a retroactive effect of its effects..."[7]

5.

This is the reason why in a dialectical materialist account of the parallax, we are ultimately dealing not only with one dimension of parallax "activity" and movement but with two interlinked ones: a two-dimensional, retroactive (objective) parallax condition of a parallax (subjective) movement, or a parallax within the transcendental itself that retroactively enables the parallax view that makes it visible. This means that there is no epistemological barrier separating us from the thing in itself; we relate to it through the very inconsistency of our relation. For if the thing in itself is parallax, there is a way of grasping it, namely through a parallax view. One general ontological implication of this is that there can never be a consistent ontology—be it materialist or idealist—simply because consistency is in a way just a necessarily false appearance.[8] We only see consistency as long as we do not see things clearly by squinting our eyes. There can be no consistent ontology (of consistency) and no ontology which, by sticking to one principle of coherence, could ever sustain itself and nonetheless explain the emergence of subjectivity. It seems a parallax is conceptually only a real parallax if we are effectively dealing with a (dialectical) parallax movement between two parallax movements (between subjectivity and objectivity).

6.

This must mean that not only subjectivity and objectivity each cannot constitute themselves coherently but also their relationship is beset by an "insurmountable parallactic gap"—a gap around which Žižek's "entire work circulates,"[9] because it is the displaced center of his dialectical materialism. In this sense, the parallax gives an account of what we mean when we speak of "negativity." If the parallax can thus never be one and unified—it is the clinamen in any one—and we must thus be dealing with a movement between two, we must also account for their relation (for the third element)—which, again, we can only do from making the move from one to the other and back (as there is no other, neutral way of doing it). The parallax de-substantializes not only substance but also the subject, and finally their relationship. There is no preordained place for the subject in any substantial framework nor is there any (even evacuated or unsubstantial) substance in the subject.[10] There is only an un-relation between subject and substance. This is implied by the parallax between two subjective and objective parallax constitutions—a swerve between a shift and a rift.

7.

This un-relational, parallactic parallax manifests in different *modes*.[11] There is, following an enumeration that one can find in Žižek, the *neurobiological parallax* (on the one hand side, we have the human face, on the other, there is the material "brainmeat,"[12] so that we have two closely linked incompatible sides); there is *the parallax of ontological difference* ("one cannot reduce the ontological horizon to its ontic 'roots', but one also cannot deduce the ontic domain from the ontological horizon, that is, transcendental constitution is not creation"[13]); there is *the parallax of political economy* (the genuine logic of politics that manifests in the historical practice of class struggle and then the critique of political economy with its logic of commodities: both hang together without any direct point of contact); *the parallax between dialectical materialism and historical materialism* (they are "essentially the same,"[14] but the latter emphasizes the difference between thought and sociohistorical being wherein being determines thought, whereas the former emphasizes that such determination only exists insofar as thought takes sociohistorical situations as what conditions it); *the parallax of the Real* ("the Lacanian Real has no positive-substantial consistency, it is just the gap between the multitude of perspectives on it"[15]); and *the parallax between desire and drive* (whenever we seek to grasp what we really enjoy in our own singular way, it seems to escape us and we seem to be entangled in things we do attempt to avoid).[16] And certainly there cannot but also be a *parallax between spirit and nature* (as the opposite and potential retroactive precondition of spirit).

8.

How does one conceive of this last parallax between spirit and nature? This is a real question because the spontaneous understanding of nature—as that which is opposed to what has (like spirit) a history in the strong sense of the term—does not seem to be historically constituted (and thus seems to simply ontologically precede spirit). We would lose the parallax if one side simply constituted the other (as in the thought that man emerges from nature). There appears to be a rather harsh difference, an antagonism between spirit and nature without any parallax. But, as Žižek once remarked about the dialectical method, "[w]hat if the point precisely *is* to not 'resolve' antagonism 'in reality', but simply to enact a parallax shift by means of which antagonisms are recognized 'as such' and thereby perceived in their positive role?"[17] How does one enact a parallax shift between spirit and that which appears to be its opposite, nature?[18]

9.

In line with Žižek's comment, it seems possible to answer this question by recourse to Hegel. One standard reading of the spirit-nature relationship in Hegel holds that spirit seeks itself—its own categories and concepts, structures, and inferential relations—in nature and thereby reaches the point where it becomes able to identify the very material potential for its own becoming in a reflective turning back onto it. The problem with such a reading is that it basically suggests Hegel knew nature only as something ultimately concocted by spirit. Thereby, it becomes unintelligible what "nature" actually was supposed to be, apart from the material medium for spirit's auto-recognition.

10.

The place where Hegel systematically deals with nature, in the philosophy of nature, is to be found in his *Encyclopaedia*.[19] The transition into "nature" in the *Encyclopaedia* is made from the previous part, the so-called small *Logic*. It has often been read in the same critical manner in which the end of the *Science of Logic*, the so-called big *Logic*, has been attacked with regard to its very end. Here the absolute idea seems to copulate with itself with the effect of releasing itself from its loins into nature.[20] This has often been taken to be both the highest peak and the purest eclipse of idealist philosophy. We only get to "nature" when after the big *Logic*, there is no immediate philosophy of nature, but another logic, the "small *Logic*."[21] After the *Science of Logic* has run its course, it must be repeated in a different, notably smaller or encyclopedic form to then be able to also repeat again the releasing birth act of nature from the bosom of the absolute idea in another form. The gist of this is that we cannot simply—as is already clear from this rather abstract reconstruction of the place of nature in Hegel's system— consider and take nature as a given; rather, we must account for how it is brought about. Whatever one makes of all the charges against Hegel, it seems clear "nature," that which is supposed to condition spirit, is a product.

11.

But is this not precisely the worst metaphysical idealism to assume that nature is a product of spirit? Wasn't this the whole point—that it is problematic to conceive of nature from the perspective of "God... before the creation of nature and of... finite spirit"[22]? This sounds like onto-theology at its metaphysical worst, and this might be why "the transition from logic to the philosophy of nature is... without a doubt one of the most difficult and frustrating transitions in Hegel's system for both critics and proponents of his thought."[23] What is it precisely that is created when "nature" is created? (The philosophy of) Nature appears after the end of the small *Logic* and before the beginning of the so-called *Philosophy of Spirit*. One way of reading this is to assume that we move from logics to nature to spirit. Nature then is conceived of the site where spirit emerges. Yet, taking into account that before the *Science of Logic* could commence its task, there had to be the *Phenomenology of Spirit*—a book that Hegel for a long time conceived of as introduction to his system, a system supposed to commence with the *Logic*[24]—it becomes obvious that in Hegel's system, there is more than the one sequential order (of logic-nature-spirit). We can also read the triadic structure by beginning with spirit that learns how to think logically and scientifically and is then able to investigate nature properly. But we can also take into account that "nature" describes the (material) condition of spirit. Spirit starts to understand it adequately as its precondition by creating a science of thought, that is, through a science of nature; hence, we get nature-spirit-logic. All of these individual sequences are repeated after having traversed all its members. Yet, the concept of "nature" seems to vary depending on the sequence.[25] And is Hegel not suggesting that we need the cognition and philosophy of nature to tell us what we are talking about when we talk about "nature"[26]? Nature seems to be torn between being a product and being a precondition of spirit, a logical deduction and a material resource. Depending from where and with what we look at it—closing the logical, the spiritual, or the natural eye—nature changes its nature.[27]

12.

To say something about nature is to say something about the transition into and/or out of nature. One can only speak of nature only if one also speaks of logic and spirit. Here we draw nearer to what appears to be the singular parallax, the parallactic parallax between spirit and nature. What does need to happen so that we can make the transition into the natural domain, so that we can begin with nature? Hegel accounts for it by introducing in §237 of the *Encyclopaedia* what he calls the "absolute idea."[28] The idea in general "is the *truth*," which means "that objectivity corresponds to the concept."[29] What does the concept here correspond to? Answer: to the insight into what the objectivity of thinking is. Thought thinking itself reaches a point where the concept of thinking corresponds to the act of thinking (the concept of thinking)—the subjective act of thinking and the objective constitution of thinking absolutely coincide or collide. Thinking analytically separates these two dimensions—because "it merely takes up its object," that is, thinking, "giving the latter full play, as if it were merely looking upon its movement and development"[30]—yet also syntheticized the two by applying "the strenuous effort of holding off one's own notions [*Einfälle*] and particular opinions which are always trying to assert themselves."[31] The absolute idea brings together theory and practice, practice of theory and theory of practice of what thinking is. With the absolute idea, we do not simply get a concept of thinking but we think the concept of thinking in such a way that we let ourselves be forced to think in a way that also detaches us, over and again, from all mere subjective associations and we thus attain a thought-objectivity. Hegel therefore identifies this unity—of thought—with what he calls the speculative method.

13.

Why does one need to introduce the concept of method here? The moment the investigation of the logical structure of thought reaches the point where we realize that this examination is what thinking is—determining and being determined by itself—we need to formulate a concept of what we have done by examining thought. This leads thought to formulate a system(atic) (approach to and) of thinking and this means to formulate thinking in terms of a method of thought that examines itself (and thus it also examines and thinks what it means to examine itself). The absolute idea is a name for the retroactive and totalizing—and in this sense methodological[32]—comprehension and articulation of what needs to have happened for thought to think thought. If the *Logic* depicts God's thoughts before the creation of the world and nature, at one point God during the process of creation stops and reflects on what she has been doing. And, in the end, God at this point could not but have had the idea that now it is done (and good in the Platonic sense of the term).[33] At this point, we reached the end of the *Logic* and of first part of the *Encyclopaedia*. Then there comes the final §244, wherein Hegel famously states, mirroring, but modifying, the last passages of the *Logic*,[34] that "the absolute freedom of the idea is that... in the absolute truth of itself, *resolves to release* [itself, F.R.] freely *from itself... as nature*."[35] The idea decides to release itself from itself, and the form in which this happens is nature.

14.

Hegel had defined in §18 of the *Encyclopaedia* the philosophy of nature as that part which scientifically deals with "the idea in its otherness."[36] The idea in its otherness is because we encounter an externality—at least if we defined the idea as the immanent entanglement of theory and practice, method and invention, tradition and progress (as Hegel did). So, we find something that is external to this dialectical knot between theory and practice of thinking. In nature—at least in nature at its most basic, which is conceptualized first as space and then as time—thought cannot and does not recognize itself. Thought had methodically established a self-determining order, but it cannot find it in nature. And it might not be entirely accidental that the second part of the *Encyclopaedia*—in its most recent published form—begins with a "Zusatz," an addendum. It is clear that the "Zusätze" are put together by the later editors of the *Encyclopaedia* from students' notes. Yet, does this suggest that Hegel commented on his text during the transition from *Logic* to nature orally (and extensively)? It appears unclear if the addendum with which the philosophy of nature begins is an addendum to the preceding paragraph (i.e., to the last paragraph of the *Logic*, i.e. §244). It is unclear, because this paragraph already has a "Zusatz" and the first paragraph in the philosophy of nature is consistently §245, which appears after the addendum. Is thus this "Zusatz" at the beginning an addendum to the addendum? Can one make the transition only by an addendum? Or is it a pure addendum without a preceding paragraph? What was Hegel commenting on when he made the transition into the philosophy of nature? The preceding paragraph? It does not seem to be the case, as the entire addendum is on the concept of the philosophy of nature in general. Might this be the only way in which we get from logic to nature, by stepping out of the succession of paragraphs and addenda? Like a pure comment without anything to comment on? Does this mean, if we want to know how nature commences—does it begin with and as a "Zusatz"—the answer might actually be: no idea?[37] Would this already be the idea in its otherness?

15.

Hegel describes the transition as a release but also in terms of a return. There is a "return to the beginning," which is "at the same time a move forward."[38] It is as if at the end of a process of thinking thought that discovers itself by inventing itself along the way, and at one point in this process, thinking reflects on the very conditions that allowed it to do what it thereby is about to complete. It has an idea of what it has done, but it does only really have an idea of what it has done if it also thinks the conditions— even if they are self-posited or produced—that enabled it to do what it did. It needs an idea of what precedes the idea. Those conditions are what conditioned thought, but thought only knows this after it started determining itself as thought (and thus also determines what it is conditioned by). At the end of the small *Logic*, it has no idea what it is conditioned by, which is why it now must take a closer look—and Hegel therefore speaks at the high point of the idea also the language of "intuition [Anschauung]."[39] Thought at the highest peak of its own self-referential theoretical and practical activity looks back over its shoulder and in returning determines what will have conditioned it all along since its own commencement.[40] Thinking to grasp purely what it is can only commence by subtracting all external determination, the whole world, history, and nature as well as any preconception to itself. Only in this way thought thinkingly determines itself. But when it purely thinks through itself, thought at one point—when it reaches the absolute idea of itself—also thinks the situation in which it thinks (and subtracting everything outside of itself might appear to be a negative way of doing so).[41] So, when thinking thinks thought, thought at one point also thinks what "it" was like when it did not think. Thought thinks "it" by attempting to leave itself out of the picture, by forming a concept of what the world was like without it. It is as if thought on its purest heights cannot but think its own demise.[42] The highest form of thought thinking thought—the absolute idea—is at the same time its lowest: thought thinking its own absence, thought becoming forgetful, oblivious, forgetting itself. This oblivion manifests as nature.

16.

This imagination of thought's own absence is different from the way in which Hegel criticizes the problematic post-Kantian conception of objective cognition that aims to subtract the subjective act of cognizing an object of experience from the cognition of this very object.[43] It is as if, strangely here, after the end of the small *Logic*, what previously seemed an unrealizable task is actually realized. But not in the same way. Hegel is not simply forgetful of his own deconstruction of problematic presuppositions. "Nature" is indeed spirit's conceptual name for the absence of spirit.[44] But everything hinges on how to read this with regard to the constitutive parallax relation between spirit and nature. Thought seeks to understand itself and therefore, as Hegel almost everywhere argues, needs to externalize itself. Pure thought externalized as such leads to pure externality, which for Hegel determines the concept of nature as it first manifests itself as space.[45]

17.

What is it to think of nature as a space (inhabited by all kinds of things) where thought is not? One can start answering this by taking recourse to an analysis, provided by Gérard Wajcman, of a phenomenon of contemporary mass media: the fascination with animal-life documentaries.[46] Wajcman suggests that the documentaries allow for the belief that in the natural realm, everything is in order and there is no distress or disorientation. Animals always seem to know what to do, when and with whom to do it, etc. The natural animal world seems happily be deprived of all the things that trouble human beings. Wajcman suggests watching animals is enjoyable precisely because they do not have the problems we have. Nature is truly external to the sphere(s) of (sexualized) spirit: "Between men and women it's been pretty messy… Not at all as it is with animals where everybody seems to know perfectly well how to do it. How, and with whom, and when."[47] Thought conceiving of the conditions of its own commencement, and thus of itself, conceives of the absence of thought in a particular way: the absence of thought is an enjoyable thought.[48]

18.

Why are we dealing with a parallax here? Not simply because thought imagines nature to be everything that thought is not but because thought imagines nature as that which precedes and thus conditions thought in such a way that we will be able to take it as a key to thought's emergence—as the anatomy of the human is the key to that of the ape, as Marx will later remark. Yet, nature is not on every level as harmoniously non-spiritual; otherwise, it would be difficult to account for the emergence of something that is not nature from within nature.[49] Nature is not the complete absence of order and lawfulness;[50] or, more specifically, not every absence is the same.[51] And nature is—this is crucial—a specific kind of absence: an absence that is linked to a peculiar material presence. For nature is not simply an invention of thought—thought finds something outside of itself[52] that it considers to mean something for itself. "Nature" is something that thought finds outside of itself and internalizes it by identifying it with the idea of its own absence.[53] Thought is thus materially dealing with something when it is dealing with its own absence—and this absence repels it, yet it is also attracted by it, because thought "is presaged in Nature."[54] What does this mean for what "nature" is? It means that thought projects onto nature that it is an embodiment of its own absence, but then forgets this same projection and hence becomes actually and effectively absent from its own projection onto nature. This cannot but mean for Hegel that nature "remains a problem."[55]

19.

Why is it a problem? Because it strangely seems to lead into the following scenario: thought seeks to understand itself better, identifies something that it finds outside of itself as material representation of its own absence—and thereby internalizes it into its process of self-understanding—but then starts thinking in a natural manner. Why natural? Because nature is at first the realm of externality, and as soon as thought identified nature as material embodiment of its own absence, it conceives of thought and nature as if the two were simply external opposites. The difference between thought and nature is thereby dealt with as if it were a difference between two bodies. Thought has a spontaneous tendency to become a problematically naturalist when it seeks to understand what it is conditioned by and posits this precondition as nature. The problem appears thus clearly: there is no logical transition from *Logic* to nature—since thought does not simply produce nature, we leave the terrain of logic. But as soon as there is nature, thought forgets that it is compelled to take material nature as embodiment its own absence. So, thought sees a logic of nature at work at its own origin. Yet, there is also no natural transition from nature to spirit (or thought), since otherwise we would never leave nature and thus there would be no spirit. Nature is and remains a problem.

20.

We think from the perspective of either nature or thought: both are tied together, mutually implied in the other, yet cancelling each other out, leading to the inner inconsistency of the respective other. Logical thought has to forget that it can only get to nature if it forgets itself. And if it does so, it forgets what it is looking at. It takes nature to be a natural given. Subsequently spirit becomes just another natural emergence (which we can only explain if we assume that nature inconsists, too). Nature does, in turn, not care about spirit's emergence; only spirit does—the planet, for example, will go on even when human life destroys itself. To depict this parallax relation between spirit and nature, Hegel has used a wonderful concept.[56] He states—according to his students' notes—that "Spirit finds in Nature... its counter-image [*Gegenbild*]." It is not an *Ebenbild*, similitude, but a counter-image to what thought thinks of itself and how it sees itself. Hegel argues, in line with Žižek, that we see nature with either the logical or the natural eye closed. Nature looks radically different each time, as does spirit in consequence as well. What we see in it is the counter-image enclosed in every image we have of spirit.

Notes

1   Slavoj Žižek, *Parallax View* (Cambridge: MIT Press, 2006), 17.
2   Žižek, *Parallax View*, 17.
3   Žižek considers the discursive status of philosophy itself to be that of the parallax view (so, of the parallax in a general manner that then needs specification)—a thesis he unfolds in his reading of Kojin Karatani. Cf. Žižek, *Parallax View*, 17 and Kojin Karatani, *Transcritique: On Kant and Marx* (Cambridge: MIT Press, 2005).
4   Slavoj Žižek, *Sex and the Failed Absolute* (London: Bloomsbury, 2020), 102.
5   Žižek, *Parallax View*, 5.
6   This is how one can read Žižek's claim that "*L'objet petit a* can be defined as a pure parallax object... the inscription of subjectivity into the object" (Žižek, *Parallax View*, 18).
7   Žižek, *Parallax View*, 24.
8   For this cf. Žižek, *Sex*, 17–65.
9   Slavoj Žižek, *Interrogating the Real* (London: Bloomsbury, 2005), 17.
10 Cf. Rebecca Comay and Frank Ruda, *The Dash—The Other Side of Absolute Knowing* (Cambridge: MIT Press, 2018), 17ff.
11 This leads to a complex combinatorics: there is a subjective parallax, an objective parallax, and a parallax of their non-relation. These three in a peculiar way mirror the different dimension of the imaginary, the symbolic and the real, so that we have to say something about the imaginary imaginary, the imaginary symbolic, the imaginary real, the symbolic symbolic, etc. and in the same way about the subjective subjective, the subjective objective, the subjective relationship, the objective objective, etc. A model for this was developed by Žižek in: Slavoj Žižek, *For They Know Not What They Do. Enjoyment as Political Factor* (London: Verso, 2008), xi–cvi.
12 Žižek, *Interrogating the Real*, 17.

13   Žižek, *Interrogating the Real*, 17.
14   Žižek, *Parallax View*, 6.
15   Žižek, *Parallax View*, 7.
16   This is not an exhaustive list—which would be impossible to give anyway. Cf., for example, also "Hegel's Parallax" (cf. Žižek, *Sex*, 97–102). Žižek also made repeated use of Sartre's claim that if one is attacked from both sides of the political spectrum, one must have hit something worth attacking, which points to the fact that the real object of a political debate can sometimes only be addressed through such a swerving, squinting movement, hitting it awry, as it were.
17   Slavoj Žižek, *The Sublime Object of Ideology* (London: Verso, 2008), xvii.
18   Obviously, one influential way of replying to this question was formulated in Engels' *Dialectic of Nature*. I will leave this text aside here, but will return to it in the nearby future.
19   G.W.F. Hegel, *Hegel's Philosophy of Nature. Part Two of the Encyclopaedia of Philosophical Sciences (1830)* (Oxford: Oxford University Press, 2004).
20   For an opposite argument, cf. William Maker, "The Very Idea of the Idea of Nature, or Why Hegel Is Not an Idealist." In *Hegel and the Philosophy of Nature*, ed. Stephen Houlgate (New York: State University of New York Press, 1998), 1–28.
21   For a detailed reading of problems related to this, cf. again Comay and Ruda, *The Dash*.
22   G.W.F. Hegel, *The Science of Logic* (Cambridge: Cambridge University Press, 2010), 29.
23   Benjamin Berger, "'The Idea that *Is*': On the Transition from Logic to Nature in Hegel's System," *Pli. The Warwick Journal of Philosophy*, vol. 31: *Hegel and the Sciences: Philosophy of Nature in the 21st Century* (2019): 69–87, here: 70. If this really is a "transition" is a crucial part of the question.
24   The details of the relationship are more complicated. For this cf. again: Comay and Ruda, *The Dash*.
25   I am here reformulating the argument of note 12, only for the three terms: logic, nature, spirit.
26   Hegel, *Hegel's Philosophy of Nature*, 4.
27   It is important to remark that neither of the three triadic sequences is convincing on its own. Reading them together explains Hegel's emphasis on the image of the "circle of circles" (cf. Hegel, *The Science of Logic*, 751) as *modus operandi* and *representandi* of philosophy. It points to the fact that one must dialecticize the three sequential orders. For a more detailed reading of this, cf. Frank Ruda, "Imagine There Is No Nature. Preliminaries for a Dialectical Ecology" (forthcoming).
28   It marks the third and final section of the doctrine of the concept, which itself is the third and final part of the logic. Cf. G.W.F. Hegel, *Encyclopaedia of the Philosophical Sciences in Basic Outline*, vol. 1 (Cambridge: Cambridge University Press, 2010), 299ff.
29   Hegel, *Encyclopaedia*, 283.
30   Hegel, *Encyclopaedia*, 301.
31   Hegel, *Encyclopaedia*, 301.
32   The *methodos* of this method is one that is identified fully only in retroaction. Only at the end will we know where the path we have been wondering on will have led us to.
33   Hegel therefore states that with the idea of method is presented as a "*systematic totality*" (Hegel, *Encyclopaedia* 1, 243)—a totality of differential determinations that determine the concepts generated on the way. All concepts generated in the path of

the *Logic* are systematically linked through the retroactive closure at the end which is brought about by the concept of the speculative method.

34 It would be worth a study of its own to examine the precise differences in the endings of the small and of the big *Logic*. I leave this aside here. Elsewhere, I showed that the *Logic* can be read as a depiction of the practical unfolding of what Badiou calls truth-procedure (which does clarify that the *Logic* is not as such—simply—an ontology, but rather accounts for transformations occurring in the discourse of ontology). Cf. Frank Ruda, "Hegel's Immanence of Truths." In *Badiou and the German Tradition of Philosophy*, ed. Jan Völker (London: Bloomsbury, 2019), 51–68.

35 Hegel, *Encyclopaedia* 1, 303. The English translation makes it quite difficult to get that the idea releases itself from itself in a specific form, namely as nature. It rather generates the kind of impression that led to all the idealist and metaphysical readings. In the 1830 version, Hegel uses "sich... frei aus sich zu entlassen [to freely release itself from itself]." G.W.F. Hegel, *Enzyklopädie der philosophischen Wissenschaften im Grundrisse [1830]*, vol. 1 (Frankfurt am Main: Suhrkamp, 1986), 393.

36 Hegel, *Encyclopaedia* 1, 46.

37 Some of Hegel's readers suggested—following Hegel's own explicit statement that "there is no transition that takes place" (Hegel, *The Science of Logic*, 752)—that therefore there is no transition from logic to nature (as it cannot be made from within the logic nor can it occur in nature)—and we here see how the link, the non-relation between the two clearly, comes to the fore. Cf. Donald Philip Verene, "Hegel's Nature." In *Hegel and the Philosophy of Nature*, ed. Stephen Houlgate (Albany: SUNY Press, 1999), 209–25, here: 220.

38 Hegel, *Encyclopaedia* 1, 303.

39 Hegel, *Encyclopaedia* 1, 303.

40 "The Philosophy of Nature itself belongs to this part of return; for it is that which... assures to Spirit the knowledge of its essence in Nature" (Hegel, *Encyclopaedia* 1, 14).

41 Which Hegel indicates by including the so-called "preliminary conceptions" at least into the *Encyclopaedia*—and it can be argued that in a very different way the *Phenomenology* fulfils a similar function for the greater *Logic*. Cf. Hegel, *Encyclopaedia* 1, 47–134.

42 Which might be one reason as to why "Physics and the Philosophy of Nature... is worse than it supposes itself to be." Cf. Hegel, *Encyclopaedia* 1, 3.

43 G.W.F. Hegel, *Phenomenology of Spirit* (Oxford: Oxford University Press, 1977), 45ff.

44 An instructive contemporary reading can be found in: Wes Furlotte, *The Problem of Nature in Hegel's Final System* (Edinburgh: Edinburgh University Press, 2018).

45 This is very different from the idea that spirit seeks in nature a yet evolving spirit as many readers of Hegel have argued. It is also remarkable that Hegel gives clear conceptual precedence to space over time—not only in line with contemporary physics but also different from the Kant of the first Critique. Cf. Hegel, *Hegel's Philosophy of Nature*, 13f.

46 Cf. Gérard Wajcman, "The Animals that Treat Us Badly," *Lacanian Ink* 33 (Spring 2009), 126–45, here: 131. For Žižek's reading of this, cf. Slavoj Žižek, *Absolute Recoil. Towards a New Foundation of Dialectical Materialism* (London: Verso, 2014), 203.

47 Wajcman, "The Animals," 131. In a sense, one can state that this is one way of finding the "universal" in the particular and empirical that Hegel talks about in §21. Cf. Hegel, *Encyclopaedia* 1, 55.

48 It is like thought regressive as if it were so drunk that it forgets what it is and becomes "Spirit estranged from itself; in Nature Spirit lets itself go (*ausgelassen*), a Bacchic God unrestrained and unmindful of itself" (Hegel, *Hegel's Philosophy of Nature*, 14).

49 This resonates with Žižek's repeated critique of the idea of a "mother nature." Cf. Slavoj Žižek, *Disparities* (London: Bloomsbury, 2019), 22ff.

50 Which is why it is also important that one thereby should not wrongly just hypostatize contingency as something that is abstract in nature and the most difficult to think or come to terms with; the absence of structure is still determined ex negativo determined. Hegel will argue for a non-coherent concept of nature. Cf. Hegel, *Encyclopaedia* 1, 216f.

51 Think of the endlessly used example of the Lubitsch joke about the difference between a "coffee without milk" and "without cream." Absence is never simply identical, or is it?

52 Hegel at the very end of the small *Logic* states that the idea "is the process of intuiting"—and intuiting suggesting one looks at something external (or externality as such). Cf. Hegel, *Encyclopaedia*, 1, 303.

53 The idea of a thought that is not yet really thought and thus immersed into nature—so thought is there but not as thought—is what Hegel also describes as "the primal (ursprünglichen) state of innocence." Cf. Hegel, *Encyclopaedia* 2, 8.

54 Hegel, *Encyclopaedia* 2, 3.

55 Hegel, *Encyclopaedia* 2, 3. Cf. also: G.W.F. Hegel, "*Vorlesungen über die Philosophie der Natur.*" In *Gesammelte Werke*, vol. 24.1 (Hamburg: Meiner, 2012), 3.

56 "This is… the goal of the Philosophy of Nature that spirit, that Spirits finds in Nature its own essence, i.e. the Notion, finds its counterpart [*Gegenbild*] in it" (Hegel, *Encyclopaedia* 2, 13).

"I Am Nothing, but I Make Everything"
Marx, Lacan, and the Labor Theory of Suture

Adrian Johnston

1. Facing the Gap: Real Abstraction and the Laboring Subject

One of Karl Marx's many famous one-liners occurs in his 1844 "A Contribution to the Critique of Hegel's Philosophy of Right. Introduction," a short but rich text containing several such one-liners. Therein, Marx, speaking in the name of the proletariat, declares, "*I am nothing and I should be everything*" (Ich bin nichts, und ich müßte alles sein).[1] Several years later, and even more famously, *The Communist Manifesto* of 1848 echoes this linking of capitalism's oppressed and exploited class with nothingness when Marx and Friedrich Engels cry out, "The proletarians have nothing to lose but their chains" (*Die Proletarier haben nichts... zu verlieren als ihre Ketten*).[2] This nothingness of the 1840s seems to designate and encompass basic notions of poverty, dispossession, alienation, and the like.

Admittedly, these 1844 and 1848 associations of the proletariat with "*nichts*" precede the mature Marx's historical materialist critique of political economy. They thus are lacking in the conceptual precision and multifaceted details of this later theoretical framework. Marx's critique of political economy arguably is born in its full and proper form only starting with his discovery of the category of surplus-value in the *Grundrisse* notebooks of 1857–8.[3] However, surplus-value is inseparable from another essential component of the capitalist mode of production, namely, commodified labor-power.

One of the claims I will advance in this intervention is that there is a significant cross-resonance between, on the one hand, the earlier Marx's 1840s invocations of laborers' nullity and, on the other hand, the status of commodified labor-power as the source of surplus-value under capitalism as per the *Grundrisse* and volumes of *Das Kapital* emblematic of the later Marx. Arguing for this first claim leads into and, in turn, is reciprocally supported by a second, perhaps surprising, claim: the Lacanian theory of subjectivity (especially as encapsulated by Jacques-Alain Miller's model of "suture," with its recourse to Gottlob Frege's account of arithmetic and the number zero) is crucial to discerning and analyzing this link within Marx's corpus between the nothingness of the proletariat and the position of commodified labor-power as the origin of surplus-value within the capitalist mode of production. Marx's associations of labor with nothing (*nichts*) should be taken very literally, perhaps even more literally than he originally intended. The third and final claim I will defend here, flowing from the first two just mentioned, is that commodified labor-power (as per a historical materialism retroactively illuminated by psychoanalysis) can be put forward as the hidden material-economic basis for the coming to light of split forms of subjectivity from Immanuel Kant and the German idealists through Sigmund Freud and Jacques Lacan.

This final claim entails supplementing Alfred Sohn-Rethel's well-known thesis about the commodity form in general being the concealed socioeconomic nucleus of Kantian subjectivity. In *Intellectual and Manual Labour: A Critique of Epistemology*, Sohn-Rethel contends that the "real abstractions" generated out of market exchange relations in capitalism form the origins of the therefrom-derived "intellectual abstractions" of the categories and concepts constitutive of the subject of Kant's transcendental idealism.[4] Sohn-Rethel's analysis, in moving from the commodity to the transcendental, moves from objectivity to subjectivity.

However, this red-thread line of thought in *Intellectual and Manual Labour*, for all its insightfulness and suggestiveness, fails to bring out a central aspect of Kant's rendition of subjectivity crucial not only for post-Kantian German idealism but for psychoanalysis as well: the status of the subject as split, as inherently and irreparably divided into discrepant dimensions. Starting with Kant, this splitting of subjectivity surfaces in the guises of rifts between the transcendental and the empirical as well as the noumenal and the phenomenal. Thereafter, variations on mismatches between the "in itself" (*an sich*) and the "for itself" (*für sich*) become refrains implicitly and explicitly organizing both German idealist and psychoanalytic theories of the subject.

A possible explanation for Sohn-Rethel's failure to articulate a historical materialist explanation for the genesis of transcendental subjectivity specifically as split, as marked by the negativity of internal self-division, has to do with his focus on commodities exclusively as nonhuman things. Sohn-Rethel, given his preoccupation with the capitalistic sphere of exchange (and corresponding neglect of the capitalistic sphere of production), zeroes in on money as the Marxian commodity par excellence, as the one commodity standing in for and exchangeable with all other commodities. He thereby conceives commodities in light of the paradigmatic commodity of currency as embodied in the guises of coins, bills, and other inert, tangible tokens.

Yet, whereas money is a unique commodity as the "universal equivalent," there is another unique commodity not done full justice to by Sohn-Rethel's *Intellectual and Manual Labour*, namely, commodified labor-power. By contrast with money as the universal equivalent, labor-power within capitalism could be characterized as the "universal exception" among all other commodities—and this for two reasons. First, commodified labor-power is universal as the real abstraction of socially necessary labor productive of all commodities, including itself, as simultaneously both use-values and exchange-values (with the latter containing the surplus-values appropriated by capital and capitalists).

Second, labor-power is exceptional in being the one and only commodity able to generate out of itself a greater amount of value than it itself costs.[5] In more technical terms, the wages paying for the production and reproduction of labor-power (with these means of subsistence being the basket of commodities as articles of consumption consumed by the bearer of labor-power and his/her dependents) amount to less exchange-value than the exchange-value of the (other) commodities produced by the capitalistic employment of this same labor-power. That is to say, labor qua commodified labor-power is the sole source of surplus-value thanks to the discrepancy between the cost of and the value produced by this labor-power. Moreover, whereas money qua universal equivalent is a commodity as an object, labor-power qua universal exception is a commodity as a subject (i.e., laboring subjectivity).

I wish to refocus attention on the subjective commodity-form of labor-power in capitalist production processes, rather than, as per Sohn-Rethel, the objective commodity-form of money in capitalist exchange processes. Doing so permits achieving a historical materialist account of the German idealist splitting of subjectivity over and above Sohn-Rethel's much more limited version of this type of account. *Intellectual and Manual Labour* restricts itself to charting the emergence, through abstractions from modernity's marketplaces, of the Kantian transcendental subject as the unified apperceptive agent underpinning Galilean-Newtonian natural scientific knowledge.

Sohn-Rethel's historical materialist analysis of the Kantian transcendental subject would be exhaustive only if one accepted a highly debatable assumption. This would be an assumption according to which the Kant of the *Critique of Pure Reason* and related texts was concerned exclusively with providing, through his transcendental idealism, an epistemological foundation for modern mathematized physics. Assuming instead, as I think one should, that the concerns and ambitions of Kant's theoretical philosophy go well beyond such a narrow focus on the quantitative and mechanical natural sciences alone, *Intellectual and Manual Labour*, despite its accomplishments, leaves much work left to be done in terms of a historical materialist recasting of German idealism and its theories of subjectivity.

Kant's "Copernican revolution" inaugurates what could be characterized as the parallactic model of split subjectivity, with the "Paralogisms of Pure Reason" of the first *Critique* being the key textual locus for this.[6] Apart from the connotations of irreparable splitting emanating from the motif of parallax—these connotations obviously are central given my focus on this occasion—parallax as a misleading visual effect will feature toward the end of my text. That said, I will not retell the story of Kant's inaugural dividing of the subject here, having already done so at length in the fourth chapter of my 2005 book *Time Driven: Metapsychology and the Splitting of the Drive.*[7] This splitting of subjectivity initiated by Kant is an enormously important and influential feature of German idealist depictions of the subject. Its importance and influence are evident in psychoanalysis, among later theoretical orientations postdating the era of German idealism. This is especially the case for Lacan's version of analysis—a version, so I will contend below, that itself yields certain crucial insights when utilized in a retroactive re-reading of Marx's critique of political economy. Specifically, I now will proceed to offer a Lacanian reinterpretation of commodified labor-power (and, along with it, the Marxian distinction between labor and labor-power) opening up the possibility of a historical materialist explanation for the coming to light of modernity's "barred S" ($\$$) in the works of Kant and his German idealist successors.

2. Labor as the Negative: The Emptiness of Work

During the February 24, 1965, session of Lacan's *Seminar XII* (*Problèmes cruciaux pour la psychanalyse* [1964–5]), Miller presents the original version of what was to become his seminal paper "Suture (Elements of the Logic of the Signifier)."[8] Miller's concept of suture is designed to capture, in quasi-formalized terms, the essence of the Lacanian theory of the split subject (i.e., the barred S [$]). More precisely, Miller translates Lacan's distinction between, on the one hand, the subject of the saying (*dire*) of enunciation and, on the other hand, the subject of the said (*dit*) of the utterance into the terms of Frege's explanation of arithmetic counting and the succession of positive whole integers.[9] This Lacanian dividing of the speaking being (*parlêtre*) subjected to the signifier between the *dire* of enunciation and the *dit* of the utterance is meant to reflect the fundamental analytic distinction between the subject (*sujet*) of the unconscious and the (partially) conscious ego (*moi*), respectively.[10]

Miller's account specifically of the number zero in Frege's 1884 *Die Grundlagen der Arithmetik: Eine logisch-mathematische Untersuchung über den Begriff der Zahl* is the key to the Millerian interfacing of Fregean formalism with Lacanian metapsychology. As per this account, zero is the one and only number endowed with the peculiar status of being not identical to itself, of amounting to a lack of the self-identity possessed by other, non-zero numbers. With positive whole integers (1, 2, 3...), one has both a general, non-empirical concept (such as "the concept of the number two") and particular, empirical instances (e.g., two pens, two cups, etc.) corresponding to this concept. In these instances, there is an identity between concept and object in which, to stay with the example of two, the concept of the number two remains identical with itself, enjoying self-identity, both in its pure conceptual form and in the guises of its empirical embodiments.

With zero, by contrast, one instead has a non-empirical concept (i.e., "the concept of the number zero") that by its own definition is deprived of any possible empirical instances. There literally are no objects corresponding to the concept of the number zero. That is to say, zero objects mean no objects whatsoever (whether pens, cups, or whatever else).

On Miller's construal of Frege, the signifier "zero"/"0" marks the impossibility of empirical instantiations of the concept of the number zero, namely, the necessary absence of objects corresponding to this strange concept. Miller designates the concept of the number zero as "zero lack" (i.e., lacking any objective incarnations) and the inscription of this lack in the form of the signifier "zero"/"0" as "zero number" (i.e., as an integer written into the series of numbers). On the basis of this, Miller maintains that the zero number as the signifier "zero"/"0" is itself the one (1) object of the concept of the number zero as zero lack. Hence, the first positive whole integer, 1, is generated by counting the singular signifier "zero"/"0." One subsequently gets 2 as the count of 0 and 1; 3 as the count of 0, 1, and 2; etc. As with set theory—Lacan himself links Georg Cantor and Frege in this way[11]—there is the void of the empty set (0 as $\varnothing$), then the set with the empty set as its one member (1 as $\{\varnothing\}$), then the set with both the empty set and the empty set counted as the single member of a set (2 as $\{\varnothing, \{\varnothing\}\}$), and so on (with 3 as $\{\varnothing, \{\varnothing\}, \{\varnothing, \{\varnothing\}\}\}$). This dynamic of signifying an absence, of translating zero lack into zero number, is what Miller baptizes "suture."[12]

Before Miller's original 1965 presentation of his Frege-inspired theory of suture, Lacan already, in the June 3, 1964, session of *Seminar XI* (*The Four Fundamental Concepts of Psychoanalysis* [1964]), equates *le sujet* with 0 as generative of the numbers succeeding it.[13] This equation of the subject (of the enunciating unconscious) with zero indeed is the central gesture at stake in Miller's recourse to Frege's model of numerical succession.[14] Throughout the twelfth seminar of 1964–5, both before and after Miller's February 24, 1965, talk therein, Lacan endorses the concept of suture *à la* Miller[15] (an endorsement repeated in the subsequent years too[16]).

Certain signifiers are identified with by the speaking subject as the load-bearing nodes in the networks constituting its very subjectivity. These (master) signifiers (S_1s) would be personal pronouns, proper names, and select nodal terms (*points de capiton*) functioning as "unary traits" (*traits unaires*) stitching and holding together the identity of the *parlêtre*. For both Lacan and Miller, such pivotal signifiers, embedded in the chains of (other) signifiers (S_2s) constituting the static, noun-like subject of utterances, are akin to Miller's zero number standing in for (or "suturing") the impossible-to-capture, kinetic, verb-like subject of enunciation, itself thereby associated with Miller's zero lack. The Lacanian-Millerian 0-subject, in its self-division between the concept of the number zero (i.e., zero lack [as $\$$]) and the signifier of this concept (i.e., zero number [as S_1]), thereby becomes productive of the infinite proliferation of successor numbers as the series of positive whole integers (from 1 to ∞ [as S_2]).

This tension between the two sides (*dire et dit* as zero lack and zero number, respectively) of the split-from-within speaking subject is continually catalytic. This antagonism animates the ceaseless, restless production of ever-more signifiers perpetually trying, but always failing, to pin down the subject of enunciation at the level of the subject of the utterance. In *Time Driven* and elsewhere, I draw out the parallels between the suture theory of subjectivity and Kant's groundbreaking move of splitting the subject between transcendental and empirical as well as noumenal and phenomenal dimensions.[17] I will not recapitulate these parallels in detail on this occasion.

But, suffice it for now to say that the innovative Kantian cleaving of the very core of subjectivity becomes a crucial inspiration for the post-Kantian idealists' various renditions of self-consciousness and the human condition in general. J.G. Fichte, F.W.J. Schelling, and G.W.F. Hegel all take up and further develop, each in his own fashions, Kant's thoroughgoing division of the subject. And, of course, Marx and Engels, emerging from the Hegelian Left of the 1830s and early 1840s, ambivalently inherit, in both conscious and unconscious ways, the complex legacies of what Engels calls "classical German philosophy" from Kant to Hegel.

However, neither Marx nor Engels evinces explicit awareness of any links between the split subject of German idealism and topics falling within their own theoretical investigations. Sohn-Rethel, with his neglect of the divided nature of the Kantian transcendental subject, is, along with the Georg Lukács of 1923's *History and Class Consciousness*, in the best of company in this instance. At most, one could claim the existence of a Marxian-Engelsian sense of indirect indebtedness to this German idealist motif via the intermediary of the Feuerbachian thematic of alienation (*als Entfremdung*). Marx and Engels certainly do not, as I presently will proceed to do, draw manifest connections between this philosophical subject and the analysis of commodified labor-power featuring centrally in Marx's critique of political economy. Yet, I hope soon to show that idealist split subjectivity and historical materialist laboring agency, with the psychoanalytic theory of the subject as a mediator, mutually illuminate one another in profound and suggestive manners.

Combining Kant, Lacan, and Miller with Marx, commodified labor-power as per historical materialism involves a subjectivity both voided (hence associable with 0) and divided (hence associable with $). Starting with the laboring subject's nothingness under capitalism, this nothingness has multiple senses and resonances within the Marxist critique of political economy (as well as elsewhere in Marx's writings, including such youthful texts as the 1844 Paris *Economic and Philosophical Manuscripts*). As I indicated at the very outset, there is initially and most obviously the nothingness of labor qua its alienation, disempowerment, exploitation, marginalization, oppression, and so on.

Beginning in the 1840s, the young Marx, via the thematic of "alienated labor" as animalistic "working to live" rather than properly human "living to work," also draws attention to the emptiness of labor in the sense of it being robbed of any satisfying significance by capitalism.[18] Industrial hourly wage-workers are fungible variables insertable into an indefinite number of mechanized production processes. Techno-scientific industrialism's divisions of labor and job markets deskill these workers,[19] reducing them to the prostitution of being mere bodies with time ("if you've got the money, I've got the time"). They have no attachment to or investment in their work, being forced, as really abstract labor,[20] into assuming a *Cogito*-like distance from and indifference to their activities and surroundings. Alienated labor is empty in its unrewarding meaninglessness and drudgery. Work counts for nothing but time lost to capital's atomized replaceable cogs of hungry, tired flesh.

However, particularly in the mature Marx's economic research, the empty, voided status of laboring subjectivity takes on additional important connotations and traits. First and foremost, there is the thesis that persons are compelled to sell themselves as laborers to capital only if and when they are deprived of the means to produce for their own self-subsistence. In the *Grundrisse*, this condition of turning people into capital's "human resources" is characterized as an "*absolute poverty*" (*die absolute Armut*) through which labor is turned into an insubstantial void in losing ownership of any of the objects of laboring (i.e., the means of production).[21] But, this zero of absolute poverty is also the laboring subject as generative of all use-, exchange-, and surplus-values in the capitalist mode of production.

This subject is, as the *Grudrisse* maintains, the "*free labourer*" as a "virtual pauper" (*virtueller Pauper*).[22] Its pauperization consists in it being reduced to possessing only its own labor-power. The bearer of this labor-power receives for it meager wages as alms. In sad truth, these alms are nothing but a small fraction of the exchange-value produced by this same impoverished subject being returned to it by capital for the mere perpetuation of its pauperized condition. Incidentally, in *Theories of Surplus-Value*, Marx equates capitalists, *rentiers*, and politicians to "respectable paupers" insofar as they are the real do-nothing sponges parasitically living off the proceeds of the labor of others.[23]

Labor's *absolute Armut* of the *Grundrisse* obviously overlaps with such better-known Marxian concepts as "primitive accumulation" and the "freedom" of commodified labor-power as its having been created in the first place through being freed from qua dispossessed of the means of production.[24] The *Grundrisse* itself elsewhere observes, "The positing of the individual as a *worker*, in this nakedness (*dieser Nacktheit*), is itself a product of *history*."[25] This history is none other than that of primitive accumulation, the original "liberation" of persons from their means of production, famously recounted in the eighth and final part of the first volume of *Capital*. The nudity (*Nacktheit*), this having of nothing but one's skin to sell (for a tanning),[26] that results from primitive accumulation's violent, lawless processes of "freeing" laborers is the zero-level of commodified labor-power as the condition of possibility for all values and wealth in capitalism.[27]

Additionally, given capitalism's zero-sum game between capital- and wage-labor, one could say that zero wages function like a mathematical attractor (and/or a Kantian regulative ideal) for the capitalist system as dominated by capitalists. Marx repeatedly indicates as much.[28] Admittedly, the necessary labor, reflected in wages, providing for the production and reproduction of labor-power never can be reduced to nothing; even the lowest subsistence level of immiserated wage labor still involves the basic requirements of these laborers' most minimal needs. Nonetheless, capital relentlessly tends to push down the wages of necessary labor so as to push up the surplus-value generated by surplus labor—and this despite various mitigating and antagonistic factors checking this tendency.

But, what about the laboring subject as split, over and above the nothingness at the base of such subjectivity? What about the division at the heart of commodified labor-power arguably analogous and related to the fundamentally divided status of both German idealist and psychoanalytic subjectivities? This has everything to do with the ineradicable discrepancy within capitalism between, on the one hand, the exchange-value of commodified labor-power (represented by wages as the cost of this power) and, on the other hand, the exchange-value of the commodities produced for capital by the labor-power capital purchases through wages.[29]

As seen apropos primitive accumulation, the voiding of pre- and non-capitalist laborers through plunging them into the absolute poverty of owning no means of production is an original and essential condition of possibility for the very existence of the capitalist mode of production. The virtual pauper as the transcendental lack of capitalism underlies commodified labor-power (just as the split subject of Kant's paralogisms of pure reason is an expression of transcendental mechanisms at the base of the edifice of subjectivity). Once thusly brought into being, capital's laboring subject as commodified labor-power thereafter suffers from a structurally intrinsic division. This gap remains necessarily unbridgeable so long as capitalism itself continues to exist. Without it, capital cannot accumulate surplus-value. There would be no "'" in M-C-M' and, hence, no capitalism.

The split at issue here has everything to do with the aforementioned status of commodified labor-power as the universal exception among commodities. As I explained above, this one commodity, unlike all other commodities, uniquely possesses the capacity to produce more exchange-values for capital in the guise of the commodities it makes than this exceptional commodity costs capital in wages as also themselves exchange-values. Surplus-value accruing to capital results exclusively from this difference between the wage cost of producing and reproducing commodified labor-power (translated through labor's C-M-C′ into other commodities [C′] it consumes as its means of subsistence) and the values of the capital-owned commodities this power creates through its application as work performed each and every working day.

The transcendental void inaugurated by primitive accumulation, the nothingness of labor reduced to a de-objectified capacity, now can be compared not only to Kant's "I, or he, or it (the thing), which thinks,"[30] but also to the Lacanian-Millerian zero lack (a comparison made all the easier by the priority of mathematics and quantification in capitalism). Through being put up for sale as a commodity on a labor market, this zero lack of unemployed, propertyless labor-power is put forward as a unit with, like zero number, the potential, if employed by owners of private property qua means of production, to be generative of additional units of value. Then, through subsequently being purchased by capital on a labor market, this zero number comes to be counted-for-one (1 as {∅}), for slightly more than nothing, as a source of surplus-value (with a counting-for-zero of zero lack as zero number preceding this capitalistic counting-for-one). And, just as 1 is the smallest positive whole integer which, as such, is closest to and succeeds 0, so too are the wages marking commodified labor-power's being counted-for-one by capital kept to a minimum necessarily below the exchange-values this labor fabricates. Finally, with commodified labor-power's movement from zero lack (primitive accumulation) to being counted-for-zero qua zero number (labor market) to being counted-for-one (employment in capitalist production process), it produces a series of other commodities analogous to 2, 3, 4, etc. as the open-ended succession of positive whole integers generated starting from 0 and 1.

3. Counting for Nothing: Transcendental Class Consciousness

So, what is to be made of these parallels between German idealist, Marxist, and psychoanalytic renditions of subjects as split? What are the implications of the above-emphasized cross-resonances between, on the one side, the $ of both philosophy and metapsychology and, on the other side, the $ of the historical materialist critique of political economy? What worthwhile conclusions, if any, are to be drawn from this network of associations between theories of subjectivity?

In 1847's *The Poverty of Philosophy*, Marx proposes and explains a number of the core tenets of historical materialism. In the fifth of seven "observations" apropos "The Metaphysics of Political Economy," he presents an insight pertinent at this juncture of my intervention. Marx raises the question of why people in the eleventh century believed certain things, while people in the eighteenth century believed other things. He then claims:

> When... we ask ourselves why a particular principle was manifested in the eleventh or in the eighteenth century rather than in any other, we are necessarily forced to examine minutely what men were like in the eleventh century, what they were like in the eighteenth, what were their respective needs, their productive forces, their

mode of production, the raw materials of their production—in short, what were the relations between man and man which resulted from all these conditions of existence (*conditions d'existence*).[31]

If historical materialism has a transcendental dimension, it would be "all these conditions of existence" as infrastructures making possible specific social totalities, with their superstructural constellations and phenomena. These constellations and phenomena include, among many other things, the sorts of ideas that manifest in the guises of philosophical/theoretical conceptions of subjectivity. Moreover, Marx's utilization of the eighteenth century as an example is especially fortuitous for my current purposes.

The split subject of Kant's theoretical philosophy certainly would count for Marxian historical materialism as a superstructural-ideational product related to the eighteenth century and its "conditions of existence." If Kant is indeed the first overt divider of (modern) subjectivity, then one could ask, following the Marx of *The Poverty of Philosophy*, why this splitting surfaces precisely in late-eighteenth-century Europe, and not in another time and place. In the historical time and place surrounding Kant, capitalism obviously has established itself. Moreover, considering the evidence I provide above of the multiple affinities between a laboring subject riven by a structural gap between discrepant exchange-values and a subject partitioned into transcendental-noumenal and empirical-phenomenal strata, this strongly hints that capitalism's commodified labor-power is an underlying (unconscious, even) historical-economic condition of possibility for the Kantian and German idealist theories of subjectivity erupting into the history of ideas starting near the end of the eighteenth century.

Engels concludes his 1886 book *Ludwig Feuerbach and the Outcome of Classical German Philosophy*, a summary of his and Marx's fraught rapport with German idealism, with the statement: "The German working class is the inheritor of German classical philosophy."[32] If my preceding analysis is justified, then the proletariat is able to be the heir and realizer of German idealism (as per Lukács[33] as well as Engels) precisely because German idealist subjectivity, starting with Kant's transcendental $, already "inherits" qua abstracts from and sublimates the proletarian subject as commodified labor-power. Thus, Engels's German working class inherits its own legacy via the detour of German classical philosophy. A sort of parallax effect is operative here: what appears to Engels to be a movement of inheriting going from German idealism treated as an object of Marxist reflection to the consciousness of proletarian subjectivity (in which Engels, along with Marx, participates) turns out to be the self-movement of the "working class" itself. The subject-position of capitalist commodified labor already pre-figures the subjects of the German idealist philosophies influencing Marxism.

The thrust of my intervention would seem, at first glance, to be in line with the thoroughgoing historicism of the likes of Sohn-Rethel,[34] Moishe Postone,[35] and numerous other representatives of post-Lukácsian Western Marxism. It would appear that I too seek to dissolve the purported universality and timelessness of German idealist philosophical subjectivity within the perpetually shifting waters of transient sociohistorical contexts. But, such is not the case.

Elsewhere, I have argued that unqualified pan-historicisms, reducing everything to the historical as evanescent, local, and so on, are neither faithful to Marx's theoretical framework nor intellectually consistent and defensible.[36] Without recapitulating those arguments here, suffice it for now to say that I view the capitalist splitting of laboring subjectivity via the creation of commodified labor-power as helping to make explicit an implicit divided status of subjects—with this status pre-existing its being made explicit in and through capitalism. Through the conditions of labor imposed by capital, the sorts of splits identified by both German idealism and psychoanalysis move from being *an sich* to (getting closer to) becoming *an und für sich*.

Therefore, the genesis of proletarian class consciousness would be a dawning awareness not only of this class's true *volonté générale* as an economic group within capitalist society but also an emergent comprehension of essential features of the transcendental layers of subjectivity. Commodified labor-power, sublated in and through German idealism, sheds light both on capitalism as a whole and on transhistorical facets of pre-capitalist and capitalist subjects alike. Paraphrasing a famous line from the 1857 Introduction to the *Grundrisse*,[37] one could say that the anatomy of the proletariat is the key to the anatomy of the peculiar *Gattungswesen* of the split subject.

Notes

1   Karl Marx, "Zur Kritik der Hegelschen Rechtsphilosophie. Einleitung." In *Karl-Marx-Ausgabe: Werke-Schriften-Briefe, Band I: Frühe Schriften, erster Band*, ed. Hans-Joachim Lieber and Peter Furth (Darmstadt: Wissenschaftliche Buchgesellschaft, 1962), 501; in English: Karl Marx, "A Contribution to the Critique of Hegel's Philosophy of Right. Introduction." In *Early Writings*, trans. Rodney Livingstone and Gregor Benton (New York: Penguin, 1975), 254.

2   Karl Marx and Friedrich Engels, *Manifest der kommunistischen Partei* (Hamburg: Phönix-Verlag 1946), 64. In English: Karl Marx and Friedrich Engels, *The Communist Manifesto* in *Selected Writings*, ed. David McLellan (Oxford: Oxford University Press, 1977), 246.

3   Karl Marx, *Grundrisse: Foundations of the Critique of Political Economy (Rough Draft)*, trans. Martin Nicolaus (New York: Penguin, 1973), 324–5.

4   Alfred Sohn-Rethel, *Intellectual and Manual Labour: A Critique of Epistemology*, trans. Martin Sohn-Rethel (London: The Macmillan Press, 1978), 6–8, 17, 20–1, 28–9, 57, 60–1, 74, 77–8.

5   Marx, *Grundrisse*, 324; Karl Marx, *Value, Price and Profit, Wage-Labour and Capital & Value, Price and Profit* (New York: International Publishers, 1976), 42–3; Karl Marx, *Capital: A Critique of Political Economy, Volume One*, trans. Ben Fowkes (New York: Penguin, 1976), 270, 279–80, 671–2, 680–1, 713–14; Karl Marx, *Capital: A Critique of Political Economy*, vol. 2, trans. David Fernbach (New York: Penguin, 1978), 113; Karl Marx, *Theories of Surplus-Value, Part I*, ed. S. Ryazanskaya, trans. Emile Burns (Moscow: Progress Publishers, 1963), 392, 397–8, 400–1; Karl Marx, *Theories of Surplus-Value, Part III: Volume IV of Capital*, ed. S.W. Ryazanskaya and Richard Dixon, trans. Jack Cohen and S.W. Ryazanskaya (Moscow: Progress Publishers, 1971), 208; see also on the topic: Maurice Dobb, *Political Economy and*

Capitalism: Some Essays in Economic Tradition (London: Routledge, 1940), 61–2; Ronald L. Meek, *Studies in the Labor Theory of Value* (New York: Monthly Review, 1956), 183; Ernest Mandel, *Marxist Economic Theory, Volume II*, trans. Brian Pearce (New York: Monthly Review Press, 1970), 86–8; M.C. Howard and J.E. King, *The Political Economy of Marx* (Essex: Longman, 1975), 42, 102; G.A. Cohen, *Karl Marx's Theory of History: A Defense* (Princeton: Princeton University Press, 1978), 189; Meghnad Desai, *Marxian Economics* (Oxford: Basil Blackwell, 1979), 20–1, 24–5, 30–1, 34–5; Ben Fine and Alfredo Saad-Filho, *Marx's Capital* (London: Pluto Press, 2016 [sixth edition]), 21, 33; Duncan K. Foley, *Understanding Capital: Marx's Economic Theory* (Cambridge, MA: Harvard University Press, 1986), 34; David Harvey, *The Limits to Capital*, London: Verso, 2006, 22–4; David Harvey, *A Companion to Marx's Capital* (London: Verso, 2010), 291; David Harvey, *A Companion to Marx's Capital, Volume Two* (London: Verso, 2013), 37.

6   Immanuel Kant, *Critique of Pure Reason*, trans. Paul Guyer and Allen W. Wood (Cambridge: Cambridge University Press, 1998), A341/B399-A405/B432, 411–58.

7   Adrian Johnston, *Time Driven: Metapsychology and the Splitting of the Drive* (Evanston: Northwestern University Press, 2005), 79–119.

8   Jacques-Alain Miller in Jacques Lacan, *Le Séminaire de Jacques Lacan, Livre XII: Problèmes cruciaux pour la psychanalyse, 1964–1965* (unpublished typescript), session of February 24, 1965; Jacques-Alain Miller, "Suture (Elements of the Logic of the Signifier)," trans. Jacqueline Rose, *Screen* 18, no. 4 (Winter 1977/1978), 24–34.

9   Johnston, *Time Driven*, 110–19.

10   Jacques Lacan, *The Seminar of Jacques Lacan, Book XI: The Four Fundamental Concepts of Psychoanalysis*, ed. Jacques-Alain Miller, trans. Alan Sheridan (New York: W. W. Norton, 1977), 139–40; Jacques Lacan, "*L'étourdit*." In *Autres écrits*, ed. Jacques-Alain Miller (Paris: Éditions du Seuil, 2001), 449, 452–3.

11   Jacques Lacan, *The Seminar of Jacques Lacan, Book XIX:... or Worse, 1971–1972*, ed. Jacques-Alain Miller, trans. A.R. Price (Cambridge: Polity, 2018), 141–2, 154; Jacques Lacan, "*... ou pire: Compte rendu du Séminaire 1971–1972*." In *Autres écrits*, 547.

12   Miller, "Suture," 30, 34; Johnston, *Time Driven*, 110–19.

13   Lacan, *The Seminar of Jacques Lacan, Book XI*, 226.

14   Johnston, *Time Driven*, 110–19.

15   Lacan, *Le Séminaire de Jacques Lacan, Livre XII*, sessions of December 16, 1964, January 20, 1965, March 3, 1965, March 10, 1965, March 24, 1965, May 5, 1965, May 26, 1965, June 9, 1965; Jacques Lacan, "*Problèmes cruciaux pour la psychanalyse: Compte rendu du Séminaire 1964–1965*." In *Autres écrits*, 200.

16   Jacques Lacan, *Le Séminaire de Jacques Lacan, Livre XIII: L'objet de la psychanalyse, 1965–1966* (unpublished typescript), sessions of April 20, 1966, May 18, 1966, June 8, 1966; Jacques Lacan, *Le Séminaire de Jacques Lacan, Livre XIV: La logique du fantasme, 1966–1967* (unpublished typescript), session of March 1, 1967; Jacques Lacan, *Le Séminaire de Jacques Lacan, Livre XVI: D'un Autre à l'autre, 1968–1969*, ed. Jacques-Alain Miller (Paris: Éditions du Seuil, 2006), 48–9, 55–6, 59; Lacan, *The Seminar of Jacques Lacan, Book XIX*, 40–8, 61, 90–1, 114–15, 138, 150, 154–5.

17   Johnston, *Time Driven*, 79–119; Adrian Johnston, *Žižek's Ontology: A Transcendental Materialist Theory of Subjectivity* (Evanston: Northwestern University Press, 2008), 13, 46, 196, 210, 248–68.

18   Marx, *Economic and Philosophical Manuscripts, Early Writings*, 322–34; Marx, *Wage-Labour and Capital*, 19.

19   Marx, *Grundrisse*, 529, 699, 700, 704.

20 Marx, *Grundrisse*, 104–5.

21 Karl Marx, *Grundrisse der Kritik der politischen Ökonomie (Rohentwurf)* (Frankfurt: Europäische Verlagsanstalt, 1967), 203; Marx, *Grundrisse*, 295–6.

22 Marx, *Grundrisse*, 497; Marx, *Grundrisse: Foundations of the Critique of Political Economy*, 604.

23 Marx, *Theories of Surplus-Value, Part I*, 218.

24 Marx, *Value, Price and Profit*, 38–9; Marx, *Grundrisse*, 459–60, 502, 508–10, 512–13; Marx, *Capital, Volume One*, 873–940; Karl Marx, *Capital: A Critique of Political Economy, Volume Three*, trans. David Fernbach (New York: Penguin, 1981), 354–5, 753–4, 1019; Marx, *Theories of Surplus-Value, Part III*, 271–2, 314–15.

25 Marx, *Grundrisse*, 375; Marx, *Grundrisse: Foundations of the Critique of Political Economy*, 472.

26 Marx, *Capital, Volume One*, 280.

27 Marx, *Wage-Labour and Capital*, 30; Marx, *Theories of Surplus-Value, Part I*, 45.

28 Marx, *Grundrisse*, 285–7, 422, 543, 557, 817, Marx, *Value, Price and Profit*, 58, 61–2; Marx, *Capital, Volume One*, 1068–9; Marx, *Capital, Volume Two*, 391; Karl Marx, *Theories of Surplus-Value, Part II*, ed. S. Ryazanskaya, trans. Emile Burns (Moscow: Progress Publishers, 1968), 547–8.

29 Anthony Brewer, *A Guide to Marx's Capital* (Cambridge: Cambridge University Press, 1984), 63; Foley, *Understanding Capital*, 34, 40, 46–7.

30 Kant, *Critique of Pure Reason*, A346/B404, 414.

31 Karl Marx, *Misère de la philosophie: Réponse à la Philosophie de la misère de Proudhon*, https://www.marxists.org/francais/marx/works/1847/06/misere.pdf; Karl Marx, *The Poverty of Philosophy* (Moscow: Foreign Languages Publishing House, 1956), 115.

32 Friedrich Engels, *Ludwig Feuerbach and the Outcome of Classical German Philosophy*, ed. C.P. Dutt (New York: International, 1941), 61.

33 Georg Lukács, "Reification and the Consciousness of the Proletariat." In *History and Class Consciousness: Studies in Marxist Dialectics*, trans. Rodney Livingstone (Cambridge: MIT Press, 1971), 117–19, 121, 142, 149, 177, 192.

34 Sohn-Rethel, *Intellectual and Manual Labour*, 199–201, 203.

35 Moishe Postone, *Time, Labor, and Social Domination: A Reinterpretation of Marx's Critical Theory* (Cambridge: Cambridge University Press, 1993), 5, 16, 81, 139–40, 171, 259, 270, 280, 369–70, 387.

36 Adrian Johnston, "Meta-Transcendentalism and Error-First Ontology: The Cases of Gilbert Simondon and Catherine Malabou." In *New Realism and Contemporary Philosophy*, ed. Gregor Kroupa and Jure Simoniti (London: Bloomsbury, 2020), 171–5.

37 Marx, *Grundrisse*, 105.

Part Three

Parallax in Aesthetics

14

Drama as Philosophy
The Tragedy of the End of Art

Todd McGowan

1. Philosophy after Art

With the development of German idealism, philosophy reaches a point where it no longer requires art to think on its behalf. As Hegel infamously puts it, "art, considered in its highest vocation, is and remains for us a thing of the past."[1] Philosophy fills the role that art did in prior epochs. The great advantage of philosophy over art is that it speaks to us in a more straightforward manner, using concepts rather than representations. In this way, philosophy is truer to the structure of our spirit, which is conceptual rather than imagistic.

Even Hegel's otherwise loyal followers decide to part company with him when he makes this claim. Some argue that Hegel simply couldn't anticipate future artistic developments that continue to render art philosophically relevant. This is the case with two of his most enthusiastic contemporary champions—Robert Pippin and Slavoj Žižek. According to Pippin, Hegel's claim that art is a thing of the past refers only to the representational art with which he was familiar, not to abstract modern art. This art accomplishes the same task as Hegel's own philosophy, which indicates that he would have embraced its philosophical importance. Pippin concludes his essay "What Was Abstract Art?" by linking these projects. He states, "What... a kind of self-authored normativity or human freedom might be is a terribly difficult question. But perhaps, over the last hundred years, and especially in the experiments of abstraction, we now have some sense of what it looks like (thus both confirming and undermining Hegel's claim about the way art could now matter)."[2] Modern art matters from a Hegelian perspective because it tackles the fundamental question of Hegel's philosophy: what does freedom from authority look like? If Hegel had foreseen the direction that post-Romantic art would take, Pippin argues, he would not have delivered a negative verdict on art's future for philosophy.

Much like Pippin (otherwise his antagonist), Žižek affirms that Hegel's proclamation about the end of art, while it correctly rejects attempts at the romantic re-enchantment of the modern world, misses the future rise of abstract art. Abstract art moves beyond the paradigm of representation. It rejects beauty as an ideal. As a result, it expresses the unfreedom that persists in modernity in a way that Romantic art cannot. The persistence of this unfreedom testifies to our need for art, a need that abstract art addresses. The novels and plays on Samuel Beckett, which Žižek celebrates, evince continued power of this art to remain a thing of the present, not the past.[3] Beckett proves Hegel wrong when it comes to art.

It is clear that Pippin and Žižek are on to something. Hegel's pronouncement of the end of art's philosophical value surely cannot be right, given the fecundity of the art that has followed in the wake of this pronouncement. The idea that the novels of Virginia Woolf and Toni Morrison, the music of Richard Wagner and Arnold Schoenberg, and the paintings of Vincent van Gogh and Pablo Picasso can say nothing that philosophy can't also say more straightforwardly stretches credulity. This is not to mention revelations of the art form that Hegel never imagined—the cinema. If we take the dismissal of art's importance in the modern world seriously, we find ourselves with a less convincing philosophical system.

As a result, Hegel's interpreters, even if they don't go as far as Pippin and Žižek, tend to focus on the continued importance of art within his system. Though some claim that art has no significant role to play, most see art as necessary but nonetheless secondary to philosophy. According to Benjamin Rutter in *Hegel on the Modern Arts*, "If the idea that art has no real place in Hegel's mature system is still defended, the balance of opinion has shifted... in favor of a more optimistic appraisal. More than one commentator has recently asserted the ongoing indispensability of the arts on a properly Hegelian conception of the modern world."[4] The philosophical importance of art has become, contra Hegel, an accepted truth across different theoretical camps.

Philosophy in the twentieth century engages in a massive undertaking to reassert the priority of art. From Martin Heidegger's invocation of art as the "*happening of truth*" to Theodor Adorno's claim that "great artworks are unable to lie" to Jacques Derrida's insistence on the priority of literature relative to philosophy, philosophers after Hegel seek to put the latter's dismissal of art irrevocably to rest.[5] Even Alain Badiou, who laments philosophy's attempt to suture itself to art and thereby deny its proper grandeur, nonetheless grants art the status of a truth procedure, which he denies to philosophy. It is as if Hegel's attempt to discount the importance of art for knowledge occasions a philosophical backlash that continues to this day.

But Hegel's dismissal of art's significance does not stem from a failure to appreciate what art has to say. More than any thinker before him, Hegel displays a profound sensitivity to the impact that art has on us as subjects. Even though he never published the *Aesthetics* during his lifetime, he gave numerous lecture courses on the arts that reflect a constant engagement with art's philosophical importance. What's more, his acquaintance with the history of art was extensive. His interpretations not only stand out on their own merits but play a major role in his philosophy. He turns to Diderot's *Rameau's Nephew* and Sophocles' *Antigone*, rather than historical events or philosophical movements, to make decisive points in the *Phenomenology of Spirit*. Art suffuses Hegel's philosophy. And yet, he proclaims its philosophical end.

The solution to this paradox lies in the structure of the philosophy that Hegel constructs. Hegel announces that art is "a thing of the past" because he believes that philosophy must become artistic. It must take art as its model if it has to remain relevant in the modern world. In order to speak to the challenge of modernity, philosophy must remodel itself on the basis of an artistic approach to its concepts. The danger is not that art will become passé but that philosophy will lose all relevance if it continues down its traditional path. It will become a series of arguments and counterarguments that no one will notice. This is the sense of Hegel's infamous statement.

Hegel takes the radical step of integrating art into his own philosophical method. As Hegel sees it, art becomes philosophically unnecessary only at the moment when philosophy becomes artistic. The absolute art form, drama, provides a paradigm for philosophy, a paradigm that Hegel himself adopts. He authors the end of art's philosophical importance at the moment he becomes the first dramatic philosopher. He does so by creating a method in which he dramatizes each theoretical position that he confronts.

The form of drama itself is not what appeals to Hegel. He does not want to see his philosophy acted out on the stage. What matters is the way that drama allows the positions that it shows to unravel themselves and expose their contradictions. This process is not confined to actual plays but exists just as clearly in novels and films. When Hegel integrates drama into his philosophy, it is drama as an enactment of contradiction—an art of dramatizing rather than theater specifically.

Obviously, Hegel does not identify cinema as the absolute form of art because it didn't exist during his lifetime. The situation with the novel is more complex. Though Hegel read many novels, he was acquainted only with novels that had yet to develop the form to the extent that drama developed. Had he known of the novels of Jane Austen or lived long enough to read Honoré de Balzac's *Père Goriot*, Hegel might have named the novel the absolute work of art or placed it alongside drama. It is certain that cinema would have had this status had he seen Orson Welles' *Citizen Kane* (1941). The novel and cinema can do what Hegel privileges drama for doing, which is why we should think of drama in the widest sense when we discuss it in relation to his philosophy.

Drama represents the absolute form of art for Hegel because it reveals the unsurpassability of contradiction, just like absolute knowing in the *Phenomenology of Spirit* or the absolute idea in the *Science of Logic*. If Christianity as the absolute religion provides the content for Hegel's system (with the infinite manifesting itself in humiliated finitude), drama gives this system its form. In no artistic medium, according to Hegel, does contradiction become more evident than in drama. This is why Hegel places drama at the endpoint of his philosophy of art. By exhibiting the necessity of the events it depicts and exploring their logic to its final conclusion, drama enables us to see the contradictions that would otherwise remain hidden. As Walter Davis points out in *Get the Guests*, "Drama represents what happens to conflicts when they are activated and drawn to their inevitable conclusion."[6] Drama makes visible what subjects cannot discover about themselves through self-reflection. It gives the lie to the story that the subject tells and the self-identity that the concept promises.

Without taking stock of how Hegel transforms philosophy, his statement about art being "a thing of the past" doesn't make sense. He relegates art's significance to the past in order to make it a present force within philosophy. With Hegel, art and philosophy cease to be separate domains. The highest form of art, drama, becomes the philosophical method. Earlier philosophers deploy concepts and elaborate arguments, but Hegel transforms philosophy into a drama. The point becomes the exploration of how a concept or mode of argument plays itself when thrust into dramatic conflict.

Hegel's philosophy takes Shakespeare, the greatest modern dramatist, as its point of departure. Through the changes that he makes to the form of philosophy, he attempts to make himself into the Shakespeare of philosophy. Even though *Antigone* is probably Hegel's favorite play—he calls it "the most consummate work of art"—he recognizes that Shakespeare goes beyond Sophocles in his depiction of contradiction.[7] *Antigone* depicts the contradiction of Greek society through an external opposition between Antigone and Creon. The conclusion of the play reveals the impossibility of any coexistence of the two necessary forms of law—the public law that Creon follows and the unwritten law of the tradition to which Antigone adheres. But Sophocles lacks the idea of modern subjectivity. The result is that it is not fully clear how Creon and Antigone necessarily produce each other out of their own internal logic. In the *Aesthetics*, Hegel states that "truly *tragic* action necessarily presupposes either a live conception of *individual* freedom and independence or at least an individual's determination and willingness to accept freely and on his own account the responsibility for his own act and its consequences."[8] With Shakespeare, this finally comes about.

In the four great tragedies, we see Shakespeare's characters confront their own contradictions that undo them from within. Hamlet, Othello, Lear, and Macbeth are all the authors of their demise. Through their self-destruction, they reveal the contradiction at the heart of modern subjectivity. Lear, for instance, wants love to coincide with recognition. His struggle with his daughters is an opposition that expresses this internal contradiction. He destroys himself by betraying the one daughter, Cordelia, who offers him love rather than recognition, while embracing Goneril and Regan, who give recognition without love. Macbeth, for his part, consciously wants power but unconsciously recoils from the horrors that power requires. He dies nominally from the sword of Macduff, but his own subjectivity leads him directly to this death. Both Lear and Macbeth destroy themselves not contingently but through the necessity of the contradictions that define their subjectivity. Drama reveals the truth of their contradiction.

Just as Shakespeare dramatizes oppositions in order to reveal their basis in contradiction, Hegel creates a philosophy in which he submits every theoretical position that he encounters to the exigencies of drama. In drama, every position discovers that it authors its own demise as clearly as King Lear. The absolute is Hegel's recognition that he himself cannot escape the self-destructive drama that he identifies in other philosophies. The absolute reveals that self-destruction is unavoidable because contradiction is unsurpassable. With Hegel, philosophy transcends art only insofar as art becomes the privileged philosophical method. This is one of the key pillars of Hegel's break from modern philosophy and from his fellow German Idealists.

2. The Argument against Argumentation

In contrast to Hegel, Immanuel Kant grants the work of art a privileged place within his philosophy. On a cursory reading, it seems that Kant has much more respect for art than Hegel. But art remains fundamentally distinct from Kant's theoretical and practical philosophy. It serves as a bridge between the two without infecting either one. Even though Kant represents a radical turn in the history of philosophy, he philosophizes through argumentation, like the thinkers before him. In this sense, there is a genuine continuity between Descartes, Spinoza, Leibniz, Hume, and Kant. Despite their differences, they all privilege traditional argumentation.

The history of philosophy is the history of philosophical argumentation. From Aristotle quarrelling with Plato over the independent existence of the idea to Schelling and Fichte disputing about objective and subjective idealism to David Lewis and Alvin Plantinga arguing about possible worlds, argumentation has constituted the core of philosophical activity. The conviction that argumentation is the privileged philosophical method has been a constant from Aristotle onward. When he recounts the history of philosophy, Hegel implicitly removes argumentation from this privileged position. Rather than employing argumentation against other philosophers in order to assert his own position as superior, Hegel creates a new form of argument: he dramatizes their philosophies to show how they undermine themselves.

When Hegel dramatizes the philosophy of Leibniz, for instance, he reveals the contradiction between the absolute status that Leibniz accords to God and the autonomy of the individual monads. In the dramatic enactment of his philosophy, Leibniz presupposes multiplicity as absolute. But because he retains the idea of agreement between the isolated monads, God must come on the scene as the monad of monads that guarantees preestablished harmony between them. When God enters, the autonomy of the monads must exit, causing the system to founder. Hegel doesn't assault Leibniz with countering argumentation but with an argument that turns to the exigencies of dramatic form.

But Hegel's campaign against argumentation in philosophy does not begin with the *History of Philosophy*. It starts in his first major publication, the essay on the difference between Fichte's philosophy and Schelling's. There, Hegel criticizes Kant for having "allowed negative argumentation to go on replacing philosophy, as before, only more pretentiously than ever under the name of critical philosophy."[9] For all Kant's novelty, he continues the centuries-long practice of argumentation that Hegel finds unsuited for philosophy. As Hegel goes on, his critique of argumentation as a philosophical method becomes sharper. It reaches its high point in the "Preface" to the *Phenomenology of Spirit*, where Hegel justifies his own method for the first time. He writes, "Argumentation... is reflection into the empty I, the vanity of its own knowing.—This vanity, however, expresses not only the vanity of its own content, but also that of this insight itself; for this insight is the negative that fails to catch sight of the positive within itself."[10] When one defends an insight with argumentation, one necessarily paves the way for an opposing argumentation implied by one's own. Argumentation is necessarily one-sided, and it implicitly suggests the opposite side as a credible alternative. As long as one remains within the domain of argumentation, there is no possibility for definitively deciding between the oppositions.

This is not to say that Hegel would have us conduct all our political contestation by dramatizing rather than arguing. One must first argue in order to have a position to dramatize. Though philosophy is always political, politics is not initially philosophical, at least in Hegel's sense. It requires argumentation in order to accomplish anything. Argumentation in politics has a local validity. Hegel does not want to eliminate argumentation from politics but to displace its priority in philosophy.

Whereas drama concludes with a clear determination by exposing a concept's contradiction with itself, argumentation represents an instance of what Hegel labels a bad infinity: it continues unceasingly between argument and counterargument. Mired in irresolvable arguments, philosophy has failed to reach any conclusions. Hegel aims to rectify this by abandoning argumentation for art—and specifically for drama.

Of course, it is absurd to argue for the abandonment of argument. This is why Hegel adds later in the "Preface" to the *Phenomenology*, "The study of philosophy is as much hindered by the conceit that will not argue, as it is by the argumentative approach."[11] The point is not to abandon argument altogether but to argue through a new method, a method that abandons the form of argumentation. Hegel does this when he integrates dramatic art into his philosophy. When we begin with a first principle and subsequently prove it, we end up articulating more than just this principle. We also imply its opposite, which triggers another philosopher to articulate an opposing argument.

The abandonment of argumentation for art (and specifically drama) renders Hegel a controversial figure in the history of philosophy. For many, he represents a departure from philosophy proper through his failure to make sustained and convincing arguments for his theoretical moves. This is undoubtedly the source of the disdain heaped on him by figures such as Bertrand Russell and Karl Popper. Even a more sympathetic commentator like Charles Taylor notes that often the arguments of the *Science of Logic* "collapse ignominiously without the underlying premiss of ontological necessity."[12] But Hegel's seemingly outmoded statement on the end of art should lead us to rethink his defects as an arguer. Hegel's arguments seem flimsy because they are a new form of argument—a drama rather than a proof. Argumentation relies on the conscious intentions of the thinker making the argument. One constructs an argument according to a line of thought that one consciously develops through careful preparation. When the unconscious manifests itself in an argument, it always does so obscured by the conscious intentions that predominate. For instance, if I argue that socialism is a superior economic system to capitalism, I undoubtedly have an unconscious motive for doing so, but this unconscious motive is completely obfuscated by the argument. Even the greatest psychoanalyst would have no way to decipher it from the argument alone. Argumentation does not make the unconscious conspicuous. The case is altogether different with drama. Hegel's turn from argumentation to drama is unthinkable outside his anticipation of psychoanalysis and its discovery of the unconscious. Drama marginalizes conscious intention in order to highlight the disruptiveness of the unconscious.

The unconscious becomes noticeable through the way that our acts exceed what we intend. When we see the enactment of a position, we can identify the unconscious through the distance that separates what the position thinks of itself and what it does. The conscious intention attempts to realize itself as an act in the world, but it cannot prevent the unconscious from hijacking the act for itself. Even the act that goes perfectly according to plan never really does because the satisfaction that it generates has to do with the subject's unconscious desire, not the fulfillment of the conscious wish. Drama has the effect of drawing attention to this disjunction.

3. The Path to Failure

In the *Phenomenology of Spirit*, the drama that Hegel enacts is clearer than anywhere else in his philosophy, which accounts for its popularity as the entry point to his philosophy. This is his most dramatic work, the philosophical dramatist at the height of his powers. The movement within this work stems from the series of contradictions that become evident once Hegel places the various theoretical positions on the stage and allows them to play out their own logic. Hegel gives each position the benefit of the doubt. He treats it as absolutely valid, allowing it to rise and fall on its own terms. Throughout the development of the *Phenomenology of Spirit*, Hegel illustrates how each theoretical position leads beyond itself to its own demise. Drama is the proving ground for philosophy. It is the site where every theoretical position endures its self-destruction. No position can escape this self-destruction—not even Hegel's own—because no position can avoid its own unconscious, which is what drama puts on display.

This is most apparent in Hegel's discussion of the master and servant. When Hegel shows us how the struggle between the master and servant takes place, it becomes readily apparent that mastery undermines itself. It is a self-annihilating quest. The master turns the other into a servant to ensure recognition, but this has the effect, as Hegel shows, of rendering the other unworthy of bestowing recognition. The master can find a worthy adversary only if one who will accept death before acquiescing, but a dead subject is, unfortunately, incapable of recognizing the authority of the master. The master's own project—the project of mastery—is a self-defeating one. The drama that it unleashes reveals that it never had any hope of success, that its failure was written into it from the beginning.

Later, when Hegel turns to the enlightenment in the section on "Spirit," he moves onto turf closer to home. Hegel himself is an enlightenment philosopher, but when he dramatizes the position of the enlightenment, its contradiction becomes evident. This is why Hegel is an enlightenment philosopher cut from a different cloth than Voltaire or Diderot. Enlightenment in Hegel's drama initially manifests itself as what he calls "pure insight." Pure insight sees religious faith as the enemy that it must destroy in order to bring about a society of autonomous subjects. Faith represents dependence on the unjustified authority of priests.

As the relationship between pure insight and faith plays out, we see that pure insight's attack on faith is actually an attack on itself. According to Hegel, faith is pure insight taken seriously, a position that emerges out of pure insight's own project. Pure insight's vilification of faith stems from its theoretical proximity, not its distance. The overriding concern of pure insight is the subject's transcendence above its natural existence. Rather than concern itself with merely making money, acquiring property, and indulging in natural pleasures, a subject should embrace the autonomy that derives from the subject's break from the natural world.

When pure insight encounters faith, it criticizes this position for actually doing what it claims to want. Faith renounces worldly goods and the logic of acquisition. Pure insight responds by criticizing faith for this renunciation that it characterizes as driven by superstition. Faith's renunciation of worldly goods demonstrates the subject's capacity for transcending its natural being, although pure insight does not recognize this and attacks faith on just this point. In this way, the drama of pure insight and faith reveals the contradiction of pure insight. It gives the lie to the purity that pure insight professes about itself. Hegel states, "this pure insight is in truth a deception, which feigns and demands an *inner* elevation, but declares that it is superfluous, foolish, and even wrong to be *in earnest* about it, to put this elevation into *actual practice* and *demonstrate its truth*."[13] Pure insight absolutely rejects faith, but the drama of the two indicates that faith is a version of pure insight with its hands dirty. By enacting pure insight's encounter with faith, Hegel shows that it doesn't want what it claims to want.

Here, the difference between argumentation and drama becomes clear. There is no way to solve an argument between pure insight and faith. Each side can see the hole in the other's argument and use this as a site for its own counterargument. Dramatizing each position, on the other hand, reveals the contradiction that undermines each position. Though we don't have to abandon the enlightenment when we recognize the contradiction in its critique of faith, we do have to revaluate the complete dismissal of religious belief as superstition. It turns out that faith is not the enemy of the enlightenment but part of the enlightenment project. Faith shows the proper disdain for our natural being, though it mistakenly invests itself in another world rather than grasping the transcendence that occurs with the emergence of subjectivity.

Though the *Phenomenology of Spirit* showcases the dramatic character of Hegel's philosophy more than his other works through its focus on the experience of subjectivity, this same privileging of drama is evident even in Hegel's construction of logic. When Hegel moves from the *Phenomenology of Spirit* to the *Science of Logic*, he brings the revolution in argument with him. The result is a logic that seems to defy its name.

Hegel describes the *Science of Logic* as completely divorced from the relation between consciousness and its object that the *Phenomenology* plays out. In this later text, he claims to present logic in its purity without the taint of experience. As this description of the project suggests, there would seem to be no room for drama in logic. Without nature or finite spirit, no possibility for the interaction of the concept with its other exists. Argumentation appears as the only path, which accords with the standard conception of logic. And yet, Hegel continues the integration of drama into philosophy even in the *Science of Logic*, the book in which we would least expect to find it.

The role of drama in the *Logic* becomes evident in the book's opening chapter, Hegel's often questioned move from being to becoming. If one examines the argument of this chapter, there is no doubt that it is completely unconvincing. The controversy surrounding this argument began during Hegel's lifetime and has not abated since. In fact, it's not entirely clear what Hegel is arguing about the relationship between being and nothing. But in *Hegel im Kontext*, Dieter Henrich notes that Hegel's only point in this opening chapter is to show the failure of beginning with being. The aim is not a successful argumentation but the dramatization of a failure.[14] Rather than constructing an argument about the relationship between being and nothing, Hegel dramatizes being and illustrates that it comes to nothing.

Hegel engages being in an interaction through which it must reveal itself. It is this drama that leads to becoming as the truth of being. If we abstractly argue that pure being is all that there is, in the manner of Parmenides, then this claim has an apparent validity. One might contest it by arguing that there is only becoming and no pure being, but there would be no way to adjudicate this argument and counterargument. We would remain caught up in a stale series of oppositions. Drama brings us from opposition to contradiction.

Once we attempt to dramatize pure being, as Hegel does at the beginning of the *Logic*, this validity immediately disappears. By imagining how pure being would act, Hegel sees that it is equivalent to nothing. Every effort to define pure being results in something other than pure being, which shows that there can be no pure beginning. Hegel writes, "If any determination or content were posited in it as distinct from an other, it would thereby fail to hold fast to its purity. It is pure indeterminateness and emptiness."[15] The emptiness that results from pure being's self-assertion leaves it identical with nothing

Hegel shows that pure being requires nothing to define itself, that it cannot do without nothing as its antagonistic actor. But nothing is not opposed to being. It is being's internal necessity, the way in which being necessarily undoes itself. When we show being in action, the nature of the relationship between being and nothing becomes evident. Being cannot hold itself separate from nothing, nor can nothing keep itself distinct from being. This occasions the transition to becoming, which is a way of resolving the contradiction of being while installing its own contradiction that will manifest itself through becoming's own drama.

Becoming is the failure of pure being or pure nothing to remain identical with itself without an internal contradiction. In order to constitute themselves conceptually, being and nothing must vanish into each other. This necessary vanishing is becoming. This dramatic structure repeats itself throughout the *Science of Logic* until the absolute idea, which parallels absolute knowing in the *Phenomenology of Spirit*. When we reach the absolute, the drama does not come to an end. Instead, the absolute installs self-destructive drama—and the contradiction it reveals—as the ultimate horizon.

4. The Philosophy That Doesn't Begin

Hegel's philosophy is a thoroughgoing rejection of the pure beginning. The beginning, for Hegel, is always just an empty abstraction. To make the rejection of the pure beginning theoretically tenable, Hegel must adopt a new form of philosophy. Argumentation depends on the articulation of a first principle that the development of the argument defends. The beginning has an absolute priority. In contrast to argumentation, drama reveals the unimportance of the beginning. In drama, what counts is the conflict that occurs, not the starting point for this conflict. Drama is a proving ground in which each position exposes itself through the contrast with how it begins. Just as Coriolanus reveals that his attachment to his mother is stronger than the cause for which he fights in Shakespeare's play, in the *Phenomenology of Spirit*, the beautiful soul makes evident its desire for the corrupted world that it criticizes. We see what argument hides when we watch a drama unfold.[16]

In his discussion of Christianity, Hegel identifies the fall as an absolute beginning rather than the loss of a pure prior state. In Hegel's retelling, the beginning is already contradictory. When Adam and Eve sin by eating the fruit from the Tree of the Knowledge of Good and Evil, they evince the conflict that inaugurates subjectivity. Their sin gives birth to them as spiritual (i.e., as thinking) rather than simply animal beings. The story of the fall disguises its status as a beginning by describing the state—life in the Garden of Eden—prior to the fall. But prelapsarian life is a fantasy produced out of the fall itself. It has no place within the drama of Adam and Eve, though it is part of their narrative of self-identity. The fall retroactively creates the illusion of a time of innocence and bliss in the Garden of Eden that humanity lost. Hegel's claim is that this prelapsarian life exists only after the fall and results from the image of the past that the fall creates.

The story of the fall is not exceptional. All stories about beginnings stumble into this same structural trap. The beginning rewrites its own necessity into history and thereby posits its own antecedents. In this way, it produces an illusory purity that never existed. Just as there was no prelapsarian life in the Garden of Eden, there is no honeymoon period in a romantic relationship, no moment before things began to go sour or become stale. From the moment the relationship commences, the forces that will ultimately destroy it are active. In fact, these forces are often what initially fuel the relationship. The beginning suffers from the same contradiction as the end, though it is hidden in one instance and visible in the other. Drama exposes the beginning for what it is, when we follow it all the way to the absolute.

Once we arrive at the end of Hegel's dialectic—at the absolute—our perspective on the beginning undergoes a complete revolution. The revelation of the absolute is that there is nothing prior to the beginning, which is precisely what a discursive approach to the beginning cannot signify. When we examine the beginning on its own terms, it seems to be the product of what precedes it, but the absolute idea reveals that the beginning actually receives its justification through what follows after it. Every beginning is in this sense an absolute beginning, an event that breaks from the past. The discursive structure of thought obscures this break, but Hegel aims to restore its decisiveness. Understanding the beginning demands that we cease looking at its antecedents and turn our attention to its effects. We can gain some purchase on what precedes the beginning by focusing solely on what it produces. The truth of the beginning does not lie in its illusory original purity but in the contradictions that it inaugurates. We only understand the beginning from the perspective of the end, which comes about through the drama that the beginning unleashes.

5. The Dialectic to Nowhere

The genius of art, for Hegel, lies in its capacity to strip away the contingency that colors ordinary reality. In the *Aesthetics*, Hegel points out, "Art liberates the true content of phenomena from the pure semblance and the deception of this bad, transitory world and gives them a higher actuality born of spirit."[17] Art attains a truth that ordinary actuality misses through its adherence to the requirements of form, which reveals the necessity of the events it depicts. We typically lament as unrealistic works of art that exclude contingency in order to follow the dictates of a certain aesthetic form, but Hegel sees this exclusion as the indication of art's superiority to ordinary reality. The contingency of ordinary reality often obscures the contradictions of our subjectivity. The necessity at work in aesthetic form makes the contradictions evident.

Ordinary reality appears contingent because it translates contradictions into oppositions. In the scenario of the encounter with the former romantic partner, I experience an opposition between the former lover and my current spouse. The encounter creates a situation in which I must choose between these two different options. But what is really at stake for me is not the decision between opposing possibilities. It is the confrontation with the contradiction of my relationship that appears—due to the distortion of ordinary reality—as an opposition. But drama reveals the contradiction that the opposition hides.

The greatest works of art are those that reveal the necessity of contradiction. This is what gives *Hamlet* its philosophical importance. Hamlet suffers perhaps more than any other fictional character from the contradictions of modern subjectivity. He insists on his own autonomy as a subject but feels the weight of traditional authority. He wants to act for the sake of justice but recognizes the insignificance of any action. He dedicates himself to knowledge but realizes the emptiness of all learning. When Hamlet appears on stage, the contradictions of modernity reveal themselves.[18] The drama of his character exposes what modernity tries to hide from itself. We see the tragic necessity that underlies modern subjectivity.

Like Shakespeare before him, Hegel illustrates how the oppositions that we construct to enliven our struggles in the world express our own contradictions while simultaneously making them seem possible to overcome. The aim of philosophy must be to lay bare the contradictions that these oppositions obscure, so that when we struggle against an antagonist, we recognize the contradiction inhering in this fight. We can defeat an opponent, but an internal contradiction always defeats us.

Hegel's insistence that contradiction is absolute bespeaks a vision of subjectivity as fundamentally self-destructive. And yet, he concludes his philosophy of art with a turn to comedy. He even claims that "comedy is fundamentally that with which tragedy comes to an end."[19] But the end of the tragic is not its erasure but the embrace of self-destruction as constitutive. We arrive at the comic, ironically, when we cease trying to transcend our self-destruction. The comic recognizes that contradiction is inescapable, which is why all humor is essentially gallows humor.

Though Hegel ends his history of art with comedy rather than tragedy, his turn to comedy is an affirmation of the insurpassability of our self-defeat. The comic figure is a figure reconciled with its self-defeat rather than struggling against it. Comedy is tragedy after giving up resistance to the tragic. Comedy recognizes that there is no escape, just as Hegel's philosophy leaves no way out. In it, resolution (*Auflösung*) serves as the name for internalizing rather than overcoming contradiction. Through this internalization of contradiction, he follows the lead of the dramatic arts.

Notes

1   G.W.F. Hegel, *Aesthetics: Lectures on Fine Art*, trans. T.M. Knox, vol. 1 (Oxford: Clarendon Press, 1975), 11.

2   Robert Pippin, "What Was Abstract Art? (From the Point of View of Hegel)," *Critical Inquiry* 29 (2002): 1–24, 24.

3   See Slavoj Žižek, *Disparities* (London: Bloomsbury, 2016).

4   Benjamin Rutter, *Hegel on the Modern Arts* (Cambridge: Cambridge University Press, 2010), 6–7.

5   Martin Heidegger, "The Origin of the Work of Art." In *Poetry, Language, Thought*, trans. Albert Hofstader (New York: Harper and Row, 1975), 15–86, here: 71; Theodor W. Adorno, *Aesthetic Theory*, ed. Gretel Adorno and Rolf Tiedemann, trans. Robert Hullot-Kentor (Minneapolis: University of Minnesota Press, 1997), 130.

6   Walter A. Davis, *Get the Guests: Psychoanalysis, Modern American Drama, and the Audience* (Madison: University of Wisconsin Press, 1994), 61.

7   G.W.F. Hegel, *Lectures on the Philosophy of Art: The Hotho Transcripts of the 1823 Berlin Lectures*, trans. Robert F. Brown (Oxford: Clarendon Press, 2014), 434.

8   G.W.F. Hegel, *Aesthetics*, 1205.

9   G.W.F. Hegel, *The Difference between Fichte's and Schelling's System of Philosophy*, trans. H.S. Harris and Walter Cerf (Albany: SUNY Press, 1977), 80 (translation modified).

10 G.W.F. Hegel, *Phenomenology of Spirit*, trans. A.V. Miller (Oxford: Oxford University Press, 1977), 36 (translation modified).

11 Hegel, *Phenomenology of Spirit*, 41.

12 Charles Taylor, *Hegel* (Cambridge: Cambridge University Press, 1975), 348.

13 Hegel, *Phenomenology of Spirit*, 339–40.

14 See Dieter Henrich, *Hegel im Kontext* (Frankfurt am Main: Suhrkamp, 1971).

15 G.W.F. Hegel, *The Science of Logic*, ed. and trans. George di Giovanni (Cambridge: Cambridge University Press, 2010), 59.

16 Alain Badiou recognizes the hostile relationship that philosophy must have to the story of self-identity, but he contends, against Hegel, that the matheme rather than drama is the proper response. He states, "philosophy is originally linked to the possibility of interrupting the story." Alain Badiou, *Le Séminaire—Parménide: L'être I—Figure ontologique, 1985-1986* (Paris: Fayard, 2014), 258.

17 Hegel, *Aesthetics*, vol. 1, 9 (translation modified).

18 In his discussion of *Hamlet*, Hegel claims, "In Hamlet's case one must say that the ending is a matter of chance. Contingency can only be of interest insofar as it is congruent with what issues from the heart. Hamlet is without support; the shoal of finitude is insufficient for him. In the background of his heart there lies death. And this inner necessity is worked out by contingent external factors." Hegel, *Lectures on the Philosophy of Art*, 436.

19 Hegel, *Lectures on the Philosophy of Art*, 437.

15

Parallaxes of Sinister Enjoyment

The Lessons of Interpassivity and the Contemporary Troubles with Pleasure

Robert Pfaller

Roughly twenty-five years ago, in the mid-1990s, happened the discovery of what I have called "Interpassivity." This discovery became possible due to a tool that Slavoj Žižek had developed for quite different purposes. Žižek had pointed at the idea, crucial for psychoanalysis, that the unconscious can be outside, that our innermost feelings can be executed by external agents. Žižek illustrated this with the example from his own experience: he likes it when television Sitcoms that include "canned laughter" laugh already in his place. So he does not have to pay attention and is not even obliged to laugh, but still can feel, as he calls it, "objectively amused."[1] This remark was directed toward this paradoxical outside existence of the unconscious as it is to be understood in psychoanalytic theory.

But this idea was just as helpful to me, as a philosopher engaged in the battles of aesthetics and of the spontaneous philosophies that surround the arts. It allowed me to tackle something that was at the time not only by coincidence *unseen* but *impossible to see* within the art field. It was a necessarily invisible issue, or a necessary non-object of aesthetic theory at the time—due to the presence of interactivity theory. Interactivity theory was in the mid-1990s an incredibly dominant theory that exerted a lot of influence and pressure upon the artists and their production. Interpassivity was at that time impossible to see due to the fundamental assumptions that interactivity theory promoted. These assumptions were: if the observers are active, if there is some involvement or participation on the side of the observers, then they gain more pleasure from observing, and they also gain more freedom—since they are not passive and just watching like "couch potatoes" that have to accept and to swallow what the artists produce; instead, they can somehow change what they swallow, and that is better and liberating.

Of course, everyone a bit familiar with philosophy knows quite well that *being active* is not a proof of *being free*. Spinoza has taught a great lecture on this: not every activity is a free activity. One can be very active, but as a servant under somebody else's command, and one can also be active for somebody else's profit. With Žižek's remark, it became possible to see that the same also goes for pleasure. It is not true that people are more happy or that they gain more pleasure the more they are involved in something. Žižek's remarks on his own TV experience proved exactly the opposite: there were some people existing who did not want to be actively involved—they did not want to change what they saw; and they did not even want to be passively involved—they did not even want to do the enjoyment part of it; they did not want to laugh. This brought us to think that the relationship between people and their pleasure is more complicated than interactivity theory had assumed. And it is also more complicated than a more general theory of the "homo oeconomicus" would assume. This theory had probably provided the pre-conscious, underlying anthropology of interactivity theory. The "homo oeconomicus" theory in its basic line would be that we try to minimize work, and to maximize pleasure. But interpassivity theory obviously proved the opposite. People do not always want to maximize their pleasures. They sometimes even want to be defended from their pleasures, and they want somebody else to enjoy in their place, vicariously.

The fact that the relationship between people and their pleasures is quite problematic became obvious only a few years later in Europe. At the end of the 1990s, it became quite clear that people have a quite problematic relationship with their pleasures. One could say that at that time most of what had hitherto been pleasures were seen "breaking bad." All the things that had previously been fun for adults, like drinking alcohol, smoking, having sex, or just flirting, wearing furs, high heels, driving cars, eating meat, and many other pleasures, all of a sudden became sinister, dark—under various suspicions, political, hygienic, environmental, and so on. We can say that at the end of the 1990s—I would claim under the massive impact of neoliberalism and its ideological ally, postmodernity—we observed a kind of parallactic move of culture: a parallactic move with regard to pleasure. Pleasure turned sinister. This sudden change can only be compared, I think, to changes that we sometimes observe in love life. There the same thing can happen. For example, your best friend, just fallen in love, tells you that a certain person is so great and can only be loved, which is completely obvious, etc. A while later the same friend starts telling you that this person is completely awful, and it is obvious that this person can only be hated. You will see this transition going on without any mediation in between. There was not a moment of doubt, or balanced opinion, or undecidedness. There was just a sudden change from one extreme obviousness to the opposed extreme obviousness.

Furthermore, this "change of opinion" was not caused by any new information that people gained about their love partners. It is not that until yesterday they thought that the beloved person was a shining beauty, but after a while, they discovered that this person never arrives in time, so that they had to think over their judgment. It is not like that. When you look carefully at your friends and when you see them falling in love, ask them what is the reason why they are in love. Write that reason down for yourself. And a couple of years later, when they separate again, ask them why they separate. Then you will find out that it is often precisely the same reason. For example, three years ago, it was wonderful because this person was so caretaking. Finally your friend found somebody who really cared. Three years later, this is unbearable because it is totally suffocating; this person takes away their breath with all that care—totally impossible. Or until yesterday, this person was witty and inspiring, and it was wonderful because this person was intellectually so brilliant. But today it is terrible because this smart ass always knows better and always has to have the last word.

Now I think precisely the same thing went on with the breaking bad of our pleasures. We did not learn that smoking, of which we had thought that it was a beautiful and innocent pleasure, was actually not so healthy, so that we had to start to change our mind about it. No. This is very nicely remarked by the American author Richard Klein in his beautiful book *Cigarettes Are Sublime*,[2] where he states that if we had not known that cigarettes are dangerous, we would never have smoked them. It is precisely the danger for our health that makes them sublime. What Klein remarks here, I think, can be generalized to all our pleasures. The damaging character pertains to every of our delights. And it is precisely that malign, or evil, dimension that makes these things sublime for us. You can even think of apparently harmless pleasures: partying, for instance. OK, but still it messes up your flat. Or you dance as if there were no tomorrow. OK, but it costs your sleep. Even if you do such apparently innocent things like philosophizing, or going for a walk, you have to be ready to waste time. You cannot say, I will philosophize now for two minutes, and then I will stop and do some other things, etc. There is always something in pleasure that challenges us to transgress our ordinary economy of resources: time, money, sleep, soberness, etc. This is what Georges Bataille has nicely pointed at with his notion of "transgression" that pertains to any of our pleasures.[3] This is precisely also the reason why the typical postmodern strategy to solve this problem, the so-called "Non-ism," does not work. Slavoj Žižek has given a nice list of examples and was one of the first who analyzed this development[4]: in the 1990s, we were all of a sudden delivered with such interesting inventions like beer without alcohol, coffee without caffeine, cream without fat, sex without body contact, politics without decisions, or art without genius. In all these practices, the malign, somehow uncanny, dimension was removed, but did we thus become more happy? Of course, not. Have you ever celebrated a party only with orange juice? I think, it does not work. This is, as Richard Klein has remarked, because it is the malign dimension that allows us to turn these things into instances of the sublime. The crucial question here is, of course, how does this parallactically work? How can some malign thing be turned into some sublime thing? And what is the parallaxis in culture, on the contrary, that succeeded at turning all the formerly sublime things into matters that have to be prohibited and policed away because they are so nasty, ugly, unhealthy, opposed to appropriate behavior, etc.?

Psychoanalysis is probably *the* theory that has remarked that pleasure is in itself something problematic and that it can become sinister. Just think of Sigmund Freud's remarks on the notion of "taboo" in Polynesian,[5] which corresponds very well to what Indo-European languages show with their always double notions of, for example, in English the "holy" and the "sacred" (or in Latin, *sanctus* and *sacer*; Greek *hosios* and *hagios*, etc.): Freud notes that "taboo" means, on the one hand, "sublime, holy," and on the other hand, it means "filthy." This is exactly what happened to our pleasures: they are on the one hand sublime, and on the other filthy. And they can turn from one appearance into the other, opposed appearance. Of course, the same goes for Freud's own notion of pleasure, and especially for his notion of "neurotic displeasure." Freud states that what patients apparently suffer from, at some point in the course of psychoanalytic treatment, they start defending. So when the analyst seems to start taking away their symptoms, they start defending their symptoms as if they were a treasure. This shows, says Freud, that there is some unacknowledged pleasure at work in the symptom, and that is what is being defended by the patients.[6] This notion of neurotic displeasure is basically what Jacques Lacan has later designated by his notion of "enjoyment" (*jouissance*). Enjoyment in Lacan's sense is, again, a kind of filthy pleasure, and a pleasure that is basically suffering[7]—a pleasure that is under most conditions experienced as displeasure.

Furthermore, beyond pointing out that pleasure can appear in its opposed form, psychoanalysis has given us another hint, which is, I think, relevant here. In his essay "The Uncanny" (Freud [1919h]), Freud describes very aptly that whenever pleasure appears as filthy or unpleasant, we do not only have to do with such displeasure but also with an agent that appears as the thief of our enjoyment. So whenever you hate your pleasure, you also find a culprit who has taken away your pleasure. I think this is very significant for the postmodern situation. If postmodernism has succeeded in turning our pleasures into displeasures, into matters of disgust and awe, it has also been very successful at producing alleged thieves of enjoyment. Prominent examples for such thieves today are, for example, refugees who threaten to take away all our pleasures, but in other discourses, the same function is fulfilled by heterosexual white men who seem to have been the big thieves of enjoyment in history—just to mention two prominent instances.

In psychoanalysis, the thieves of enjoyment have basically two shapes. One is the mythical "primordial father" who enjoys everything (all the tribe's females) and castrates everybody else (all the tribe's males); and the other is the *doublegaenger* who does the same. The *doublegaenger* is that other ego who has access to enjoyment, takes away your enjoyment, and enjoys in your place; thus, the *doublegaenger* is the prominent figure of the thief of enjoyment in Freud's theory, in his essay "The Uncanny."

Now it is important here how the parallactic shift from filthy to sublime pleasure can be managed. It may be helpful to recall a little bit of theology, if you allow me to enter this foreign terrain for a moment. I have developed this point in my recent book *Erwachsenensprache*.[8] If you briefly put a very rough picture of religious history before your eyes, one may perhaps state this: Of course not all religions do have Gods, as Emile Durkheim has remarked.[9] But in case that religions do have Gods—is it then not significant that the older a religion is, the younger its Gods can be? So older religions have very young Gods, and some very old religions only have young Gods, where all Gods are children. In religions that we are a bit familiar with—ancient Greece, ancient Rome—you find all kind of divine ages, but among them you find a number of child Gods, infant Gods with a pretty childish behavior: so, for instance, you have little Eros, this naked little boy with his bow and arrow, who shoots at mortal people, totally irresponsibly. This is how you can explain why people fall in love with entirely inappropriate partners, like the doctor father or the psychoanalyst or whoever may occur. The Greeks and Romans explained this inappropriateness by the fact that it was not the most responsible God who shot around with his love arrows. And, of course, in Greek and Roman antiquity, you do not only find children Gods but also drunk Gods, like Dionysus; you also have sexually greedy Gods, divine men and women who were constantly after human beings, trying to seduce or to rape them, taking on the shapes of animals; and you have very jealous Gods, childishly vain Goddesses who start the Trojan war, a total massacre, just because three Goddesses compete about who is the most beautiful among them. Attempting to come to a general judgment, we have to say that Greek and Roman antiquity not only placed their Goddesses and Gods above themselves, intellectually and morally, but placed them quite often below themselves— as even more silly and foolish than the humans, and morally even less responsible than the human beings. The younger a religion is, I would claim, the more its Gods move upward. In Catholicism, you still have a certain heritage of this ancient heritage, a certain childish personnel—not exactly Gods, but at least you have baby Jesus, and you have a number of naked little angels that emerge in the Christmas decorations in the streets with their naked little asses. So there is still quite some fun with these holy personnel from the heavens that come down to earth at some times of the year. In Protestantism, of course, this has been completely erased; you have just one God, and this God is very old and wise, knows everything, even your innermost motivations, and is, of course, not sexually greedy or after you—anything of this kind is far below this God. So what does this mean, if we can describe the religious development like this? Psychoanalytically speaking, we can say: modern people only feel observed *from above*, by an agency that reads their innermost feelings and longings. This is very similar to what Sigmund Freud coined his notion of the *superego* for. That is also an eye that looks down upon you, and into you, from above. Ancient Gods, on the contrary, looked at you *from below*. And they did not look into you. They just looked how things appeared.

In our culture we have still preserved a certain respect for this kind of observation, for example in terms of politeness. When we perform acts of politeness, it is not that we care, like upper Gods, about how things are meant. We only care about how it looked. And even if we meant it very honestly, it is a shame if it did not work on the level of appearance. Not ourselves, and not the others, but somebody else could be very disappointed and find this utterly shameful if we do things improperly. We have a lot of skills for doing this properly, so that the appearance of politeness can be established and maintained. All of us have a lot of knowledge about, for example, what it means to shake a hand. It has to have a certain speed, not too fast, not too slow; it has to have a certain firmness; you must not squeeze too much, but also not too little; you must not to leave the other's hand too early, and not too late; and so on. So there is a lot of competences that we apply here, and if something goes wrong, we feel a bit ashamed, although we know perfectly well that we meant it honestly. Yet politeness was not fully established, and that means that we somehow disappointed a lower agency of observation: one that only cares for appearances and does not look into our innermost motivations. This can sometimes be even very shameful. Even if you have the most honest feelings, when you, for example, while attending a funeral, want to express your sympathy and condolence with, let us say, the mourning widow, but unfortunately, precisely because you are so moved, you stumble and fall upon the widow, and together with her fall into the open grave, etc. You may have meant it very honestly, and you were actually very sad, but still it looked like slapstick, and the whole ceremony may appear jeopardized and may have to be repeated because this was so shameful.

This means that we have got some implicit knowledge about this looking at ourselves from below: looking not at our intentions but only at our appearances. This is, of course, of crucial importance also for psychoanalysis, a theory that cares very much for appearances. It is the whole issue of the initially quoted statement by Žižek referring to Lacan's sentence that "the unconscious is outside." This is precisely a reference to this fact that psychoanalysis does not ask how you meant it but instead listens to what and how you said it or how you performed it and reads this appearance.

Now, what can be learned here from ancient Greek culture? I think the crucial point here is *that these infantile, silly Gods that looked at people from below nevertheless were Gods and still deserved a certain respect and obedience for that*. Not people believed in Gods at that time, but on the contrary, as it were, the Gods believed in human beings, and these had to act accordingly, in order not to disappoint the Gods' expectations. So even if what these Gods wanted was silly, people had to respect them and pay tribute to them. So if they were very silly and just wanted to be entertained, people had to organize—just like today's television programmers—something for them in order not to get bored. One had to give them some sports, or some music, Olympic Games, and display human happiness, so that these Gods did not get bored and start throwing lightnings upon people.

Sigmund Freud remarks this difference that separates us from the ancient world in a footnote to his "Three Essays on the Theory of Sexuality," where he states that ancient people's relation to sexuality was completely different from that of us moderns. Freud states,

> The most striking distinction between the erotic life of antiquity and our own no doubt lies in the fact that the ancients laid the stress upon the instinct itself, whereas we emphasize its object. The ancients glorified the instinct and were prepared on its account to honour even an inferior object; while we despise the instinctual activity in itself, and find excuses for it only in the merits of the object.[10]

The ancients (to put this into another, maybe more precise translation) "celebrated the drive": the key to this remark, I think, relies in the notion of celebration, since you do not celebrate when you want. Celebration is an obligation—a duty that is deserved mostly to young, silly Gods.

As a consequence, in culture we have to do with two different types of objects. We have to do with profane objects that are *allowed*, like mineral water, or beer (here in Bavaria, you can order a pint of beer for lunch even if you are a policeman or a soldier)— completely profane, at least up to a certain amount. But you cannot order champagne with your *Schnitzel* or your *Weißwurst*. That would not only be a strange choice but you would even feel a bit uncanny if you did that. Champagne belongs to a different kind of drinks that are *either forbidden or obligatory*. When your colleague at the office or the other professor has got their birthday, of course, somebody will come with a bottle of champagne; and while otherwise it may be completely prohibited to drink alcohol, now the opposite is the case, and now it is obligatory to drink champagne. Even if the doctor has forbidden it to you, you must take a little bit of champagne and congratulate the birthday girl or boy. The objects that pertain to the order of the sacred have these modalities: on the one hand, they are forbidden; on the other, they are obligatory. I think this is the solution to the problem of the ambivalence of pleasure in culture—a solution that will maybe allow us to see the pleasures under their sublime aspect again.

Culture has this crucial function, as it were, to reconcile the individuals with their enjoyment and with the sacred objects—by the help of a command. So when I sit at home at night, studying philosophy, but some friends come by and knock at my door, saying, "Robert, you have read enough for today; come with us now for a beer, as we have got to celebrate something...," then I gladly come with them, and then the glass of beer that I hold in my hand becomes a proof to me that life is worth living for. The next day, I may not even want to *think* of beer. But under this command, beer becomes something sublime to me.

So we have to acknowledge that people are not spontaneously hedonist. On the contrary, people are pretty reluctant to enjoy at the moment when they perceive the pleasure as something pertaining to the sacred, and then only a command by culture can help them to transgress this limitation and to transform this filthy sacred object into a sublime one. Then, of course, they enjoy this tremendously—and what they enjoy is precisely the power of their group or collective to transform this object into a sublime object. This is the crucial point in the perception of these objects, and in the perception of others that today mostly appear as "thieves of enjoyment," primordial fathers who tackle us with some offer of alcohol, or the smoker who wants to offer us a cigarette, and so on—terrible characters that penetrate our innocent intimacy and homoeostasis these days, in postmodernity. I think the crucial question of perception here is always, do we perceive the other as someone who transgresses a boundary, that transgresses a prohibition; or do we see the other as someone who follows an obligation, someone who respects a duty. This is the crucial difference in how we perceive others. David Foster Wallace, in his talk "This Is Water," has given a nice example of how this perception changes our judgments fundamentally. He says, when I drive in traffic by car, and somebody overtakes me in a very ruthless, dangerous way, so that I have to break, then I get very angry, of course, and I want to shoot him to the moon. Because I think, I follow the rules, and the other doesn't. The other is a total lawbreaker, someone that does not follow any rules. Psychoanalytically this means, we are castrated, but the other somehow escaped castration—a kind of primordial father on four wheels. But, Foster Wallace says, this is just a matter of imagination. We imagine it to be like this. We imagine that the other's not following any rules is the enjoyment that he has taken away from us. A very questionable enjoyment, by the way. Would you like to have this enjoyment? Imagine that the Bavarian police sends you a letter saying, "Dear Madam, dear Sir, we have learned that tomorrow is your birthday, and, as a little gift from the Bavarian police, you can drive on the Bavarian highway tomorrow as crazily and ruthlessly as you want, without being punished." Would you accept this present? Here we encounter again what Freud says in his essay on the uncanny: when the *doublegaenger* appears, it is about stealing a pleasure from you that you actually would not want to have. But still you are very angry that the other takes this presumed pleasure away from you. So, Foster Wallace says, it is my imagination, or your imagination, to think that the other were the thief of your enjoyment (psychoanalytically speaking, the other is the cause of your castration, while he has remained uncastrated). But, Foster Wallace states, we can also form a completely different imagination. We can, for instance, imagine that the other has got a terribly wounded child on his backseat—a child that I cannot see from my position of view—and probably he has got to bring this wounded child to a nearby hospital as fast as possible. In this case, would not everybody be glad to give way to this driver? We would not be angry at him for driving so dangerously. On the contrary, one would be glad to help him with this task. So the key question here is: do I perceive this other as somebody who just wants something, for example, to drive like a madman? Do I see this other—psychoanalytically speaking—as homogeneous, that is, as someone who is like "at home" in this nasty pleasure that is forbidden to us? So that I am a foreigner to this pleasure, but the other is at home in it? Or do I see the other as just as split as myself, as someone who has to follow a duty? Can I see him maybe as someone who is even ashamed about the fact that he has to drive like a madman, but still feels he has to do it in order to save the child? If I am able to see the other in this way, as split just as myself, then I do not have a problem in solidarizing with him. I think this is today the crucial problem in culture. We do not see the other as someone who is split. Instead we see him as someone who is completely at home in his filthy enjoyment that he, miraculously, can bear and enjoy, whereas we, subjected to rules, to castration, subjected to health requirements, environmental requirements, requirements of decent behavior, and so on, are completely deprived from that. The fact that we homogenize the other is the reason why we often say things like, for example, "Dear Madam, dear Sir, if you have to do this, then please do it at home."

Twenty or thirty years ago on the contrary, it was pretty obvious to people that these things were not matters of "doing it at home." In the photo albums of our parents and grandparents, one finds them smoking when they were in public. They smoked just as they dressed a bit more elegantly when they went out. Smoking belonged to their public appearance. It was a tribute to appearance and to politeness. At home they often did not smoke; they did only under the condition that they had guests. So even non-smokers always had a small collection of cigarettes and cigars at home for the case that guests would arrive. Then one had to be elegant and generous and offer them some. This was the condition under which smoking took place at home. Today, on the contrary, we regard smoking as something totally filthy that can only belong to the private person, not to the "public man" and to the order of appearance. It cannot be a duty; it must be an addiction, we assume.

This is why I think that we have today to relearn the lessons of ancient Greek religion (a few traces of which have survived in Catholicism): that there are silly Gods that sometimes demand from us silly things; things that can become pleasures, due to demands that allow us to transform filthy matters into sublime ones. Only under this condition that we feel observed from below, we become able not to see our filthy pleasures only as awful. This is why I have suggested a small modification to the Freudian "topography" of the psychic apparatus with its agencies of "super-ego," "ego," and "id." In the Freudian picture, only the super-ego is conceived as an agency of observation. But actually, if we take Freud's own remarks seriously—especially his reference, in "The Uncanny," to Heinrich Heine's novel *Gods in Exile*, where the ancient

Gods themselves have become filthy and threatening, because they are not celebrated anymore—then we can say: maybe from below, from the "id" do not only emerge nasty drives; maybe also the id is something that observes us, from below, and brings with it some nasty duties. Sometimes we have to drink, or to smoke, or to utter silly formulas of politeness; sometimes we have to talk to others, and be generous or charming; sometimes we may even have to do sex; etc. So there can be a lot of silly duties that can be commanded by silly Gods. But the fact that we perceive them, with their eyes, as duties allows us to turn these silly things into sublime things. Everything here depends on the question whether we regard these lower agencies as agencies of observation, that is, of duty, and not just as agencies of drives. This is why I have suggested to call this lower agency of the psychic apparatus not the "id" but the "under-ego." The under-ego is the agency that observes us, only cares for appearances, and causes us to see things that we ourselves are pretty reluctant to do as duties. Thus it helps us to overcome our limitations. So, for example, when I come to a bar with dimmed light and elegant atmosphere, with smooth jazz coming from the loudspeakers, then I hear the voice of a lower God that tells me, "Robert, now please do not order mineral water here." This is how the lower psychic agency helps us to become more elegant, generous, and sovereign, to go for life as it is worth living for, and not only serve life as servants of its preservation, as Georges Bataille has aptly put this. Then our pleasures, all of a sudden, present themselves from their sublime side. And the other that we hitherto perceived in a postmodern way as a thief of our enjoyment all of a sudden turns out to be a comrade, a helper to experience the pleasure as sublime, and as something that can be shared in solidarity—and as something that is pleasant precisely due to the solidarity. This is not only an issue of "how can we maximize pleasure?" or "how can we have pleasure at all, instead of experiencing it as appalling and filthy?" This is also an inherently political question. It epitomizes the absolute minimum standard of good life that must not be undergone. This is not a matter of that kind of good life that yuppie people stress other people with—of endless refinement of food and holiday destinations. Instead, it is that very minimum standard of good life without which you would not have any life at all that merits its name. People lacking this notion of a minimum standard of good life would not even know what to politically fight for. This is the reason why, in Bertolt Brecht's poem, the Paris communards of 1871 in their "resolution" declare to their enemies that they have decided to fear henceforth *bad life more than death.*"[11]

Notes

1   Slavoj Žižek, *Liebe Dein Symptom wie Dich selbst! Jacques Lacans Psychoanalyse und die Medien* (Berlin: Merve, 1991), 50.
2   Richard Klein, *Cigarettes are Sublime* (London: Picador, 1995).
3   See Georges Bataille, *The Accursed Share. An Essay on General Economy*, vols. II & III (New York: Zone Books, 1993).
4   Slavoj Zizek, "Psychoanalyse und deutscher Idealismus," *Mesotes. Zeitschrift für philosophischen Ost-West-Dialog* 1 (1992): 5–14; Slavoj Zizek, "Passion in the Era of Decaffeinated Belief," *The Symptom* 5 (Winter 2004). Available online: https://www.lacan.com/passionf.htm (accessed March 2, 2020).

5   Sigmund Freud, "Totem und Tabu." In *Studienausgabe, Bd. IX* (Frankfurt am Main: Fischer, 1993), 287–444, here: 311.

6   Sigmund Freud, "Jenseits des Lustprinzips." In *Studienausgabe, Bd. III* (Frankfurt am Main: Fischer, 1989), 213–72, here: 220.

7   Jacques Lacan, *The Seminar. Book VII. The Ethics of Psychoanalysis, 1959–60*, trans. Dennis Porter, notes by Dennis Porter (London: Routledge, 1992), 184; Dylan Evans, *An Introductory Dictionary of Lacanian Psychoanalysis* (London/New York: Routledge, 1997), 91f.

8   Robert Pfaller, *Erwachsenensprache. Über ihr Verschwinden aus Politik und Kultur* (Frankfurt am Main: Fischer, 2017); Robert Pfaller, "The Sub-Ego. Description of an Inferior Observing Agency," *Problemi* LVII, nos. 11–12 (2019): 143–56.

9   See Emile Durkheim, *The Elementary Forms of the Religious Life* (London: Allen & Unwin, 1976).

10   Sigmund Freud: "Three Essays on the Theory of Sexuality." In *Standard Edition*, vol. 7 (1905), 125–245, here: 149.

11   Bertolt Brecht, *Die Gedichte von Bertolt Brecht in einem Band* (Frankfurt am Main: Suhrkamp, 1984), 653.

16

Nautical Positioning
Navigating with Whitehead's Process-Ontology

Eva Schürmann

If, in an effort to discover in parallax, a productive theoretical figure by means of which our general unease about our world relations were to be expressed beyond the subject-object dichotomy, then many parallax thinkers avant la lettre can be found: Nicholas of Cusa and his concept of a "coincidence of opposites," Spinoza's anti-cartesian monism, Leibniz's substance pluralism, Fichte's transcendental idealism, Hegel's Kant-critical dialectic, Schopenhauer's conception of representation resp. imagination, and Merleau-Ponty's perceptual phenomenology. Each of these theories marks an important stage within ontology-critical thought that seeks to grasp what happens when a subject's consciousness, experiencing itself, relates to a world that is obviously not simply "given." Because of the consequence of the division of being into a subjective and an objective part further oppositions follow: such as the one of spirit and matter as well as freedom and causality, or culture and nature.

Spinoza, in direct reaction to Cartesian dualism, takes offence at the conception of two substances whose accordance can never be made plausible. Leibniz's pluralistic monades leave behind the binary correspondence of mind and matter. Schopenhauer expects the productive dissolution of aporetic subject-object relations through his concept of *representation* (German *Vorstellung*, meaning *idea* as well as *imagination*) since they contain both: a representing self as the form of realization of a represented object. However, since such a concept of representation sounds all too mentalistic, Merleau-Ponty will, in the twentieth century, expect more from the concept of perception. Its corporeal foundation has a less idealistic bias but follows the same critique of the subject-object dichotomy.

All these voices could be recalled and retraced here, if the chapter's ambition would be to present a critical history of ontology and to shed light on the problems connected with it, like, for instance, the debates between realism and idealism. But the systematic problem does not exclusively and not primarily exist with regard to the question of

For helpful explanations of Whitehead's philosophy I am very grateful to Michael Hampe; for the translation to Dominik Finkelde; and for his cognitive support, as always, to Gerhard Dirmoser.

how to understand the subject-object-ontology as the relation between a wordless and incorporeal cogito-ego, which is confronted with an object as composed of lifeless and mechanistic matter. Rather, the problem already exists where our thinking about being as a totality is too static due, for example, to the "law of identity" and "the principle of sufficient reason." Both laws commit us to a logic of determination(s) that cannot do justice to process-dynamics, fissures, or ruptures (in the sense of nonlinear developments), phase transitions, interactions, and contradictions that characterize being from the outset. This is where, according to the considerations developed in the following sections, parallax comes into play, namely as a concept with the help of which an identifying, linear-causal and determining thinking can be circumvented.

Taking parallax as a starting point, a dualistic subject-object-ontology is not only erroneous if or because the relationship of an already overestimated subject of domination is thought undialectically with regard to an always simplified understanding of the world as object; what is more crucial is that further multifactorial interactions between mind and world are added to the spatiotemporal conditions of their reciprocal movement and situation. If neither subject nor object are ever completely identical with themselves, because their situatedness is changeable at every moment in which new constellations constantly arise, other facets become recognizable (but also new actualizations result and interdependent influences assert themselves), then one encounters the traces of an ontology process theoretically conceived. There are also a number of important key witnesses, whose names are, however, significantly less well-known in the history of philosophy than those philosophers mentioned above.

I am thinking, for example, of the epistemologist Gaston Bachelard, the paleontologist Pierre Teilhard de Chardin, and the mathematician and philosopher Alfred North Whitehead. The philosophical views of these thinkers naturally differ in detail. What they have in common, however, are a few basic motives, such as the criticism of any form of substance thinking and the ambition to shed light on a unified theory of the world. They take offence at the fact that human self- and world-relations usually disintegrate within the history of ideas into a scientific-objectivist and a subjectivist description. They criticize that once these descriptions are separated, they can no longer be brought together, and the understanding of the world thus collapses into completely incommensurable perspectives. This interpretation of being as expressed in unconnected systems of description leads to a whole series of problems, of which the mind-body problem is only one, although probably the most severe. What is called the "explanatory gap" in the philosophy of mind, however, does not only concern the question of how neuronal states become personal experiences and brain physiological processes become qualitative experiences. It also concerns the relationship between freedom and causality as a whole. As a consequence, ontology is segmented into different areas: On the one hand we have the front-line position of subjectivity in the sense of a "domain ontology" of the private, of feeling, arbitrariness, and mere opinion. And on the other hand, we have the sphere of what is "objective" in the sense of what is factual within absolutely existing or timeless natural laws.

To explain ourselves as responsible and rational agents is no longer possible in such an ontology, since it lacks an explanation of how the phenomenally experienced world of cultural, historical, and social practice is supposed to be able to have evolved from the "matter" for which the history of nature stands for. In this universe, full of atoms, comets, and planets, full of physically explicable (and also inexplicable) phenomena, such as black holes or dark matter, there are, in an ontic sense, also phenomena such as music and art, religion and politics; there are cathedrals, progress in law, struggles for freedom, and normative convictions, as well as a history of science influenced by cultural history and socialization. Phenomena of this type are either not due to the laws of nature or are connected to them in a way that requires explanation, which cannot be dissociated from these laws.

Of course, parallax is not by itself a self-explicative key concept for a better understanding of being and the world. In order to be able to become one, it must be spelled out in certain intentions and integrated into a larger theoretical framework, especially if, as in my case, it has to be developed in its significance for aesthetics. I have to go into more detail for this and would like to refer (from the tableau of possible connections or systematic interfaces mentioned at the beginning of this chapter) to a thinker whose cosmological conception of ontology is very well suited to unfold parallactic subject-object relations: Alfred N. Whitehead.

Whitehead is undoubtedly an extravagant thinker whose terminology is not easily accessible and who, probably for this reason, is still not as well-received in Germany as he deserves.[1] But his neologisms are, for good reasons, indebted to the insight that the problems of subject-object thinking are at least partly due to a bewitching grammar and hypostasizing language of the philosophical tradition. In Whitehead's process-teleological thinking, aesthetics occupies, as we will see, a key position, because all reality is understood from an elaborate concept of value-based experience. He considers logic and aesthetics, science and art to be equally original and equally truthful forms of what reality exploration stands for. He does not resign himself to the fact that in the midst of a physically describable icy space of matter and antimatter, of suns, and planets orbiting each other, there is also what he calls "the civilized universe."[2] (By this he does not only mean discourses like law and politics or symbolic forms like language and art but the fact that there is a striving for truth and a sense of beauty at all.) The civilized universe must be explainable and understandable within the natural universe. It cannot be put aside of an "actually" objective, material understanding of reality as being "merely" a subjective sphere of error-prone opinions. Therefore, if the idea of parallax is a theoretical figure by means of which dynamic variability, spatiotemporal transition, and moving positionality can be conceptualized, then one would be wise to look up Whitehead. Within his process ontology, subjective and objective processes form a relational connection that is more than a change of perspective or dialectical mediation. He unfolds a metaphysics of the possible in which there can be no talk of ever completely identical original states, but in which the experiencing and the experienced form a context of creative realization in inexhaustible diversity.

To explain this in detail, I proceed in the following three steps. First I explain by the help of a picture of nautical positions what for me is productive in parallax as a theoretical figure of thought. Second, as briefly as possible, I will trace Whitehead's quasi-nautical process-ontological theory in some basic ideas in order to establish what parallactic relations could be. In the third part, the concepts gained from this will be suitable for qualifying aesthetics as an index of experience and a sphere of value from which a parallactic understanding of ontology can be made plausible.

1. Nautical Interrelations

What is special and enlightening about parallax as a concept can best be explained with the help of an analogy, which I will elucidate with a recourse to the history of marine navigation. For the central idea of parallactically conceived subject-object relationships is not, according to my thesis, that we have different views depending on the observer and on the object. This would be nothing new compared to any perspectivism that has always emphasized the standpoint dependence and the relationality of reality. Already Wittgenstein's comments on aspect seeing proved adequately that a figure offers different possibilities of perception, which the beholder can realize differently in the act of perception. But such "gestalt-switch" figures as Jastrow's duck or Necker's Cube are usually bi-stable. One cannot constantly see or discover something new or different in them.

In the case of Wittgenstein's example, a motionless observer sees either a rabbit or a duck, period. From the perspective of nautics, on the other hand, we know the importance of parallaxes for position- and distance-determination under the conditions of continuous motion of all the variables of reference in play. Angle measurements, which arise when one orients oneself from moving locations on changing horizons, help to calculate one's own position or the distance from the target location. "Position marks nautically the temporarily occupied location of a moving object that floats, which is important for course changes."[3] If we take this useful determination of location as the starting point for parallactic subject-object relationships, we both do not think of them from the outset as fixed and statically locatable conditions.

Through navigation, we know how moving observers align themselves in the moving medium of water according to a changing starlit sky. Nautics is therefore the appropriate paradigm for the development of what is likely to be productive about parallax. The nautical sciences have existed for at least 5500 years; but in Europe people have only been navigating with the help of compass needles for about 800 years (much earlier so in China), and with the help of astrolabes for about 500 years. Before that, one was dependent on keeping sight of the coastline and the position of the sun. At night, people in the northern hemisphere oriented themselves to the constellation of the Big Dipper and the Polar Star. On the high seas one was always advised to orientate oneself according to the position of the stars. Therefore, the ephemeris of the astronomer Johannes Müller, later called Regiomontanus, is a milestone in the history of maritime navigation. Columbus and Vasco da Gama used these star charts on which the starlit sky is recorded in relation to the earth at a given time. Such astronomical tables do not determine position values once and for all, but in relation to a determining coordinate system at a certain time and for a certain period of time, namely in the case of Regiomontanus for constellations of the years 1475 to 1506. A more precise determination was only possible with the help of sextants.

Accordingly, a nautical concept of a position inevitably identifies something only as a temporary, changeable momentum of a process. In the nautical world we find a model of continuous motion of all relations involved in the determination of a position. Analogous to this, it becomes apparent that parallactically conceived subject-object relationships cannot simply be thought of in "presence-ontological terms." What something is or isn't is always different and has to be questioned anew, because it owes itself to multifocal and multiperspective processes that result from the dynamics of both moving observers and changing perceptions. This goes beyond, I think, what Žižek considers to be the decisive property of parallax:

> The standard definition of parallax is: the apparent displacement of an object (the shift of its position against a background), caused by a change in observational position that provides a new line of sight. The philosophical twist to be added, of course, is that the observed difference is not simply "subjective," due to the fact that the same object which exists "out there" is seen from two different stances, or points of view. It is rather that, as Hegel would have put it, subject and object are inherently "mediated," so that an "epistemological" shift in the subject's point of view always reflects an "ontological" shift in the object itself.[4]

This is true, but it is not enough if we expect a revised understanding of the terms "subjective" and "objective." A revision of ontology also requires a revised concept of identity. Something is, whatever it is, only in relation to countless other entities and in the spatiotemporal transitoriness of interdependent and interacting relations. We are no longer dealing here with comparatively simple, because bi-stable aspect changes, but possibly with temporarily unrecognizable aspects that are different today compared to yesterday or completely imperceptible from certain points in space.

On the basis of a concept of nautical positionality, it becomes impossible to think of an identical subject as a materially existing counterpart of a static object. To think according to nautics means not being able to deduct the epistemic position from the ontic determination. The nautical observer knows that she herself is in the middle of what she wants to measure or determine. Remembering her own speed of movement, in moving oceans and under the changing starlit sky, she navigates through a space-time that relativizes everything. Instead of asking for identifiable conditions, she perceives recognizable constellations and realizable possibilities against the background of changing horizon lines and ever new parallaxes.

So much for my understanding of parallaxes as nautical interrelations. It may remind us that at any moment from any position, aspects of objects become perceivable which are only transitory findings in dynamic stances. For a parallactic ontology, as I will now show, one finds in Whitehead a proponent of utmost importance.

2. Whitehead's Relational Ontology

Whitehead's cosmological process ontology is both science-oriented and science-critical. It takes into account the individual biological and physico-chemical findings of the individual sciences by never losing sight of the fact that natural reality consists of innumerable, simultaneously occurring, and interacting events on atomic and molecular, biochemical, and electromagnetic levels. But this does not cause him to abandon the first-personal and qualitative experience of this reality. Not only do experiential facts belong to reality just as much as other facts, but we know of all facts only through experience, which therefore cannot be excluded under any circumstance.[5] It is this form of abstraction that Whitehead criticizes above all else, both in the natural sciences and in philosophy. According to his conception, reality consists from the outset not merely of objectively measurable facts that are identical with themselves and that have also, as in Locke's work, secondary qualities. The entire distinction between primary and secondary qualities is based on a spatiotemporal localization and fixation of properties such as the mass or weight of a body on a supposedly primary level. The latter subsequently degrades, then, into other properties such as color or temperature to a rather vague position "within us," that is, in the mind, in feeling, or in suspiciously mistrusted acts of perception. Such a conception of being, however, abstracts from any concrete experience and individual realization of what is ontic. As a result, the unbearable "explanatory gap," mentioned above, arises between matter, supposedly raw or dead, and enigmatic spiritual phenomena that somehow emerge from matter. Whitehead criticizes this way of thinking as the "bifurcation of nature" which lacks the unification of a scientist-naturalistic view of the world, on the one hand, and a humane self-understanding as beings, on the other, beings who are capable of acting rationally and responsibly, historically and socioculturally.

> This theory which I am arguing against is to bifurcate nature into two divisions, namely into the nature apprehended in awareness and the nature which is the cause of this awareness. The nature which is the fact apprehended in awareness hold within it the greenness of trees, the song of the birds, the warmth of the sun, the hardness of the chairs, and the feel of the velvet. The nature which is the cause of awareness is the conjectured system of molecules and electrons which so affects the mind as to produce the awareness of apparent nature. The meeting point of these two natures is the mind, the causal nature being influent and the apparent nature being effluent.[6]

Although the mechanistic model of nature can be used with an astonishing amount of success, numerous incoherencies like erroneous ideas of cause and effect or truth and opinion follow. Only within the bifurcation theory do primarily scientific findings appear as actually truthful,[7] while real individual experiences are discredited as subjective opinions. By contrast, the "philosophy of organism" opens up a completely different theoretical framework.[8] In it there are actual entities, occasions, and events, which have psychophysical properties and which coexist in internally determined and externally creative relations with each other. They can grasp each other ("prehend") and experience, feel and perceive each other in different gradations.[9] The essential ability of actual entities consists in being able to make or have experiences that become conscious to different degrees and realize qualities of feeling and perceiving on an elementary level. These entities have the character of events that form connections ("nexūs") with each other: "an event is a nexus of actual occasions inter-related in some determinate fashion in some extensive quantum… for example, a molecule is a historic route of actual occasions, and such a route is an 'event.'"[10] The central position of the basic categorical concepts of event and nexus results from Whitehead's critique of the philosophical tradition of substance thinking.

> The classical ontology is "beautifully simple. But it entirely leaves out of account the interconnections between real things. Each substantial thing is thus conceived as complete in itself, without any reference to any other substantial thing. Such an account of the ultimate atoms, or of the ultimate monads, or of the ultimate subject enjoying experience, renders an interconnected world of real individuals unintelligible.[11]

An important feature of Whitehead's ontology is the status it gives to the modality of the possible. Reality is not identical with everything "that exists," but the respective, temporary actualization of possibilities. Alongside the "actual entities" there are the so-called "eternal objects," which are timeless forms or undetermined possibilities of that which has to be individually realized each in a particular way. Eternal objects are not, like Plato's ideas, hierarchically higher-valued, but a modal dimension of possibility that is still open in the way of how it will be actualized. "Concrescence" is what Whitehead calls the realization of universal forms through actualized entities. "Concrescence" from the Latin *concrescere* etymologically means growing together, but also condensing, emerging, forming. We will return to this later on, for the importance of the concrete in Whitehead's thinking can hardly be overestimated. For now, we may assert that "concretus" is the perfect participle passive form of *concrescere* and, as such, literally means "that which has been condensed," that which has arisen from movements that grow together.

The philosophy of the organic does not think of nature as a "passive, instantaneous existence of bits of matter,"[12] but takes into account the changing constellations of possibility and reality. Even a single cell is understood as a nexus of many actual entities. Consequently, a whole living being consists of an immense number of real individuals and plural nexūs. In this way, new formations constantly manifest and actualize themselves, grow together to new potentials, which, in turn, are only partially realized, etc. Spontaneity and unexpected developments are no longer inexplicable in these inexhaustible processes of becoming, but are completely coherent.

> We have to "think of the material world as basically not a shifting configuration of substantial things, but a nexus of events, or processes. We are to think of the existence of a mountain as a long process, and the existence of an individual atom in the mountain as a connected series of vibratory processes."[13]

What Whitehead calls "the contemporary world" consists of innumerable simultaneously occurring processes and events that make up everything that is.

> On a moonless night, the faintly luminous stretch of the sky which is the Milky Way is an Appearance of the contemporary world, namely, it is a great region within the "Receptacle" of that world as it appears. But the Reality whose functioning issues in that Appearance, is a flux of light-energy travelling through the utmost depths of space and, to our imaginations, through illimitable time.[14]

The decision as to whether our perception of such reality can be adequate cannot depend on either the subject or the object alone. Rather, the simultaneously perceivable region of reality consists, in turn, in the "nexus of real processes"[15] and is, thus, multifactorially conditioned. Questions such as "what guarantees the correspondence of a subjective perception with reality" and "when is it possible to have a reliable knowledge of objective facts" are mistaken from the outset. They are based on all-too-simple and fixed ideas of what a subject is, or an object, or what both are in their relation to one another. Hume had simplified the relationship between sensory perception and object all too much by "conceiving an initial bare occurrence of sense-impressions devoid of essential relationship to other factors in experience."[16] Behind every sensory experience lies "a terrific tale of complex activity omitted in the abstraction."[17] If one thinks, for example, of the complexity of cellular processes and the interaction of functional circuits in the organism, one will agree with Whitehead here. At any given moment, a sensory perception meets another "region" of reality, which can be pre-empted according to the preconditions of their respective organisms.

One can see how far such a description deviates from the usual bivalent, causal-logical understanding of subject and object, because a sense-datum causes not simply and automatically its own unambiguous registration. After all, the senses can also deceive. Rather, every perceptible thing appears only under complex realization conditions and within individual, spatiotemporal constellations: "[T]he resulting appearance… expresses the issue of a Law of Nature, belonging to that cosmic epoch and to those more special conditions within that epoch."[18] To question and to clarify is "whether the animal body and the external regions are not attuned together, so that under normal circumstances, the appearances conform to natures within the regions."[19] The question of correspondence (between perception and reality, the experiencing and the experienced) presents itself as a question of "truth-relations,"[20] of which there are different types. Sensory perceptions can realize truth relationships in varying degrees. They are largely determined by what an organism can apprehend from what is happening within its simultaneous present region of reality. For example, according to their organic abilities, bats can perceive sound waves in a cave that are not perceptible to humans. Dogs extract some sort of information from smells that are imperceptible to cats, and so on. To speak of an "objective content" is therefore an inadequate expression and an abstraction altogether, because everything that can be apprehended exists only as the possibility of an act of experience. When it is actually (ap-)prehended, it is *not* possible to abstract from the qualities of concrete experience of someone who prehends it. A consequence is that truth can no longer exclusively function as a propositional category of verification—with science, allegedly, incorporating the sum total of empirical facts. Science has no monopoly on truth and objectivity.

For process ontology, on the other hand, there are constantly changing parallaxes, and that means more than just perspectives. The entire framework of theoretical thinking is no longer that of a subject taking up or changing one point of view in order to focus on another aspect of an object; rather both, subject and object, are effects of interdependent processes. What is called subject elsewhere is, according to Whitehead, only an occurrence of actual entities that are or can become objects for respective other entities by being experienced (as data for their own development). With the neologism "superject," he wants to escape the pitfalls of the subject-object terminology.

> For Kant, the world emerges from the subject; for the philosophy of organism, the subject emerges from the world—a "superject" rather than a "subject."... the feeler is emergent from its own feelings.[21]

In the present context, we can limit ourselves to emphasize the abolition of linear cause-and-effect relationships, which is introduced by the term "superject." There is, from the outset, no such things as a substantial subject or a "given" object, and between the two an unambiguous relationship. As "subject" we refer, rather, to that which arises in and from an encounter of different processes through experience. Subjectivity is realized in the having and making of experiences.

Whitehead calls "fallacy of misplaced concreteness"[22] an error in reasoning that occurs in the process of deeming the result of an abstraction to be something concrete. We usually consider given things to be concrete in their materiality and consider our experience of them to be subjectively diverse. But something is concrete only in the way we experience it. If we detach things from this context, we incorrectly transform the abstract into a concrete datum. In this context Whitehead criticizes also what he calls a "simple location." This is yet another misleading abstraction that fixes things in spatiotemporal positions. From the insights of the physical sciences of his time, he deduces "the entire abandonment of the notion that simple location is the primary way in which things are involved in space-time."[23] The fallacy is to pinpoint concrete entities at defined space-time locations.

> To say that a bit of matter has simple location means that, in expressing its spatio-temporal relations, it is adequate to state that it is where it is, in a definite finite region of space, and throughout a definite finite duration of time, apart from any essential reference of the relations of that bit of matter to other regions of space and to other durations of time.[24]

For instance, the question of where exactly the color spectrum of a sunset is located cannot be answered by fixing it either to the sky or to the eye. The sunset is, rather, as experience the effect of a combined interaction of the sun, the molecules in the atmosphere, the eye, and the brain. These entities are necessary components for the perception of color. The fact that entities prima facie have a circumscribed form and are located in a specific place is abstracted from the processual event-form that they take on in larger contexts. "Entities" are events in the passage of space and time.

Obviously, Whitehead's ontology is strongly reminiscent of Leibniz. But Whitehead's relationship to the history of philosophy is selective;[25] he only partially follows Leibniz, whom he also criticizes for both linking "the terms 'perception' and 'apperception'... too closely... to the notion of consciousness" and to "the notion of representative perception." Whitehead "reject[s]" both terms mentioned above.[26] In contrast, for him the expressions "feeling" and "prehension" are more appropriate:

> But there is the term "apprehension".... Accordingly, on the Leibnizian model, I use the term "prehension" for the general way in which the occasion of experience can include, as part of its own essence, any other entity, whether another occasion of experience or an entity of another type. This term is devoid of suggestion either of consciousness or of representative perception."[27]

Whether he does justice to Leibniz is not of interest to us here. Of importance is his conviction that we must not imagine "actual entities" as Leibnizian monads. They are "unified events in space and time. In some ways, there is greater analogy with Spinoza's modes; that is why I use the terms mode and modal."[28]

Indeed, Spinoza's monism and Leibniz's pluralism sometimes enter Whitehead's thinking in a strange amalgamation. For him, the unity of the universe is thought to be the precondition for plural multiplicity. Not infrequently, his description of spirit and matter is reminiscent of the Spinozian model of an aspect change at the attribute level, for example when he writes: "There are two routes of creative passage from a physical occasion. One is towards another physical occasion, and the other is towards the derivative reflective occasion."[29] Similarly, Whitehead's creativity as a "category of the ultimate" resembles without doubt what Spinoza calls "natura naturans." Nevertheless, Whitehead does not think in terms of a psychophysical parallelism but in terms of a bipolar unity. A remark often quoted for its poignancy is worthy of reiteration here: "No one ever says, Here I am, and I have brought my body with me."[30]

Indeed, no one would express himself like that. Yet we are very familiar with the opposite phenomenon: to be physically present while with one's thoughts elsewhere. In Whitehead's ontology mind and matter are not parallel attributes of a monistic substance, but everything that is, exists in a psychophysical bipolarity. Neither are bodies purely material, nor are mental processes purely spiritual. We are once again dealing with various forms of actualization of event relations. The more an event repeats the connections from which it arises, the more "physical" it is. The more an event deviates creatively and innovatively from the correlations, the more spiritual it is. However, since identical initial states never prevail, no event is a mere repetition or completely "mindless." Conversely, no event can be totally new but always repeats something from its ancestral contexts. Everything that is, is thus more or less physical or spiritual. Creativity as a decisive characteristic of an inexhaustible variety of "interrelations"[31] follows from this on a cosmological level. Reality does not simply exist in the form of things and facts that are identical with themselves. Reality exists only in a constantly changing process of unfolding and interweaving possible forms and realizing events. In them something that

is parallactically recognizable or hidden is constantly renewed. Creativity is "an order…
in virtue of which second after second, minute after minute, hour after hour, day after
day, year after year, century after century, age after age the creative energy"[32] originates
from the unity of a perceiving center of experience and perishes therein.

With Whitehead, parallax can thus be understood as an ontologic-theoretical
concept, because, as I wanted to show, the nautical positionality of events, occasions,
and actual entities can no longer be grasped with the grammar of subject and object,
but requires a different terminology. Identity logical determinations go wrong, because
ontologically we are not dealing with things and states, but with events under the
conditions of respective spatiotemporal constellations. Parallactically conceived relations
of mutual entanglements, enablings, effects, and realizations that empower organisms
to experience something as well as that which is experienced—via the connection
("nexus") of both—can no longer be described in categories of the mind and its object.
These relations discard an understanding of subjectivity that misses itself within false
identity logics when it locates itself in a simple locality. A new understanding of being
and of the world becomes recognizable. It takes into account the transitory nature of our
nautical positions in a medium of continuous change. In this contemporary universe,
new parallactic shifts are constantly occurring. Vocabularies like Whitehead's may not
unhinge the subject-object-grammar, but they do allow other descriptions of it. Now,
given the centrality of the concept of experience, Whitehead's focus on aesthetics follows
consequently. That is the reason why we have to turn to aesthetics in the last section.

3. A Parallactic Ontology of Aesthetic Experience

As we have seen, Whitehead's process-theoretical metaphysics recognizes in
perceptual and sentient experience a key dimension of all that is real. In this respect,
it is only reasonable that aesthetics in the sense of its word origin of Αισθητοσ (the
perceivable) must play a primary role in such a system of thought. Whitehead has not
developed an explicitly formulated aesthetic, much less a philosophy of art.[33] But with
this cosmological meaning of aesthetics in general and of the qualitative experience of
value in particular, he is an aesthetician by nature, because he understands everything
that is real as being bound by sentiment[34] and value: "Value is inherent in actuality
itself."[35] He describes as aesthetic significance "the sense of being one actuality in a
world of actualities."[36]

In this speculative aesthetic, art is only one of many phenomena of the civilized
universe that requires explanation. In the same way, we encounter in this universe what
we used to call, since Schleiermacher, "sense and taste for the infinite": "the infinitude
of actuality, hidden in its finitude of realization."[37] So, the experience of aesthetic value
is in no way limited to art. It is equally well realized in everyday life, in metaphysical
and spiritual questions or in the face of individual experience of the beauty of nature.[38]
Whitehead particularly appreciated the poetry of English Romanticism, namely
Wordsworth and Shelley, and he certainly also has his own theory of symbols, which
was further developed by Susanne K. Langer. More important in the present context,
however, is what I would call the "aisthetic dimension" (i.e., grounded in perception) in

Whitehead's conception of reality, within which art is only one of several types of truth relationships. This conception is itself aisthetic, because "'feeling' is used as a synonym for 'actuality'."[39] However, various gradations must be differentiated. In the face of psychophysical bipolarity, concepts or activities of feeling, perception, and experience must not be understood from the outset as either sensual grasping or cognitive grasping, but rather as various transitional forms and interrelations of a cosmic bipolarity. Whitehead considers any ideal of "pure" understanding to be mistaken anyway. Concepts are always clothed in feelings. Experiences realize certain realities in various gradations from feeling and sensation to reflection and perception from inexhaustible variations of possibilities. Such experiences are not value-neutral: "Our enjoyment of actuality is a realization of worth, good or bad. It is a value experience. Its basic expression is—Have a care, here is something that matters!"[40] So reality is a totality of the outwardness of many facts and the inwardness of experiencing these facts.[41]

All degrees of prehension take place in a process of contrast formation. This Whiteheadian theory of contrasts (terminologically a bit unintelligible), owes its existence to the need for new vocabularies. One must not think here of color contrasts or figure-ground constellations. On the contrary, Whitehead means syntheses and pattern formation, "modes of synthesis of entities in one prehension, or patterned entities."[42] Contrast is a category of existence because everything that exists—and, as we have seen, this also includes possibilities—can be combined with everything else to form patterns. Complementary poles intertwine in contrasts and combine to form something new.[43] One of the most important contrasts is between "affirmation" and "negation." "All aesthetic experience is feeling arising out of the realization of contrast under identity."[44]

In cosmic interrelations, all individual beings arrange themselves in this way with others in a concise manner, so that new, specifically individualized patterns emerge and vanish again and again. In certain contrasts, manifold possibilities for current realities become concrete; different parts combine to form a new pattern in the sense of forming unity.

There are two characteristics of the contrasts understood in this way, which must now concern us more closely: (1) they are always actualizations of possibilities, and (2) they are concretization of a universal. Both aspects are constitutively interconnected without being identical. The universal is a quality of the whole of being, and it offers the potentials whose realization in each individual case means an individualization through which something becomes something specific. Reality is therefore necessarily actual and concrete, while the universal has the ontological status of the possible. Let us recall that "eternal objects" (possibilities or forms) are in their relation to actual entities not what platonic ideas would be toward copies. Rather, they are like indeterminate possibilities for certain actualities and general forms for special concretizations: "The realm of forms is the realm of potentiality."[45] In finite individuals, infinite possibilities of variation are realized in a process of inter-reliant growth to form certain contrasts ("concrescence"). Thus, concretizations are individual creative syntheses.

Timeless forms are realized by actual entities. Whitehead calls this (in another and somewhat idiosyncratic use of language) "exemplification." Unlike Nelson Goodman, he understands it primarily as the realization of an indefinite possibility in a specific individual event. This means that, among other things, the possible and the real grow together concretely. Exemplification is concretization and the latter is actualization. In Goodman's famous "exemplification" of a tailor's swatch (or fabric sample), it is important to replace a concept of representation as a substitute use of signs with a better concept.[46] The sample possesses properties to which it simultaneously refers;[47] that is, it refers not only conventionally to something that is completely different from itself. In Whitehead's thinking, instead, it is more important to consider the modal and ontological differences between the possible and the actual/real or the universal and the particular, which grow together in exemplary contrasts. Exemplification is the individualized realization of a universal form. The terms "particular," "concrete," "universal," and "individual" are not always used by Whitehead in the same way as we know them from other contexts. When we speak here of the "universal" and the "particular," we do not use these terms in either the Kantian or the Hegelian manner.[48] Whitehead's use of them is based rather on a *pars-pro-toto*-logic: "patterned contrasts, so that the prehensions of the whole of its parts produces the fullest harmony of mutual support."[49]

Indefinite possibilities become certain individualities, because the latter are to be understood as parts of a cosmic whole, where the universal in its form of a universal being and the individual in the sense of the particular stand both in connection with one another within modal distinctions. As we have seen, possibilities belong to existence as much as realities, although it is difficult to speak of givenness here: "For example, the total multiplicity of Platonic forms is not 'given'. But in respect of each entity, there is givenness of such forms."[50] They exist inasmuch as they can be exemplified by actual entities, but they become real only through concrete actualizations. In concrete terms, then—let us recall the fallacy of misplaced concreteness—we are precisely not talking about artificially isolated and identity-logically fixed particles of matter that are the actual patterns into which experiences of contrast merge (coming from the stream of potentialities).

A specific quality of experiencing values conveys the beautiful.[51] In addition, there are other value bonds of the true and the good, and no "region of reality" can be limited exclusively to one of these values. Thus, for example, mathematics and morality are equally concerned with ideals, and thus with a transcending of finite reality in the orientation toward an infinite possibility. Common to all these normative values, however, is, again, that they make up the "civilized universe," which must be understood within a spectrum of continuity with the "natural universe." The universe can be changed by thoughts, because realized thoughts are preceded by timeless forms as a mode of possibility. But the way in which these thoughts are realized is a question of the "contemporary world." In the same way that a variable in mathematics can represent various things, namely either any number or a very specific quantity, eternal objects offer general potentials, but their realization through actual entities is tantamount to an increase in determinacy. For example, in a formula such as $y = x^2$, only very specific numbers can be used for the variables, such as 4 and 2, 9 and 3, 16 and 4, etc., not any number. The context of the variables (actual entities) "forces" the numbers which enter the equation into certain patterns of ordered pairs. Similarly, the universal form of the color red can be actualized differently by Rubens than by Josef Albers, or differently by a tomato than by a strawberry.

If we experience a poem or a piece of music as beautiful, it is due to the original value of human experience. It expresses a normative responsiveness that, according to the systematic whole of Whitehead's ontology, is not simply personal taste. "Beauty is a quality which finds its exemplification in actual occasions: or put conversely, it is a quality in which such occasions can severally participate. There are gradations in Beauty and in types of Beauty."[52] It would not be coherent to assume that a work of art tells someone something because that particular person happens to have a mind that is sensitive to certain phantasmagoria. Conversely, however, the responsiveness to beauty suggests that art is a value sphere of its own kind. Only at this point does art come into play as a specific type of truth-relation. "[T]he indirect interpretative power of Art [expresses] the truth about the nature of things."[53]

What makes any form of proposition true is that there are places in space and time in the world where something is true. When something becomes concrete in the way described above, then something finite is realized (or exemplified) out of infinite possibilities. Art is an ontologically excellent sphere of the concrete. Every single work of art is an innovative creation, through which something is realized that does not exist precisely because of expected causal chains but whose spatiotemporal fit is the result of a creative effort, through which the connection between part and whole is revealed.

> In the greatest example of any form of art, a miraculous balance is achieved. The whole displays its component parts, each with its own value enhanced; and the parts lead up to a whole, which is beyond themselves, and yet not destructive of themselves.[54]

Whitehead distinguishes between civilized and non-civilized creatures by their capacity for universality:

> The hermit thrush and the nightingale can produce sound of the utmost beauty. But they are not civilized beings. They lack ideas of adequate generality respecting their own actions and the world around them. Without doubt the higher animals entertain notions, hopes and fears. And yet they lack civilization by reason of deficient generality of their mental functionings.[55]

From the ability to become a universality, therefore, derives a characteristic of what is special with regard to human civilization. It sees itself as part of a cosmic whole. Similar to Leibniz's monads, which are impossible mirrors,[56] works of art, according to Whitehead, exemplify something that must somehow be given as a possible form in order to become an actual reality, but that at the same time unfolds only a possible partial aspect of a/the whole. And since not everything can be perceived at all times, it might only be temporarily recognizable. In other words, artworks exemplify nautical parallaxes. But there can only be a correspondence of artistic exemplification with the simultaneous world if the parallaxes are perceived with care, which present themselves to a person in motion within a location/position in time. If this succeeds, a new pattern of the infinite and the finite, the universal and the particular is actualized. In the best case, the actualization of a new pattern occurs that exemplifies what otherwise would remain "unseen"[57] and conceptually incomprehensible.

One may find such arguments, apparently borrowed from Platonic and German idealism, as too harmonizing. In fact, these considerations are based on the idea of beauty as a cosmic harmony. The work of art as protest, or as an expression of existential despair and anger, does not feature in them. But Whitehead's philosophy is a metaphysical and speculative aesthetic, not a description of everything that is addressed in art. Nor is Whitehead's possibly conflictive and forgetful focus no longer our topic here. I simply wanted to show that parallax can be illuminated with Whitehead and Whitehead, in reverse, with parallax. We find in his aesthetic cosmology a real alternative to the subject-object-ontology, which leaves too many questions open.

Let us recall the starting point of the metaphysical question: how is a "civilized universe" *naturally* possible? How is it possible that in a seemingly meaningless, largely empty, and incomprehensibly large universe, phenomena such as art and religion, law and culture exist without there being a common basis on which to trace these two universes? Civilized subjects experience normative aesthetic or ethical significance, but we have no explanation for this. Epistemic and ontological explanations fail because of the complete disconnectedness of the so-called objective cognition, on the one hand, and qualitative first-person, social and cultural experience, on the other. Whitehead's answer to this problem is that if there is to be a continuity between the experiencing and the experienced, then works of art, world religions, and other spheres of value as parts of the natural universe must be naturally explainable as well.

> [O]ur existence is more than a succession of bare facts. We live in a common world of mutual adjustment, of intelligible relations, of valuations, of zest after purposes, of joy and grief, of interest contracted on self, of interest directed beyond self, of short-time and long-time failures or success, of different layers of feeling, of live-weariness and life-zest.[58]

Notes

1   "A philosopher who is ambitious in the theory of science, interested in cultural theory, inspired by religion, and inclined towards extreme linguistic innovations, provides for most people of our time connections of too many incompatibilities" (Michael Hampe, *Alfred North Whitehead* (Munich: Beck, 1998), 180).

2   Alfred North Whitehead, "VI Civilized Universe." In: *Modes of Thought* (New York: Free Press, 1968), 105–26; also the fourth part of Alfred North Whitehead, *Adventures of Ideas* (New York: Free Press, 1967).

3   Odo Marquard, *Skeptische Methode im Blick auf Kant* (Freiburg: Alber Verlag, 1958), 54.

4   Slavoj Žižek, *The Parallax View* (Cambridge, MA: MIT Press 2006), p. 17.

5   Whitehead goes so far as to say, "that apart from the experiences of subjects there is nothing" (Alfred North Whitehead, *Process and Reality* (New York: Free Press, 1979), 252).

6   Alfred North Whitehead, *The Concept of Nature* (Cambridge: Cambridge University Press, 1955), 30f.
7   "The bifurcation theory is an attempt to exhibit natural science as an investigation of the cause of the fact of knowledge." Whitehead, *The Concept of Nature*, 30f.
8   See Spyridon A. Koutroufinis, *Organismus als Prozess* (Freiburg: Alber Verlag, 2019) as well as the "introduction" to the German translation of Whitehead's *Modes of Thought*, written by Stascha Rohmer: Alfred North Whitehead, *Denkweisen* (Frankfurt am Main: Suhrkamp, 2001).
9   Acts of feelings form the positive type of prehensions. Whitehead, *Adventures of Ideas*, 233.
10   Whitehead, *Process and Reality*, 80.
11   Whitehead, *Adventures of Ideas*, 132f.
12   Whitehead, *Modes of Thought*, 115.
13   Victor Lowe, *Understanding Whitehead* (Baltimore: Johns Hopkins University Press, 1966), 17.
14   Whitehead, *Adventures of Ideas*, 247.
15   Whitehead, *Adventures of Ideas*, 432f.
16   Whitehead, *Modes of Thought*, 122.
17   Whitehead, *Modes of Thought*, 121.
18   Whitehead, *Adventures of Ideas*, 247.
19   Whitehead, *Adventures of Ideas*, 251.
20   Whitehead, *Adventures of Ideas*, 246ff.
21   Whitehead, *Process and Reality*, 88.
22   Alfred North Whitehead, *Science and the Modern World* (New York: Macmillan, 1925), 51.
23   Whitehead, *Science and the Modern World*, 128.
24   Whitehead, *Science and the Modern World*, 84.
25   It is to Christoph Kann's credit that he has traced Whitehead's selective understanding of the classics of the history of philosophy: *Fußnoten zu Platon. Philosophie Geschichte bei A.N. Whitehead* (Hamburg: Meiner Verlag, 2001). "Here, too, the typical Whitehead approach to tradition can be observed: the intention of a selective reception of suitable basic positions is accompanied by sometimes radical criticism" (204, translation D.F.).
26   Whitehead, *Adventures of Ideas*, 233f.
27   Whitehead, *Adventures of Ideas*, 234.
28   Whitehead, *Science and the Modern World*, 70.
29   Whitehead, *Religion in the Making* (Cambridge: Cambridge University Press, 1926), 89.
30   Whitehead, *Modes of Thought*, 114.
31   Whitehead, *Religion in the Making*, 64.
32   Whitehead, *Religion in the Making*, 98.
33   Which only means that he did not dedicate a book of his own to these topics. Implicitly he has an aesthetic metaphysics and a speculative aesthetic. Some of this can be found in Reiner Wiehl, *Philosophische Ästhetik zwischen Immanuel Kant und Arthur C. Danto* (Göttingen: Vandenhoeck & Ruprecht, 2004), chapters 4 and 5.
34   For example, he goes so far as to say that "[a]ll order is therefore aesthetic order, and the moral order is merely certain aspects of aesthetic order." See Whitehead, *Religion in the Making*, 91.
35   Whitehead, *Religion in the Making*, 87.

36 Whitehead, *Modes of Thought*, 120.
37 Whitehead, *Modes of Thought*, 113.
38 It would be interesting to elaborate here the systematic interconnections between Whitehead and Iris Murdoch, because her idea of a gradual gradation of reality, which we can reach through attentive aesthetic perception, is promising for further investigation. See Iris Murdoch, *Sovereignty of Good* (London: Routledge, 1970).
39 Whitehead, *Religion in the Making*, 91.
40 Whitehead, *Modes of Thought*, 116.
41 Whitehead, *Modes of Thought*, 116.
42 Whitehead, *Process and Reality*, 22.
43 This is not by chance reminiscent of Merleau-Ponty, who explicitly speaks of "entrelacement" in such cases.
44 Whitehead, *Religion in the Making*, 101f.
45 Whitehead, *Modes of Thought*, 69.
46 cf. Eva Schürmann, "Ästhetik als exemplarisches Philosophieren mit Kunst." In *Ästhetik. Denken und Disziplin. Workshop der Deutschen Gesellschaft für Ästhetik*, ed. Juliane Rebentisch (2017). Available online: http://www.dgae.de/kongresse/das-ist-aesthetik/#denken-und-disziplin.
47 "Exemplification is possession plus reference," Nelson Goodman, *Languages of Art. An Approach to a Theory of Symbols* (Indianapolis: Bobbs-Merrill, 1968), 53.
48 For Hegel, what is individual is the unity which the pure concept forms through the negation of the opposites of the universal and the particular. See for example: "Taken in an abstract sense, universality, particularity, and individuality are the same as identity, difference, and ground. But the universal is what is identical with itself *explicitly in the sense* that at the same time the particular and the individual are contained in it." G.W.F. Hegel, *Encyclopaedia of the Philosophical Sciences in Basic Outline* (Cambridge: Cambridge University Press, 2010), §164.
49 Whitehead, *Adventures of Ideas*, 344.
50 Whitehead, *Process and Reality*, 43.
51 Whitehead distinguishes "beauty" as a cosmic harmony quality from "beautiful" as a quality of a concrete.
52 Whitehead, *Adventures of Ideas*, 252.
53 Whitehead, *Adventures of Ideas*, 249.
54 Whitehead, *Modes of Thought*, 62.
55 Whitehead, *Modes of Thought*, 3f.
56 Thus I read the paradox of windowless "point de vues sur l'univers": Eva Schürmann, *Darstellen und Vorstellen* (Paderborn: Fink Verlag, 2018), chapter 4, scene 4.
57 Whitehead, *Adventures of Ideas*, 207, 349.
58 Whitehead, *Religion in the Making*, 68.

17

Feeling at a Distance, or the Aesthetics of Unconscious Transmission

Tracy McNulty

One of Freud's most fundamental insights is that for the human being; whose perception of reality is mediated by an unconscious fantasy that no one shares; there is no possible access either to the natural environment or to our fellow man. As a result, each and every one of us is consigned to a fundamental solitude concerning the free drive and its effects upon the organism and the psychic apparatus. What I will explore in the following sections is the paradoxical corollary of this position, namely the affirmation that human reality is fundamentally transindividual and intersubjective, traversed by a quest that impacts each and every human being but that belongs to no one in particular.

This point is made by Freud himself, most memorably when he claims that living men retain in their unconscious the traces of the long-ago murder of the primeval father: an example I will return to at the end of this chapter. But its implications for thinking about unconscious transmission, especially as it is relayed by the body, were explored by Freud only in speculative terms and have been left largely unexamined by later psychoanalysts.

An important exception is Jacques Lacan, who not only develops Freud's insight but understands it both as the driving force of an analysis and as essential to the eventual creation of the analyst. Lacan follows Freud in affirming that the unconscious quest that animates the analysand finds expression through his body, in the form of symptoms, repetitive behaviors, or unmotivated acts. More surprisingly, however, he claims that the analysand's act causes what is at work in his own body to impact the body of the psychoanalyst—and this despite the fact that this unconscious quest, and the act to which it gives rise, is not an object of conscious knowledge or representation for the analysand and does not pass through speech. In his seminar on "The Psychoanalytic Act" (1967–8), Lacan advances that the analysand's act is not something the analyst can know, interpret, or anticipate but something by which he is "struck" both psychically and in his body, where it leaves its traces or impressions.

We can infer from Lacan's argument—for reasons I will explain below—that this "striking" occurs at a specific moment in an analysis, and indicates that the cure has entered its final phase. In the early part of an analysis, the analysand addresses the analyst as an other in the social link: an other who might respond to the subject's appeal or take responsibility for his suffering. If the analyst refuses to respond to these appeals, it is in order to confront the analysand with his fundamental solitude concerning what acts in his body—and to call forth dreams and symptoms that might allow him to construct a knowledge about what, until now, has been repeating in silence. In this early phase, then, we might say that the analysis emphasizes not only the absence of any Other who might be able to respond or treat but the unbridgeable distance separating the analysand from the analyst.

In contrast, what "strikes" the analyst in the analysand's act—as opposed to his pleas for help or demand for recognition or love—is what Lacan calls the object (a), the object-cause of desire that acts in and through the subject. Its impact supposes that the analysand has traversed the logical moment in an analysis that Lacan calls "separation," which is marked by the fall of the seduction fantasy and the entry into castration. The seduction fantasy is defined by the repression, or "alienation,"[1] of unconscious desire. It represses the subject of the unconscious, and the erotogenic body in which it dwells, by propping up the illusory consistency of the ego and encouraging it to seek satisfaction in the social sphere or in relations with others. Inasmuch as the moment of separation entails a detachment from the ego and the ideals that shore it up, it can be understood at least in part as a separation from the social and the identifications that sustain it— and, with it, the recognition that the object that causes the subject's desire is a psychic object, specific to him or her, that has no consistency and no worldly equivalent.

Unlike the imaginary object the analysand had vainly sought in relations with others, the object-cause of desire is a (purely) mental object that does not, properly speaking, exist, and that cannot therefore be perceived, named, or represented. Like a black hole—which cannot be observed directly, but is known only by the way it warps space-time—it is an object we know solely by its effects. It acts in the subject's body, mobilizing an unconscious quest that pushes the subject to act in ways that are at odds with natural aims and societal ideals. Unlike the unified body image that supported the ego by providing it with an illusory coherence, the body mobilized by the object a is the *corps morcelé* or erogenous body carved out of the organism by the drives: the site of inscription and transmission of experiences and mental representations that have never been conscious, that find expression only in unwilled acts and involuntary feelings. Through this body, the object a seeks to create a path for itself by means of the subject's act.

More surprisingly, however, it also acts upon others. Paradoxically, the analyst is most impacted or affected not by the narrative or the demands that the analysand addresses to him as an other in the social link but by unconscious acts that pass through the body, whose stakes are particular to the unconscious desire of a specific subject and illegible outside the framework of his or her fundamental fantasy. At this point of maximum opacity or illegibility, a barrier is breached, and something that is not an object of conscious representation or knowledge is transmitted from one subject to another. It is this action, and the effects it produces in those it "strikes," that attests to the end of an analysis—and, under conditions I will describe shortly, to the creation of the analyst.

The impact of this object across multiple subjects makes a unique contribution to the problem of parallax, especially as Slavoj Žižek has allowed us to understand it in relation to the object of unconscious fantasy. The end of analysis can be understood less as a severing of subject and object than as a shift in the relationship between them that entails a new openness to the object-cause of desire in its properly aesthetic dimension, its unpresentability. But it also inaugurates a subject-object relation that is not only unresolved or unreconciled but is defined by what I will characterize as an *intersubjective relay* that traverses human subjectivity, whose manifestations are aesthetic in nature. One important consequence is that separation in its analytic stakes does not merely affirm the subject as a discreet individual, released from all responsibility to and for others. While it certainly involves a liberation from parental and cultural demands and ideals, separation must not be understood as a turn away from the collective as such. To the contrary, it necessarily involves a renewed commitment to humanity, above and beyond the imaginary of the social tie.

Here I will explore this premise through three examples. The first is clinical, while the second and third belong to the domain of political aesthetics. If "separation" is concerned with the liberation of desire, then each of these examples shows in a different way that desire is itself transindividual, and not a private affair. All of them illuminate in different ways the aesthetic function of the body, or the transmission of an unpresentable object from one subject to another whose "sign" is feeling. In each case, I want to focus on a specific manifestation of this aesthetic function, what I will call "disinterested feeling."

1. The Pass

My clinical example concerns the procedure of the Pass, which Lacan invented in 1967 as a means of verifying the end of an analysis. He devised this procedure during the period when he was first conceptualizing, in his seminar on "The Psychoanalytic Act," the impact of the analysand's act on the analyst's own body—an insight that becomes fundamental to the logic of the Pass and the creation of the analyst that is its aim. In the Pass, a candidate who has reached the logical term of an analysis testifies about his experience to two witnesses, or *passeurs*, who are, in turn, charged with transmitting that testimony to a cartel of analysts. The candidate—who is called the *passant*—speaks about his experience as an analysand and attempts to transmit something of his relation to the object that causes desire. Yet the pass is concerned not primarily with what the passant has managed to say about his analysis but with something that is fundamentally unsayable or unaddressable, and that therefore passes through the body. This real object, transmitted by an act of the unconscious, is what Lacan calls the object a. It is not an object of conscious observation or recording but something that is at once transmitted by a body and received by a body, depositing itself in the bodies of the two passeurs without their knowledge.

For an analogy we might look to the study of trauma, which confirms that what is unspoken in the life of one person can find expression in the body of another—for example, through the intergenerational transmission of trauma from a parent or grandparent to a child. A distinctive feature of the Pass, however, is that the procedure brings together three people who are not otherwise connected, who may be complete strangers. The passeur, in other words, is a disinterested spectator, with no personal stake in the experiences of the person speaking. Moreover, the aim of the procedure is to verify whether the passant has reached the end of analysis. It is concerned not so much with the transmission of trauma or with the unfinished business of that speaker but rather with the transmission of the object-cause of desire. So why, we might ask, are the bodies of these disinterested witnesses required to confirm it? My thesis is that in registering its impact, they show the *object a* to be something that is not only unique to the passant, singular and discreet, but inseparable from the quest of humanity—of the human subject as such.

Over the past few years I have twice served as a passeur, or witness, in this procedure. On both occasions, the experience of listening initially felt like a non-experience, as though I were merely a spectator or a witness to something that did not fundamentally concern me. In each case, however, I came to see—albeit only much later—that I had, in fact, been the vehicle for a transmission whose stakes completely eluded me at the time. In my first experience, six months elapsed between the hearing of the passant's testimony and my reporting of that testimony to the cartel. During that period, I had experienced two unusual symptoms that troubled me for several months. Only after giving my testimony to the cartel did it begin to dawn on me that each of these symptoms was related in some way to the experience of listening to the passant. More precisely, they seemed to inscribe in my body something that the passant was unable to put into words, but that had nevertheless been transmitted to me unconsciously. One of these symptoms was a sudden spike in blood sugar, serious enough to make me undergo testing for diabetes. It now seemed to me that this transitory symptom—which attested to the malfunctioning or even failure of the regulatory apparatus controlling insulin, and thus the body's defense against something indigestible—was due to the effects of the passant's testimony on my body.

I wrote about this experience in some detail in a previous essay,[2] and since then, it has given rise to a whole project on unconscious transmission that continues to develop and unfold. Initially I considered this symptom to be the expression of my own *resistance* to what was being transmitted, a defensive reaction against something that was invading my body. I still believe this is at least partly true. Sometime later, however, I had the opportunity to speak with the passant about our respective experiences of the Pass. When I mentioned my transitive diabetes, the passant was momentarily speechless. It turns out that his mother had been diabetic, and that the management of her disease—which eventually resulted in her death—had occupied much of the family's attention when he was a child. Up to this point, however, he had never thought that her disease had any particular significance for his own psychic life. Now, on the contrary, he realized that her diabetes, and the peculiar feeling it had inspired in him as a boy, had in some obscure way evoked for him the excess of femininity itself: that of his mother, first of all, but also the feminine demand that had overwhelmed him in experiences with romantic partners, and even perhaps a part of his *own* femininity that had never managed to find expression. Despite the importance of this cluster of thoughts and feelings, neither his mother's symptom nor his sense of being overwhelmed by femininity had in any way figured in his testimony. Even in this context, that is, it had remained something fundamentally "unaddressable," something he could neither formulate for himself nor address to someone else.

The symptom of uncontrolled blood sugar that I developed following the Pass is something that has cropped up in my own life on a few different occasions. Most of the time, therefore, this has been "my" symptom, giving expression to an excess in my own body that could not be fully managed. In my own life, it is definitely related to the question of femininity. On this occasion, however, I am tempted to say that "my" symptoms were no longer mine, but were giving expression to something that transcended me. It wasn't so much "my" femininity that found expression in this symptom, that is, but Femininity *as such*: something that exceeded my particular subjectivity.

So what am I claiming? That the Pass is an instance of telepathy? The short answer is yes. There would be no psychoanalysis if this unspoken, unconscious transmission were not a reality. Most of the time, the analyst doesn't speak at all; and yet she is nevertheless able to transmit, to cause to be imprinted upon the unconscious of the analysand, certain questions that drive the transference. Hence the importance of the Pass as a confirmation of the end of analysis, especially for someone who wishes to work as an analyst. The logic of transference supposes not only that the object-cause of the analyst's desire is able to act wordlessly upon the body of the analysand[3] but also that the analyst is not going to block the transmission coming from the unconscious of the analysand in an act of counter-transference. In the broadest sense, then, it implies an openness to the human subject.

What I have called the "unaddressable" within the subject, following Willy Apollon,[4] could be understood as the cause of his or her desire. But this unaddressable also connects the subject to something larger than himself: what Apollon calls the "human quest." In this case, the passeur takes something further, sustaining a kind of relay.

But why do I want to say that this is about humanity as such, and not just about one or two individual subjects? This is where I want to turn to political aesthetics, to explore what it reveals about this "feeling at a distance" (*tele-pathy*) and its stakes for intersubjective transmission. Both examples help to illuminate one of the most striking features of the procedure of the Pass: the fact that the two passeurs who receive the transmission are *disinterested spectators*, who, unlike the analyst, know nothing about the experiences of the person speaking and who further have no personal stake in it. My hypothesis is that registering its impact, they show the *object a* to be something that is not only unique to the passant, singular and discreet, but inseparable from the quest of humanity—of the human subject as such.

2. Kant on the French Revolution

My second example concerns the sublime feeling that Immanuel Kant identifies with a specific manifestation of enthusiasm, which he understands as a sign that something formless and unnamable has been transmitted from one subject—or one people—to another. I am thinking of the late essay from the *Contest of the Faculties* entitled "A Renewed Attempt to Answer the Question: Is the Human Race Continually Improving?," which was published near the end of Kant's life. The question Kant raises is whether it can be asserted that the human race is constantly progressing for the better and, if so, *how* it can be asserted. "In human affairs," he writes, "there must be some experience or other which, as an event which has actually occurred, might suggest that man has the quality or power of being the *cause* and… the *author* of his own improvement."[5] Kant specifies that

> the occurrence in question does not involve any of those momentous deeds or misdeeds of men which make small in their eyes what was formerly great or make great what was formerly small, and which cause ancient and illustrious states to vanish as if by magic, and others to arise in their place as if from the bowels of the earth.[6]

It is not the act of a singular great man or world-historical actor. Instead, he writes,

> We are here concerned only with the attitude of the onlookers as it reveals itself *in public* while the drama of great political changes is taking place: for they openly express universal yet disinterested sympathy for one set of protagonists against their adversaries, even at the risk that their partiality could be of great disadvantage to themselves. Their reaction (because of its universality) proves that mankind as a whole shares a certain character in common, and it also proves (because of its disinterestedness) that man has a moral character, or at least the makings of one. And this does not merely allow us to hope for human improvement; it is already a form of improvement in itself, in so far as its influence is strong enough for the present.[7]

Kant then turns to the example of the recent French Revolution and asks if this event can be considered to constitute a sign that humanity is continually improving. Kant is writing in 1795, when the Terror has run its course and the triumph of the counter-revolution is all but assured: so the question is very topical, and its answer far from obvious. Nevertheless, Kant concludes in the affirmative. The reason is not that the revolution can be determined with certainty to be good or bad, a step forward or a great calamity. All of those possibilities remain open. Indeed, Kant writes,

> The revolution which we have seen taking place in our times in a nation of gifted [*Geistreich*] people may succeed, or it may fail. It may be so filled with misery and atrocities that no right-thinking man would ever decide to make the same experiment again at such a price, even if he could hope to carry it out successfully at the second attempt.

Nevertheless, he continues,

> I maintain that this revolution has aroused in the hearts and desires of all spectators who are not themselves caught up in it a *sympathy* which borders almost on enthusiasm, although the very utterance of this sympathy was fraught with danger. It cannot therefore have been caused by anything other than a moral predisposition within the human race.[8]

Evidence of humanity's progress is found in the sympathetic enthusiasm experienced by the *disinterested spectator* of the revolution, who may be distant in space or time. In other words, the spectacle of a people in revolution is a sign of progress in humanity because *we feel something* when we contemplate it, even today. This feeling establishes that humanity is indeed a subject, an author or cause of its own progress, and not a pure abstraction.

Kant goes on to characterize the sympathetic enthusiasm of the onlookers as a "sublime feeling." Recall that, for Kant, the sublime is not an attribute of objects or events; we cannot say that the French Revolution, or for that matter any other object or datum of experience, is sublime. Instead, the sublime is something we *feel* when confronted with the magnitude of a phenomenon or event that overwhelms us, confronts us with our impotence, but that also causes us to discover our calling as subjects, which is that of having to supply a presentation for the unpresentable.

The first point I want to make is that Kant's discussion of the French Revolution inflects in a new way the requirement of "distance" that is so central to the Analytic of the Sublime.[9] There Kant specifies that manifestations of natural might, like an erupting volcano or a tidal wave, may be judged sublime, but only on the condition that the spectator remains at a certain distance. Without that distance, which mitigates the mortal threat they represent, the feeling aroused by the spectacle can only be terror, and not sublimity. On the rare occasions when Kant takes up a political example, like this one, this requirement of distance is sometimes interpreted to mean that Kant has in mind a purely vicarious experience, from which the spectator remains safely disengaged and aloof. In his remarks on the revolution, however, Kant treats this distance not only in terms of disinterestedness but in terms of *transmission*: what is transmitted to those who witness without being directly involved, as opposed to the complex range of feelings—elation, terror, hope, fear, and so forth—that are felt by the actors in those events. It is this capacity for transmission that suggests we are dealing with something larger than ourselves, more important than our own survival.

Jean-François Lyotard captures this dimension very well when he asks of Kant's essay: "what is *delivered* in enthusiasm"?[10] The question suggests that the witnessing at issue here is not a passive, disengaged spectatorship that leaves the onlooker fundamentally unchanged. Instead, enthusiasm attests to the fact that something has been "delivered" to the spectator, even deposited in her, that impacts or transforms her in some fundamental way. Kant himself describes enthusiasm as an agitation, a "shaking," that may be expressed as a "rapid succession of attraction and repulsion for the same object."[11]

Crucially, then, this enthusiasm—while "sympathetic"—is also involuntary and unwilled; it implies neither affirmation, assent, nor identification. It has nothing to do with the spectator's political views or commitments, or the elation or fear he might feel at the prospect of the revolution's success. If sympathy for the revolutionaries is "universal," despite those differences, then it is something one feels without willing or wishing it, and that may well run counter to the explicit views or tastes of the person so affected. It is not only involuntary, therefore, but potentially unwelcome: a feeling that forces itself upon us, whether we like it or not.

Lyotard brings into relief a second point that is implied in Kant's analysis, but not explicitly stated: namely, that sublime feeling implies a *body* that receives the mark, imprint, or blow of transmission. Kant had already emphasized not only that we are seeking to prove the existence of a tendency within mankind as such, within the "human race as a whole," but also that this humanity must be considered "not as a series of individuals" but as a "body [*Körper*] distributed over the earth in states and national groups."[12] Lyotard's reading develops this further and allows us to appreciate that "body" should be understood here not merely as a metaphor for the "human race" considered as a whole but as something more akin to the body at stake in psychoanalysis: the site of inscription of memory-traces that are unable to find any conscious representation, and that therefore find expression only as feelings that have no stable ideational content. Lyotard even describes the pathos of enthusiasm as something akin to a drive response: it is, he writes, an "energetical sign, a tensor of desire [*Wunsch*]."[13]

This reading makes clear that the enthusiasm of the disinterested spectator is never a mere witnessing, since the event "delivers" something to the onlooker, impacts her materially, and demands a response, a relay, from the subject thus affected.[14]

A third key point to stress in Kant's argument is that the subject whose "progress" is at issue here is "humanity," and not merely a specific party or people. Humanity is something larger than the revolutionaries, larger than the French people, larger even than the citizens of the earth at a given moment. This is why the enthusiasm of the disinterested onlookers is at once involuntary and universal. When a person, or people, acts, we can approve or disapprove, feel exaltation or apathy. But when *humanity* is in action, it is impossible simply to remain a spectator.

Similarly, I felt in my initial experience of the Pass testimony that I was there *solely* as a spectator, a witness of something that did not fundamentally concern me. Only retroactively was I forced to recognize that I was not only a spectator, and that my body had been enlisted to transmit something greater than my "own" subjectivity. There is no possibility of remaining a mere spectator when one is confronted with the desire of a subject, a desire that transcends all limits.

Kant's argument also helps to illuminate the stakes of the symptom in my last example, by distinguishing what might be described as the aesthetic function of the symptom—the registration and transmission of the unaddressable—as distinct from its role in repression. We usually think of hysterical conversion as the manifestation of a conflict between the ego and an unconscious desire, which is inscribed somatically as a symptom that gives expression to both tendencies simultaneously— and in so doing allows the unconscious fantasy that has been repressed to keep operating in silence without the hysteric's knowledge. The symptom is not a pure impasse, however, since it is also the expression of something acting in the subject that pushes to find an outlet—no matter how forcefully it is repressed. In this sense the symptom constitutes not only a retreat from psychic reality but a means of constructing and transmitting a real that is not otherwise accessible. It gives expression to one important dimension of aesthetics, namely the presentation of the unpresentable.

Willy Apollon amplifies and extends this insight when he cautions that in each analysand, the analyst must be alert not only to the problems and impasses she faces but in how the unaddressable within her both carries within it something of the human quest and moves it forward.[15] Understood in this way, the hysterical symptom bears witness to or transmits an object that is not merely particular to the fantasy of that subject but that traverses human experience. When we consider the great hysterics of the seventeenth century and afterward,[16] it is apparent that the hysteric, in the wake of the age of reason inaugurated by Descartes, becomes the guardian, for a part of humanity, of an experience that is alien to language or unaddressable. She keeps the flame alive and assures its relay, even if she knows nothing about it.

3. Aesthetics and Unconscious Transmission

I want to conclude by connecting this aesthetic relay to Freud's tracking of the unconscious transmission, through history, of a long-forgotten experience that is relayed and sustained only through the feelings of human receivers who are distant in space and time. It too is concerned with a transindividual subject, even with humanity itself.

I am thinking of the final lines of *Totem and Taboo*, where Freud concludes his reconstruction of the primeval murder of the father with these remarkable words:

> No one can have failed to observe... that I have taken as the basis of my whole position the existence of a collective mind, in which mental processes occur just as they do in the mind of an individual. In particular, I have supposed that the *sense of guilt* for an act has persisted for many thousands of years and has remained operative in generations which can have had no knowledge of that act. I have supposed that an emotional process, such as might have developed in generations of sons who were ill-treated by their father, has extended to new generations which were exempt from such treatment for the very reason that *their* father had been eliminated.[17]

Freud supposes not only that a feeling of guilt has persisted for thousands of years but that it endures among human beings who live in an environment in which *the father no longer exists*, since totemic and matriarchal societal forms have long since displaced the primal horde ruled by an all-powerful father. The sense of guilt therefore concerns an object that is not part of the environment at all, and whose effects must therefore be distinguished from the organism's response to environmental pressures. Something of human history is transmitted solely through feelings and cannot be verified by any other means.

Freud's argument is not only a speculative thesis, however, but predicated upon what he discovers in the body of the apostle Paul. Paul complains that he "feels in his members"—in his body—a sinfulness that pushes him to act in ways he does not will, but that his mind is powerless to control.[18] The guiltiness he feels concerning what "dwells in his flesh" is not merely "his" guilt, however—a guilt that might have some object or referent in his own life—but a guilt afflicting humanity as such. Freud understands it as an unconscious inscription of the repressed truth of the Hebrews' murder of Moses, and more distantly of the guilt felt by the entire human race as a result of the primeval murder of the father that it repeated and reactivated.[19] The body of Paul is thus the transmitter of something that traverses humanity, but that needed a body—*his* body—in order to express itself.

Paul's feeling of guiltiness is where Freud's reconstruction of the Moses story begins, and not biblical tradition, the historical record, or any other piece of evidence Freud considers along the way. This feeling is significant because it attests not only to the murder itself but also to the long-term consequences of the "delivery" or relay of the act in feeling. Almost as significant for Freud is the case of Goethe, who "feels certain"—apparently based on no evidence whatsoever—that Moses was murdered by the Jews (*Moses* 114). While another person might view this conviction on Goethe's part as a bit of idle speculation that has no basis in reality, it carries tremendous weight for Freud. Because Goethe *felt* it, Freud is certain that something is at stake there.

What I find remarkable in these and other works is the extent to which Freud always tracks historical transmission through the feelings of specific bodies, feelings that attest that something has landed. This attention to feeling might explain why Freud is so interested in the works of other writers: not only major literary figures like Goethe and Shakespeare but academic and scientific writers whose accounts he consumes voraciously despite the fact that he is rarely convinced by what they have to say. In almost every case, it seems to me that what interests Freud is not so much the authority or expertise each writer brings to the topic, or even the specific interpretation he or she provides but rather: *what did this person see? What did this person feel?* It is the testimony of a subject he seeks, and not the judgment of an expert. This is especially palpable in Freud's short essay "Moses of Michelangelo." On the one hand, Freud observes that most commentators have not really responded to the sculpture at all, but only to the biblical narrative, and thus to a discourse or interpretive framework that would impose a meaning upon the sculpted form. On the other, a few of them really *do* see or feel something that exceeds that interpretation and attests to how the writer's body has been impacted or struck by an act—in this case, the act that traversed the body of Michelangelo as he sculpted the form.

In each of these examples, we could say that something is transmitted to a "spectator" of the most disinterested type: someone who did not even "see" the original event, who knows nothing of it, who could have no stake in it, and yet finds himself or herself profoundly affected and even weighed down by this transmission. Each of these human receivers becomes for Freud a privileged divining rod, their bodies like radio towers relaying a signal from humanity's distant past.

Notes

1   Alienation and separation are for Lacan the two slopes of the fantasy, $ \Diamond a. The first enables the repression of the corps morcelé through identification with the mirror image, which provides the "armor of an alienating identity." Jacques Lacan, *Écrits*, trans. Bruce Fink (New York: W. W. Norton, 2007), 78.

2   Tracy McNulty, "Untreatable: The Freudian Act and Its Legacy," *Jacques Lacan: Psychoanalysis, Politics, Philosophy and Science*, ed. Agon Hamza and Frank Ruda, *Crisis and Critique* 6, no. 1 (April 2019): 227–51.

3   I have explored this thesis through a reading of the "Specimen Dream" that opens
     the second chapter of Freud's *Interpretation of Dreams*, the Dream of Irma's Injection.
     When Freud the dreamer peers into Irma's throat to find his own symptoms staring
     back at him, what he encounters is the agency of his own object within the body
     of his patient. It is thus the bodies of these patients that attest to the object that
     acts in Freud. Initially, this object is a source of anxiety and trepidation for Freud:
     associating to the "dirty syringe" that the dream identifies as a possible cause of Irma's
     infection, Freud wonders whether he might have inadvertently caused or aggravated
     Irma's symptoms through medical malpractice. Ultimately, however, I argue that the
     dream analysis allows us to understand the "dirty syringe" as a figure of the analyst's
     act, which, unlike the act of the medical doctor, must reactivate and even aggravate
     the patient's symptoms in order to allow what is acting in the body to find expression.
     After the turning point marked by this dream and its analysis, Freud doesn't hesitate
     to inject his patients with his "dirty syringe," to retrigger the symptom or call forth
     the drive. McNulty, "Untreatable," 232–9.
4   Willy Apollon, "The Act, a Psychoanalytic Concept," trans. Tracy McNulty, *(a) The
     Journal of Culture and the Unconscious* (2013).
5   Immanuel Kant, "A Renewed Attempt to Answer the Question: Is the Human Race
     Continually Improving?" In *Political Writings*, ed. Hans Reiss, trans. H.B. Nisbet
     (Cambridge: Cambridge University Press, 1970, 1991), 181.
6   Kant, "A Renewed Attempt," 182.
7   Kant, "A Renewed Attempt," 182.
8   Kant, "A Renewed Attempt," 182.
9   Faced with a manifestation of natural might like an erupting volcano or a tidal wave,
     the human spectator can only feel small.
10   See the chapter of the same name in *Enthusiasm: The Kantian Critique of History*,
     trans. Georges Van Den Abbeele (Stanford: Stanford University Press, 2009), 21–42.
11   Cited by Jean-François Lyotard, "The Sign of History," trans. Geoff Bennington. In *The
     Lyotard Reader*, ed. Andrew Benjamin (London: Blackwell, 1991), 393–411, here: 404.
12   Kant, "A Renewed Attempt," 181.
13   Lyotard, "The Sign of History," 404.
14   In other words, something acts upon the spectator: it isn't just a "spectacle" that one
     contemplates like a picture (or like a "game," in Kant's language).
15   Training Seminar in Lacanian Psychoanalysis, Quebec City, Quebec, 2019
     (unpublished).
16   On this subject, see Michel de Certeau's magisterial study, *The Possession at Loudun*,
     trans. Michael B. Smith (Chicago: University of Chicago Press, 2000).
17   Sigmund Freud, *Totem and Taboo: Some Points of Agreement between the Mental
     Lives of Savages and Neurotics*, trans. and ed. James Strachey (New York and London:
     W. W. Norton, 1950), 195–6.
18   Epistle to the Romans, chapter 7.
19   Sigmund Freud, *Moses and Monotheism*, trans. Katherine Jones (New York: Random
     House, 1939), 109–10.

The Dream That Knew Too Much
On Freud, Lacan, and Philip K. Dick

Dominik Finkelde

1. Introduction

This chapter is a continuation of my theory on non-wakefulness that describes the extent to which it is only in mental states of *dogmatic slumber* (Kant) that we human beings build up apparently coherent forms of experience.[1] Non-wakefulness protects our consciousness from supernumerary properties of what there is and helps us to combine segments of reality from a basically inexhaustible multitude of facts, things, and circumstances into reasonable clusters of states of affairs shared and maintained *phantasmatically* with others. Social reality rests on selection processes to shape "what is the case" without giving its share of being to that which is suppressed, through that which is the case. Slavoj Žižek, to whom the theory of non-wakefulness is partly indebted, next to Jacques Lacan, speaks of the homogenizing power of ideology. The latter is "not an illusion masking the real state of things but... an (unconscious) fantasy structuring our social reality itself."[2] The Austrian philosopher Robert Pfaller extends this thesis with his concept of "interpassivity."[3] It stands for the possibility to outsource one's beliefs into belief-systems of others which gives people the possibility to fantasize reasons of their actions as belonging to themselves even if they have with regard to certain deeds no clear and distinct rationale of what they are actually doing and why they are doing it.

Now the concept non-wakefulness will be expanded in the following sections with a theoretical exploration of the experience of awakening from dreaming, especially, but not exclusively, in nightmares. This is done to lay bare a mutual permeation, on the one hand, of the non-wakefulness of our everyday life through, on the other hand, experiences of awakening through dreaming. Jacques Lacan prepared the way for the arguments presented here in his Seminars of the 1960s. According to him, reality, as that which is, results through a parallactic contortion of the aforementioned slumbering states of wakefulness (i.e., of not-wakefulness) on the level of our everyday consciousness. However, these mental states rest, and this is decisive, on experiences of awakening through dreaming. The chiastic relationship is explained with the help of the Aristotelian concepts "tyche" and "automaton," which Lacan presents in Seminar XI (*The Four Fundamental Concepts of Psychoanalysis*) from 1964.[4] He shows that the psyche in her dream work can encounter truth values that, due to repression mechanisms in the waking state, maintain non-wakefulness in everyday life. This may happen when inner-psychic instances of censorship, as determined by Freud, lower their force fields. Unacknowledged wishes, repressed desires, grievances, and perversions then have the opportunity to produce a synesthetic play of the imagination in the dream rebus.[5] Often this rebus appears to be nothing more than absurd. But as Freud has prominently pointed out, there is "method in this madness." The latter gives the psyche the possibility of a catharsis-like cleansing, even if Freud sees, in contrast to Wilfred Bion, for example, the therapeutic power of the dream guaranteed solely by the analyst's capacity for interpretation.

The chiastic relationship between slumbering wakefulness and awakening in and through dreams will be discussed in the following sections in more detail, since its epistemological significance for man's cognitive faculties to make experiences through and within his lifeworld has not been given much attention in contemporary philosophy. While it is indeed true that dreams have been a recurrent theme of philosophical investigation from Aristotle, via Descartes to Kant,[6] the philosophical interest in this matter, however, has waned in the twentieth century, especially since Norman Malcolm's anti-Cartesian arguments from 1953 and 1959. Following individual remarks made by Ludwig Wittgenstein, dreams, Malcolm argues, are only retrospectively transferred back from the waking state via the memory of the dreamer and as such cannot be verifiable like ordinary memories through others.[7] The status of experience cannot be granted to them. This leads Malcolm to the thesis "[that] the concept of dreaming is derived, not from dreaming, but from descriptions of dreams, i.e. from the familiar phenomenon that we call 'telling a dream.'"[8]

Daniel Dennett reinvigorated in 1976 the debate again in his famous article "Are Dreams Experiences?"[9] In addition to critical replicas made by Hilary Putnam[10] and Thomas Nagel,[11] he points out some hasty conclusions of Malcolm's opinion. In particular, Malcolm underestimates, so Dennett, the abilities of future neuroscientific dream research. Dennett's own, so-called "videocassette theory of dreaming" remains, however, despite his own assertions, ultimately very similar to Malcolm's opinion. According to Dennett, the dream is, figuratively speaking, inserted into the awakening consciousness like a cassette in a video recorder. It can be interpreted, but the interpretation must not be based on the assertion that the dreaming consciousness itself makes experiences. In addition to this, Dennett makes no secret of the fact that essential insights of Freud are negated. This becomes particularly clear when he, in a speculative thought experiment, draws the future picture of neuroscientific dream research in which scientists can determine the contents of the dream even with more precision than the dreamer herself.

Essential Freudian concepts like the dream's secondary revisions, the differentiation between latent dream thoughts and manifest dream content, or the theory of retroactive causation of traumatic experiences in and with the help of dreams are not covered by this theory anymore. After all, a latent dream thought can only be revealed from the manifest dream content if the dream is assumed to be identical with the mental experience of the psyche (when dreaming) and thus is as a form of experience. Therefore, dreams are not, according to Lacan, as the sleep researchers J. Allan Hobson and Robert McCarley believed to be able to show in their studies on REM sleep, "motivationally neutral."[12] Rather they are filled with motivational content. This thesis has recently been confirmed in neuroscientific sleep and dream research by Mark Solms, among others.[13] As far as I can judge, he is to be credited, after the so-called "Freud Wars" were fought especially in the 1990s, for having united Freud's findings with contemporary sleep and dream research and within the philosophy of mind.

Lacan aptly illustrates the above-mentioned conviction of a chiastic entanglement between slumbering wakefulness (= non-wakefulness) and awakening dreaming in the tale of the Taoist philosopher Chuang Tzu (fourth century BC).[14] After Chuang Tzu dreams one day of being a butterfly, he wonders after waking up whether he could not also be a butterfly who, in turn, dreams that he is Chuang Tzu. The value of the story should not be dismissed by saying that a dreaming butterfly is empirically absurd. The tale's argument wants to show how, according to Lacan, the butterfly constitutes the framing in which Chuang Tzu can desire and thus lead his everyday life. The phantasm of being a butterfly, with the various associations of being able to fly, and of freedom and beauty that are semantically contained within it form the illusion of an unconscious in relation to the complementary illusion of the ego function in everyday life. In this case, then, Chuang Tzu is indeed Chuang Tzu within symbolic reality—although on the level of his unconscious desire, he is also this mental object, which is a butterfly. The latter as symptom is interpreted by Lacan even more than by Freud as a condition of a subject's being split.[15] The phantasm of the dream is complementary to the phantasmatic effect of our ego function in everyday reality. This reality is virtually "constructed" by various forms of inner-psychological defense mechanism. Therefore, one could say that not only is the one who dreams a dreamer but so too is the one who does not stand up to dreams and then seeks refuge in the mental state of being awake (i.e., being non-awake).

In order to determine more precisely the relationship of the chiastic entanglement of non-wakefulness in the waking state and of awakening in dreaming, the following sections of this chapter will present examples for further explication. The first comes from the field of art, more precisely from the short story "Exhibit Piece," which was written by the US-American science fiction author Philip K. Dick and then loosely turned into the episode "Real Life" of the TV-series *Electric Dreams*. The second example refers to the much-commented dream of the "burning child," which Freud analyzes in chapter seven of *The Interpretation of Dreams*. On the basis of both examples, the parallactic change of perception is to be demonstrated. They lead to objects changing their ontological status along two mutually exclusive mental modes of perception (i.e., waking and sleeping and their various intermediate forms). At first glance, this does not sound surprising, because dreamed (or fantasized) objects have a different ontological status by definition compared to non-dreamed objects. The former lack the correlate in space-time. And with this in mind, the epistemic change of the status of the subject (from waking to dreaming or from dreaming to waking) naturally also changes the ontological status of the objects perceived. What will be examined here, however, is the fact that both mental states are each the basis of a guarantee of the ontological consistency of the respective other.[16] In dreams, we can encounter objects whose truth values we could not have perceived in the state of waking, due to censorship instances—but which still *linger on* in the mind. And it is precisely these experiences that the concept of parallax between non-wakefulness, in being awake, and wakefulness, in being in dreams, seeks to capture. In other words, dreaming is examined not only in terms of the extent to which the epistemic change of a subject's point of view leads to an ontological change of status on the part of the object and vice versa but also in terms of the extent to which the objects of the waking state and the objects of dreams, due to a constitutive non-coincidence, have always referred to each other in their various ontological statuses. No mediating third reconciles them. This can be experienced in everyday life. Neither can one say, "Now I am falling asleep" when one falls asleep, since one is already asleep at the same moment, nor can one say, "Now I am waking up" when one wakes up, since one already has woken up. This makes it possible to distinguish between waking and dreaming epistemically and yet to determine that both their non-coincidence and codependence is an ontological factor for the mind-world relationship; that is, these mental states are factors that affect ontologically the basic structures of reality. From here on we may understand Lacan, who in Seminar XI remarks to what extent the philosophy of psychoanalysis directs us, allegedly, "into the direction of idealism."[17]

2. "Real Life"

The episode "Real life" of the TV-Series "Electric Dreams" takes place in a not-too-distant future, in which the two protagonists, George and Sarah, each lead their successful professional lives. George is the CEO of a high-tech company, and Sarah is a member of a special police squad. However, it soon turns out that both George and Sarah are one and the same person. What they have in common is a distinct dream state, already familiar to us from the above-mentioned Chuang Tzu story. Because when one of the two, George or Sarah, goes to sleep, the other wakes up and starts his or her day. A sleep simulator, which George apparently codeveloped, enables the entanglement. It promises customers who buy it relaxing holidays from one's ego function, which constantly is under epistemological and normative strain. And the product's inventors have truly read their Freud to the letter, because the dream device promises to track down hidden and repressed desires of the sleeping person and—according to Freud's theory of wish fulfillment—to make them virtually relivable. Complications come to light when it turns out that both George and Sarah are haunted by unresolved traumas. Suddenly neither of them knows which world is modally necessary (because it is fundamental) and which one is contingent (arbitrary/derived), or the fantasized complementary substitute fantasy of a repressed truth. George suffers from the loss of his wife who was lost in a murder. Sarah suffers from being the survivor of an attack on her police squad. To her it is obvious that her life must be derived from George's fantasies, because against the background of her guilt of being the only survivor, she repeatedly asks her life partner the same question over and over again: "What have I done to deserve a life like this?" Living lives that are, apparently, too good to be true, Sarah and George are overcome by the neurotic (and finally psychotic) suspicion that they evade what is essential to each of their lives by simulating some other life. Robust reality of waking does not take priority over the vague reality of dreaming. Trauma is for both some kind of "sufficient reason" of their being.

Numerous insights, especially from Freud's latter period, shape the dramaturgical structure of the episode. In "Remembering, Repeating, and Working-Through" (1914),[18] Freud devotes himself to finding reasons for pathological repetition. In neurotics like George and Sarah, it can put an extreme strain on life in the form of recurring unpleasant memories. As Freud himself recognized, however, this contradicts his understanding of the pleasure principle, which, as a principle of homeostasis, rejects the repetition of stressful thoughts and experiences. According to Lacan, Freud's concept of repetition has nothing to do with recognition or with anamnesis in the Platonic sense[19] but with the fate of an encounter that happens as if by chance, but in fact has only waited to return.[20] This points to the impossibility of the subject to resolve a trauma that formally inscribes itself in the psyche through the very process of becoming a subject. And the question: "What have I done to deserve a life like this?" points to such a trauma. It stands, as Lacan writes, for "a rendezvous with the real to which we are called, but which eludes us."[21] Trauma occurs when the "subject, insofar as he thinks as *res cogitans,* does not meet it," that is, the source of trauma.[22] It is "that which always comes back to the same place…. The whole history of Freud's discovery of repetition as function becomes clear only by pointing out in this way the relation between thinking and the real."[23] Every reflection of the subject, every psychoanalytical reflection, reaches its limit here. Memory cannot overcome it. This "limit… is known as the real."[24]

Lacan mentions the Spinozistic formula: *cogitatio adaequata semper vitat eandem rem.* He translates it as: "The adequate thought, *qua* thought, as the level at which we are, always avoids the same thing—if only to find itself again later in everything."[25] The individual cannot recognize what is in his head and in what way her thinking is getting out of the way of something that cannot be met head-on. The instance of misrecognition happens in the back of one's thoughts, which leads to the fact that consciousness cannot get away from that which had an impact but now cannot be confronted.[26]

In the story of Chuang Tzu as retold by Lacan, the motif of trauma seems at first glance to play no role. But under the forced choice analyzed by Lacan, which is hidden in the act of every subject's becoming, a psyche cannot do without its alter ego and thus without non-coincidence. In Chuang Tzu's text, it is the butterfly that keeps the frame of hidden and suppressed desires open. It enables Chuang Tzu to be identical with himself. Lacan writes: "In fact, it is when he was the butterfly that he apprehended one of the roots of his identity—that he was, and is, in his essence, that butterfly who paints himself with his own colors—and it is because of this that, in the last resort, he is Chuang Tzu."[27]

The fate of George and Sarah exemplifies the same codependence of two mutually exclusive personifications of the mental. George experiences his reality as co-constituted by Sarah and vice versa. The one apparently lives some kind of dream of the other and can thus maintain the virtuality of non-wakefulness in everyday life, as a CEO or as a police detective, which, in turn, revolves around the gap of a stressful experience. Or to put it another way: George lives his dogmatic slumber, the reality surrounding him, in its hard-to-bear objectivity, through Sarah's handling of her own trauma in her dreams. Sarah can be herself through her dream of George. George is her medium of transference from the ego function to another ego of her own.

3. Awake in a Dream

The fact that Lacan recognizes a decisive insight of psychoanalysis in this structural codependence of a chiastic entanglement of non-wakefulness during the day and awakening in dreams is reinforced by the fact that, following his analysis of Chuang Tzu, he comes to speak of the famous dream of the "burning child," which Freud describes in the seventh chapter of *The Interpretation of Dreams*. A father is haunted by this vision as he falls asleep during the death watch of his deceased son. During the dream the child confronts him with the words: "Father, can't you see that I'm burning?" Horrified by the encounter, the father wakes up and sees small flames in the adjoining room where his son is laid to rest. A candle had fallen on the bed and left burn marks on the sheets.

This dream is parallactic as it brings to the fore a hidden knowledge of the father, namely, his responsibility. According to Lacan, the father could not have confronted this in a waking state. It is triggered by a coincidental event, the toppling of the candle, which takes on, allegorically speaking, the structural role of the dream simulators in the episode "Real Life." The psyche of the dreaming father does not interrupt the dream when he experiences the flickering from the room next door, but rather the psyche integrates the event out of the paradoxical need to prolong the traumatic encounter with the dead-living son. This confirms, on the one hand, a function of the dream emphasized by Freud, namely, "to be the guardian of sleep,"[28] insofar as the father, indeed, continues to sleep; while, on the other hand, the prolongation provokes the confrontation with a repressed guilt. The dream as guardian of sleep leaves too much time for an unconscious guilt to materialize into that which cannot be met. A truth value of traumatic proportions confronts the psyche, as in the case of George and Sarah. Repressions have enabled the father to live in a slumbering state of non-wakefulness or in the "dogmatic slumber" of his everyday life. Only the parallactic shift from the slumbering state of non-wakefulness to the awakening dream provokes the confrontation with the hidden object of desire in its traumatic dimension: to have the deceased son both alive and burning before the eyes. The existence of this object may well be presumed even in a state of non-wakefulness, and yet the father can only encounter this object in a dream. Lacan states: "Father, can't you see I'm burning? What is he burning with, if not with that which we see emerging at other points designated by the Freudian topology, namely, the weight of the sins of the father."[29]

Starting from the moment of contingency, when the candle tips over onto the deathbed, the encounter with what cannot be met takes its course. It begins with the light of the flames flickering in the room next door pushing their light through the eyelids of the sleeping father. This contingent element of sensory perception coming from the outside world is integrated into the dream rebus.[30] The deceased son comes to life. This enables the encounter, which, in turn, marks a first narrative attempt of the psych's self-therapy to confront the traumatic object of desire with its full emotional impact.[31] This moment can last seconds or minutes, since our consciousness is not bound in dreams to the subjective form of time. But more important is the temporal form of chance, because it is the condition of a *rendezvous* with the real. So how exactly is the accidental toppling of the candle to be interpreted? Lacan does it with the Aristotelian terms "tyche" (fate or luck) and "automaton" (chance). They underline how subjectivity is by definition out-of-time, or in the words of Kirstin Hyldgaard, to whom this article is indebted: "the subject is a matter of bad timing."[32] Aristotle mentions the two concepts in his *Physics* (book II, chapters 4–7, 196a–197b). He points out that they are not compatible with his so-called four causes of being (i.e., matter, form, effect, purpose) as explanations of change and movement in the world. "Tyche" as a subcategory of "automaton" stands for a random event. Purely random events can be experienced by animals, to quote Aristotle, "other than man and to many inanimate objects. So we say that the horse came automatically, in that it was saved because it came, but it did not come for the purpose of being saved."[33] But this notion does not hold for "tyche." Fate as the outcome of luck seems here to follow in accordance with an intention,[34] without which a clear originator of the intention cannot be identified.

The utility of Aristotle's differentiation for psychoanalysis is apparent, because prior to Freud, a slip of the tongue may have been perceived only as an arbitrary event in contingent chains of occasions ("automaton") but not as an event of fate ("tyche"). After Freud, a hidden purpose comes into play: for example, by conveying a message in opposition to a speaker's intention. A peculiar shape of the Aristotelian concept of final causality stands out here, albeit (apparently) in opposition to Aristotle's line of argument. In the case mentioned, only the unconscious knows about this "final cause," because, as Lacan says, "we are always called to the real.... The real is that which always lies behind the automaton, and it is quite obvious, throughout Freud's research, that it is this that is the object of his concern."[35] It is "the chapter of my history that is marked by a blank or occupied by a lie: it is the censored chapter. But the truth can be refound; most often it has already been written elsewhere, namely," on "my body," in "my childhood memories."[36] An unconscious desire permeates censorship mechanisms of the psyche and accidentally says something meaningful or acts out in dreams or memories. Contingency and final causation coincide.

"Tyche" reveals its own form of final causation, as the dream of the burning child shows. The dream as a frame of desire processes guilt via displacement and condensation. It then leaves the psyche partially recovered at the point where it wakes up with horror. A parallactic change from the awakening dream state to the slumbering state of non-wakefulness takes place. In this sense, the dream is a kind of catalyst of an exchange with that which cannot be encountered. It mediates, as Petra Gehring aptly says, "between an unreal actuality and a possible (healthy) reality of tomorrow. One unreal actuality makes the other of an encapsulated suffering… something to talk about (in the case of success)."[37]

4. Sins of the Fathers

According to Lacan, the philosophy of psychoanalysis leads, "at first sight… in the direction of idealism."[38] This is supported by the fact that the basic structure of reality is not able to come to its adequate ground due to the influence of what Lacan calls the Real. People are called to a rendezvous with all kinds of its forms. Fateful encounters like that of Chuang Tzu and the butterfly or that of the father with the burning child are not exceptional phenomena of a few chosen people. They are experiences that people, although often less oppressive, repeatedly have in everyday life when they are surprised by unpleasant memories or wake up exhausted from their dreams. According to Lacan, the real prevents "the reality system" from evolving without tribulations since reality without pleasure-seeking subjects would only be identical with itself.[39] That is why it, the real, is "the motive force of development."[40] This does not mean that "life is a dream." Reality, according to Lacan, is always "en souffrance," "in abeyance,"[41] both individually and collectively, because of that which cannot be encountered. For this reason, the psyche is chiastically wound into slumbering states of being non-awake and into awakening states of dreaming. Both mental states determine themselves and help to cathartically catch up with multiple levels of repression processes, at least to some extent.

Similar to Sarah's fate in "Real Life," a fundamental sin or trauma reveals itself as the hidden origin of human liveliness. Or, according to the terminology repeatedly used in this chapter, non-wakefulness is written into being in order to keep the trauma on which reality surrounding us rests, in general, at a distance. And just as Sarah and George seemingly can no longer bear the non-wakefulness of their everyday lives and repeatedly have their "rendez-vous with the real," so too does the father seek to escape his guilt by waking up. The encounter with his deceased son was ultimately *only a dream.*

Lacan emphasizes the ontological insight of the chiastic entanglement of non-wakefulness and of awakening from dreams with reference to the fact that people, by definition, carry the burden of their symbolic debt with them. He writes: "The sins of the father—are they not born by the ghost in the myth of Hamlet, which Freud couples with the myth of Oedipus? The father, the Name-of-the-father, sustains a structure of desire with the structure of the law, but the inheritance of the father is that which Kierkegaard designates for us, namely his sin."[42]

Becoming a subject demands the subordination of all kinds of invocations/appellations that enable the child to adapt to the desires of others. But just as the neck of a bottle pushes back a part of the bottle's contents, so too can only a small portion of desires of the growing child be rescued into the ego function. What is left behind is not gone, only lost and out of sight of the mind's cognitive abilities. In repetitions, it bumps into the ego function and generates a psycho-symbolistic surplus-value that the psyche cannot bring to nil. Lacan's talk of the "sins of the fathers" marks the absence of a sufficient reason for normative orders. The present is forced into repetitive loops of memory: the remembrance of what was never fully experienced. Reality is inevitably, therefore, always costructured by the unconscious, for the gap in the law, the "sins of the fathers," is nothing that remains external to man. They recur in many forms: from social production processes of goods that generate new superego forms of subjugation to commemorative rituals that see themselves as forms of determinate negation.

In Freud's dream of the burning child, the father encounters an object from which he had previously been spared by an unconscious structure of suppressed reality. Just as the spirit of old Hamlet communicates to his son the traumatic and threatening truth of him being murdered (encumbering thereby the young Hamlet's social role as "prince of Denmark"), so too the burning child communicates a truth to the father.

After the encounter, though, the latter can indeed say, as I have mentioned, "Thank God. It was only a dream." But this dream was more than an illusion. It was the parallactic change that for a moment had revealed another ontological basic structure of reality, on whose suppression non-wakefulness rests.

The episode "Real Life" ends in tragedy. George destroys his dream simulator and, thus, cuts his correlation to Sarah. But, to the surprise of the audience, it is Sarah who dies in the very same moment. This makes the audience suddenly aware that it was actually her consciousness and her dream simulator through which she dreamed of him, of George, the way he, George, dreamed of her. The structure of a mutual chiastic interpenetration now becomes obvious. It differs from causal and grounding relations. With Freud and Lacan, one could say that Sarah loses the frame through which she had maintained her image of reality with herself at the center in the struggle with her trauma. She has lost contact with a dimension of her unconscious that, as function or role, is played by the butterfly in the story of Chuang Tzu. If this frame disintegrates, then the dream as a current conversation with what cannot be put into words breaks down. In this case, the psyche no longer has any possibility to transfer via the catalyst of dream fragments meanings detached from words into the order of the signifier. Curiously, even before George destroyed his dream simulator, it was he who has had the firm conviction that it absolutely had to be his life that was the real one and not Sarah's. But in the end, Sarah suppressed his longing for her happiness in order to provoke the erasure of her ego function in the impossible choice for what is Real in "Real Life."

Notes

1   Dominik Finkelde, "Non-Wakefulness," *The Philosophical Journal of Conflict and Violence* 3, no. 2 (2020): 92–107.
2   Slavoj Žižek, *The Sublime Object of Ideology* (London: Verso, 1986), 33.
3   Robert Pfaller, *Interpassivity. The Aesthetics of Delegated Enjoyment* (Edinburgh: Edinburgh University Press, 2017).
4   Jacques Lacan, *The Seminar, Book XI (The Four Fundamental Concepts of Psychoanalysis)*, trans. Alan Sheridan (New York: W. W. Norton, 1998).
5   After all, we humans can only approach each other as social beings under the cognitive effort of hiding or suppressing our egoisms, aggressions, and perverse fantasies.
6   Christopher Dreisbach, "Dreams in the History of Philosophy," *Dreaming* 10, no. 1 (2000): 31–41.
7   Norman Malcolm, "Dreaming and Skepticism," *The Philosophical Review* 65, no. 1 (1956): 14–37; Norman Malcolm, *Dreaming* (London: Routledge & Kegan Paul, 1959).
8   Malcolm, *Dreaming*, 55. "If a man had certain thoughts and feelings in a dream it not more follows that he had those thoughts and feelings while asleep, than it follows from his having climbed a mountain in a dream that he climbed a mountain while asleep" (Malcolm, *Dreaming*, 51–2). See also C.S. Chihara, "What Dreams Are Made On," *Theoria* 31 (1965): 145–58.

9   Daniel Dennett, "Are Dreams Experiences?" *The Philosophical Review* 85, no. 2 (1976): 151–71; "The Onus Re Experiences: A Reply to Emmett," *Philosophical Studies* 35 (April 1979): 315–18.

10   Hilary Putnam, "Dreaming and 'Depth Grammar'" (1962), as reprint in *Philosophical Papers, Vol. 2.: Mind, Language and Reality* (Cambridge: Cambridge University Press, 1986), 304–24.

11   Thomas Nagel, "Dreaming," *Analysis* 19, no. 5 (1959): 112–16.

12   See Ritchie E. Brown, Radhika Basheer, Robert McCarley et al. "Control of Sleep and Wakefulness," *Physiological Reviews* 92, no. 3 (July 2012): 1087–187, 1133.

13   According to Solms "dreaming can be switched 'on' and 'off' by a neurochemical pathway which has nothing to do with the REM oscillator in the pons." This discovery is important because instead of a reduction of dream sequences to brain regions that trigger REM sleep, Solms, quoting Panksepp, refers to the upper brain regions of the so-called frontal lobes. Their influence on dreaming frees dreaming from the assumption that dreaming is only a purely mechanical and contingent neuron fire without any consciousness-intrinsic causes. The latter thesis is supported among others by Solms in opposition to J. Allen Hobson. Solms: "[T]he function of this higher brain pathway… is to 'instigate goal-seeking behaviors and an organism's appetitive interactions with the world'… These are precisely the functions that Freud attributed to the 'libidinal drive'— the primary instigator of dreams—in his theory" (Mark Solms, "The Interpretation of Dreams and the Neurosciences," *Psychoanalysis and History* 3, no. 1 (2001): 79–91, 84).

14   Lacan, *Seminar XI*, 76.

15   Sigmund Freud, *The Interpretation of Dreams*, trans. James Strachey. In *The Standard Edition of the Complete Psychological Works*, vols. IV and V (London: Hogarth Press, 1953), here: vol. V, 678. In his *Introductory Lectures* he writes: "[A] dreamless sleep is the best, the only proper one. There ought to be no mental activity in sleep; if it begins to stir, we have not succeeded in establishing the foetal state of rest: we have not been able entirely to avoid residues of mental activity. Dreaming would consist in these residues. But if so, it would really seem that there is no need for dreams to have any sense" (Sigmund Freud, *Introductory Lectures on Psychoanalysis*, in *The Standard Edition of the Complete Psychological Works*, vol. XV (London: Hogarth Press, 1961), 89). Freud does not believe that dreaming is an explicit psychological work that helps the dreamer to overcome emotionally unpleasant experiences. This task is the sole responsibility of the analyst. The principle role of dreaming is only to guard sleep and to watch over and regulate sleep during the return of the repressed. Wilfred Bion saw this differently. He started from the conviction that the analysand who brings a dream to the analyst has himself already done part of the deciphering work that Freud reserves for the analyst.

16   This enables numerous intermediate forms between waking and sleeping/dreaming, as we know them from experiences of daydreaming or from experiences of the so-called lucid dreams.

17   Lacan, *Seminar XI*, 53.

18   Sigmund Freud, "Remembering, Repeating, and Working-Through," in *The Standard Edition*, vol. 12, 147–56.

19   Lacan, *Seminar XI*, 47–8.

20   Lacan: "What is repeated, in fact, is always something that occurs… *as if by chance.* This is something that we analysts never allow ourselves to be taken in by, on principle. At least, we always point out that we must not be taken in when the subject tells us that something happens to him that day that prevented him from realizing his wish to come to the session" (Lacan, *Seminar XI*, 54).

21   Lacan, *Seminar XI*, 53 (translation changed).

22   Lacan, *Seminar XI*, 49 (translation changed).

23   Lacan, *Seminar XI*, 49 (translation changed).

24   Lacan, *Seminar XI*, 49.

25   Lacan, *Seminar XI*, 49 (translation changed).

26   Lacan "[A]n act, a true act, always has an element of structure, by the fact of concerning a real that is not self-evidently caught up in it" (Lacan, *Seminar XI*, 50).

27   Lacan, *Seminar XI*, 76. Lacan continues: "It is when he is away that he is Choang-tsu for others, and is caught in their butterfly net. This is why the butterfly may—if the subject is not Chang-tsu, but the Wolf Man—inspire in him the phobic terror of recognizing that the beating of little wings is not so very far from the beating of causation, of the primal stripe marking his being for the first time with the grid of desire" (76).

28   Freud, *The Interpretation of Dreams*, 678.

29   Lacan, *Seminar XI*, 34.

30   Lacan describes a similar moment in *Seminar XI* on the basis of his own experience, when he hears a knocking shortly before awakening. Consciousness remains in some kind of limbo since sense data have not interconnected yet with the faculties of perception. "I must question myself as to what I am at that moment—at the moment, so immediately before and so separate, which is that in which I began to dream under the effect of the knocking which is, to all appearances, what woke me. Observe what I am directing you towards—towards the symmetry of that structure that makes me, after the awakening knock, able to sustain myself, apparently only in a relation with my representation, which, apparently, makes of me only consciousness. A sort of involuted reflection—in my consciousness, it is only my representation that I recover possession of" (Lacan, *Seminar XI*, 56-7).

31   Freud would reject this thesis because, according to him, the dream itself does not (as it does for Bion) already have a therapeutic function. The dream can only gain this function through the interpretation of the psychoanalyst.

32   Kirsten Hylgaard, "The Cause of the Subject as an Ill-Timed Accident." In *Lacan. Critical Evaluations in Cultural Theory*, vol. 1 (London: Routledge, 2003), 228-42: here 231.

33   Aristotle, *Physics Books I and II*, trans. William Charlton (Oxford: Clarendon Press, 1992), 197b, line 15, p. 36 (translation changed).

34   Aristotle, *Physics*, 196b, lines 21-4, p. 34.

35   Lacan, *Seminar XI*, 54.

36   Jacques Lacan, "The Function and Field of Speech and Language in Psychoanalysis." In *Écrits. The First Complete Edition in English*, trans. Bruce Fink (New York: W. W. Norton, 2006), 197-268, here: 215.

37   Petra Gehring, *Traum und Wirklichkeit* (Frankfurt a. M.: Campus, 2008), 185.

38   Lacan, *Seminar XI*, 53.

39   Lacan, *Seminar XI*, 55.

40   Lacan, *Seminar XI*, 55.

41   Lacan, *Seminar XI*, 56.

42   Lacan, *Seminar XI*, 51.

Notes on the Contributors

- **G. Anthony Bruno** is Assistant Professor in Philosophy at Royal Holloway University of London. He has published articles on freedom, mortality, pantheism, and idealism in *History of Philosophy Quarterly, Idealistic Studies, Dialogue: Canadian Philosophical Review*, and other journals. His current research concerns the development of logic in post-Kantian philosophy and its relation to systematicity, contingency, and subjectivity. He is coeditor of *Skepticism: Historical and Contemporary Inquiries* (Routledge 2018) and editor of *Schelling's Philosophy: Freedom, Nature, and Systematicity* (Oxford University Press, 2020). His recent article is "Schelling on the Possibility of Evil: Rendering Pantheism, Freedom, and Time Consistent," *Northern European Journal of Philosophy* 18, no. 1 (2017), 1–18.

- **Dominik Finkelde SJ** is Professor for Epistemology and Contemporary Philosophy at the Munich School of Philosophy. He has published on contemporary philosophy and German Idealism, especially on Hegel, Kant, Frege, Wittgenstein, and Badiou. Recent publications include *Idealism. Relativism, and Realism. New Essays on Objectivity Beyond the Analytic Continental Divide*, edited with Paul M. Livingston (De Gruyter 2020); *Excessive Subjectivity. Kant, Hegel, Lacan, and the Foundation of Ethics* (Columbia University Press 2017), "Lack and Excess/Zero and One. On Concrete Universality in Dialectical Materialism," *Philosophy Today* 63, no. 1 (2019), 55–71; "Anamorphosis and Subjectivity in the Space of Reasons," *Philosophy Today* 64, no. 1 (2020), 117–36.

- **Markus Gabriel** is Chair for Epistemology, Modern and Contemporary Philosophy at the University of Bonn and Director of the International Centre for Philosophy. He has also held positions at the New School for Social Research and the University of California, Berkeley. His research interests include German Idealism, as well as both ancient and contemporary analytic philosophy. He has published extensively on a wide variety of philosophical topics both historical and systematic. His noted publications on realism, in particular, are: *Fields of Sense. A New Realist Ontology* (Edinburgh 2015); *An den Grenzen der Erkenntnistheorie: Die Notwendige Endlichkeit des Wissens als Lektion des Skeptizismus* (Alber 2008); and *Transcendental Ontology: Essays in German Idealism* (Bloomsbury 2013).

- **Graham Harman** is Distinguished Professor of Philosophy at the Southern California Institute of Architecture. He has published on the metaphysics of objects and developed an object-oriented ontology. He is a leading proponent of Speculative Realism and the series editor of *Speculative Realism* published by Edinburgh University Press. His most recent books are: *Art and Objects* (Polity 2020) and *Skirmishes: With Friends, Enemies, and Neutrals* (punctum 2020).

- **Adrian Johnston** is Distinguished Professor in and Chair of the Department of Philosophy at the University of New Mexico at Albuquerque. He has published extensively on Dialectical Materialism and German Idealism. His recent publications are: *A New German Idealism: Hegel, Žižek, and Dialectical Materialism* (Columbia University Press 2018) and *Prolegomena to Any Future Materialism, Volume Two: A Weak Nature Alone* (Northwestern University Press 2019).

- **Thomas Khurana** is Professor of Philosophy at the University of Potsdam. He was Heisenberg Fellow at Yale University, Theodor Heuss Visiting Lecturer at the New School of Social Research in New York, and Humboldt Fellow at the University of Chicago. He has published on Kant, Hegel, Heidegger, Wittgenstein, Adorno, Foucault, Derrida, Cavell, Brandom, Agamben, Walther White, and others. Among his recent publications are his book *Das Leben der Freiheit: Form und Wirklichkeit der Autonomie* (Suhrkamp 2017), the edited collection *Negativität: Kunst - Recht - Freiheit* (Suhrkamp 2018), and his paper „I do not cognize myself through being conscious of myself as thinking`: Self-Knowledge and the Irreducibility of Self-Objectification in Kant", *Canadian Journal of Philosophy* 49 (2019), 956–979.

- **Anton Friedrich Koch** is Professor of Philosophy at Heidelberg University. He held visiting professorships at Emory University (Atlanta, USA), and at the University of Chicago. His field of research is epistemology and ontology, drawing from Plato, Aristotle, Kant, Hegel, Heidegger, and analytic philosophy. His recent books are: *Hermeneutischer Realismus* (Mohr Siebeck 2016) and *Die Evolution des logischen Raumes* (Mohr Siebeck 2014). Some recent articles are: "Die Mittelstellung des Wesens zwischen Sein und Begriff," A. Arndt/G. Kruck (ed.), *Hegels "Lehre vom Wesen". Hegel-Jahrbuch Sonderband* (DeGruyter 2016), 9–20; "Neutraler oder hermeneutischer Realismus?," *Philosophisches Jahrbuch* (2015), 163–72.

- **Paul Livingston** is Professor of Philosophy at the University of New Mexico. His work focuses on the philosophy of mind, philosophy of language, phenomenology, and political philosophy. He has published widely on twentieth-century and contemporary philosophy, especially on Badiou, Wittgenstein, Heidegger, and Dummett. His recent publications include the monographs *The Logic of Being: Realism, Truth, and Time* (Northwestern 2017) and *The Problems of Contemporary Philosophy* (co-authored with A. Cutrofello, Polity 2015). His recent article is "The Sense of Finitude and the Finitude of Sense," *Semantics and Beyond: Philosophical and Linguistic Investigations* (Ontos Verlag 2014).

- **Todd McGowan** teaches theory and film at the University of Vermont. He is the author of *Emancipation After Hegel: Achieving a Contradictory Revolution* (Columbia University Press 2019); *Only a Joke Can Save Us: A Theory of Comedy* (Northwestern University Press 2017); *Capitalism and Desire: The Psychic Cost of Free Markets* (Columbia University Press 2016), *Universality and Identity Politics* (Columbia UP 2020). He is the editor of the Film Theory in Practice series at Bloomsbury and coeditor of the *Diaeresis* series at Northwestern University Press.

- **Tracy K. McNulty** is Professor of French and Comparative Literature at Cornell University. Her research interests include contemporary French Philosophy, psychoanalytic theory (especially Freud and Lacan), and political Theory. Her recent publications are: *The Hostess: Hospitality, Femininity, and the Expropriation of Identity* (Minnesota University Press 2007) and *Wrestling with the Angle: Experiments in Symbolic Life* (Columbia University Press 2017).

- **Christoph Menke** is Professor of Philosophy in the Department of Philosophy at the Goethe University Frankfurt am Main. His book publications in English include *The Sovereignty of Art: Aesthetic Negativity in Adorno and Derrida* (MIT Press 1998) and *Law and Violence: Christoph Menke in Dialogue* (Manchester University Press 2018); *Kritik der Rechte* (Suhrkamp 2018).

- **Robert Pfaller** is Professor of Philosophy and Cultural Theory at the University of Art and Industrial Design in Linz, Austria. He is the author of numerous articles and books on psychoanalysis, popular culture, and the predicament of contemporary forms of enjoyment. His recent publications are: *Das schmutzige Heilige und die reine Vernunft* (Fischer Verlag 2008); *The Pleasure Principle in Culture: Illusions without Owners* (Verso 2014); and *Erwachsenen-Sprache. Über ihr Verschwinden aus Politik und Kultur* (Fischer Verlag 2017).

- **Nina Power** is an independent researcher with a specialization in contemporary critical and social theory. She is the author of *One-Dimensional Woman* (Zero Books 2009) and multiple articles on modern French philosophy, Germany philosophy, Marxism, and feminism.

- **Dirk Quadlieg** is Professor of Cultural Philosophy at the University of Leipzig, Germany. He has published numerous articles on Hegel, social theory and on contemporary culture with regard to modern forms of reification. His recent publications are: *Differenz und Raum zwischen Hegel, Wittgenstein und Derrida* (Transcript 2007), "On the Dialectics of Reification and Freedom: From Lukács to Honneth—and back to Hegel," *Symposium. Canadian Journal of Continental Philosophy* 17, no. 1/2013, 132–49; *Vom Geist der Sache. Zur Kritik der Verdinglichung* (Campus 2019).

- **Frank Ruda** is Senior Lecturer in Philosophy at the University of Dundee, Professor at the European Graduate School (Saas Fee/Malta), and Adjunct Professor in the School of Marxism at Capital Normal University in Beijing, China. His most recent books include *The Dash—The Other Side of Absolute Knowing*, with Rebecca Comay (MIT Press 2018); *Reading Marx* with Slavoj Žižek and Agon Hamza (Polity 2018); and *Indifferenz und Wiederholung* (Konstanz University Press 2018).

- **Eva Schürmann** is Professor of Philosophical Anthropology and Cultural Philosophy at the University of Magdeburg. She has published on aesthetics and phenomenology with articles on Merleau-Ponty, Spinoza, and on questions of representation and imagination within the philosophy of mind. She is the author of multiple articles and the books *Vorstellen und Darstellen* (Wilhelm Fink 2018) and *Seeing as Practice* (Palgrave MacMillan 2020).

- **Slavoj Žižek** is Professor at the European Graduate School in Switzerland and International Director of the Birkbeck Institute for the Humanities, Birkbeck College, University of London. He authored numerous books, including *Less Than Nothing. Hegel and the Shadow of Dialectical Materialism* (Verso 2012) and *Absolute Recoil: Toward a New Foundation of Dialectical Materialism* (Verso 2004).

- **Alenka Zupančič** is Research Adviser at the Institute of Philosophy of the Slovenian Academy of Science and Arts and Professor at the European Graduate School, Switzerland. She is the author of numerous articles and books on psychoanalysis and philosophy, including *What Is Sex?* (MIT Press 2018); *The Odd One In: On Comedy* (MIT Press 2008); *The Shortest Shadow: Nietzsche's Philosophy of the Two* (MIT Press 2003); and *Ethics of the Real. Kant and Lacan* (Verso 2000).

Index of Names

Index of Subjects

CPSIA information can be obtained
at www.ICGtesting.com
Printed in the USA
LVHW061934240223
740134LV00010B/115

9 781350 253377